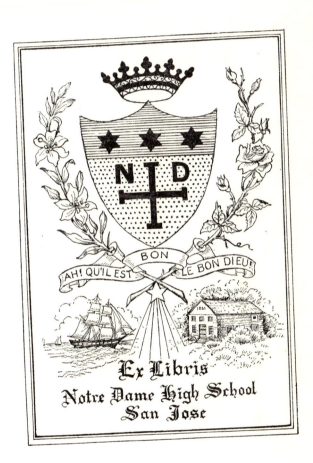

BON

AH! QU'IL EST   LE BON DIEU!

Ex Libris
Notre Dame High School
San Jose

GREEK HISTORY

BY

M. L. W. LAISTNER

PROFESSOR OF ANCIENT HISTORY
IN CORNELL UNIVERSITY

D. C. HEATH AND COMPANY

BOSTON   NEW YORK   CHICAGO

ATLANTA   SAN FRANCISCO   DALLAS

LONDON

938
L14

3 D 2

550

PREFACE

THE very kind reception accorded to my *Survey of Ancient History*, as well as actual inquiries or suggestions made by several university teachers, have seemed to justify the publication of the present volume. As it is an expansion of pages 1 to 367 of the *Survey*, it may be well to offer a word of explanation regarding the plan followed in its compilation. Though the book is mainly devoted to the Hellenic world, it was thought desirable to retain the early chapters on the Near and Middle East; and some additional matter has been incorporated in the sections on the social and intellectual life of Babylonia and Egypt. In the main part of the book the chapters on the political history of the Greeks have been left unchanged save for occasional minor additions or alterations. The economic history of Greece and the development of the Athenian constitution, on the other hand, have been treated more fully than was possible in the *Survey*. Large additions have also been made in the chapters devoted to literature, thought, and art in the archaic and classical periods. Finally, the single chapter in the *Survey*, entitled *The Hellenistic Age*, has disappeared; in its place the reader will find two much longer chapters, each subdivided into two sections. The amount of space thus given over to the two centuries after Alexander will hardly, in the light of our present knowledge, be regarded as disproportionate to the importance of the age.

My sincere thanks are due to Messrs. Methuen and Co., Ltd., for permission to cite some passages from A. Erman's *Literature of the Ancient Egyptians*, and to the Society for the Promotion of Hellenic Studies for leave to reproduce the Frontispiece and Plates 25 and 26.

M. L. W. L.

CORNELL UNIVERSITY
ITHACA, N. Y.
DECEMBER, 1931

CONTENTS

LIST OF PLATES

LIST OF MAPS

GREEK HISTORY

INTRODUCTION

SOURCES AND CHRONOLOGY

THE sources from which the modern historian reconstructs the history of the Ancient World are of the most varied character. There are formal histories like the masterpieces of Thucydides and of Livy. There is a great body of other Greek and Latin writings in prose and verse, which, insofar as they illustrate or are expressions of Hellenic and Roman civilization, must be regarded as historical material. These literatures have been transmitted through centuries and have not been appreciably increased by modern discoveries. He would be a sanguine man indeed who looked forward with any confidence to the recovery of a considerable body of Greek and Roman literature now lost.[1] On the other hand, the archæological and epigraphic material continues steadily to increase.

While the beginnings of serious epigraphic studies reach back to the eighteenth century, scientific excavation of historic and prehistoric sites dates only from the middle of the nineteenth. Especially during the last fifty years a mass of monumental and inscriptional evidence has accumulated; with its help many aspects of ancient civilization, on which the surviving literatures of Greece and Rome, or such monuments as have remained

---

[1] In spite of the recovery from the rubbish heaps of Egypt of Aristotle's *Constitution of Athens*, a portion of an important Greek historical work of the early fourth century B.C., some pæans of Pindar, poems by Bacchylides, the *Mimes* of Herondas, and some other literary fragments hitherto unknown, the vast number of *papyri* from Egypt have added singularly little to our knowledge of Greek literature and thought. On the other hand, they have immensely increased our knowledge of the economic and legal and administrative history of the Hellenistic and Græco-Roman periods.

above ground through the ages, throw little or no light, have been at least partially illumined. Yet there would seem to be a danger in the very wealth of this new material, and in its too exclusive use. It is possible to be so overawed by the quantity of pottery unearthed on an unimportant site, or by a mass of *papyri* illustrating but one human activity during a short period and in a restricted area, as to attribute to these a historical significance out of all proportion to the information that they offer. Again, it will rarely be possible to write a continuous history of a state or of a long epoch, if the material available for their reconstruction is wholly or mainly archæological and epigraphic. Such material may be abundant for one era and most scanty for another. Thus, while there is plentiful evidence for Egyptian history during the fourth, fifth, sixth, and twelfth dynasties, and again for the eighteenth and those that follow, the intervening ages are still extremely obscure. What greater contrast could one find than between Greek history during the fifth and fourth centuries B.C. on the one hand and during the third century on the other? Or, between the two centuries from Cicero to Hadrian and the century and a half that follow? In the former instances the historian has both abundant literature and archæological material from which to fashion his mosaic of ancient history; in the latter the literature is either non-existent or so poor in quantity or quality as to make any reconstruction largely a matter of guess-work.

A further danger, which is one of method, is more radical. There are extensive periods of Greek and Roman history for which the student has the guidance of historical works. But the accounts of the ancient historians are in the main concerned with political, military, and constitutional history. The speeches of the Attic orators or of Cicero deal primarily with political affairs or judicial business; and even Cicero's voluminous correspondence, invaluable historical source though it be, chiefly illustrates the public and the social life of the governing class at Rome between 65 and 44 B.C. To a less degree we learn also about the equestrian or financial class. Cicero's interests scarcely pass beyond those limits, and we look in vain for information about the life and activities of the mass of the people in Rome and Italy. This being the character of the most important literary sources available at that time, it was inevitable that the older generation of modern writers on Greek and Roman history — men like Niebuhr, Thirlwall, Grote — should treat mainly of political, military, and intellectual history. The accumulation of archæological and epigraphic material has enabled more recent scholars to enlarge the picture of the Greek and Roman world, by adding to their narrative sections on economic development, or on social history and institutions. Yet the new method of reconstructing the past sometimes seems in danger of being carried too far. Political, military, and constitutional history is relegated to second place, and page after page is devoted to the treatment of social or economic history.

The more brilliant the reconstruction of these aspects from the recently found material, the greater the danger that the picture of Greek and Roman history is out of focus. For, ultimately, where ancient histories have survived, they must necessarily form the framework on which the modern student has to build up his reconstruction of ancient history. In view of the character of those histories a properly balanced reconstruction should give first place to those aspects of the ancient world which they illuminate. Besides, while in the case of the ancient kingdoms of the Near and Middle East political history is synonymous with the history of dynasts and dynasties, so that a certain distaste on the part of the modern reader for the continual rivalries, the endless wars, the egotistical aggrandizement of eastern potentates, is intelligible and excusable, in the case of the Greeks and Romans — at any rate during a great part of their history — political affairs, both at home and abroad, were the concern of the citizen body as a whole. Thus, to give but one example, an account of the Greek city-states from the sixth to the fourth century B.C., which relegates to a secondary place the political history and institutions of that period, can only be radically false and one-sided. In fine, the disproportion between political and social history, and the gross overemphasis of the latter in more than one recent publication on ancient history, necessitate the repetition of a truism, that it is impossible for a student to understand the social institutions and life of any people until he has a clear grasp of that people's political development and history.

Whereas some consideration will subsequently be given in their proper chronological place to the more noteworthy historical and other writers of Ancient Greece, it is convenient at this point to offer some remarks on the materials which have been broadly designated archæological sources. By these are meant the remains of ancient cities and buildings, objects of art of most divers kinds, implements of domestic use or from the workshop, coins, pottery, and inscriptions. Utensils made of baked clay are cheap; unless they are meant for ornament and are therefore elaborately decorated, they can be easily and inexpensively replaced; and, though they may be broken, the fragments are almost imperishable. Broken pottery will be thrown aside by the inhabitants of a settlement, so that in time a dump or rubbish heap will accumulate. And, even if the settlement be abandoned, the dump will remain as a record of the site's former occupation. Again, it was a common practice among ancient peoples to bury with their dead articles such as these had used during their earthly life. Pottery is not only the commonest form of such grave furniture, it is also the most important to the modern student of ancient civilization. In the prehistoric period of any country, or in any era of which written records are meagre or absent, potsherds are indeed precious historical material. If pottery be present in any quantity at a given site, the stratification will enable the excavator to establish some form of chronological scheme. It may provide evidence, too, for commercial, or for less friendly, intercourse between the inhabitants of different regions; and something may be learnt from it of the culture and conditions of life of its makers. The depth of such deposits is sometimes very considerable; in the mound of Tell-el-Hesy, in southern Palestine, the different strata together totalled a depth of some sixty feet; at Cnossus in Crete the Neolithic deposit amounted on an average to twenty-six feet, representing many centuries of human occupation.

Many kinds of substance have been used for the recording of inscriptions, while their content is of almost infinite variety. The material is mainly determined by the natural resources of a country. In Mesopotamia, where both stone and wood were scarce, clay was usually employed; in Egypt, stone and papyrus.

But wood, wooden tablets smeared with wax, leather, and skins, in short, any substance presenting a reasonably smooth surface, have been used at various times and places as writing material. The contents of an inscription — using the latter word in its widest sense — may be almost anything. It may be no more than a person's name, it may be a letter, a bill, a curse, a chronicle, an official document, a funeral éloge.

Apart from late writers like Manetho and Berossus (both lived in the third century B.C.), and foreigners like Herodotus and Ctesias, no formal histories of the great oriental kingdoms and dynasties have survived. The epigraphic records on the other hand are abundant for some periods, scanty or lacking for others. Doubtless chance and the ravages of time have operated very greatly to effect this unequal preservation of written sources. But warfare and the accompanying destruction of material things are no less the cause of many gaps in our knowledge; and, in addition, we must not leave out of sight the possibility that a people might deliberately seek to suppress, or at least take no trouble to preserve, the memory of some part of its history. Modern ignorance concerning the period of Hyksos domination in Egypt is due not merely to the material factors already noted, but to the desire of the Egyptians of the eighteenth and later dynasties to forget this unhappy period of their national growth. Conversely, the deliberate act of one of Assyria's last kings, Ashurbanipal, in collecting a great library of cuneiform tablets, which modern excavation has retrieved, has put at our disposal exceptionally full material for studying the latest and most glorious centuries of Assyrian history.

But in Greek history, too, there are periods of considerable length for whose political history the existing literary evidence is restricted in amount and inferior in quality. This is the case, for example, with Greece in the third century B.C., but the epigraphic material is fortunately abundant. Finally, there are aspects of Greek civilization about which we should be almost wholly ignorant, save for the preservation of numerous inscriptions. But for these, to give but one instance, the development of school and higher education in the Greek world of the last three centuries B.C. would be very obscure.

As the city-states developed and their political and economic life became more complex, written records grew rapidly in quantity. The various kinds of official documents kept in the public archives were inscribed on rolls of *papyrus;* these — leaving aside the special case of Egypt — have long since perished. But, happily, copies of the more noteworthy texts were often made on more durable material, stone or bronze, and set up in the market and other public places. It is to the recovery of these, often in a sadly mutilated condition, that we owe much of our knowledge of certain aspects of ancient Greek civilization. Moreover, as a stereotyped phraseology gradually became fixed for many official transactions and decrees, damaged inscriptions can frequently be restored by the expert with a very high degree of certainty. There is an immense variety of such records and we cannot do more than indicate the character of a few. There are remains of law-codes, like that from Gortyn; [1] official lists of priests and magistrates; resolutions or decrees passed by civic assemblies; treaties made between two or more states; and the official transactions of city-councils and city-magistrates. Of great value, too, are many documents referring to the undertaking or completion of public works, and to state income and expenditure; [2] furthermore, leases and contracts, as well as gifts or bequests made by public-spirited citizens, and in the Hellenistic age also by princes, to city-governments for a great variety of purposes. [3] Nor, finally, must the many records of purely private transactions be overlooked.

An introductory chapter to a general survey of ancient history must necessarily include some reference to the methods of reckoning time used by the ancients, and to the general principles on which the chronology of ancient states has been reconstructed. The modern reader is so accustomed to seeing the birth of the Founder of Christianity taken as the starting point for reckoning historical events both forward and backward, that he tends to forget that, while there was a certain unity due to the fact that ultimately all time-reckoning depends on observation of the heavenly bodies, in detailed practice there was great diversity. The use of both the lunar year and of the solar is extremely ancient. Babylonia and Egypt may be said to share the honor of evolving systems of time-reckoning and methods of expressing

[1] Cf. below, page 149.   [2] Cf. below, page 316.   [3] Cf. below, page 429.

conveniently the intervals between, and the succession of, events, on which all subsequent chronological schemes are based. The contribution of Babylonia was the greater, for the familiar divisions into years and months, and of the day into two sets of twelve hours each, appear to have originated there. The Babylonians, however, followed the lunar year, so that frequent intercalary periods were necessary to keep the months in proper relation to the seasons. It is remarkable that their method of expressing successive events in official documents was for centuries so primitive and cumbersome; for we can hardly call otherwise a system in which a particular year is named after some important event, or else the year after such and such an occurrence. In Egypt the reckoning by a solar year of exactly 365 days was in use from earliest times. As it was not the practice to intercalate a day every four years, the months in time lost all relation to the seasons, and corrections do not appear to have been made in the calendar with any regularity or frequency. Again, the dating of events as occurring in such and such a year of King X was clumsy; it has also caused much difficulty to the modern student of Egyptian history. For there is often great uncertainty about the length of a particular king's reign. The system followed by the Assyrians marks a great advance on earlier usage. They, in their official documents and computation of events, followed the more convenient method of naming each year after an official or magistrate. It was a method analogous to that in use at a much later date in the majority of Greek city-states and in Rome. Many such lists of Assyrian magistrates (*limmu* lists) have been preserved; they are invaluable not only for dating events in Assyrian history, but for reconstructing the chronology of other countries, for example, of Egypt. It must be admitted that the dating of reigns and events in Egyptian and Mesopotamian history prior to the middle of the second millennium B.C. is still attended by many uncertainties, and the dates, reckoned in terms of years B.C., which are given in modern histories, must therefore be regarded as approximate rather than as precise.

Both in the Greek city-states and in Rome the lunar year formed the basis of the calendar, with the inevitable result that some inaccuracy in the relation between calendar and seasons

was more or less constant. In Greece the lunar year was reckoned as 354 days, and it was therefore 11 days short of the solar.
In order to bring the two into harmony, an intercalary month
was inserted every two or three years. Thus, in Athens, to the
last quarter of the fifth century, a lunar-solar cycle of eight
years with three intercalary months was in force. For a time
this cycle was superseded by a nineteen-year cycle, devised by
the astronomer Meton; though this gave a somewhat more accurate computation, it was still short of exact. Later, the Athenians reverted once more to the eight-year cycle. So far as we
know, no other Greek state devised a more efficient calendar.
The usual method of dating events was by reference to the chief
magistrate in a given year (*e.g.* at Athens, the senior archon, at
Sparta, the senior ephor); but, even on official inscriptions, we
do not find such indications of date before the middle of the fifth
century. The dating by Olympiads, that is to say, by a four-
year period computed on the celebration of the Olympian festival (traditional date of the first Olympiad, 776 B.C.), was
never used in public or private business, or in official documents. And, though relatively a far more convenient system of
reckoning, it was not even adopted by historical writers before
the third century B.C.

There are other facts which may increase our difficulty in
trying to equate ancient and modern dates exactly. For example, the calendar year in different city-states started at different seasons. At Athens it began in midsummer; hence to
represent a given Attic year accurately in modern reckoning it
is necessary to indicate two years. In this way the first archonship of Themistocles, which began in mid-July, 493, and lasted
till mid-July, 492, must be expressed by a double date, 493–492.
Again, in Athens, from the fifth century on, the ten committees
of the Council each officiated for one-tenth of the year. To
bring this reckoning into complete accord with the calendar
year of twelve months sometimes creates difficulties.

The Jewish calendar, which is still in use among that people
for religious purposes, is likewise lunar. The year is divided into
twelve months of twenty-nine and thirty days. To make up the
difference between the lunar and the solar year a thirteenth
month is periodically inserted, usually every three years.

Finally, we must note the practice of reckoning in eras, that is to say, dating the history of a country by the years after some event of outstanding importance. Of such eras a goodly number were introduced at different times, but for the most part their use was restricted to comparatively small areas. Of the few which were widely adopted, and existed for a prolonged period, one instance will suffice. The so-called Seleucid era, which began in the autumn of 312 B.C., was followed for many centuries in the countries included in the one-time Syrian empire. Among many of the Jews of the Near East its use continued at least as late as the eleventh century A.D.; and it survives to the present day among some Christian sects and their Mohammedan neighbors in Syria.

CHAPTER I

MAN IN THE STONE AGE

I would then that I lived not among the fifth race of men, but either had died before or had been afterward. For now verily is a race of iron. Neither by day shall they ever cease from weariness and woe, neither in the night from wasting, and sore cares shall the gods give them. Howbeit even for them shall good be mingled with evil. Hesiod, *Works and Days*, 174–179. (Mair's translation.)

A VERY old myth, once perhaps current among many peoples though varying in details, teaches that mankind, since man's creation, has passed through several stages, each of considerable length. According to the commonest form of the legend there were four such eras, but the early Greek poet Hesiod, adding one to the number, describes successively five: the Golden, the Silver, the Bronze, the Heroic, and the Iron Ages. The idea underlying this myth is one of the progressive degeneration of mankind, the story of man's gradual decline from a god-like character and existence. Modern archæological science, too, distinguishes a number of stages in the history of man; but, reversing the pessimism of legendary fancy, traces man's continuous advance in material culture, and his social and political evolution. These stages or periods of material progress have been conveniently named after the substances which men have in each case used to fashion the implements on which they chiefly depended for their means of subsistence. Thus it has become customary to refer to the Early Stone (Palæolithic) Age and the Late Stone (Neolithic) Age, the Copper and Bronze Ages, and, finally, the Iron Age. But it should be noted at the outset that, though such a classification is very convenient for defining the general course of man's material progress, and for distinguishing very approximately the main stages of a long journey, it would be a serious error to assume that these epochs were sharply marked off one from the other. On the contrary, the more evidence accumulates, the clearer it becomes that there was no break in continuity between the Palæolithic and the Neolithic, or between the Neolithic and the Copper-Bronze Ages. Rather, one merged gradually into the other, so that, for example, the earliest users of copper or bronze tools in a given area continued side by side with these to use stone implements or arms.

The remains of the Palæolithic Age have been found in river drifts and valley deposits, in caves, and in rock shelters, over a very wide geographic area; namely, in Syria, North Africa and Egypt, central Europe as far as Bulgaria, South Russia; above all, in England, France, and the Spanish peninsula. So far no finds of Palæolithic objects are attested for Macedonia and Greece or for the islands of the eastern Mediterranean. By far the densest distribution is in France and Spain; it is from the Early Stone Age remains brought to light in those two countries that the slow evolution, representing the passage of many thousands of years, of Palæolithic man, his tools, and his art, can best be studied in unbroken continuity from the first beginnings down to the advent of the Neolithic Age. Very slowly man learnt to improve with his hands the rough stones and flints which at first he had used much as he found them in nature. These flints are of various types, serving as knives, cleavers, scrapers, and axes. Even in the earliest period of the Palæolithic Age man acquired the art of chipping pieces from a flint core and fashioning them into sharp-edged tools. Excavators have in different areas discovered what may be called Palæolithic workshops, that is to say, Palæolithic deposits of flints with the cores from which they had been flaked. A further stage of development is reached with the use of animal bones for making implements. At last, with the greater diversity and immensely improved character of their tools, men were enabled to advance culturally with relatively much greater speed. It is to the latest period of the Palæolithic Age that belong numerous and most varied examples of earliest man's artistic skill. Carving or sculpture in the round, incised drawing, low relief, and painting — all these methods of portraying human or animal figures he learnt to master. In all probability he modelled or

carved rude figurines in the round before trying his hand at
reproducing figures and objects on a flat surface, whether by
incision or by painting. For the latter processes demand a
somewhat greater measure of skill. Yet it is precisely in these
that Palæolithic man attained to the greatest degree of success.
The paintings, drawings, or engravings of reindeer, bison, horses,
wild goats, and other animals, which are to be seen in the caves
of the Dordogne in France or in the Altamira cave in northern
Spain, show an astonishing realism or naturalism, and testify to
the keen powers of observation possessed by the artists who
made them. No less striking is the minute skill displayed in
engraving figure designs on reindeer horns and bones, which
were either used as implements or intended as votive offerings.[1]
In either case we may suppose that the representations of wild
animals on them were believed to be, as it were, good magic, in
one case insuring success to the hunter who used a spear point
or harpoon so engraved, and in the case of votive gifts to procure in a more general way a plentiful supply of game. Human
figures, especially in paintings and drawings, are much rarer,
and the surviving examples show that Palæolithic man failed to
display the same artistic aptitude in portraying his fellows.
Probably, indeed, he had less skill in this respect because less
practice, if we are right in assuming that his primary impulse in
drawing and engraving was utilitarian rather than artistic. One
discovery of immense importance in the history of human progress can now be said with certainty to have been made in the
last period of the Palæolithic Age, the art of making fire. Momentous as was this new knowledge, it does not appear to have
been at all fully utilized. For it is only in the Later Stone Age
that those crafts for which the use of fire is essential began to be
developed.

Compared with the slow cultural advance of man in the
Palæolithic period progress in the Neolithic Age is rapid. Man
of the Late Stone Age used more varied materials; he showed
greater constructive ability in fashioning and constantly improving his implements; he displayed an inventive genius and
a social sense, which led to far-reaching developments. The dis-

---

[1] There is a magnificent collection of such decorated reindeer horns in
the museum at St. Germain-en-Laye, about twelve miles from Paris.

tribution of Neolithic remains is extremely wide; it extends from Scandinavia and England to North Africa and Egypt; from France and Spain in the West to Anau in central Asia (West Turkestan).[1] Though there are certain characteristics common to all this widely diffused culture, there are also many variations and differences in the material objects found in various Neolithic stations and graves. Hence archæologists have been enabled to distinguish some nine or ten regional groups, besides making various classifications, especially of the ceramic fabrics. Thus we can distinguish between the Neolithic culture of the Alpine and of the Danubian area, or the western from the eastern Mediterranean type. Other phases, again, are found in Egypt, Syria, Susa, and Anau.

The making of clay vessels, which is one of Neolithic man's important inventions, may well have been, up to a point, due to an accidental discovery. In a general way it is true that the earliest pot fabrics are imitations of more primitive containers; for example, in the western Mediterranean region, wooden bowls and vessels made from matted rushes, in eastern countries, the gourd. To procure greater density, or to protect the pots from the action of fire while the contents were being heated, a coating of clay might be applied. This, when exposed to the action of fire, hardened, and it was but one step further to fashion an all-clay pot in imitation of a gourd or rush vessel. The principle of reinforcing rush-work with clay is also found in late Neolithic building. Although it must be admitted that the Neolithic period has no naturalistic paintings or drawings to show, to match the best of the Palæolithic cave pictures, Neolithic man was by no means devoid of an æsthetic sense, which he manifested in other ways. Much of the later Neolithic pottery shows great diversity of shapes, precision of form, fineness of texture, and equal firing, to a truly remarkable degree. For, at that time neither the potter's wheel nor the kiln had yet been invented. Again, we can trace a gradual evolution of design; at first it is quite primitive, finger impressions made on the wet clay, which, on being baked, left a rude pattern on the surface of the vase. Then, simple linear ornaments began to be incised or painted in

[1] For completeness be it added that both the older and the younger Stone Age can be illustrated by finds in China and Japan.

more regular designs on the vessels. In the latest stage the whole pot may be covered with regular, and often very elaborate, geometric or spiral decoration. To Neolithic man's accomplishments as a maker of stone implements far in advance of Palæolithic tools, and as a potter, we may further add his skill in textile work, using this term in a wide sense to include spinning, weaving, netting, and basket making. Examples of such work have been preserved, but they are necessarily scarce owing to the perishable nature of the material.

Of far-reaching importance, too, was the domestication of animals (horse, ass, ox, sheep, pig, goat, dog), and of plants, which was now first effected. Yet the most striking characteristic of Neolithic man was his gradual realization that, to use Aristotle's famous phrase, man is a political being. In other words, not only did men by degrees abandon the nomadic and hunting modes of life, but they learnt to join together in groups and form communities, and to lead a more stationary existence. Indeed, the immense advance in material progress, which has already been outlined, was only possible because men realized the need of coalescing into settled communities and of collaborating in the satisfaction of their daily wants. Corporate action was especially manifested in Neolithic building. In such villages and stations as have been unearthed the ground plans of the huts show that these were sometimes square or rectangular, sometimes circular. They were built of branches and flexible twigs bound together by clay. Especially noteworthy are the lake-dwellings found in Switzerland, northern Italy, and some other districts. They are formed of square huts built on artificially constructed platforms, which in turn were supported by wooden piles driven into the bed of the lake. Some of these belong to the latest period of the Neolithic Age, but continued to be inhabited in the early Bronze Age; the lake-dwellings of Italy, however, do not appear to have been formed before the conclusion of the Stone Age.

But the most remarkable examples of engineering skill in the Neolithic epoch are to be found in the megalithic monuments. These occur in many places, but are most numerous in western Europe, especially in France. The names given in Brittany to these structures have been taken into general use by prehis-

STONEHENGE

toric archæologists. *Menhirs* are single large stones set on end; sometimes a number of such are arranged in a circular or oval formation (*cromlech*), sometimes they occur set up in a series of parallel rows (*alinement*). A *dolmen* is composed of several vertical stones surmounted by a single flat slab placed horizontally. The enormous size and weight of these stones fill the spectator with wonder how Neolithic men performed the feat of setting them on end, or — still greater feat — of transporting them for considerable distances from the place where they were originally found.[1] While the dolmens were certainly burial chambers, the purpose of the other types of megalithic monuments is still obscure. It is now definitely established that regular inhumation was already practised in the late Palæolithic Age, but it was earth-interment of the simplest character. Neolithic burials, on the other hand, were often far more elaborate. They were made in caves, both natural and artificial, under large boulders, or cut into the solid rock, in stone cists, or in the more elaborate stone chamber of a dolmen.

It has been convenient to portray the chief characteristics of the Neolithic area as a whole, but it is important to bear in mind that the duration of the Neolithic Age in different regions within that era varied enormously. Broadly speaking, it is in the South and East that men first learnt the use of metal, and in the North and Northwest that the Later Stone Age lasted longest. Thus, in Elam copper was in use perhaps as far back as 5000 B.C., and the earliest traces of man in southern Mesopotamia show that he was already familiar with metal. In Egypt copper was known by the middle of the fourth millennium and in Crete not much later. On the other hand, in Britain and in Scandinavia the Stone Age lasted to approximately 2000 B.C. The transition from one to the other, at whatever period it occurred, was very gradual. In some areas, as in Egypt and Crete, the transitional process can be traced with fair completeness; hence it has become convenient to dub the age, during which the use of stone and metal tools went on side by side, Sub-Neo-

---

[1] For example, several of the Breton menhirs attain to a height of from thirty to thirty-five feet; the enormous fallen monolith at Locmariaquer, now broken into several pieces, when intact was nearly seventy feet long. The largest of the menhirs in southern France do not exceed about fifteen feet.

lithic, Eneolithic, or Chalcolithic. That there was considerable commercial intercourse between the inhabitants of different regions during the Neolithic Age has been proved beyond question. The discovery in Neolithic graves in western Germany of necklaces made of Mediterranean shells, or the presence of the volcanic glass, called obsidian, coming from the island of Melos, in different parts of the eastern Mediterranean, are but two instances of such early trade relations. At the same time, owing to the chronological reasons given above, the Neolithic Age cannot be satisfactorily separated from the Copper-Bronze Age in a matter affecting different geographic areas at the same date. At this point it is enough to allude to the facts, since a fuller treatment of the topic may be reserved for a survey of the Bronze Age civilization of the Mediterranean area.

CHAPTER II

THE LAND OF THE TWO RIVERS

> *As for the land of Sumer and Akkad, I collected
> the scattered peoples thereof, and I procured food
> and drink for them. In abundance and plenty I
> pastured them, and I caused them to dwell in a
> peaceful habitation.* — From an inscription of
> King Hammurabi. (L. W. King, *Letters and
> Inscriptions of Hammurabi*, iii, p. 191.)

1. POLITICAL DEVELOPMENT AND HISTORY TO *c.* 1900 B.C.

IT was convenient in the previous chapter to sacrifice chronological order and to sketch as a whole the general character of
Stone Age culture. We must now revert to a more detailed
consideration of those regions of the Near and Middle East
in which the earliest historic kingdoms took their rise. We
must begin with that district of Asia, lying between the rivers
Euphrates and Tigris, which is itself but a part of that larger
area to which the name, the Fertile Crescent, has sometimes
been applied.[1] The two great streams which enclose this land
of the two rivers both rise in the Armenian highlands, and at no
great distance from one another. The Euphrates, after a tor-
tuous course through the Taurus and Anti-Taurus ranges, enters
the north Syrian plain by Samosata. From here to the Persian
Gulf the length of the river is almost twelve hundred miles at
the present day, but at the beginning of the historic period was
much less. For the process of silting-up has been so extensive
through the centuries that the sites of ancient cities, which
c. 3000 B.C. were on or close to the sea, are now a hundred miles
inland. The Tigris, whose upper course is much shorter, passes
through the hill-country of Assyria, and emerges into the plain

---

[1] By the Fertile Crescent is meant that wide semi-circular area bounded
on the south by the Persian Gulf and Indian Ocean, on the east by the
Iranian mountains, on the north by the Armenian highlands, and on the
west by the Mediterranean and Red sea.

near Tekrit. The two streams gradually converge, so that on the thirty-fourth parallel of latitude they are only a little more than a hundred miles apart, while in the neighborhood of Baghdad the width of the intervening plain narrows down to twenty miles. Since in ancient times the Euphrates followed a slightly more easterly course, the narrowest part of the plain may not have been more than fifteen miles from river to river. Below this point the interfluvial land widens again, and it is this region, with its rich alluvial soil, which corresponded to the kingdom of Babylonia, and, earlier still, to the lands of Akkad and Sumer. Only a very few cities belonging to this political area lay a little further to the north.

The hilly and mountainous country situated to the east of the lower Tigris was the land of Elam, corresponding roughly to the modern Persian provinces of Luristan and north Khuzistan. Its mountains are the southern extension of the ancient Zagros range, the central portion of which formed the eastern boundary of Assyria. Excavations conducted on two Elamitic sites, Susa and Musyan, have shown that the region was inhabited at a very early date (before 4000 B.C.) by a people whose earliest remains seem to show that they were at the end of the Neolithic and the beginning of the Chalcolithic Ages. Though there are certain affinities between the early Elamitic pottery and the earliest wares found in Mesopotamia on the one hand, and those un-earthed at Anau in west Turkestan on the other, the evidence does not at present warrant any definite ethnological conclusions being drawn from these remains. It is, however, abundantly clear that, from very early times, the inhabitants of Elam and Mesopotamia were in close contact, which, more often than not, took the form of warlike relations.

At the earliest date of which we have any record Babylonia had become the home of two peoples who were racially quite distinct, the Semites and the Sumerians. Which of these two races first settled in this region is still a disputed question; nor does the existing evidence permit us to draw any certain conclusions about the earlier home of the Mesopotamian Semites, though both Arabia and Asia Minor have been suggested. Again, several theories have been put forward regarding the original home of the Sumerians. The regions about and beyond the Caspian, central Asia, and India have all been so proposed, but none of these hypotheses is free from difficulties. Recent discoveries in Sind and in the Punjab have revealed ruins of a civilization which bears marked resemblance to the Sumerian. Tentatively the earliest of these Indian remains may be assigned to the beginning of the third millennium; we are warned, however, that the differences between the two cultures are by no means negligible.[1] The balance of probability seems to be slightly in favor of an original central Asiatic home, from whence several migrations took place. The earliest may have brought the Sumerians to Mesopotamia, while a later wave of peoples, akin to them, found its way to the Indus valley. At all events it is certain that when we first meet the Sumerians in Mesopotamia they are culturally far ahead of the earliest Semitic settlers.

Of the surviving lists of early Sumerian kings some at least belong to a very early date. Much later (end of the third millennium) are accounts of early Sumeria, which were composed by scholars and poets at a time when the Sumerians had lost their political independence and had been merged in a Semitic kingdom. Such writings, however good as literature, depict the realm of legend not of history. There are stories of a great deluge and of a very early unified kingdom of Babylon, as well as of various dynasties in city-states, of which the chief were at Kish in the North and at Erech in the South. The mythical king of Erech, Gilgamesh, became the central figure in many Sumerian legends, and the hero of a Sumerian, and later of a Semitic, epic. Even though these poems and tales are legendary, there can be no doubt that, underlying them, is a sound, if rather shadowy, historical tradition of a Sumerian occupation of southern Mesopotamia, extending over many centuries. Indeed, in more than one instance recent discoveries have shown the names of very early kings, hitherto regarded as quite mythical, to have been in fact historical. But, apart from isolated examples like this, the latest archæological explorations as a whole give startling sup-

---

[1] Cf. the warning in *Antiquity*, ii (1928), p. 82: "Recent excavation, whilst confirming the previous evidence of close connexion with the Sumerian civilization of Mesopotamia, has also revealed striking differences, and it is proposed to recognize this fact by substituting for the name Indo-Sumerian, formerly given to the newly discovered culture, that of Indus."

port to the belief that those legends enclose a very solid kernel
of historic truth. In the most recent excavations at Ur graves
were opened up, which certainly antedate the first dynasty of
Ur, and may do so by several centuries. Not only were some of
these burials in vaulted chambers of limestone and brick, showing a most advanced architectural technique, but the funeral
furniture laid with the dead is even more remarkable. Gold,
silver, and copper vessels, silver lamps, jewelry of gold, lapis,
and carnelian, ostrich shells encrusted with mother of pearl and
lapis lazuli, delicately modelled figurines of gold, and beautifully
worked daggers — all these are convincing proof of two important historic facts. In the first place, by the second half of the
fourth millennium B.C. the Sumerians had developed a material
culture far in advance of any contemporary civilization, not ex-
cepting Egypt; secondly, the artistry and craftsmanship revealed in these objects presuppose centuries of previous cultural
development. To cite the words of the fortunate discoverer of
these treasures, C. L. Woolley, "The earliest of the graves . . .
bear witness in their contents to a civilization already old and
with centuries of apprenticeship and development behind it." [1]
If then these objects may be dated about 3500 B.C. — and they
cannot be much later — the beginnings of Sumerian occupation
of Mesopotamia must be placed well back in the fifth millennium.

When, from about 3200 B.C., historical data for Mesopotamian history begin to be more definite and rapidly become fuller,
we find a great number of city-states in both the northern half
(Akkad) and the southern half (Sumer) of this region. In
Akkad the Semitic element is already becoming strong and continues to increase steadily. The history of the next twelve
hundred years in Mesopotamia is both a chronicle of almost
continuous warfare and political rivalry, in which the ruler of
first one, and then another, city temporarily subjugates one or
more of his neighbors, and also it is a record of a racial struggle,
in which the more vigorous, though less artistic, Semitic stock
ultimately triumphs, and the Sumerian is submerged. The
Semites learnt much from their neighbors; they took over the

---

[1] *Antiquity*, ii (1928), p. 17. The reports of the excavations at Ur are
to be found in the *Antiquaries Journal*.

Sumerian method of writing and adapted it to their own Semitic tongue. The Sumerian language, save as a vehicle of religious ideas and ritual, by degrees passed out of use.

Existing records are too few and too sporadic to enable one to give anything like a consecutive account of early Sumero-Akkadian history. Ur, Erech, Adab, Lagash, Umma, Kish, Opis, seem to have been the politically more powerful or culturally more advanced cities (Cf. Map 1). The ambitions of their rulers (*patesis*) made fighting an almost continuous occupation for at least a goodly portion of their subjects. From time to time the *patesi* of one city, being endowed with greater ability or ampler material resources, succeeded in bringing under his control one or more adjacent or rival communities. He would emphasize the greater power and dignity that he had won, by assuming the more impressive title *lugal*, which may be rendered king. What methods were adopted to administer his enlarged territories is quite obscure. We may suppose that the conquered cities were obliged to pay tribute, and their governors forced to swear fealty to the *lugal* as overlord. The death of the *lugal* was generally the signal for the subject cities to reassert their political independence. The *patesis* of Lagash appear to have exercised power in Mesopotamia for an unusually long period. King Ur-nina, the founder of a dynasty about 2900 B.C., is known from reliefs, on which he is pictured in the midst of his family. He is credited with improving the irrigation in his territories by building canals, and is known for his religious zeal, which took the form of numerous dedications to the gods. The character of the third ruler of Lagash, Eannatum, was more warlike. He claimed to have conquered the peoples of Umma, Opis, Erech, and Ur, to have laid low the powerful city of Kish, and even to have warred successfully against the Elamites. It has been questioned whether he was really as remarkable a conqueror as his inscriptions record. At all events a sculptured slab survives as a memorial of his prowess. On it several scenes are depicted: we see the king setting out to war at the head of his army, and the formal burial of his slain troops. We see, too, the enemy's dead, who are left unburied, and vultures are shown devouring them and carrying off their heads. From this grim piece of realism the slab has been dubbed the "Stele of the Vultures."

Information about the successors of Eannatum is at present
very scanty; but it seems clear that Eannatum's wide conquests, even if his account thereof be strictly accurate, were not
lasting, and, further, that the relations between Lagash and her
near neighbor, Umma, were a source of constant anxiety. Situated on the opposite side of a canal, the men of Umma could

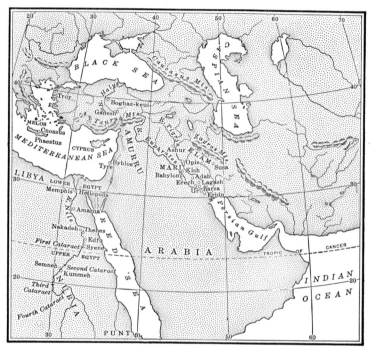

EGYPT AND THE NEAR EAST IN THE THIRD MILLENNIUM B.C.

interfere with the water supply of Lagash, and we now know
that the feud between the two communities was old-standing.
For, perhaps a century before Ur-nina's time, the king of Kish,
Mesilim, who was then (about 3000 B.C.) a power in the land,
had acted as arbitrator and had delimited the boundaries of the
two cities. The "Stele of the Vultures" had also been set up as
a boundary-stone. For about a century after Eannatum periods
of peace and war alternated in the political history of Lagash
and Umma, and the last independent *patesi* of Lagash was des-

tined to be overthrown by the ruler of Umma. It happens that a goodly number of documents from the time of Urukagina of Lagash (about 2700 B.C.) have been recovered. They show him to have been, not indeed a man of war, but a would-be social reformer. He aimed at improving the status of the laboring population, more especially by restraining the priestly and official classes, of whose greed and exactions many instances are quoted. These well-meant reforms naturally brought him the hostility of the more powerful among his subjects, and perhaps his rapid defeat at the hands of the ruler of Umma, Lugalzaggisi, and the reduction of Lagash, might at least have been postponed, if Urukagina could have relied on the full loyalty of all his subjects.

Lugalzaggisi's warlike progress was meteoric. He conquered Erech and made it his capital. When, somewhat later, he styled himself "king of the land of Sumer," it was no idle boast, for he really had brought city after city under his political control. His ambition did not end here, for he next turned his attention to the land of Amurru (*i.e.* Syria). "When he conquered from the rising to the setting sun, (the god) Enlil smoothed his path from the lower sea (*i.e.* the Persian Gulf) across the Tigris and Euphrates as far as the upper sea (*i.e.* the Mediterranean)," is the impressive statement of an inscription, in the later part of which is a list of important Sumerian cities who had acknowledged his overlordship.

Though there can be no doubt that for several centuries Semitic influence and power had been steadily growing in the northern district of Akkad, no Semitic dynasty had hitherto succeeded in winning a dominant position comparable to that held by Lugalzaggisi for a quarter of a century, or even to that enjoyed by the ablest of the rulers of Ur. With the arrival of Sharru-kin (Sargon) of Agade and Kish we enter on the first period of Semitic domination in Mesopotamia. Sargon's career of conquest was remarkable and his reign a long one (about 2637–2581 B.C.). The systematic reduction of the Sumerian cities, and the winning of undisputed mastery over the two lands of Sumer and Akkad, were followed by a series of foreign expeditions of which unhappily no detailed accounts have survived. It is clear, however, that he invaded the mountainous

country of Elam, and, besides laying siege to and capturing
Susa, occupied also some of the lesser Elamite towns. Even
more ambitious were his campaigns in the Northwest. Sargon
claims to have brought all the western lands as far as the
Mediterranean sea under his sway, and to have penetrated as
far as the Taurus mountains; indeed, there is now reason to
believe that he conducted an expedition even farther northward, into central Asia Minor, the region which at a later date
was to become the centre of the Hittite empire. For fifty-five
years Sargon ruled over his dominions, though the peace of his
later years was disturbed by rebellions. On his death many
of his subjects rose in revolt, and Sargon's elaborate political
structure was disrupted. Such disturbances were but too common in the oriental monarchies, especially during the earlier
period, and they show the dangers inherent in the quasi-feudal
system of government, in which, on the death of the ruler, each
or any prince of a dependent city might see an opportunity for
his own advancement by force of arms.

Some years later an even greater conqueror appeared in the
person of Naram-sin. His relationship to Sargon is disputed;
probably he was Sargon's grandson. Like his grandfather,
Naram-sin ruled over his people for more than half a century;
again our records are scanty and not free from difficulties. He
had to put down serious risings in the kingdom that he inherited,
on the first occasion soon after his succession, and again after
one of his foreign expeditions. Thus we see how a fairly prolonged absence from his seat of government might jeopardize
entirely the safety of his throne. His foreign campaigns took
him into the Zagros mountains in the East and as far as Kurd-
istan in the North. Whether Naram-sin's overlordship extended
to northern Syria and the Mediterranean, as Sargon's had done,
is not clear. There is no doubt about a great expedition to the
southeast, for it is referred to on the base of a diorite statue of
Naram-sin: "Naram-sin, the mighty, king of the four regions
of the earth, conqueror of nine armies in one year . . . He
conquered Magan and defeated Mani(um), prince of Magan.
In their mountains he quarried stones and bore them to his
city of Akkad. And he made thereof a statue of himself and
dedicated it to the god . . ." By the land of Magan is probably

meant the eastern or southeastern portion of the Arabian peninsula. The best-known monument of Naram-sin is the so-called
Stele of Victory, on which is commemorated the king's defeat of
King Satuni in the latter's kingdom situated in the Zagros
mountains. Naram-sin is seen ascending a steep mountain
followed by his army; he has just slain his opponent, who lies
wounded on the ground. Naram-sin himself is armed with
spear, bow and arrow, and battle-axe, and wears a helmet on
his head, but apparently no body armor. His men are armed
with bows and arrows and spears (Plate 1).

After Naram-sin's time the authority of Akkad began to
wane. The mountain tribes of Gutium had caused trouble to
the more peaceful inhabitants of the plains. Under the later
kings of Akkad such raids became more frequent and more
destructive. Finally, these rude mountaineers overran Sumer
and Akkad, where they appear to have exercised control for
more than a century. For a while a dynasty at Erech seems
to have ruled in Sumer, only to be ultimately overthrown by
the men of Gutium. The *patesis* of Lagash were more fortunate
and more powerful. Even in the time of the kings of Akkad,
the rulers of Lagash, though vassals of the former, had enjoyed
considerable independence and power. They seem to have
maintained their position even when the oppression of the rest
of the land by the kings of Gutium was at its worst. It happens
that exceptionally full records have been recovered illustrating
the reign of one of the later *patesis* of Lagash, Gudea. His
numerous inscriptions bear witness to his great piety, which
manifested itself in the erection of temples and dedications to
the gods. For this purpose he imported building-stone, cedar
and other costly woods, gold and copper, from distant lands.
Incidentally these statements afford an indication of extensive
commerce at this period, extending to the Taurus mountains and
Syria in the West, and to Arabia in the Southeast. Gudea's rule
lasted for many (forty?) years; it appears to have been marked
not only by piety to the gods but by justice and care for his
subjects.

It was a prince of Erech, Utukhegal, who brought the oppression of the Gutium dynasty over Sumer and Akkad to an end;
but information about these countries is extremely sparse until,

about 2300 B.C., a new dynasty arose at Ur. Its founder was Ur-engur, to whose importance as a law-giver we shall have occasion to refer later. Otherwise he is somewhat overshadowed in the existing records by his successor, Dungi, who is reputed to have reigned for fifty-eight years. His rule marks the last great Sumerian revival in Mesopotamia; at the same time it was a period during which Sumer and Akkad were once more under the ultimate control of a single ruler. Dungi styled himself both "king of the four regions of the earth" and "king of Sumer and Akkad"; as a conqueror he sought to rival Sargon and Naram-sin. He waged war against the Elamites and the mountain tribes of the Zagros range, and northern Mesopotamia and Assyria were effectively controlled by him. That his empire extended over Syria and as far as the Mediterranean is possible, but cannot in the present state of our knowledge be regarded as certain. That a part of Asia Minor was under the political control of Dungi, as has recently been suggested, must for the present be regarded as pure speculation. The empire of Ur-engur and Dungi fell to pieces under their successors; more than that, no Sumerian dynasty ever again attained to political power, and the Sumerian element in the population of Mesopotamia, which seems to have been growing steadily less for several centuries before this time, gradually disappeared or was merged in the Semitic.

Toward the end of the third millennium very important political developments occurred which radically altered the whole situation in Mesopotamia, and culminated in the establishment of the first Babylonian empire. The two main factors which operated so powerfully to change the political situation were the increased power of the Elamites and the appearance in the land of the two rivers of a new wave of Semites. Hostilities between Elam and the cities of Sumer and Akkad go back almost to the beginning of Mesopotamian history, and we have had occasion to refer more than once to wars between these neighboring countries. Hitherto, however, the advantage, so far as our very imperfect records allow us to form certain conclusions, seems generally to have been on the side of the Sumerian or Semitic princes. Of the growth of Elamite power in the second half of the third millennium nothing is known, but it was sufficient ultimately to give the Elamites a permanent hold on Sumer for a century. The last king of the Ur dynasty, Ibi-sin, was defeated by a coalition of the Elamite king and the chief of Mari, a considerable principality on the western side of the middle Euphrates. The Mari prince, Ishbi-irri, then established himself at Isin, and was the founder of a Semitic dynasty which endured for nearly two hundred years. A rival Semitic dynasty at Larsa came to the fore about the same time; for a while the two, whose relations seem at first to have been unusually harmonious, controlled most of the land. Later, Isin in alliance with the Elamites attacked Larsa, and a Semitic was replaced by an Elamite ruler there. But these new allies did not remain on good terms permanently; some forty years after they had made common cause against Larsa, the king of Isin himself succumbed to his Elamite neighbor.

But the most momentous occurrence during these two centuries, between the fall of the Ur dynasty and the establishment of the first Babylonian empire, was the settlement of a body of west Semitic (Amorite) invaders in Babylon. Geographically Babylon was situated on the western borders of Akkad, being on the western bank of the Euphrates a little below the point where the two rivers approach to within twenty miles of one another. Though inhabited from early times, Babylon was politically unimportant in the Sumero-Akkadian period. Maintaining at first a precarious existence in face of the powerful princes of Isin and Larsa, the new Amorite rulers of Babylon preserved their independence and in time began to encroach on the territories adjacent to their city. Even so, at the accession of the sixth in the line of Babylonian kings, Hammurabi (1947–1905 B.C.), the greatest power in the land was the Elamite king of Larsa, Rim-sin, who destroyed Isin and made himself master of all Sumer and at least a part of Akkad. Hammurabi was king of Babylon for over forty years; but, though he seems to have captured Isin and Erech early in his reign, it was not until he had been on the throne for thirty years that the great and final clash with the Elamites came. From this war (about 1918 B.C.) Hammurabi emerged triumphant. Rim-sin was captured, his Elamite allies were defeated, and the whole of Sumer and Akkad was brought under the sway of the Babylonian monarch. In the North

Hammurabi's authority extended as far as Assyria; for in a military despatch reference is made to "two hundred and forty men of the king's company . . . who have left the land of Ashur and the district of Shitullum." Hammurabi's son and successor, Samsu-iluna, ruled almost as long as his father, but his kingdom was disturbed and even threatened by foreign peoples, who under his successors encroached more and more, and finally, about 1750 B.C., brought the Babylonian dynasty to an end. These new political developments in Mesopotamia and the adjacent countries, since they to some extent inaugurate a new era, must be postponed to a later chapter.

2. MESOPOTAMIAN CIVILIZATION

Social and economic life in Mesopotamia at the time of the first Babylonian dynasty can be reconstructed with considerable fullness, thanks to the copious documentary material which has been recovered by the excavator's spade. Thus, there are available numerous letters of Hammurabi and his successors, as well as a substantial body of inscriptions. Above all, in 1901 the French archæologist De Morgan discovered at Susa in Elam a large slab inscribed with the now famous code of laws which has made Hammurabi's name immortal (Plate 2). For Mesopotamian civilization prior to Hammurabi's time the available material is far less abundant and much more scattered. Nevertheless, though it is often very hazardous to use the evidence of one age to illustrate the history of another, the risk in the present case is relatively slight. For, where the life and habits of a people were so largely determined by geographical and climatic conditions, which in the land of the two rivers have varied little through the ages, it is safe to assume that many of the conditions which are well attested for c. 2000 B.C. had existed with little change for centuries before. This would be especially true of what was by far the most important occupation in that region, agriculture.

As far back as our records go, we find allusions to irrigation and to the building and upkeep of canals, which branched off from, or connected, the two rivers, and formed a perfect network of waterways. The snows melting in Armenia in the early spring cause an enormous increase in the volume of water carried down toward the sea by the Euphrates and Tigris. In April and May the rivers are at their highest, and cause heavy inundations in the plains; in June the waters gradually fall. The plain-dwellers from earliest times had two problems to face; on the one hand, they must prevent the flood-waters from standing and converting large tracts of territory into marsh land, unfit for cultivation. On the other hand, they must so husband their resources that there would be enough water available for the fields during the hot summer months, when the rivers were at their lowest. It causes no surprise, therefore, that, even in the earliest epigraphic records, we meet with allusions to canal-building and to proper irrigation, which was of such vital importance to every Mesopotamian community. We have already seen how the question of the water-supply was a constant anxiety to the rulers of Lagash, and involved them in frequent hostilities with the neighboring city of Umma. The inscriptions of both Ur-nina and Urukagina record the construction of canals, while a similar attention to irrigation is found in documents of Ur-engur, the founder of the third dynasty at Ur. The letters of the Babylonian dynasty have numerous allusions to this same topic, and the code of Hammurabi contains many ordinances which testify to a careful supervision of all waterways. Nor must it be forgotten that the larger canals, like the rivers, were extensively used for purposes of navigation and transport. Occasionally, in spite of every care being taken, disasters might occur. In the twenty-sixth, and again in the thirty-eighth, year of Hammurabi serious floods devastated the land, and doubtless caused much misery. The task of keeping the canals themselves clear by dredging, as well as seeing that the canal-banks were in good repair, entailed constant attention and much labor. For the upkeep of the banks the farmers through whose plots the canal flowed were responsible. If a cultivator was careless in keeping his portion of a dike in proper condition, and his negligence caused loss to others, the code provides that he must make good the loss. On the other hand, such a regulation as this, "if a man owe a debt and (the god) Adad inundate his field and carry away the produce, or through lack of water, grain have not grown in the field, in that year he shall not make any return

of grain to the creditor, he shall alter his contract tablet, and
he shall not pay the interest for that year," [1] shows that there
was a good deal of sound equity in the code.

The population of Babylonia, as we find it in Hammurabi's
day, was made up of three groups: an upper class, a lower class
of free men, and a servile class. The barrier between the first
and second seems to have been rather rigid. The upper class
must have been a very heterogeneous one, including not only the
landed nobility and the priests, but the numerous public officials
and the wealthier traders and merchants. The lower class was
made up of small farmers, craftsmen, artisans, and so forth. In
the sense that these seem to have had no political influence
they may be regarded as half-free; but, inasmuch as they were
liable to some military service, and could own property and
slaves, they are almost as sharply separated from the servile
class as from their superiors. That slavery was a very ancient
institution is beyond doubt; what is remarkable is that the
slaves had certain privileges which we do not find in other ancient slave-holding societies. For example, a male slave might
marry a free woman; the children of such a marriage would be
free. Again, slaves, though legally regarded as chattels, could
nevertheless acquire some property of their own, which, on the
death of a married slave, would pass to his wife and children.
One remarkable feature of Hammurabi's code has never been
satisfactorily explained. The punishments are extremely severe
and framed on the principle of exact retributive justice, best expressed in the Biblical phrase, "an eye for an eye, a tooth for a
tooth." Nevertheless, there are two scales of punishment, one
for the upper class, one for the humbler folk, and members of the
former are punished more severely than the latter. It has been
suggested that the distinction indicates an original difference of
race, but this explanation creates as many difficulties as it solves,
and the problem must for the present be regarded as unsolved.

Of a great part of the land the monarch himself was the owner;
much, too, was "owned" by one or other of the gods, that is to
say, for practical and mundane purposes, it was under the control of the priests. Thus it is probable that a relatively small
portion of all the territory suitable for cultivation was privately

[1] Code of Hammurabi, § 48.

owned. The actual agricultural work, whether the land was
royal domain, temple property, or privately owned, was carried
on partly by slaves, partly by the poorer class of free men, who
were in effect small tenant farmers. Their living was at all times
precarious, since the tithes or payments to the landlord were
heavy; and in addition they were, as we have seen, liable for the
upkeep of the canals, on which the success of their crops depended. Moreover, in spite of the fertility of the soil, the labor
and the anxieties of the farmer were many. Land in Mesopotamia, if not kept under cultivation, rapidly became overgrown
with weeds. Growing crops must be protected from birds and
insects; while a swarm of locusts in the spring might ruin a
whole year's work. The field crops that were most extensively
grown were wheat, barley, and spelt. Hardly less important
than these for the essential food-supply was the cultivation of
the date-palm. Cattle- and especially sheep-rearing were carried on intensively; for wool, together with grain and the produce of the date-palm, formed the most important articles of
export. The "honey" used for sweetening was in reality date-
syrup; for bee-keeping, though known on the Middle Euphrates
and in Assyria at a later date, was not practised in Babylonia.
From fermented date-syrup a highly intoxicating beverage was
prepared. Of fruit-trees, the fig and the pomegranate were
most successfully raised. Cattle were used for plowing and for
draught purposes, but the universal beast of burden was the
donkey. Recent discoveries have shown that the horse and
the war-chariot were already known in Mesopotamia at the
beginning of the third millennium; but probably the horse
was used only for military and not for domestic needs. One
special class of agriculturists in the time of the first Babylonian
dynasty is of peculiar interest. The military forces were made
up partly of a standing army, partly of a citizen militia, levied
as need for it arose. To the members of the standing force,
the professional soldiery, the king regularly assigned lots of land.
These their sons inherited, but with the liability to serve in the
army as their fathers had done. Thus it is in Babylonia that
we first meet with such military occupiers, a class found in
later centuries, for instance, in Egypt and in the Roman empire.
The official class was very numerous. In the earlier period of

Mesopotamian history a quasi-feudal system obtained; consequently, the *lugal's* officials were relatively few in number, because the government of cities conquered by him was left to the
local chiefs or *patesis*, after they had made their submission to
him. The efforts of Sargon and Naram-sin, and later of Ur-
engur and Dungi, to form a more unified state out of Akkad and
Sumer, must have resulted in an increase in the number of royal
officials, who to a great extent replaced the local chiefs or magistrates. Under the Babylonian dynasty this process was carried much farther. Hammurabi or Samsu-iluna governed their
dominion through their own officials, and the monarch concerned himself not only with their conduct but with that of their
subordinates. The most numerous body of officials was those
charged with the collection of taxes and tribute. All classes had
to pay tribute to the king; in Hammurabi's time even temple
lands were not exempt. The payment of tribute was either in
kind or else in gold, silver, or copper. The ingots of metal were
stamped to guarantee their weight and purity. Remission of
taxation was a very exceptional reward, which the monarch
sometimes bestowed on specially deserving officials.

The conditions under which the lower class lived in the towns
were a good deal better than those endured by the small-farming
population. The craftsmen seem regularly to have been organized in associations or gilds; at the head of each was a kind of
president or master, who acted as intermediary between the
members of his craft and the officials in such matters as taxation or recruiting for the army, in a manner curiously reminiscent of the professional corporations and their *magistri* in the
Roman empire. The master craftsmen also took pupils for
instruction. The length of such apprenticeships, as extant
articles of agreement show, varied greatly and depended on
the trade to be learnt. They might be completed in little more
than a year or they might last as much as five. The absence
in Mesopotamia of stone and timber suitable for building meant
that these materials must be imported from outside. Even
palaces and temples were constructed of brick and tiles, though
here and there stone might be used for some special part or
decorative feature. The wood of the palm was indeed employed
in building, but it was of exceedingly poor quality. For fine

pillars and massive doors cedar from Lebanon and other hard woods were transported at great expense by the rulers in Babylonia. For ordinary purposes the substances ready to hand were exploited with great skill. The long reeds abounding in marshy districts could be utilized for building, furniture, and in other ways. But, above all, clay was plentiful and good, and all manner of utensils could be fashioned in pottery which in other countries would be made of wood or metal. The demand for water-pipes, casks, chests, lamps, spinning-whorls — all made of baked clay — in addition to vases of every shape and size, both for everyday use and for ornament, made the potter's calling the most widely followed of all the crafts. Although metal had been known from very early times, it was, since all of it had to be imported, still relatively scarce during the third millennium. Copper, which in the beginning had been used in a pure state, was in time alloyed with lead or antimony, and, later still, with tin, to produce the harder and more durable bronze. Iron was indeed known in Hammurabi's day, but it was scarce and dear. Of extreme antiquity, as shown, for example, by the finds from Ur, was the expert working of the precious metals, alone or in conjunction with lapis lazuli and other precious and semi-precious stones. The value of silver remained relatively great, seeing that as late as *c.* 2000 the ratio of gold to silver was as high as 1 : 6. The regions from which the various metals were obtained cannot be specified with any certainty.

The most recent excavations at Ur have revealed a part of the town-site; even after the loss of its political independence Ur must have continued to be one of the more important cities in Babylonia. The remains of houses and streets thus laid bare belong to the period of the first Babylonian dynasty. The houses were carefully built in such a way that the lower courses of the walls were of burnt bricks, and the upper courses of mud brick, very accurately joined together. They were roomy, too, for there can be little doubt that many of them had an upper story. The ground floor contained a general living-room, domestic offices, and, sometimes at least, a private chapel; a staircase led to the more private rooms above. Thus, we are at liberty to deduce that the standard of comfort enjoyed by the town-dwellers was reasonably high, a conclusion that is also borne out by the material objects, and by the evidence of numerous private letters of this age, recovered from various Mesopotamian sites.

Nothing is more remarkable than the highly centralized and carefully organized administration under which the subjects of Hammurabi lived, as illustrated particularly by the careful administration of justice. These Babylonians seem to have been as fond of litigation as the Greeks of the fourth century B.C. are said to have been. Thus we may properly conclude this section with some further remarks on the code of Hammurabi and on judicial affairs in general. When the code was first deciphered, Hammurabi was hailed as one of the world's great legislators. Though further discoveries have shown that he hardly deserves such a title, his claim to be regarded as an administrator of undoubted eminence is beyond dispute. Since the code was discovered considerable remains of an earlier Sumerian law-code have been recovered; a comparison of the two codes makes it clear that Hammurabi's legal ordinances were based on the earlier Sumerian laws. For these the founder of the third dynasty of Ur, Ur-engur, may be largely responsible, for he was noted for his attention to justice and good order. Yet much that the Sumerian code contained was, in all likelihood, not so much express legislation by a particular ruler, as a codification and writing down of custom and customary law, existing long before and till then handed down by oral tradition. Hammurabi's code contains nearly three hundred headings, but most of them are very brief. They deal with a great variety of topics.[1] Some citations will best make clear the strange contrast between the crudest application of the *lex talionis* and a civil law of considerable juristic refinement, which we find side by side in the code. Thus, on the one hand we find the retributive principle carried to extreme lengths:[2]

[1] The following is a brief summary of the contents: §§ 1–5, penalties for false witness and unjust judge; §§ 6–25, criminal offenses; §§ 26–41, regulations respecting military service; §§ 42–126, civil law, especially as governing contracts of various kinds; §§ 127–194, the law of the family and divorce regulations; §§ 195–227, punishments; §§ 228–277, ordinances regulating prices, hire of labor, and building operations; §§ 278–282, slaves.

[2] The citations that follow are taken from *The Code of Hammurabi* by

STELE OF NARAM–SIN

Plate 1

STELE CONTAINING THE CODE OF HAMMURABI

Plate 2

195 If a son strike his father, they shall cut off his fingers.

196 If a man destroy the eye of another man, they shall destroy his eye.

202 If a man strike the person of a man who is his superior, he shall receive sixty strokes with an ox-tail whip in public.

218 If a physician operate on a man for a severe wound with a bronze lancet and cause the man's death; or open an abscess (in the eye) of a man with a bronze lancet and destroy the man's eye, they shall cut off his fingers.

229 If a builder build a house for a man and do not make its construction firm, and the house which he has built collapse and cause the death of the owner of the house, that builder shall be put to death.

230 If it cause the death of a son of the owner of the house, they shall put to death a son of that builder.

It is difficult to believe that the law was ever fully enforced, or that the savage punishments for criminal offenses were regularly carried out. It is more reasonable to suppose that the code lays down the maximum penalty, leaving it to the discretion of the judges to fix a lighter punishment in specific cases. On the other hand, it was the mark of an enlightened government to hold the towns and their magistrates responsible for the maintenance of law and order in their respective communities, as exemplified in paragraph 23:

23 If the brigand be not captured, the man who has been robbed, shall, in the presence of God, make an itemized statement of his loss, and the city and the governor, in whose province and jurisdiction the robbery was committed, shall compensate him for whatever was lost.

Again, the provisions of the code, as well as contemporary letters, make it clear that the position of women was juridically more favorable than in other ancient communities. The laws governing marriage and divorce seem less to the woman's disadvantage than the provisions of the Greek or earlier Roman law. The following quotations are a fair sample of this part of the code:

138 If a man would put away his wife who has not borne him children, he shall give her money to the amount of her marriage

R. F. Harper (University of Chicago Press; 1904). The numbers refer to the sections.

settlement, and he shall make good to her the dowry which she brought from her father's house, and then he may put her away.

141 If the wife of a man who is living in his house, set her face to go out and play the part of a fool, neglect her house, belittle her husband, they shall call her to account; if her husband say "I have put her away," he shall let her go. On her departure nothing shall be given to her for her divorce. If her husband say, "I have not put her away," her husband may take another woman. The first woman shall dwell in the house of her husband as a maidservant.

142 If a woman hate her husband, and say, "Thou shalt not have me," they shall inquire into her antecedants for her defects; and if she have been a careful mistress and be without reproach and her husband have been going about and greatly belittling her, that woman has no blame. She shall receive her dowry and shall go to her father's house.

We may conclude with one or two citations from that part of the code which regulates business transactions:

59 If a man cut down a tree in a man's orchard, without the consent of the owner of the orchard, he shall pay one-half mana of silver.

60 If a man give a field to a gardener to plant as an orchard and the gardener plant the orchard and care for the orchard four years, in the fifth year the owner of the orchard and the gardener shall share equally; the owner of the orchard shall mark off his portion and take it.

61 If the gardener do not plant the whole field, but leave a space waste, they shall assign the waste space to his portion.

104 If a merchant give to an agent grain, wool, oil, or goods of any kind with which to trade, the agent shall write down the value and return (the money) to the merchant. The agent shall take a sealed receipt for the money which he gives to the merchant.

105 If the agent be careless and do not take a receipt for the money which he has given to the merchant, the money not receipted for shall not be placed to his account.

Various courts existed for the administration of justice and for carrying the provisions of the code into effect. In the past, judicial authority would appear to have been mainly in the hands of the priests, and trials would then be conducted in a portion of a temple set apart for this purpose. In Hammurabi's time, however, such priestly jurisdiction had well-nigh ceased, though the administration of the oath fittingly remained one of the duties of the ministers of religion. The documents of the period refer to "king's judges" and "city judges"; one of the regulations of the code lays down severe penalties against a judge who shall have reversed an earlier judgment, the implication being, of course, that he did so from corrupt motives:

> 5 If a judge pronounce a judgment, render a decision, deliver a verdict duly signed and sealed and afterward alter his judgment, they shall call that judge to account for the alteration of the judgment which he had pronounced, and he shall pay twelve-fold the penalty which was said in judgment; and, in the assembly, they shall expel him from his seat of judgment, and he shall not return, and with the judges in a case he shall not take his seat.

Severe penalties were also imposed on false witnesses. The litigant had the right of appealing directly to the monarch, if he considered that he had not been justly treated by the judges before whom he had appeared. The numerous letters of the period are largely concerned with litigation arising out of leases, sales, contracts, and so forth; there are some, too, which record the intervention or the decision of the king himself in cases which had been brought to his notice, either by way of appeal or in some other manner. Thus it is abundantly clear that, although there was as yet no sharp distinction between civil and criminal offenses, though the penal ordinances are crude, the Babylonians, like another branch of the Semitic race, the Hebrews, had a high respect for the sanctity of the law.

3. Religion and Thought

The dwellers in Mesopotamia were polytheists. The earliest stages in the evolution of an elaborate pantheon can no longer be discerned; for, as far back as the fourth millennium, not only was the number of deities, male and female, very large, but lists of them had been drawn up by priests, their functions had been defined with some clearness, and they had been grouped in order of precedence and power. At a time when Mesopotamia was studded with numerous independent cities, each had its own patron deity who was regarded as its lord and

owner. With such a multiplicity of divinities it was natural
that similar functions should have been attributed to many.
It was also an obvious development that the political prominence
of a particular city-state should, as it were, react upon its tute-
lary god; in other words, the divine guardian of a city, whose
rulers conquered others and thus created a larger political
organism or even an empire, ceased to be of merely local importance and was worshipped over a wider area. The god,
Marduk, who in earlier centuries had been one of a number of
minor deities, but whose cult was especially centred in Babylon,
became during the age of Hammurabi and his successors the
premier divinity of the Babylonian empire. At that time the
great New Year's festival was held in his honor and lasted no
less than eleven days. Again, when more than a thousand years
later Assyria became the strongest state in the Near and Middle
East, the old local god of Ashur, called by the same name as
his city, became by far the most important figure in the pantheon.

The sun (Shamash) and moon (Sin) received worship in
various centres; prominent also was the cult of Adad, the god
of thunder and storms, who was particularly feared because the
manifestation of his wrath brought destruction to crops, to
irrigation-works, and to cattle. Terrible, too, was Nergal, the
ruler of the underworld; he was regarded also as the sender of
plagues, wars, and other disasters. Usually a female divinity
was associated with each male god; but, whether worshipped
alone or jointly with their lords, these goddesses were for the
most part subordinate, just as their functions were commonly
less clearly defined. The outstanding exception was Ishtar,
daughter of Sin, who in time attained to a unique influence.
Her character was twofold, since she was honored now as the
goddess of love, now as the invincible warrior goddess. Since
in astronomy she was identified with the Morning and Evening
Star, her symbol on artistic representations was a star with
eight or sixteen rays.

Besides the major personages, of whom but a few have here
been named, there was in the Babylonian pantheon a multitude
of deities of lesser rank or of those whose influence was never
more than local. In addition, the belief in spirits and demons

was deeply rooted in men's minds. The malignant demons especially were believed to be incessantly plotting against mankind. They were bringers of disease and madness, they destroyed cattle and flocks, they sought in every way to harm the human race. Many of them are described or portrayed in art as monstrous creatures with human bodies and animal heads. They were particularly dangerous after nightfall, lurking in lonely and desert places, near tombs, or under the shadow of ruins. The natural concomitant of these beliefs was that the greatest attention was paid to magic, incantation, and divination. Moreover, since the evil spirits were believed to cause sickness of every kind, the practice of medicine could never develop along strictly scientific lines. The code of Hammurabi is proof, indeed, that already at that time various surgical operations were attempted; with what degree of success we cannot tell. It is true that the greater part of the surviving medical texts belongs to the Assyrian and late Babylonian periods. Yet there is no doubt that much of the information that they contain goes back to a far earlier age. The Babylonian physicians used an extensive pharmacopeia, botanical and mineral; also, the diagnosis of some diseases which can be identified seems to show that careful clinical observations were made. Nevertheless the function of the doctor was too often subordinate to that of the expert in magical rites. To foretell the future various methods were in use, the most widespread being the inspection of sheep's livers. This organ was regarded as the seat of the sensations and of life itself; inferences were drawn from its shape and the shape of its different parts, from its markings, color, and so on. The soothsayers who practised liver divination were required to undergo a long period of training. To help the learner, clay models of a liver were constructed. Vertical and horizontal lines were drawn on it and the needful information was inscribed in each section. Examples of such practical aids to divination have been recovered by excavation. Another form of predicting the future was by observation of the stars; for, although the great age of Babylonian astrology came only at a much later date, we cannot doubt that considerable progress had been made by the time of Hammurabi, both along the line of astrology and of a scientific observation of the heavenly bodies. Divination by dreams, and by pouring water into oil or *vice versa* (lecanomancy) and then observing the shapes formed by one fluid when added to the other, were yet other means of prognosticating what was in store for man.

Although, then, the greater portion of the texts dealing with ritual, magic, divination, and star-gazing belongs, as has already been indicated, to the Assyrian and neo-Babylonian epochs, it is clear that by *c.* 2000 a substantial body of literature on these topics had already accumulated. Moreover, not a little of this lore went back to Sumerian times; and, since Sumerian remained the language of cult and religious ritual, it was necessary for priests and soothsayers to be in some degree bilingual. From the need of trained ministers of religion and of scribes there arose schools, organized in connection with the temples and conducted therein. And, though little that is definite is known about the curriculum as a whole, certain surviving texts give some indication of the educational ends that were kept in view.

The system of writing used in Mesopotamian lands was exceedingly complicated. Originally it is likely to have been purely pictorial, each sign or picture representing a given object. But already in the oldest extant Sumerian inscriptions the majority of signs has been conventionalized, even though a few of the archaic picture-signs survive. The Sumerian script was taken over by their Semitic neighbors and conquerors. Its adaptation to a Semitic language was, however, difficult, because the structure and phonetic system of the two languages differed greatly. The written signs became quite conventional. In this fully developed writing, to which the name, cuneiform (wedge-shaped), has been given, each sign represents a syllable. Complicated though it was to write a script in which, when fully elaborated, there were not less than five hundred signs, cuneiform had a remarkably triumphant career. Its use spread to Elam in the east and to Asia Minor in the northwest. It was adopted in Mitanni, and by the Hittites and Assyrians. From these last its use spread at a later date to the inhabitants of the kingdom of Van, and, finally, it was used by the Persian kings for their monumental inscriptions. Besides, by the middle of the second millennium the Babylonian language and script had come into general use for diplomatic communications throughout the Near and Middle East, so that even the Egyptian kings communicated in it with their native vassals in Syria and with the independent rulers of the Asiatic kingdoms. When Accadian (Babylonian) became the language of ordinary intercourse, bilingual dictionaries and phrase-books began to be compiled, in order that the pupils who attended the temple-schools to be educated as priests and scribes, after they had mastered the intricacies of writing their own, might further acquire the complicated idiom of the Sumerian tongue. Other texts used in training for various special callings were composed to teach liver divination, astronomy, and astrology, as well as mathematical tables and lists of arithmetical problems. Mathematical knowledge, apart from the simple arithmetic needed by every one in his daily life, was chiefly studied in connection with star-lore, and also for the more immediately practical purpose of land-measurement and surveying. Several plans have survived from the third millennium on which a given field or tract of land has been divided up into several smaller parcels, precise measurements of length, breadth, and area being appended.

The bulk of the poetic literature was religious. Hymns and prayers, often of great length, were composed in honor of particular divinities, many being designed for ritual use at the important festivals. Such literary works, in which the achievements of Marduk, Shamash, or some other god were set out at length, thereby acquired some of the characteristics of epic poetry. Many parts of the elaborate Sumerian mythology and legends, which, of course, lived on long after the extinction of their authors, were embodied in epic compositions. Such were the *Creation Epic*, the *Descent of Ishtar* into the underworld, the *Descent of Nergal*, and epics of various heroes, of which the *Epic of Gilgamesh* was the most famous. It is significant for the understanding of the Sumerian and Babylonian mind that the leading motive of many of these heroic lays is the question how man may escape death and attain to perpetual life. The *Epic of Gilgamesh* has survived primarily in a redaction of the seventh century B.C.; but portions of a version that is some fifteen hundred years older, as well as fragments of the tale in one or other of the languages of Asia Minor, prove that the substance and main features of the poem had undergone little change. It was divided into three parts. The first treats of the struggle between Gilgamesh and a divinely created rival for power in his earthly kingdom at Erek. It concludes with the victory of Gilgamesh and the conclusion of a pact with Engidu, his late opponent. The second division of the poem describes the various adventures of the two heroes, ending with the death of Engidu. In the concluding section of the epic Gilgamesh, who has been filled with a terror of death by his comrade's end, sets out in quest of everlasting life. In the course of his travels he accomplishes many heroic feats and on two occasions almost succeeds in his main task, only to fail at the last moment. Resigned at last to the fact that he, like all mortal things, must perish, he is enabled by the permission of Nergal, to commune with the ghost of the deceased Engidu. The poem ends with the phantom's description of a rather cheerless underworld. The pessimistic strain, which is by no means rare in the religious poetry, is not infrequently found also in the ethical treatises, collections of moral maxims, and proverbs, which together form a substantial body of literature. Fables too were popular; and, even if they ended with a moral, they served also to satisfy the pleasure which, the world over, and especially in the East, is derived from a well-told anecdote.

CHAPTER III

EGYPT TO THE CLOSE OF THE MIDDLE KINGDOM

> *Adore the king, Nematre, living for ever, in*
> *the midst of your bodies. Enthrone his majesty*
> *in your hearts. His two eyes, they search every*
> *body. He is the Sun, seeing with his rays. He*
> *illuminates the Two Lands more than the sun-disk.*
> *He makes the Two Lands green more than a great*
> *Nile. He hath filled the Two Lands with strength.*
> — From an Inscription of the XIIth Dynasty
> (J. H. Breasted, *Ancient Records of Egypt*,
> i, p. 327).

ANCIENT EGYPT, for all practical purposes, may be regarded
as synonymous with the valley of the Nile from Syene (Assouan),
just north of the twenty-fourth parallel, to the Mediterranean
Sea, a distance of rather more than five hundred miles. South of
this region, and geographically not a part of Egypt proper, lay
Nubia, the country of the Nile cataracts. It was, at least in
part, conquered and annexed to Egypt by the beginning of the
second millennium B.C. The long stretch from Memphis (near
the modern Cairo) to Syene, called Upper Egypt or the Upper
Kingdom, is a valley bordered by limestone hills and ridges. Its
width between Memphis and Thebes averages ten to twelve
miles; south of Thebes it becomes very narrow, not exceeding
an average of two miles across. Lower Egypt, or the Delta (so
called from its triangular shape, resembling the fourth letter of
the Greek alphabet), has a sea-front of about one hundred and
fifty miles, and a depth of about a hundred miles. On the west
of Egypt was desert relieved by occasional oases and inhabited
by Libyan tribes; westwards of the Delta was an approach to
Egypt by which on several occasions in their history the Egyptians were threatened by hostile invaders. To the east of the
Nile valley are rocky wastes through which one or two difficult
caravan routes led to the Red Sea. Eastwards of Lower Egypt

43

there was a causeway of immemorial antiquity to southern Syria. It followed the coast-line closely, but at certain times of the year it was liable to be flooded by sudden spring-tides. By another caravan route the traveller passed over desert and threaded his way past the northern spurs of Mt. Sinai, on his way to Palestine and beyond.

The isolation of Egypt and its inhabitants from other parts of the Ancient World has so often been stressed that a word of caution will not be out of place. The land of the Nile is not easy of access from either the west or the east; yet there were no insuperable obstacles in the way, even for large hostile armies or hordes of invaders. The Hyksos, the Assyrians, and the Persians, all attacked Egypt successfully from the east, while the onsets from the west were only less disastrous to her because less well-organized and attempted by smaller bodies of invaders. If, then, we seek an explanation for the fact that the Egyptians were never a colonizing people, and that their import and export trade was always relatively small, as compared with that of other ancient countries, we shall find it rather in the immense fertility of the Nile valley, which made Egypt self-sufficient and its inhabitants, as a whole, content to remain in the land of their birth. This fertility was entirely due to the river and its annual inundations of the adjacent valleys; for in Upper Egypt rain is a very rare occurrence, and even in the Delta rain-fall is slight and happens almost only in the winter months. Much depended on the right depth of the Nile floods. If the inundation was excessive, large tracts of country might be rendered unfit for cultivation; if it was insufficient, hardship and even famine were the result. When the river begins to fall, after the maximum inundation at the beginning of October, it leaves the land covered with mud deposits of remarkable fertilizing properties. The prosperity, then, of the people depended wholly on the satisfactory flooding of the arable soil.

In a previous chapter it has been noted that implements of the Old Stone Age show that the country was already inhabited at that early date. These objects are found in the sandstone and limestone hills which shut in the river valley; but they are not sufficient to enable us to form any clear picture of Palæolithic man in this region. Remains of Neolithic man, chiefly graves and their contents, are however very abundant in Upper Egypt, especially at Nakadeh.   This site, after which some Egyptologists have named the Neolithic civilization of Egypt, or at least the later phases of it, the Nakadeh culture, is a little to the north of Thebes and close to the point where the chief caravan route branches off from the Nile valley through the Wady Hammamat to the Red Sea.   We cannot doubt that Lower Egypt, too, was already inhabited in the Late Stone Age;   the non-discovery of remains there is due to the more destructive action of the river in the flat land of the Delta.   Neolithic man in Egypt was a remarkable craftsman.   The pottery which he made is well baked, and, though hand-made, is almost as accurate in form as if it had been turned on the wheel.   Much of it is decorated, and, besides this, is carefully polished, and toward the end of the period, even glazed.   Flint tools and weapons of very fine workmanship abound;   but the most remarkable fruits of patience combined with skill are stone vases of various shapes. Not only soft stones, like steatite, were used, but granite and alabaster.   These vessels are full of beauty and the craftsmanship displayed in the carefully carved spouts, handles, and ears for suspension, is quite admirable.   The Neolithic villages were commonly surrounded by mud walls;   the houses were constructed of mud and reeds, or else were built entirely of mud brick.   The most ambitious attempts at portraying human and animal figures are found on slate slabs or palettes, which were sculptured in low relief and belong to the end of the predynastic period.   Their primary purpose was to grind down green malachite, which was manufactured into paint and used for personal adornment.

In the latest period of the Neolithic Age the two lands of Upper and Lower Egypt seem respectively to have been unified politically into two kingdoms.   Details of this organization and of the internal administration we possess none.   But in later ages the first historic dynasty that was recorded was one founded by a man who succeeded in uniting Upper and Lower Egypt under his sceptre.   According to ancient tradition this was Menes or Mena.   On the other hand, the earliest kings recorded on extant monuments are a king of Upper Egypt, whose royal name was indicated by the sign of a scorpion;   a king of Upper Egypt,

Narmer, who, as appears from a ceremonial palette representing his triumph over his neighbors in the Delta, made himself master of Lower Egypt as well; and Aha, whose tomb has been discovered at Nakadeh. In view of these historic names, Egyptologists disagree about the historical character of Menes, and it has been suggested that Menes is really a legendary figure or title, which to later ages embodied the earliest monarchs of the first dynasty, under whom Lower and Upper Egypt were united into a single kingdom. It is, however, more probable that Aha is the divine or "Horus" name of Menes, and that he consolidated the work of unifying the two kingdoms which had been begun by his immediate predecessor, Narmer. Hence in later times he, and not Narmer, was regarded as the founder of the first dynasty.

Much uncertainty also still exists regarding the race or races to which the Egyptians at the beginning of the dynastic period belonged. It is at present impossible to form any final conclusions, for the ethnological theories put forward in recent years by different experts, it must be admitted, largely contradict one another. The earliest inhabitants were probably of a stock closely akin to their neighbors in Libya and related also to the earliest inhabitants of Crete and other eastern Mediterranean islands. They were a short, dark, dolichocephalic type. That they were somewhat more distantly related to the most western branches of the Semites is also probable; but their original home, like that of the Semites themselves, cannot be definitely fixed. At the end of the predynastic period the Egyptians first became acquainted with the use of copper, and this knowledge they probably owed to Asiatic immigrants who filtered into Lower Egypt. Further discoveries, especially in southern Mesopotamia, may well show that the debt owed by the earlier Egyptians to the Mesopotamian peoples was far more considerable than has hitherto been supposed. That there was at this early date also an admixture of peoples from northern Syria, or even Asia Minor, whom some writers describe as "Armenoid," is the most problematic hypothesis of all, and must for the present be discounted. It is unfortunate that, owing to the humid character of the Delta, remains of the earliest period of Lower Egyptian history are virtually non-existent.

The beginning of Dynasty I may be dated about 3200 B.C., and is therefore roughly contemporary with the earliest historic dynasty at Ur. The capital was at first at Thinis in Upper Egypt; but, some time during the IIId Dynasty, it was moved to Memphis, which, though in Lower Egypt, was close to the Upper Kingdom, and was therefore found to be a more satisfactory centre of government. The task of governing a country of such peculiar geographical structure must have been one of great difficulty. If we knew more about the latest years of the predynastic period, we should probably find that the work of the conquering kings was to weld together a number of tribes and principalities, whose chiefs subsequently became the king's vassals. Indeed, it is probable that the administrative units, or nomes (Greek *nomos*), into which Egypt was divided, were not merely artificial divisions, but largely based on the smaller tribal or political groups in the country during the Nakadeh period. The rulers of the earliest dynasties seem to have followed a policy of centralization of government in the capital, thus restricting as much as possible the influence and power of the nobility, who were in many cases descendants of once independent chiefs. The division into nomes was firmly established by the time of the IVth Dynasty (*c.* 2700–2550). Normally there were forty-two of these, twenty-two in Upper and twenty in Lower Egypt. Each was governed by an official nominated by, and solely and directly responsible to, the king.

The Egyptian monarchy was theocratic and, being theocratic, was absolute. The monarch combined within himself three functions. He was chief priest, he was commander-in-chief, and he was the judicial and administrative head of the state. The threefold character of the ruler as priest, general, and magistrate, is, of course, found in other early monarchies; but it was the special interpretation of the priestly functions of the king which gave to the Egyptian monarch a divine character not easy to parallel elsewhere. His claim to be the highest priest in his realm — the chosen intermediary between his people and the divine powers — was founded on the belief that he himself was the earthly incarnation of a god, who did not lose his divine nature during a transitory life on earth. He bore various titles which had reference to his divine character, of which the most

important was that which described him as the son of Ra, the
sun-god, or, at a later date when a syncretism of Ra and the god
of Thebes, Amen, had taken place, of Amen Ra.[1] There is no
indication that the Egyptians ever believed that, on the death
of the king, the crown passed to his son or nearest male relative
by divine right. The practice of some monarchs of the XIIth
Dynasty of associating a son with themselves as co-ruler, must
be regarded as purely a matter of political expediency, to insure
the succession in the family. For, often enough, the succession
on the death of a king passed to the strongest man, irrespective
of his kinship to the deceased.

With the last king of the IIId Dynasty, Snefru, we enter a
period about which it is possible to form a clearer picture than
of the earliest dynastic era. It is the age of the great pyramids,
an age, besides, about which for the first time we have a certain number of contemporary documents; these become more
copious during the Vth and VIth Dynasties. To the period of
the Vth Dynasty belong the oldest writings of a literary character that have so far been recovered. Finally, the Vth and,
above all, the VIth Dynasties correspond to an age of marked
political expansion beyond the frontiers of Egypt proper.

No remains of Ancient Egypt are more familiar than the
pyramids, those vast tombs erected by Snefru near Sakkarah
and at Gizeh by the greatest kings of the IVth Dynasty,
Khufu (Cheops), Khafra, and Menkaura. They were erected
by the respective monarchs during their lives, as the resting-
places in which their bodies would be housed after death. They
were surrounded by flat-topped tombs of much humbler proportions, which were the burial places of their chief courtiers.
The largest of all the pyramids, that of Khufu, is four hundred
and fifty feet in height. Its vastness bears witness both to the
engineering skill of the early Egyptians and to the immense
resources of the monarch; for over two million limestone blocks,
each weighing on the average more than two tons, went into
its construction. Yet it might well be asked whether any

---

[1] The importance of Ra in the Egyptian pantheon dates from the Vth
Dynasty, as will be pointed out below. The older god of light, Horus,
first in sanctity ever since predynastic times, then begins to occupy a
position subordinate to Ra.

despot ever set his subjects to a more profitless and unproduc-
tive task than this.   It has been well observed that the concentration of tombs of kings and their courtiers in the vicinity
of the capital, Memphis, is emblematic of the political organization of the Old Kingdom.

The government was a personal autocracy exercised by the
Pharaoh, and the nobles and officials who carried on the administration were closely dependent on him.[1]   His chief minister, or vizier, was at this time usually a member of the royal
family.   The nomarchs, or governors of the nomes, besides
being charged with the general control of their province, were
responsible for the proper collection of taxes, and had limited
judicial powers besides.   The highest judicial court was in the
capital and met under the presidency of the vizier.   Office
tended to become hereditary in certain families.   A son who
had at first filled a subordinate position, succeeds, on his father's
death, to the higher office thus vacated, provided the king's
good-will continues to be his.   Even the highest officials seem
to have been frequently moved from office to office, as we see
from the biographical inscription of Methen, who flourished
under Snefru.   After holding many minor appointments he
rises to the highest governorships, holding successively no less
than twelve, partly in Upper, partly in Lower, Egypt.[2]   The
general character of the government remained the same under
the rulers of the Vth Dynasty.   Perhaps the most notable
feature is the growing importance of the worship of the sun-
god, Ra.   While the kings continued to erect pyramids for
their own use after death, they also sought visibly to glorify
the god, whose "sons" they were, by setting up temples or
monuments in his honor.   Before the end of the dynasty the
disadvantages inherent in a highly centralized government, if
the ruler was weak, must have become very apparent; for,
under the kings of the VIth Dynasty a radical change in the
methods of administration can be observed.

But, above all, the VIth Dynasty was an age of foreign con-

[1] Cf. E. Meyer, *Geschichte des Altertums* (3d ed.) i, 2, p. 187.   The word
Pharaoh is a corruption of two Egyptian words meaning "royal house."
By this circumlocution direct reference to the divine monarch was avoided.
[2] Translated in Breasted, *Ancient Records of Egypt*, i, pp. 76 ff.

quest and wars. Extant records inform us of travels undertaken by high officials and of military expeditions to the south and southeast of Egypt. Numerous graves excavated in Lower Nubia have proved that this region was, during the earliest period, inhabited by people who were racially the same as, or very closely akin to, the inhabitants of Upper Egypt. Already under the kings of the Ist Dynasty the political control of the Egyptian monarch reached as far as the first Nile cataract. Both under Pepi I and his son, Pepi II, the records seem to show that these rulers extended their sovereignty also over the region between the first and second cataracts, and generally overawed the negro tribes of Upper Nubia.[1] The earliest Egyptian reference to negroes belongs to this period, and there is no doubt that considerable numbers of them found their way northward as far as the district of the first cataract and settled there. Other expeditions are recorded against the desert tribes of the Sinai peninsula and southern Palestine. These important operations were trusted to one, Uni, who, from a subordinate position, rose under Pepi I to become first a judge and later the king's chosen general. Under the successor of Pepi I, Mernere, he became governor of the South. The long autobiographical inscription in his tomb at Abydos is the most important document extant for this period. The necessity for chastising troublesome neighbors was not the only reason for activity near Sinai; the desire to keep a firmer grip on the peninsula, in order more fully to exploit its mineral wealth, doubtless influenced the king greatly. His astonishing activity as a builder and restorer of temples led Pepi I to develop the red granite quarries near Syene. Expeditions by sea and land to Punt (Somali coast) were mainly commercial in their object. From there, as well as from Upper Nubia, the Egyptians procured gold, ivory, ebony, ostrich feathers, and incense. Such expeditions did not always pass off without accidents or loss of life. One of Pepi II's officials appears to have been assassinated by a desert tribe while making ready for a sea voyage to Punt.

[1] Dynasty VI lasted approximately from 2425 to 2240 B.C. Pepi I is said to have reigned over 50 years and Pepi II, who succeeded as a child of six and lived to be a centenarian, ruled 94 years.

The administrative changes which gradually came about during this dynasty were so drastic that the system in the end was the very antithesis of the centralized government characteristic of the three preceding dynasties. With some justice the VIth Dynasty has been described as a feudal monarchy. For, whereas the king's authority in religious and secular matters continued to be supreme, the power and independence of the provincial governors become very marked. They reside permanently in their respective nomes, only occasionally visiting the capital. Their official designations vary — city-governor, head of the nome, as well as different titles of nobility and rank — their offices tend to become hereditary, thus completing the change of Egypt from a country governed by an autocrat in his capital to one administered largely by a hereditary nobility, owing allegiance to the king, but all-powerful in their provinces. The process of change is the exact converse of that which we have already observed in the earlier period of Mesopotamian history. The danger obviously inherent in this new régime, if the king was a minor or else a weak ruler, did not fail to make its appearance in due course. The successors of Pepi II were short-lived nonentities, and the nobles took to war among themselves. The two hundred and fifty years (*c.* 2240–2000), from the end of Dynasty VI to the last rulers of Dynasty XI, are still extremely obscure. It was seemingly an age of civil war, during which one dynasty, centred for a time at Heracleopolis, maintained authority over a large part of Egypt, but was then challenged and finally overthrown by a rival dynasty at Thebes. Finally, by the efforts of the last but one of the XIth Dynasty monarchs, the two Egypts were reunited under a single ruler.

With the XIIth Dynasty we at last reach a period of Egyptian history for which there is abundant documentary and other evidence. Incidentally, some of the inscriptions refer with gratitude to the fact that an era of anarchy and disunion has at length been succeeded by one of peace, prosperity, and good government. This copious evidence justifies the belief that in material welfare and in artistic achievement this age and the period of the XVIIIth and XIXth Dynasties form the two most brilliant epochs in the long history of Egypt down to Ptolemaic and Roman times. The XIIth Dynasty lasted for two hundred and twelve years.[1] In the troubled years preceding it, Egyptian control over neighboring countries like Nubia must have relaxed or ceased entirely. The kings of the XIIth Dynasty had to do all over again the work of conquest accomplished by the rulers of the VIth. Operations in Nubia are thus heard of with some frequency, especially under Senusret I and Senusret III. The former set up a monument by the second cataract, commemorating his victories over the native tribes of this region. But the country was not thoroughly subdued till the time of Senusret III (Plate 3); he conducted no less than four expeditions into the cataract region. A little way to the south of the second cataract, at Semneh and Kummeh, two inscribed boundary stones were set up in the eighth and the sixteenth year of the king's reign. In addition, forts were built here on an island in the river and on the hills overlooking this point. Remains of four forts in Lower Nubia, that is to say, between the first and second cataracts, testify still further to the thoroughness of the Egyptian occupation. The inscribed boundary stones are of great interest. The one severely restricts the immigration of negroes from the South. They are forbidden to navigate the Nile below this point; only individual negroes, who are genuine traders, shall, for this purpose, be admitted north of the Egyptian frontier. The second inscription is a rather boastful notice, in general terms, of the king's achievements; but one paragraph, in which the conqueror exhorts his successors to maintain this frontier line, is worthy to be cited:

Now, as for every son of mine who shall maintain this boundary, which my majesty has made, he is my son, he is born to my majesty, the likeness of a son who is the champion of his father, who maintains the boundary of him who begat him. Now, as for him who shall relax it, and shall not fight for it, he is not my son, he is not born to me. — (Breasted, *Ancient Records*, i, p. 296.)

[1] The following are the rulers of the XIIth Dynasty with approximate dates:

Amenemhet I, 2000–1970	Senusret III, 1887–1849
Senusret I, 1980–1935	Amenemhet III, 1849–1801
Amenemhet II, 1938–1903	Amenemhet IV, 1801–1792
Senusret II, 1906–1887	Queen Sebeknefrure, 1792–1788

The overlapping of dates is due to the practice, followed by some of the kings, of associating their sons with themselves on the throne.

Save during the period of Hyksos domination, Nubia remained a part of the Egyptian kingdom. Its inhabitants came more and more under the influence of Egyptian civilization; but the rule of the Pharaohs over this dependency seems mostly to have been exceedingly harsh. Under an autocracy, which treated a large part of the population of Egypt little better than serfs, despotic misrule over an alien race is scarcely surprising. Contemporary documents also refer to several expeditions to Punt, and to the precious commodities brought back from that distant region. The northwest and northeast frontiers of Egypt were also exposed to attacks from time to time; we hear, for example, of a Libyan war under Amenemhet I. It is possible that these neighbors of Egypt gave trouble again during the later years of this dynasty. Exploitation of the Sinai peninsula was more intense than ever before. Doubtless military action was needed at times against the desert tribes; but the only definite notice of this kind known so far is one which records an expedition into southern Palestine in the reign of Senusret III. There can be little doubt that it was a mere punitive raid and not a serious attempt to bring that country under permanent Egyptian control. It is recorded on a stele set up by one of the king's officers, Sebek-khu, who had seen his first military service as a young man on one of the Nubian campaigns, and who at this time had been advanced to command the reserve troops. Of the general condition of Syria at this date we get a glimpse in the autobiographical inscription of a noble, Sinuhe, who had become a political exile and was finally restored to favor by Senusret I. During his long absence from Egypt, Sinuhe travelled extensively in Palestine; for some time he lived with a tribal chief, Emuienshi, who held him in great honor and whose daughter he married. He fought, too, under the standard of his father-in-law against hostile neighbors. For the rest, his was a simple pastoral and agricultural life, forming a marked contrast to the luxurious and artificial atmosphere of the Egyptian court.

In their administration the monarchs of the XIIth Dynasty were able to steer a middle course between the methods of the IVth and of the VIth Dynasties, mainly because they were strong rulers. The monarchy was in fact more powerful than it had ever been; at the same time the king could afford to entrust the vizier and other high officials with extensive powers, so that the local nobility and the nomarchs, whose positions continued to be largely hereditary, were effectively kept in check. While this system is a combination of a central government with a quasi-feudal régime, it is also a distinct step in the direction of the highly elaborate bureaucratic organization which was perfected during the XVIIIth and XIXth Dynasties. Indeed, it is very probable that the power of the hereditary landed nobility was finally broken under the later rulers of the XIIth, especially under such princes as Senusret III and Amenemhet III. If, on the one hand, the governors of the nomes were closely controlled by the king, they, on the other hand, enjoyed very extensive authority in the provinces that they administered. Not only the agricultural population and rural districts, but also the towns, were under their general supervision; they were responsible for the collection of tribute and taxes within their nome, and for its punctual delivery to the royal treasury. We have no means of ascertaining the general character of their government; undoubtedly everything would depend on the individual governor. That it was ever as perfect as Ameni claims that his administration under Senusret I was, may be doubted. But, if we make allowance for a certain amount of oriental hyperbole, which characterizes most of the sepulchral inscriptions, we may still believe that Ameni's government was equitable and clement. He says of himself:

There was no citizen's daughter whom I misused, there was no widow whom I oppressed, there was no peasant whom I repulsed, there was no shepherd whom I repelled, there was no overseer of serf-laborers whose people I took for (unpaid) imposts, there was none wretched in my community, there was none hungry in my time. When years of famine came I plowed all the fields of the Oryx nome, as far as its southern and northern boundary, preserving its people alive and furnishing its food, so that there was none hungry therein. I gave to the widow as (to) her who had a husband; I did not exalt the great above the small in all that I gave. Then came great Niles, possessors of grain and all things, (but) I did not collect the arrears of the field. — (Breasted, *Ancient Records*, i, pp. 252–253.)

The judicial courts in the cities were in the hands of judges appointed by the king. Census lists, used both for taxation purposes and for the levying of troops, were kept in the capital

STATUE OF SENUSRET III

Plate 3

HEAD OF THUTMOSE III

Plate 4

and were under the general control of the vizier. The army at
this time was composed partly of regular troops, partly of militia raised in the nomes as required, partly of non-Egyptian
levies, especially Nubians. In this matter, too, the practice of
the XIIth Dynasty is halfway between that of the Old Kingdom
and of the XVIIIth and following dynasties.

With the end of Dynasty XII we enter on one of the most
obscure, as it certainly was one of the most disastrous, periods
of Egyptian history. In the scheme of Manetho there are
five dynasties to fill up the two centuries, during which the
land of the Nile fell first into internal anarchy and then became
the prey of a foreign invader. The fragmentary list of kings,
preserved in the famous Turin papyrus dating from the XIXth
Dynasty, also contained many names of what must, for the
most part, have been very ephemeral rulers. Briefly stated,
it would seem that the early kings of Dynasty XIII failed to
hold their kingdom together. First one and then another of
the hereditary nobility rebelled and maintained a precarious
independence. Thus, many of the kings whose names are
recorded were, even for the brief period of their nominal
kingship, not rulers of Egypt in fact. We cannot say whether
the country was already quite in the grip of anarchy, when
it was attacked by foreign assailants, or whether the invasion
was in part responsible for the break-up of the kingdom.
The later royal names in the list are largely those of foreign
kings. Who these invaders were, whom the Egyptians of a
later age referred to generally as "Shepherd kings," — the
name Hyksos, now in general use, is a Grecized form, used by
Josephus, of two Egyptian words — is still a moot point. In
a general way there can be no doubt that the Hyksos invasion
of Egypt was the ultimate outcome of a wide-spread clash
of peoples, and of *Völkerwanderungen*, whose repercussions
were felt throughout the Near and Middle East, as will appear
in a subsequent chapter. It is not in the least necessary, or
even likely, that the men who thus invaded Egypt towards
the end of the eighteenth century B.C. were racially homogeneous. If the rank and file were in the main Semites from
Syria, it is possible that their leaders, some of whom for a time
sat on the throne of the Pharaohs, were of Aryan stock and akin

to the princes of Hatti and Mitanni. To the Hyksos kings Manetho would assign two dynasties (XV and XVI); but, for reasons already indicated in the Introduction, it is not possible to trace either their conquest or their rule with any precision or in any detail. Lower Egypt suffered first and altogether more severely than the Upper Kingdom. Even if we allow for exaggeration on the part of later chronicles which refer to this era, the invaders proceeded ruthlessly. They maltreated the inhabitants, they burnt and pillaged the Delta in such a way that it did not fully recover its prosperity for over a century. The resistance of Upper Egypt was stouter, and the Hyksos only gradually extended their power southwards. Indeed, it is questionable whether they at any time exercised complete control in this part of the country. When the war of liberation began, that is to say, toward the end of the seventeenth century B.C., it was the men of Upper Egypt who took the lead in the revolt against the foreign despots, and bore the brunt of the fight for national independence.

The success of the Hyksos in overrunning so great a part of Egypt must have been partly due to the unsettled internal condition of the land on their approach. Partly their victories must be credited to their superior tactics, and especially to their superior armature. This is particularly true of their horses and war-chariots; for these formed a weapon of offense far more effective than any which the Egyptians could produce at that period. The Egyptians in time learnt the value of them; as pictures on monuments of the XVIIIth Dynasty show, the war-chariot had then become a regular and much valued part of the Egyptian military forces. The later Hyksos kings are to some extent known from monuments. The most notable seems to have been Khian, who dedicated statues of himself at Bubastis. Traces of him, moreover, have been found outside Egypt. The lid of an alabaster vase bearing his name was found by Sir Arthur Evans at Cnossus in Crete immediately under a Late Minoan I deposit; in Mesopotamia, near Baghdad, a small lion inscribed with Khian's royal name was recovered. These later monarchs became to a great extent Egyptianized; they adopted Egyptian manners and court etiquette, and even worshipped Egyptian gods. It has been pointed out that the Hyksos control over Upper Egypt was probably never complete; certainly, toward the end of their domination, an Egyptian dynasty (XVIIth) ruled at Thebes, though technically these princes were doubtless vassals of the Hyksos. But it was these rulers of Thebes who started the rebellion against the foreigners, a struggle which continued for about forty years with varying fortunes. The capture of Memphis by the Egyptians was the beginning of the end. The Hyksos were confined to the Delta, and at last they were driven out of Egypt altogether. The Egyptian prince under whose banner the Egyptians were liberated from alien rule, was also the founder of the XVIIIth Dynasty, Ahmose I. That he was a statesman and organizer as well as an able soldier was proved by the successful manner in which, after crushing two revolts in Egypt and recovering Nubia, he consolidated his position, and, after two centuries of anarchy and disruption, made the land of the Nile again a united kingdom under a single ruler.

CHAPTER IV

THE STRUGGLE FOR SYRIA

> *And even as I protect thee, so will I protect thy son; but thou, Duppi-Teshup, protect the king of the land of Hatti, the land of Hatti, my sons (and) my grandsons hereafter. And the tribute which was imposed on thy grandfather and thy father, — 300 half-shekels of pure refined gold of first quality together with precious stones they sent to the land of Hatti — that do thou send likewise. And cast not thine eyes on another. Thy ancestors paid tribute to the land of Egypt, but do thou send it not.* —
> From a treaty between Murshilish II, King of Hatti and a Chief of Amurru. (J. Friedrich, *Hethitische Texte*, ii (1926), pp. 12–13.)

So far we have considered separately the earlier history of Mesopotamia and of Egypt. By the middle of the second millennium B.C. very great political changes had come over the whole of the Near East, and for several centuries to come the political history of Egypt is inseparably linked with that of the Asiatic kingdoms. At the outset we must briefly touch upon the early development of several of these states. In every case our information about them — be it Assyria, Mitanni, the Hittite kingdom, or the rulers of the Sea Country who wrested southern Babylonia from the last kings of the first Babylonian dynasty — is still woefully deficient.

It is probable that some Sumerians had found their way to Assyria and had settled there by *c.* 3000 B.C. It may also well be that a Semitic colony came there at an early date. But we cannot tell how rapidly the progress of fusion of the two races progressed, or the extent to which force was used by the Semitic invaders. Ultimately the Sumerian stock here was submerged as it was in the South. During the third millennium Assyria was a small state, over which the more powerful kings of the South — Sargon, Naram-sin, Dungi —

exercised a protectorate. It is more remarkable to find a Semitic colony making its way into Asia Minor and settling there soon after the beginning of the third millennium B.C. From Kara-Euyuk, near Kaisariyeh in Cappadocia, a number of cuneiform tablets, written in the Akkadian-Semitic tongue, are known, which prove the existence there of a flourishing community. Though its members worshipped the god Ashur, the view that they were Assyrian colonists seems untenable; at that early date Assyria was not in the position to send forth settlers to another land. Besides, the affinities between this settlement of Ganesh, or Kanes, and the Babylonian-Semitic culture are marked. Hence it is more likely that the founders of Ganesh were part of a Semitic body of colonists which left Mesopotamia early in the third millennium B.C.; of them one part found its way to Ashur, the other went farther afield into Asia Minor. There are reasons for supposing that the whole body started originally from Kish. We have referred in an earlier chapter to an expedition of Sargon of Akkad into Asia Minor. Its purpose was to help the citizens of Ganesh against a neighboring state which had caused them trouble. Sargon was only prevailed upon to undertake this enterprise after urgent representations had been made to him by the Cappadocian city. His timely aid saved Ganesh from destruction, and the place continued to be of considerable importance for centuries. Its interests appear to have been primarily commercial — at all events, the deputation which went to interview Sargon and implore his aid consisted of merchants. Also, the Kara-Euyuk tablets, which may be dated about 2000 B.C., deal almost wholly with business.

Already in the time of Hammurabi's son, Samsu-iluna, (c. 1904–1867 B.C.), the political troubles began. First, the most southerly part of the kingdom, corresponding roughly to the old land of Sumer, broke away and was ruled by an independent dynasty of sea-kings, about whom we know little more than some names, partly Sumerian, partly Semitic. Much about the same date a new people, the Cassites, dwelling in the hill country of Zagros, conducted their first raid into Mesopotamia. Nevertheless, the Babylonian dynasty survived for another century, although its last five monarchs ruled over a greatly reduced kingdom. The end came about 1750 B.C., but it was neither Cassites nor sea-kings who destroyed Babylon, deposing the last king of the Babylonian dynasty. It was another people, the Hatti or Hittites, who swooped down on Mesopotamia from the interior of Asia Minor.

The origin of this people, whose kings from the fifteenth to the thirteenth centuries ruled over a realm embracing most of Asia Minor and disputed with the Pharaohs for control in Syria, is still unsolved. The inhabitants of the kingdom were certainly not all of the same ethnic stock. Whereas the bulk of the population was, as far as our records allow us to judge, autochthonous, with a strong Semitic admixture, as in the case of Ganesh, the ruling class, at the time when Hatti was politically powerful, was part of an Aryan or Indo-European body of invaders who, soon after 2000 B.C., began to push their way westward from central Asia. Another such wave of conquering immigrants settled about the same time in northern Mesopotamia on the east of the great semi-circular bend made by the Euphrates between latitudes 38° and 36°. The earlier dwellers in this region were probably racially akin to their neighbors in Asia Minor, and Mitannians are heard of before the end of the third millennium B.C. But the kings of Mitanni, as this district was called, who somewhat later made of it an important kingdom, were Aryans and worshipped Indian gods. Finally, the Cassites also were of Indo-European stock. Thus, in all three cases it is only the ruling caste, so far as we know at present, who represent the immigrant, Aryan element. We have no means of ascertaining whether these invaders acted at all in concert. In 1750 B.C. Babylon was destroyed by an invasion of Hatti, but the conquerors did not remain in the land. Shortly afterward (in 1749 or 1746?) the Cassite prince, Gandash, seized the Babylonian throne and founded a dynasty which ruled in Babylon for six centuries. Probably there was no concerted action between the two bodies of invaders; but the Cassites, who had troubled Babylonia before, simply seized their opportunity to make themselves master of a large portion of Mesopotamia, when the capital city had been laid waste by the Hatti. The kingdom now ruled over by Gandash and his successors was territorially much smaller than

the realm of Hammurabi. The sea-kings in the South held
out for about half a century before they finally succumbed
to the new rulers of Babylon. In the North, Assyria for a
brief space was a state of some importance under a king,
Shamshi-Adad II (c. 1700–1680 B.C.), whose warlike ardor
carried him beyond the boundaries of his kingdom into the
Armenian highlands and into northern Syria. Yet it was a
short-lived triumph. For the next three centuries Assyria
became again a weak kingdom, dependent politically on one
or other of its more powerful neighbors.

The political upheavals which have been briefly indicated
had at the beginning reacted on Syria also, and ultimately
on Egypt. For the Hyksos, whom in the main we must regard
as Semitic (Canaanite and Amorite?) tribes, were either forced
southward by pressure of a new people from the north, or else
they may actually have been led to Egypt by some early Hittite
chiefs, the records of whose prowess excavation has not yet
recovered.

When, about 1500 B.C., the darkness surrounding the earlier
history of the Hittites begins to be dispelled, we find a Hittite
kingdom firmly established in central Asia Minor, with its
capital at Hattushash on a hill overlooking the modern village
of Boghaz-Keui. Architectural and sculptural remains were
already to some extent known to exist on this site, which com-
mands a point where several highways of immemorial antiquity
meet, before the place was scientifically excavated by Hugo
Winckler in 1906–07. The fortifications of the citadel were constructed of heavy polygonal blocks. A large palace or temple,
whose ruins have been thoroughly uncovered, was built mainly
of brick on lower courses of stone. A massive entrance gateway is flanked on either side by a great stone lion. Smaller
fortifications were placed on several of the surroundings emi-
nences; also, at a little distance from the citadel and town,
there is a series of rock sculptures, which unhappily are so
badly weathered that the interpretation of the subject represented is quite uncertain. A religious procession of persons,
advancing from two sides and meeting in the middle, appears to
be depicted. Among the figures we seem to recognize the great
Mother goddess of Anatolia and her male consort, also the

priest-king of Hatti and a number of Hittite warriors dressed
in tunic and sleeved upper-garment, shoes with turned-up
points, and high conical hat. They were armed with swords,
bows, and spears. The character of these sculptures at Boghaz-
Keui is closely similar to that of many monuments and rock
sculptures known in other parts of Cappadocia and beyond.
For this style of art can be traced in the West as far afield as
Mt. Sipylus and the vicinity of Ephesus, and in the South
as far as northern Syria. To the historical student, however,
the most important discovery made by Winckler at Boghaz-
Keui consisted of a large number of inscribed clay tablets.
Some of these Hittite archives are written in Babylonian-
Semitic and could be deciphered with comparative ease. But
more are composed in Anatolian dialects, of which the latest
investigators would distinguish not less than six. Although
immense progress in elucidating these texts has been made by
Hroszny, Forrer, and other scholars, so that their general content can be ascertained with fair certainty, much still remains
to be done, both in deciphering tablets still unread and in
improving the interpretation of the others in matters of detail.
Nor has it been possible to classify these dialects with certainty;
in the main they appear to be Indo-European, but they contain
considerable foreign elements. All these archives, whether
couched in Semitic or in the local dialects, were written in
cuneiform script, which the Hittites had learnt from their
Semitic neighbors. Besides this script, more primitive pictographic writing is known from Hittite monuments, but this
still awaits decipherment.

Of eight early Hittite kings we at present know very little
that is definite. The third in the list, Murshilish I, captured
Aleppo and subsequently conquered Babylon, an achievement
probably identical with the destruction of that city and the
deposition of Samsu-ditana in 1750 B.C., to which reference
has already been made. After the eighth monarch there is a
gap in our information. When we come to the second series
of kings, beginning in the middle of the sixteenth century, we
are on firmer ground. For it is under this dynasty that Hatti
became a first-class power, and its kings sought to rival the
Pharaohs of the XVIIIth and XIXth Dynasties as conquerors

and rulers of empire. We cannot tell how extensive the earlier Hittite realm was, though the exploits of Murshilish I suggest that it may have extended to northern Syria and have included a good deal more than the Halys crescent. In any case, if such a greater Hittite kingdom existed for a while, it seems to have dropped to pieces again. For the earliest kings of the second series, as it would seem from the scanty extant records, conducted war with varying success against Aleppo, and had rivals for the control of southern Cappadocia and northern Syria in their neighbors, the Harri. The fourth king of the dynasty, Shupiluliuma, achieved such military success that he brought all Cappadocia and the region between the Halys and the upper Euphrates under his control, and advanced the frontiers of his realm to northern Syria and northern Mesopotamia. Since it is under him that the first serious clash between Hatti and Egypt occurred, we must now go back to consider the foreign policy of the Pharaohs of the XVIIIth Dynasty.

The founder of that dynasty, Ahmose I, did a great work in restoring peace and order in his disrupted kingdoms. It was left for his successors to undertake what, in the first instance, was a war of retaliation against Syria from whence the late oppressors had come. It is a moot point whether Amenhotep I invaded Syria, but it is certain that the third ruler of the dynasty, Thutmose I, did so. Though he might subsequently claim to have conquered all Syria to the Euphrates, his expedition was in truth no more than a raid on an extended scale. There was no single power in Syria and Palestine at that date to unify the country against an invader. Instead we find there a large number of tribes and small principalities, which were frequently at war one with the other. Northern Syria, except the region between the Lebanon range and the sea, seems to have been to some extent a protectorate of Mitanni. The territory, which in the Egyptian records is called Naharina, included the land between the Orontes and the Euphrates, as well as Mitanni proper on the east. For a half a century after Thutmose I's campaign no more is heard of Egyptian attacks on Syria. If the Egyptian monarchs declared a protectorate over Syria at this time, it can hardly have been very effective.

On the contrary, it seems clear that some effort was made by the Syrian communities to coöperate, in the event of renewed hostilities from Egypt. For, when finally Thutmose III in 1479 B.C. entered on his first Syrian expedition, he found a formidable coalition arrayed against him under the leadership of the prince of Kadesh.

If military prowess be the test of eminence, Thutmose III might deserve to be called the greatest of the Pharaohs (Plate 4). He conducted no less than seventeen campaigns into Syria; the history of his achievements, retold in considerable detail, survives in the form of annals inscribed on the walls of the temple of Amen at Karnak. In his first invasion Thutmose advanced as far as the undulating country to the south of Mt. Carmel, without encountering any serious opposition. But here, close to Megiddo, the historical original of Armageddon, he was confronted by an allied force of Syrian tribes. Thutmose's plan of battle differed, we are told, from that advocated by his general staff; nevertheless, on the morrow his strategic dispositions proved to be justified, for the Egyptian troops after a lengthy contest won a decisive victory. This was followed by the investiture and capture of Megiddo, and ample spoils were taken from the enemy. In successive years Thutmose followed up his first conquests systematically. Thus, step by step, he gained control of Phœnicia and the hinterland. His eighth campaign brought him to the Euphrates and to the borders of Mitanni. The king of Mitanni sent tribute, even as the king of Assyria had done some years before. His land campaigns Thutmose supported by naval operations off the coast, finally receiving the voluntary submission of Yantanai, which can be identified with fair certainty as the island of Cyprus. The record of Thutmose's exploits ends with the seventeenth campaign, in which he effectively quelled a general rising against Egyptian authority. Once more Kadesh played the part of leader. Though the Egyptian monarch reigned for another dozen years, he does not appear to have warred in Syria again.

During his lifetime the suzerainty of Egypt extended well-nigh to the Taurus. Neighboring states were overawed and paid tribute; besides those already mentioned, the Hittite king, it should be noted, also found it politic to appease the great conqueror with gifts. Judged by later events the steps taken to keep an effective hold on the conquered territory were not very satisfactory. The Syrian chiefs were in the position of vassals to the Pharaoh. Younger members of their families were taken to the Egyptian court, there to be educated after the Egyptian manner. Occasionally the king sent his own officials on a tour of inspection through the dependencies; in addition, some garrisons were left behind to guard important strategic points. Yet, all this was not enough; for, ultimately, the loyalty-compelling force was the prestige and power of the Egyptian king alone, and Egyptian conquerors had the same experience as the Mesopotamian warrior kings of an earlier age. Almost immediately after the death of Thutmose III a serious rising against Egyptian authority was organized in the Lebanon district. The new king, Amenhotep II, who had been associated on the throne with his father for a few years, must needs inaugurate his independent reign by a punitive expedition into Syria. Besides achieving his immediate object, the king invaded Mitanni.

Subsequently more peaceful counsels prevailed. Mitanni became a subject ally of Egypt, and good relations between the two states were further cemented by a royal marriage. For Thutmose IV married a daughter of King Artatama of Mitanni. Of the purpose and results of an invasion conducted by Thutmose IV into Syria we know nothing. Yet the mere fact that it was needed is significant; it shows that the Egyptian hold over her Asiatic subjects was none too secure. Under the latest kings of Dynasty XVIII the bonds holding together the empire won by Thutmose III became weaker and weaker. Finally they broke altogether, and it became necessary for the early rulers of the XIXth Dynasty to attempt the subjugation of Syria afresh. However, the later years of the XVIIIth Dynasty, or more precisely the reigns of Amenhotep III and IV, are a period of quite exceptional interest to us, because of the ample, and in some ways unique, documentary material available for their study. It is on this age that light is especially shed by the Boghaz-Keui documents; but, above all, it is to it that the so-called Amarna archives belong. These, which come from the new capital founded by Amenhotep IV in Upper Egypt, consist of about 350 whole or partially preserved tablets, and, with the exception of a few lists of offerings, are all letters and despatches. They may be briefly grouped as follows:

1. Letters between Amenhotep III and Amenhotep IV and the Cassite rulers of Babylon.
2. Correspondence between Amenhotep IV and the king of Assyria.
3. Correspondence between Tushratta, king of Mitanni, and Amenhotep III and IV.
4. Two letters from the king of Hatti to Amenhotep IV.
5. A number of letters to the Egyptian kings from Abd-Ashirta, prince of Amurru.
6. Letters from his son, Aziru, to Egypt.
7. A very large collection of communications from the prince of Gubla (Byblos in Phœnicia), Rib-Addi, to the Egyptian kings.
8. Letters from Artahepa, governor of Jerusalem, and other Palestinian letters to Egypt.

Outwardly, during the greater part of Amenhotep III's reign, the imperial power of Egypt seemed still to rest on secure foundations. The rulers of Babylon and of Mitanni are in the one case friendly to Egypt, in the other case in close alliance. Assyria at this date still acknowledged the overlordship of Mitanni. The unknown quantity was the new Hittite monarch, Shupiluliuma, who ascended the throne shortly before 1400 B.C.; but the Egyptian king certainly did not recognize the danger to be apprehended from this quarter. However, there can be no doubt that Shupiluliuma was the chief instigator of the unrest and finally the rebellion against Egyptian authority which came to a head in Syria during the last years of Amenhotep III. The Amorite prince, Abd-Ashirta, and, after his death, his son, Aziru, very successfully played a double game. They attacked the coastal cities of Phœnicia, which held staunchly to Egypt, assuring the Egyptian government that they were helping to defend Phœnicia from the possible attacks of the Hittite king, who was raiding Naharina and Mitanni. In spite of constant despatches from the loyal prince of Byblos, Rib-Addi, who revealed the full treachery of the Amorite chiefs, the Egyptian kings were supine and unconvinced. When at last, shortly before the death of Amenhotep III, a punitive expedition was sent against Abd-Ashirta, it wrested from him Simyra, seized by him a year or two before, and momentarily checked Amorite intrigues. But, on the accession of a new Egyptian monarch,

Amenhotep IV, the situation in Syria rapidly grew worse. A more wide-spread revolt from Egypt culminated in the loss of both Simyra and Byblos, whose prince, Rib-Addi, was killed by Aziru. The last named, till then most adept in duplicity, so far overreached himself that, after he had made his peace with Egypt on terms favorable to himself, he was forced to become the vassal of Hatti. A portion of the treaty imposed on him by Shupiluliuma has actually been recovered among the Boghaz-Keui archives.

With the loss to Egypt of all northern Syria and of Phœnicia, her ally, Mitanni, was dangerously isolated. At a most critical moment King Tushratta was murdered by one of his own sons, Artatama; in the anarchy that followed the neighbors of Mitanni saw their opportunity. The Assyrian king proclaimed his independence and seized the eastern region of Mitanni, whose parricide ruler acquiesced in what the insecurity of his own position did not allow him to combat. After some years of great distress in Mitanni, Shupiluliuma, to whose court another son of Tushratta, Mattivaza, had fled for protection, interfered by force of arms. The Assyrian king was obliged to give up his ill-gotten gains, and Mattivaza was set up on the throne of Mitanni as the vassal of Shupiluliuma, whose daughter he also married. The chronology of these years is still very uncertain, but it is clear that a year or two before Amenhotep IV's death (1358 B.C.) all Syria had been lost to Egypt. Shortly before Shupiluliuma died he concluded a treaty with Egypt, which left northern Syria in Hittite hands, while the position of southern Syria and Palestine was left undefined.[1] It was for the Egyptians to recover those lands, if they could. It was a great empire that Shupiluliuma on his death

---

[1] It is uncertain which Egyptian king concluded the treaty with Shupiluliuma. If the latter died in 1359, it must have been Amenhotep IV. If, on the other hand, Shupiluliuma's dates are a little later, so that he did not die till c. 1349 B.C., the Egyptian king may have been Harmhab. In the *Cambridge Ancient History*, vol. ii, we find the treaty tentatively assigned to Harmhab in two places (pp. 134 and 318), yet in the second passage the dates of Shupiluliuma are given as 1411–1359. On p. 264 the treaty is assigned to Amenhotep III or his successor. The synchronistic tables (pp. 694 and 700) assign the treaty to Harmhab, the year of his accession being given as 1346 or 1350. Yet the death of Shupiluliuma is there placed in 1359.

(1359 b.c.?) left to his son Arnuandash. He reigned only a few
years and was succeeded by his brother, Murshilish II. The
Boghaz-Keui archives contain a number of treaties concluded
by this prince with neighboring peoples. An agreement with
the Amorite prince, Duppi-Teshup, was calculated to keep the
Hittite protectorate over northern Syria secure.[1] Equally
illuminating are the pacts made with the chiefs of Hapalla
(Aleppo?) and of Mira and Kuwalija. From another Hittite

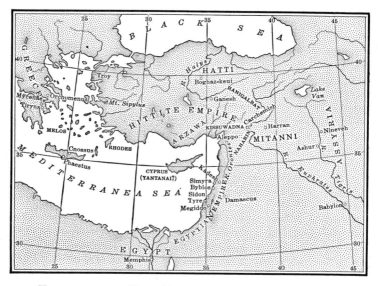

EGYPT AND THE NEAR EAST IN THE 14TH CENTURY B.C.

document we know that Murshilish, at the beginning of his
reign, conducted campaigns for several years against Arzawa.
It would seem that after a successful war these smaller states,
which were in some sort of dependence on the king of Arzawa,
became separate principalities under chiefs who were, like
the ruler of Arzawa himself, vassals of Hatti. Though it has so
far been impossible to fix precisely the geographical situation
of these place names, there can be little doubt that Arzawa
was the extended region in Asia Minor, which lay to the south
and southwest of Hatti and was later called Cilicia, Pisidia, and

[1] Cf. the citation at the beginning of this chapter.

Lycia. In the Amarna letters a king of Arzawa corresponds as an independent prince with Amenhotep III; subsequently the kingdom had come under Hittite suzerainty before the wars of Murshilish, which were presumably necessitated by an attempt of the king of Arzawa to regain complete political liberty.

We have seen, then, that the Hittite empire reached its greatest extent under Murshilish II. In the meantime, the XVIIIth Dynasty in Egypt had closed after the short-lived reigns of several weak rulers. The early kings of the next dynasty were made of different stuff and were filled with ambition to restore the foreign empire of Egypt. The second of the line, Seti I, began by attempting the recovery of Palestine and Phœnicia. This region, which the Hittites had never tried to control, had seceded *en masse* from Egypt during the weak foreign government of Amenhotep IV. Seti I's campaigns were aimed at cowing the natives and especially at reasserting his sovereignty over the coastal cities of Phœnicia. Amurru's loyalty to Hatti seems to have wavered about this time; for Benteshina, prince of Amurru, in league with Egypt, stirred up a rebellion against Hittite authority. The revolt was put down by Murshilish's successor, Muwatallish (Mutallu), who deposed Benteshina. Later, we find this prince restored as ruler of Amurru by Hattushilish III, whose vassal he remained. Seti I in his fourth year met and defeated a "Hittite" army in the Orontes valley; probably the defeated force was mainly composed of local tribes who owed allegiance to Hatti. A treaty between Seti and Muwatallish, as far as the last named's interests are concerned, can merely have reasserted the *status quo;* for Hatti still controlled northern Syria.

A more serious threat to Hittite sovereignty in that region came in the time of Seti's successor, Ramses II. Nor was the Hittite king unmindful of the more serious attack which threatened his imperial interests south of the Taurus. For Muwatallish collected troops and raised levies in all parts of his dominions; these he led in person against the invader. In the valley of the Orontes, close to Kadesh, the two armies met in 1296 B.C. Though, at the end of a long day's fighting, in which Muwatallish showed superior strategy and Ramses's troops better discipline and superior powers of defense, the Egyptian monarch could claim to be master of the field, it was a Pyrrhic victory. Ramses had lost a whole division of his army and was no nearer to attaining his real objective. Subsequently, for about fifteen years, Ramses continued his campaigns in Syria. North of Phœnicia he failed to get any permanent hold on the country; nor does he seem appreciably to have weakened the authority of Hatti in that region. Eight years after Muwatallish's death his brother, Hattushilish III, negotiated a treaty with Ramses in 1280 B.C.[1] Of this important document we possess two incomplete copies of the Egyptian and considerable fragments of the Hittite version. There is a historical preamble, setting out the earlier relations between the two high contracting parties, and a reaffirmation of the treaties made by their predecessors. The two kings undertake to abstain from all aggressions on each other's spheres of influence and conclude a defensive alliance against mutual enemies, whether these be recalcitrant subjects or foreign states. There are also provisions for the extradition of political fugitives, who are to receive an amnesty in their respective countries, and against the permanent settlement of Egyptians in Hittite and of Hittites in Egyptian territory. It is beyond doubt that the Egyptian sphere of influence hereafter did not extend beyond the Phœnician coast, and that Amurru continued to be a Hittite protectorate. If we seek for a reason why Hattushilish took the initiative in coming to terms with his rival — and this seems to have been the case — we can probably find it in the marked growth of Assyrian power at this date. Shalmaneser I attacked Hittite dependencies, when he entered the old land of Mitanni and Hanigalbat which lay to the north of it. It was therefore to Hattushilish's interest to be at peace with his old enemy, Egypt, and to continue, as his predecessors had done, to foster good relations between Hatti and the Cassite rulers of Babylon. Under Hattushilish the Assyrian peril was averted, nor was it in fact that power which, half a century later, brought the Hittite empire to an end.

---

[1] Muwatallish died in 1288 and was succeeded by his young son, Urhiteshupash. In 1281 the latter was displaced by his uncle, Hattushilish III, the younger brother of Muwatallish.

The existing documents of Hattushilish are more numerous than those of any other Hittite monarch; one is of quite exceptional interest, being a long autobiographical account of the king up to the time when he was firmly established on the throne. Strongly religious in tone, — for Hattushilish piously attributes all his success and his preservation from many dangers to his patron goddess, Ishtar, — it is also full of romance. Hattushilish was the younger son of Murshilish II, and, being sickly in his youth, was made a priest of Ishtar. On the accession of his elder brother, Muwatallish, he was given an important province to administer, which aroused the jealousy of the previous governor, a man destined to be his life-long enemy. The latter's attempt to calumniate Hattushilish to the king failed. Hattushilish next saw much military service in different parts of Asia Minor; later still he was with his brother during the campaign against Ramses II. Then he had again to combat false accusations, brought against him by his old rival, who, in addition, seems to have caused him serious losses during his absence at the war. Having at last surmounted all these difficulties, he, on his brother's death, acted as regent for his nephew, who was apparently a minor when he became king. In time this youth tried to restrict his uncle's power, a circumstance which led to civil war and in the end to Hattushilish's occupation of the throne. This triumph Hattushilish owed mainly to his having previously won the prominent nobles to his side. His nephew and his old rival, who had supported the young king to the last, were both banished. Some little while before his accession Hattushilish had taken to wife the daughter of a priest of Ishtar. It is much to be regretted that this interesting record refers only in quite general terms to Hattushilish's own reign. In more or less stereotyped language the king states that he had received the homage of vassals, while princes of equal rank had sent him gifts. Of his former enemies some had now sought alliances, others had been utterly defeated by him.

It remains to chronicle one further episode in the relations between Hatti and Egypt. A dozen years or so after the treaty, Hattushilish paid a state visit to Egypt, and with him went his daughter. Her nuptials with the Egyptian monarch were doubtless celebrated with becoming pomp, while the fact that the two royal houses were now related by marriage helped to ensure future friendship between the two states.[1]

[1] The following are the kings of the XVIIIth and XIXth Dynasties with approximate dates:

XVIIIth Dynasty		XIXth Dynasty	
Ahmose I	1580–1558	Ramses I	1321
Amenhotep I	1558–1545	Seti I	1321–1300
Thutmose I	1545–1514	Ramses II	1300–1233
Thutmose II	1514–1501	Merenptah	1233–1223
Queen Hatshepsut	1501–1479	Amenmose	1223–1220
Thutmose III	1479–1447	Ramses–Siptah	1220–1214
Amenhotep II	1447–1420	Seti II	1214–1210
Thutmose IV	1420–1412		
Amenhotep III	1412–1376		
Amenhotep IV (Akhenaten)	1380–1362		
Smenkhkere	1362–1360		
Tutenkhamen	1360–1350		
Ai	1350–1346		
Harmhab	1346–1322		

CHAPTER V

EGYPTIAN CIVILIZATION

Egypt . . . has wonders more in number than
any other land, and works too it has to show as
much as any land, which are beyond expression
great; for this reason, then, more shall be said
concerning it. — Herodotus ii, 35 (tr. Macaulay).

1. MATERIAL CULTURE

ALTHOUGH no caste system existed in Ancient Egypt, and no
sharp cleavage between an upper and a lower class of free men,
as it is found in Babylonia, the population in practice was made
up of three or four groups, whose life and material prosperity differed greatly. We must, in fact, distinguish the official class, the
town dwellers, the agricultural population, and the priests. In
addition to these free men there was a very numerous slave class.

Since agriculture was the oldest as well as the most important
occupation, the farming class might justly be regarded as the
backbone of the nation. Yet, inasmuch as the landowners
were the king himself, the priests, or the nobles, the average
farmer is not likely to have eked out much more than a pittance
for himself and his family. He was, in truth, little better than
a serf; though he might suffer oppression and wrong, he might
find it a long and difficult business to obtain redress.[1] In a
year of poor harvest the rural population would of course be
the first to suffer, and such years came from time to time, in
spite of the care taken by some of the Egyptian monarchs to
supplement nature and the Nile by canalization and by building reservoirs. Such was the purpose of Lake Moeris, constructed during the XIIth Dynasty by Amenemhet III; another
artificial lake was built a little to the west of Thebes by some
king of the XVIIIth or XIXth Dynasty. The system of canals

---

[1] Cf. the long story of the Eloquent Peasant, of which there is a good
English version by A. H. Gardiner in *Journal of Egyptian Archæology,*
ix (1923), pp. 5–25.

was intricate and old-standing; whether the proper maintenance of these was undertaken and defrayed by the state or
whether the farmers were, as in Babylonia, partly or wholly
responsible for the upkeep, we do not know. At all events,
from early times an official register was carefully kept of the
annual rise and fall of the river.

The crops chiefly cultivated were wheat, barley, and durra
(*sorghum vulgare*); the last-named, however, seems to have been
much less popular than it is in modern Egypt. Of great importance, too, was the growing of flax, since linen was the universally used material for clothing. No less ubiquitous was the
date-palm, while other fruits, as well as vegetables and flowers
in great variety, were grown extensively, either for ordinary use
or for the tables of the rich. The usual livestock — cattle,
sheep, goats, and pigs — was successfully reared. Oxen were
used in agricultural operations, while the ass was the commonest
draught animal. The horse, introduced from Syria or beyond
in the Hyksos period, was thereafter essential in the army. The
camel, though known, does not appear to have been employed
as a beast of transport save to a very limited extent.

The town dwellers were occupied in every variety of handi-
craft and in trade and commerce. From excavated town sites
we can see that the majority of houses were small and of simple
design, — a central courtyard on which a number of rooms
opened, — and that the streets were narrow. The new city,
built to be his capital by Amenhotep IV, was exceptional for its
more spacious roads and houses. The jewelry, furniture, and
the artistic productions generally, whether of the XIIth or the
XVIIIth and following Dynasties, reveal the astonishing skill
of the craftsman, as well as the luxury which surrounded the
king and the wealthy class. Much of the raw material was of
necessity imported from outside Egypt: from the Sinai peninsula, where the mines continued to be intensively exploited
after the repulse of the Hyksos; from Syria, and more especially
from Phœnicia and the Lebanon region; from Punt, whither the
queen Hatshepsut in the ninth year of her reign (*c.* 1493 B.C.)
sent five ships which returned laden with precious commodities
of all kinds; and, lastly, from Nubia. This country during the
Hyksos period passed almost entirely out of Egyptian control.

Plate 5

TEMPLE AT EDFU IN EGYPT

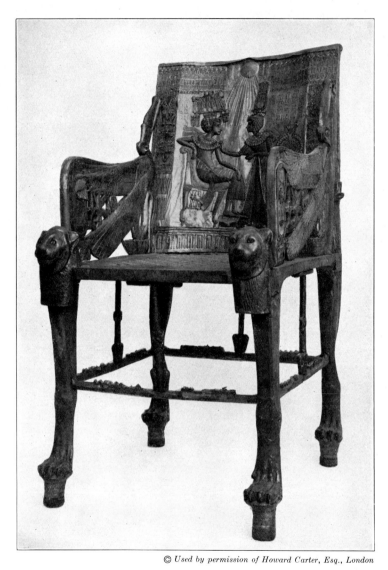

THRONE FROM THE TOMB OF TUTENKHAMEN

Plate 5a

The kings of the XVIIIth Dynasty reasserted their authority in Lower Nubia, and, under Thutmose III and Amenhotep III, the frontier was advanced to the fourth Nile cataract. Some of the royal expeditions extended even farther south than this, perhaps as far as the sixth cataract; but we have no evidence that this remote region was permanently an Egyptian protectorate.

The general condition of peasants and city-dwellers altered little through the ages. Many crafts were of immemorial antiquity. The potter's wheel only became known in the Old Kingdom, but fine vases were already being produced in the predynastic era. Glazing pottery and making blue glass from copper frit are proved by extant specimens to be exceedingly old. The elaborate offerings buried with persons of rank often included wooden models of the dead man's retainers engaged in their various callings. Many such survive and graphically represent different agricultural operations, the brewing of liquor, boats and their crews, or craftsmen at work.

The official class from the time of the XVIIIth Dynasty must have been very numerous. The administration was now highly centralized, and the work was carried on by a graded bureaucracy. The governor of Thebes, who acted as viceroy when the king was absent on any foreign expedition, was, after the monarch himself, the most important person in the realm. From the time of Thutmose III a second viceroy was appointed to act in Lower Egypt, his official residence being at Memphis. In the tomb of one of the southern governors of the age of Thutmose III, Rehkmire, there survives a long and famous inscription, from which much can be learnt about the duties and powers of that high office. Briefly, the governor was entrusted with the direction of the entire administration, with one noteworthy exception. Although he was ultimately responsible for the collection of taxes and inland revenue from the various local authorities, he did not direct the finances of the country. The treasury was in charge of another high official who was responsible solely and directly to the king. Thus for his supplies the governor must needs apply to the monarch himself; obviously this meant an important check on any over-ambitious viceroy. The local officials, of course, differed greatly in status; in places of strategic importance the control was purely military, while elsewhere, though the descendants of local chiefs and landed aristocracy still ruled in name, the real power was vested in a sheriff appointed by the king.

Of the administration of law in Egypt during the Middle and New Kingdom we really know far less than in the case of Babylonia with its Sumerian and Semitic codes. That the law had been in some form or other codified before the XVIIIth Dynasty may be deduced from a statement that the vizier, who was head of the judiciary, shall have before him the forty rolls of the law when he is passing judgment. So far as Egyptian legal practice can be appraised, the civil ordinances regulating property, contracts, testamentary succession, and the family were worthy of a highly civilized people; the criminal law, with its use of torture for witnesses, whether free or slave, and its constant appeal to magic was still of a rather primitive and savage character. Besides courts at the two chief centres of Thebes and Heliopolis, we can safely postulate the existence of inferior courts in the more important cities of the two kingdoms. We do not hear that the priests, who by the XVIIIth Dynasty not only formed a class by themselves but began to become exceedingly powerful outside the religious sphere, possessed or could legally exercise jurisdiction. On the other hand, we may be sure that, as their power grew, they could exert their influence on any branch of the administration. The earlier monarchs of Dynasty XVIII, especially Thutmose III, had lavished gifts on Amen, to whose favor they attributed their success in war and their prosperity at home. The ministers of the god, the Amen priests, welcomed a royal generosity which promoted their own power. Save for a brief check under Amenhotep IV they became continuously more powerful till, from the time of the XXth Dynasty, they dominated even the monarchs themselves. Both politically and economically the effects of Akhenaten's aberration were disastrous to Egypt. We have already seen how her Syrian empire dropped away; at home the people as a whole suffered from the exactions and tyranny of officials and tax-gatherers, as well as from the depredations of the soldiery. The administration became hopelessly corrupt because supervision by the central authorities had virtually ceased. Local authorities connived with the collectors of revenue in the nefarious task of fleecing the masses. The chief credit for restoring order in Egypt, and thereby enabling her people to recover their prosperity, seems to belong to Harmhab, whose surviving edicts are a historical source of great value. This man, who had filled important military and administrative posts in Lower Egypt, was, thanks largely to the powerful support of the Amen priesthood, elevated to the throne some twelve years after Akhenaten's death. In that interval three short-lived rulers — the second of them was Tutenkhamen, the unearthing of whose tomb was one of the most sensational discoveries of recent years — were king in name more than in fact.

From early times the most characteristic expression of royal power and magnificence had been the erection of funerary or religious buildings. Such, for example, were the pyramids set up by the kings of the Old Kingdom. Pyramid building was to some extent revived by the monarchs of the XIIth Dynasty, but these later structures, the result of a conscious archaizing, are not comparable, either in size or workmanship, with the great tombs of Cheops and his successors. Rather, the most impressive buildings of the Middle Kingdom were temples like that set up at Heliopolis in honor of the sun by Senusret I, or the so-called labyrinth at Hawara built by Amenemhet III. This was an elaborate complex of halls and colonnades in the centre of which stood a pyramid, the last resting place of that monarch. Many of the nobles, too, built themselves fine tombs, the walls of which were covered with decoration in painting and relief. Long autobiographical inscriptions often accompanied the ornamentation, and much of the epigraphic material from which our knowledge of Egyptian history is derived is in this form.[1] During the Hyksos occupation many of the older buildings must have been destroyed or badly damaged. The rulers of the XVIIIth Dynasty vied with one another in restoring old structures and building new ones. Thus Queen Hatshepsut lavished great wealth on the construction of a temple at Deir el-Bahri. The building was dedicated to Amen and also commemorated the queen's father, Thutmose I. Thutmose III's activity as a builder was displayed in various

---

[1] Cf. for instance the inscription of Ameni of which a part is cited above on page 54.

parts of his kingdom, but even his prodigality seems to have been surpassed by Amenhotep III. The most ambitious monument set up by him has unhappily not survived. It was a mighty funerary temple at Thebes, standing on the western bank of the Nile, and would appear to have been of unexampled magnificence. All that now remains are two colossal statues of the king, familiar to later ages as the statues of Memnon.[1] After Amenhotep III's time a marked decline in architecture set in. Later kings continued to build extensively; indeed, the extravagance of Ramses II went further than that of any of his predecessors. He restored, often with an utter absence of taste, and he set up a great variety of new monuments. But, to take but one instance, compared with earlier funerary temples, that which Ramses built for himself (the so-called Ramesseum at Thebes) is vulgar and pretentious. In place of the fine architectural proportions on which the artists of an earlier age had expended infinite care, the spectator viewing Ramses' temple finds nothing but immense and clumsy size. Under the successors of this king the decline in architecture, as in the other arts, was even more rapid.

Besides architecture, sculpture in the round and in relief, wall-painting in *tempera*, miniature carving, and the work of the jeweler and goldsmith were intensively and successfully cultivated at all periods. In portraiture two apparently contradictory tendencies can be noted. On the one hand, from early dynastic times strict artistic conventions were followed, the observance of which gives many Egyptian statues a stiff and lifeless appearance, however admirable the technical execution. On the other hand, as the amount of Egyptian sculptures has greatly increased, thanks to continuous excavation, it has become clear that at all times down to Dynasty XIX a love for more naturalistic or realistic presentation of the subject existed among some Egyptian artists. There were men, particularly during the fourth and the twelfth dynasties, who produced portrait statues of unsurpassed individuality. Even greater is the realism which we find in the representations of Akhenaten

[1] There is a most interesting essay on these colossi and on stories connected with them in the late Lord Curzon's *Tales of Travel*, published in 1923.

and his family, whether in sculpture or in painting (Plate 5*b*). Ultimately formalism triumphed. There was much deliberate archaism as well, coupled with a vandalism displayed by later Pharaohs, which took the form of usurping the statues of older kings and putting their own names thereon. Occasionally bad taste went even farther, and the face was worked over so as to resemble a little more nearly the features of the reigning prince.

2. RELIGION AND THOUGHT

In religion the Egyptians, like the inhabitants of Mesopotamia, were polytheists. Already in the predynastic period we find various types of deity coexistent in the Egyptian pantheon. For, side by side with the nature-worship which found its expression in the cult of the sun-god or the god of the air, we are confronted with a large group of divinities who appear to have been originally tribal totems. Of the earlier and stricter form of this totemism nothing is known; for, as far back as our records go, we already find it greatly modified. The crocodile totem has become Sebek, the crocodile god; the falcon totem has similarly been transformed into Horus. In either case the deity was represented in human form but with animal head. Different in origin from either of these two classes of deities was a god like Osiris, who would seem to have been at first a dead king or hero and who was portrayed in purely human shape, and abstractions, like Maat, the goddess of justice; and these mark the latest stages in the formative process of the Egyptian pantheon. Of the innumerable gods and goddesses whose worship is attested, the majority was never of more than local significance. At the same time political circumstances not unlike those that have been noted in Mesopotamia might convert a local into a national deity. The falcon-headed Horus, who had already become god of all Lower Egypt before the conclusion of the predynastic era, became the national god of the whole country after the unification in the Ist Dynasty of Upper Egypt and the Delta. Another important process that went on continuously and helped to weld originally divers elements into a more compact whole was religious syncretism. At the same time it brought small groups of divinities into such prominence and to such influence that their cults quite over-shadowed all others. The earliest religious writings, the so-called Pyramid Texts, of the fifth and sixth dynasties demonstrate that the rulers of that period especially promoted the cult of the sun-god, Ra. As we have seen,[1] the worship of Horus, so far from being set aside, was merged in that of Ra. Under the XIIth Dynasty, the god of Thebes, Amen, became the chief divinity of the pantheon; his identification with Ra-Horus was rapid.

The evidence of surviving monuments and of the greater portion of religious texts justifies the statement that the pre-dominant feature of Egyptian belief was the fear of death. We have seen the immense labor and cost expended by rulers and their nobles, from the time of the Old Kingdom onwards, on providing a sumptuous resting-place for themselves after death. Thus originated pyramids, or rock-cut tombs, or funerary tem-ples. The man of the people, it is true, could not afford such luxurious sepulture; but all, rich and poor alike, were animated by the same conviction that the dead were actually living in their tombs, and that, like gods and men, they required the physical sustenance of food and drink. Thus elaborate mor-tuary cults existed from the earliest times; and, with the aim of preserving the dead body as far and as long as possible, the practice of mummification was adopted. Instances of this last are known from the IInd Dynasty; it developed rather slowly, and was at first confined to members of royal or noble families. In later centuries the custom became more wide-spread, until, in the time of the New Kingdom, even the poor had recourse to a simple form of embalmment. Much of the extant literature is characterized by a profound pessimism, although it is only fair to add that the gloomy tone of a given composition often reflects the wretched political and social conditions of the writer's age. And it has been seen how in Egyptian history periods of political stability and material prosperity tended to alternate with epochs of unrest and widely prevalent distress. We thus see that the sad tone of much of the literature is due to other causes than the fear of death and its underlying religious ideas.

The so-called Prophecy of Neferohu was seemingly composed

---

[1] See above, page 48.

during the XIIth Dynasty; but it is in the form of a prophecy delivered to King Snefru of the IIId Dynasty foretelling the disasters that will befall Lower Egypt for many years after his death, until at last Amenemhet I — the founder of the XIIth Dynasty — will come to the rescue from the south and will restore the unity and fortunes of Egypt. The distressful years between the end of the sixth and the middle of the eleventh dynasties are portrayed even more vividly in the *Admonitions of a Prophet:* [1]

Nay, but corn hath perished everywhere. People are stripped of clothing, perfume, and oil. Every one saith: "There is no more." The storehouse is bare, and he that kept it lieth stretched out on the ground.

* * * * * * * * *

Behold, the rich man sleepeth thirsty. He that once begged him for his dregs (?) now possesseth strong beer.

Behold, they that possessed clothes are now in rags. He that wove not for himself now possesseth fine linen.

Behold, he that never built for himself a boat now possesseth ships. He that possessed the same looketh at them, but they are no longer his.

And yet, as specimens of the more popular literature show, the Egyptians as a whole were not only a patient but a cheerful people, making the most of the simpler pleasures of life. The truth is that we meet with other real or apparent contradictions in the writings that survive. The many examples of moral instructions, a favorite literature in the schools, do not for the most part offer more than guidance in worldly affairs, rules of etiquette, and so forth. Nevertheless, if they do not inculcate higher moral conduct, there is at least one substantial fragment, written probably in the Middle Kingdom, in which a loftier ethical standard is set. In the *Instruction for King Merikere* we come across the following sentiments: [2]

The judge who judged the oppressed, thou knowest that they are not lenient on that day of judging the miserable, in the hour of carrying out the decision. Ill fareth it when the accuser is the Wise One (Thoth, god of wisdom?). Put not thy trust in length of years; they regard

---

[1] Cited from A. Erman, *The Literature of the Ancient Egyptians;* translated by A. M. Blackman (London: Methuen, 1927), pages 99 and 101.

[2] *Op. cit.* pages 77–78. "They" and "them" must clearly mean the judges of the dead.

a lifetime as an hour. A man remaineth over after death and his deeds
are placed beside him in heaps. But it is for eternity that one is there,
and he is a fool that maketh light of them. But he that cometh unto
them without wrong-doing, he shall continue yonder like a god, stepping
boldly forward like the Lord of Eternity.

The doctrine implied in this passage, that virtue is its own
reward and that reward or punishment in the Hereafter will
depend on whether a man has led a good or a bad life on earth,
would seem to be all but unique in the extant literature of
Egypt. To some extent this may be accidental, and one cannot
deny the possibility that many, whether members of the educated priesthood or ordinary men, may have believed in and
acted on such moral principles. Nevertheless it seems impossible
at present to reconcile such an ethical code with the beliefs and
practice for which surviving documents furnish abundant illus-
tration. The widely held belief in the efficacy of magical power
(*Hike*) is attested from the earliest times and reached its fullest
expression, as far as the extant literature is concerned, in those
collections of magic *formulae* and spells, for use particularly at
funeral obsequies, that are preserved in *papyri* of the New
Kingdom and now go under the somewhat misleading title of
The Book of the Dead. In other words, it was customary to
bury such spells inscribed on rolls of *papyrus* with the deceased.
The poor man had to be content with a brief selection of
magical sentences, such as could be written on a small strip
without great expense. The wealthy sometimes had scrolls
of great length, containing more than one hundred spells, buried
with them. Since it was believed that *Hike* had a more compelling power than ordinary prayer over the gods and over the dead,
the burial of these *formulae* was intended to smooth the way of
man after his decease. For, if he recited them in the correct
way, with the proper observance of ritual forms, his entry into
the next world was assured, or at least greatly facilitated. From
the ethical point of view the regrettable thing was that this was
held to be enough, and that the deceased's manner of life —
good, bad, or indifferent — was a negligible matter, provided
his appeal to *Hike* was made strictly in the manner prescribed.

Much has been written concerning the religious reforms of
Amenhotep IV. However they be judged, it is at least certain

Mansell

QUEEN NEFERTITI

Plate 5b

that they represent no more than a short and abnormal phase in the religious history of Egypt. Modern writers, struck by the emphasis laid upon the cult of a single divinity in a land which had been for centuries polytheistic, seem to have attributed to Amenhotep's monotheism a greater profundity and originality than is warranted. The cult of the sun-god was as old as Egyptian civilization. By the time of Amenhotep III, if not before, it had attained not only exceptional importance, but had taken a form unlike that of the earlier worship of Ra. Amenhotep III had regarded the sun's disc, called in Egyptian Aten, with peculiar reverence; it was left for his son and successor to exalt this cult to the exclusion of all others. Amenhotep IV came to the throne as a child; he was apparently still in his teens when, in the sixth year of his reign, he changed his name to Akhenaten, "pleasing to Aten," and tried to enforce this worship solely in his kingdom by abolishing all other cults and persecuting their adherents, especially the priests of Amen. He forsook the old capital at Thebes and on the site of the modern Amarna founded the city of Akhetaten. There, with his courtiers, he lived a devotee of the cult, which saw in the sun, whose disc alone the eye could see, the source of all life and growth. Though outwardly his subjects might have to conform, Akhenaten's new religion did not obtain any great hold on the people. On the contrary, opposition to it, if latent at first, was strong, and within ten years of the king's death the new monotheism was rooted up and the worship of Amen was restored with greater pomp than before. Now, religious poetry was abundant in Egypt, consisting of hymns in honor of various deities, while verses in honor of the ruler, be it on his succession to the throne or to commemorate some striking victory over his foes, were also in part of a religious character. The extant hymns to the sun's disc, which were the outcome of Akhenaten's reforms, stand rather apart. They are not, indeed, specially remarkable for ethical content; but their joyous tone and freedom from artificiality make them unusually attractive, as a specimen will show: [1]

When it is dawn and thou risest in the horizon and shinest as the sun in the day, thou dispellest the darkness and sheddest thy beams. The

[1] *Op. cit.* page 289.

Two Lands keep festival, awake, and stand on their feet, for thou hast raised them up. They wash their bodies, they take their garments, and their hands praise thine arising. The whole land, it doeth its work.

All beast are content with their pasture, the trees and herbs are verdant. The birds fly out of their nests and their wings praise thy ka (person). All wild beasts dance on their feet, all that fly and flutter — they live when thou arisest for them.

The ships voyage down and upstream likewise, and every way is open, because thou arisest. The fishes in the river leap up before thy face. Thy rays are in the sea.

The surviving literature of Egypt, though considerable in bulk, is perhaps somewhat disappointing to the ordinary reader, and that for several reasons. Much of it consists of religious texts following a formal pattern and often enough couched in language that is obscure even to the specialist. Many of the stories and tales are written in an artificial style with much repetition and much oriental symbolism. These must sometimes strike even the student of the original texts as tedious and strange; in translation even the stylistic beauties, on which the Egyptians laid so much stress, necessarily are lost. Furthermore the manner in which many of the texts have been preserved has resulted in the fact that few of the literary productions are entire and not defaced by passages that have been destroyed by time or else become unintelligible in transmission.

The Egyptians devised a method of writing very early; doubtless it began by being a picture-writing in which each symbol was a representation of a particular object. But far more than this was needed, if it was to become an adequate medium for the expression of even simple ideas. And, in fact, the process once begun went through several stages, until a series of purely phonetic and alphabetic signs was evolved. Since, however, some of the older pictographs were also retained, both the writing and the reading of Egyptian always remained a complicated art, even though every thought could be adequately expressed through this medium. It was only the class of scribes which mastered these difficulties, and it was from them that the numerous administrative bureaucracy in the New Kingdom was necessarily recruited. The schools existed for the training of this class. Much of the literature that has come down to us has survived on the potsherds or flakes of limestone on which the schoolboy had written out his task. Consequently, mistakes are frequent and often so serious that it is no longer possible to recover the sense of many passages. With so complex a system of writing, and because of the presence of many archaic words in the older literature of the Middle Kingdom — the classics from which suitable selections were picked for the instruction of the young — one cannot wonder at the resulting errors and confusion. Especially popular were the collections of moral sayings, to which reference was made above. These were generally in the form of *Instructions* given by a king or highly placed official to his son or subordinate, and had the double purpose of teaching good conduct and manners and of serving as models of literary style.

The examples of secular poetry from Egypt are mostly brief and fragmentary; folk-songs, love-songs, and doggerel verse such as was sung by workmen at their daily task are all represented.

When we turn to the scientific knowledge of the Egyptians, we find that they must from early times have had a substantial acquaintance with arithmetic and practical geometry applied to the mensuration of land and to the construction of large buildings. For although existing mathematical *papyri* date either from the Middle Kingdom or after, the necessities of agriculture and the evidence of massive structures like the pyramids prove that calculation, which followed a decimal system, was a very old science. Astronomy appears to have been mainly a matter of observation, not of mathematics; in addition, both it and medicine were inseparable from the belief in and practice of magic. In medicine, indeed, there seems to have been retrogression. It is clear from the medical *papyri* that many of the Egyptians had keen powers of observation. At the time of the Old and Middle Kingdoms the medical practitioners appear to have had marked skill in diagnosis; they had some knowledge of anatomy, they carried out simple surgical operations, and they used a pharmacopeia of marked diversity. But later, under the New Kingdom, their scientific thought and experiments became dominated and warped by magic and superstitious practices.

CHAPTER VI

THE BRONZE AGE CIVILIZATION OF THE MEDITERRANEAN AREA

According to oral tradition Minos was the earliest prince to acquire a fleet. He conquered the greater part of what is now the Greek Sea, and he became master of the Cyclades and was the first coloniser of most of them, after driving out the Carians, and established his own sons there as governors. — Thucydides, i, 4.

NOTHING illustrates better the immense advance in our knowledge of early civilizations, brought about by archæological exploration during the past half century, than the discovery of a great pre-Hellenic culture in the eastern Mediterranean. Just as no one until the beginning of the present century dreamed of the existence of a great Hittite empire in Asia Minor in the middle of the second millennium B.C., so, too, it was not until the discoveries of Schliemann, from 1870 onwards, at Hissarlik, Tiryns, and Mycenæ, and the no less sensational excavations of Sir Arthur Evans at Cnossus from 1900, that it became evident that the lands later occupied by the Greeks had been, for several thousand years before, the home of a civilization no whit inferior to the contemporary cultures of Asia and Egypt. Brief allusions in classical Greek authors, like Thucydides, to an early pre-Greek maritime empire centring in Crete, which had hitherto been treated as fables, were seen to be historically justified; [1] while the examples of decorative art, described in the Homeric poems and so long believed to be the outcome of poetic fancy, are now known to reflect the memory of Minoan and Mycenæan arts and crafts.

A regional survey of Bronze Age civilization in the Mediterranean must properly begin with the island of Crete, where the oldest remains precede by sundry centuries those from other

[1] Cf. the quotation at the head of this chapter.

Aegean sites. The surprising discoveries of Evans at Cnossus in Crete naturally led to intensive exploration and excavation in other parts of the island, in which British, American, Italian, and Greek archæologists have all achieved important results. Thus, more than twenty town sites, varying in size and importance, — some are as yet only partially excavated, — six votive caves, and some two dozen miscellaneous sites are now known. All of these lie in the eastern two-thirds of the island; for it is a remarkable fact, not yet adequately explained, that the western portion of Crete (all that part lying west of an imaginary line drawn southwards from the modern village of Retimo) has so far no pre-Hellenic remains to show. Of all these Cretan sites Cnossus is easily first in importance, for two reasons: the discoveries from there are richer than those made in any other place, and it is only at Cnossus that excavation has yielded an unbroken series of objects from the Neolithic Age down to the dawn of the Hellenic period. With the help of undoubtedly Egyptian objects unearthed in Crete and others found in Egypt, which were a puzzle to Egyptologists until the discoveries in Crete showed that they were Cretan, Evans was able to formulate a chronological scheme for the pre-Hellenic culture in that island. He distinguished three main eras, each of which he subdivided into three shorter periods. To the newly revealed culture he gave the name, Minoan.[1] Though further discoveries have led to occasional modifications in the dating proposed by Evans, there is no doubt about its correctness in the main.

In a previous chapter (p. 4) it has been noted that deep Neolithic deposits at Cnossus show that the site had been inhabited continuously for centuries before the first appearance of metal. Copper first makes its appearance soon after the middle of the fourth millennium; but its use must at first have been very restricted, so that we have here an admirable instance of gradual transition, lasting several centuries, from the Later

[1] Evans' term, though not free from objections and attacked in some quarters, has come to stay. But the term Minoan must be confined to Crete. For the pre-Greek civilization of the eastern Mediterranean as a whole perhaps the best name is Aegean. Minoan will then = the Cretan phase of this culture. For the nine Minoan periods see the note at the end of this chapter.

Stone Age to the fully developed Bronze Age. With the beginning of the second Early Minoan period material progress became notably more rapid. The fullest evidence for Cretan civilization at that stage (the first half of the third millennium) comes not from Cnossus, but from the little island of Mochlos and the town site of Vasiliki. The construction of the houses was remarkably substantial. The lower courses of the walls were of stone, while above were placed layers of sun-dried brick, strengthened by cross-beams forming a framework for the whole. The inside of the walls was covered with lime-plaster colored red. Already the builders showed a taste for simple internal decoration; later this developed into the elaborate buon frescoes, which are among the most remarkable relics of Cretan art. Painted pottery occurs sparingly at first; but in the Early Minoan II and III periods it becomes much more abundant and its decorative design more ambitious. Above all, in the last stage of the Early Minoan Age the potter's wheel and the kiln have come into use, the result being a noteworthy advance in ceramic technique. Of great interest, and for chronological purposes of great value, are numerous stone vases found at Mochlos and elsewhere in Early Minoan deposits. Some of these are importations from Egypt, others are Cretan imitations of Egyptian work. This evidence for early contact between the two countries is very significant; as will be seen hereafter, relations between Crete and the Land of the Nile continued unbroken for fifteen hundred years. Small marble figurines from the Cyclades discovered on Early Minoan sites are similarly an indication of intercourse between Crete and some of the smaller islands of the Archipelago.

The great palaces at Cnossus and at Phæstus in the south of the island, which attained their greatest extent and magnificence at the beginning of the Late Minoan period, had been rebuilt and enlarged more than once; for their beginnings go back to the second half of the third millennium (Middle Minoan I–II). A certain irregularity in the plan of the palaces is therefore not surprising. Extensive traces of burning make it clear that some serious catastrophe took place toward the end of the Middle Minoan III period. Probably the damage was caused by an earthquake; at all events it did not interrupt the occupation of the sites, for the palaces were rebuilt without delay, and at the same time were enlarged. To the first half of the second millennium belong not only these two reconstructed palaces, but the smaller country-house at Hagia Triada near Phæstus, and also some of the best preserved Cretan town sites, for example, at Palaikastro, Zakro, Gournia, and Tylissos. The houses varied in size, while the usual building material is sun-dried brick. Dwellings with two stories were probably not unusual, at all events among the more prosperous citizens. The general plan of the Late Minoan palace at Cnossus deserves somewhat more detailed description; that at Phæstus, though on a smaller scale, was very similar in its general arrangement. The whole complex of buildings at Cnossus is grouped around an open rectangular court, measuring approximately 190 × 85 feet. There were entrances to the palace on the north, south, and west. What has been conveniently described as the official and religious part of the palace lay on the western side of the court. Behind this group of buildings a series of parallel store-chambers was situated. There the excavator found, still *in situ*, a great number of mighty jars once used for the storage of grain and other supplies (Plate 7*a*). This row of magazines opened out into a long gallery running north and south. In the official part of the palace lay the throne room containing still in position a throne of plastered and painted gypsum. The walls were once decorated with frescoes; two griffins flanked the doorway. The block of buildings on the east of the great court made up the residential part of the palace. On this side one of the most impressive sights of the palace confronted the spectator, a grand staircase of five flights, and a colonnaded hall on the ground floor (Plate 6*b*). There were probably four stories to the palace building. From the first, great care was taken to ensure an adequate water-supply and a good system of drainage (Plate 7*b*). For, in addition to the elaborate drains and piping of the Late Minoan I palace, we have the testimony of clay pipes of excellent workmanship, which date from the first Middle Minoan Age.

When we survey the material culture of Crete during a thousand years (*c.* 2400–1400 B.C.) as a whole, we are struck not only by the divers forms in which their artistry manifested it-

self, but by their astonishing technical skill. From the end of
the Early Minoan period the Cretan potters had favored two
styles of ceramic painting, light decoration on a dark, and dark
designs on a light background. While both methods of ornamentation went on side by side, the former style was most popular in the Middle Minoan, the latter in the Late Minoan era.
Again, though there was at all times great diversity in the
shapes, the Middle Minoan craftsman was most skillful in making small vases, whose fabric is often of astonishing thinness and
delicacy. The so-called Kamares ware was the finest achievement of the Middle Minoan potter. On a black or very dark
ground a polychrome design was painted in white, purple, and
red. In the Late Minoan period the finest vases are of larger
size, high jars and high-stemmed cups, with elaborate plant
and marine designs painted in dark colors on a cream or buff
background.

Specimens of the goldsmith's and metal-worker's art, though
naturally far rarer than pottery, are no less masterly in execution. Several of the finest examples of gold-work have not actually been found in Crete; but the two famous gold cups from
Vaphio in southern Greece (Plate 11) and the wonderful bowl
discovered quite recently by Swedish excavators at Dendra were
either Cretan importations, or, if made in Greece, their technique is so similar to Cretan work that they may be cited as
examples of Minoan art. Among the most beautiful objects
found at Hagia Triada are three vases of steatite, fashioned, as
their shapes suggest, in imitation of metal work and once covered with thin gold foil. Depicted on them in low relief are various scenes, for instance, a boxing match and a procession of
harvesters. Engraved gems and seal-stones, figurines carved in
ivory or modelled in ivory and gold, objects in bronze, and delicate inlay-work, as in a gaming-board of ivory, crystal, and
blue paste, all these illustrate the multiplicity of Cretan arts
and crafts.

Finally, we must note the frescoes. Inevitably these are all
in a very fragmentary condition, and the glory of their original
coloring has faded. Yet sufficient remains to show how varied
was the palette and how admirably naturalistic the drawing of
the Minoan painter, both in the Middle and the Late Minoan

a

b

CNOSSUS: *a.* So-called Theatral Area; *b.* Grand Staircase

Plate 6

a

b

CNOSSUS: *a*. Magazine of Storage Jars; *b*. Stone Drains
Plate 7

periods. Apart from their interest as works of art, these wall-
paintings are particularly valuable evidence for the appearance
and dress, and, to some extent, the religion and amusements, of
the pre-Hellenic Cretans. The dress of the men is very simple,
consisting usually of nothing more than a loin-cloth and a short
skirt or kilt over it (Plate 9). Cloaks, which are depicted here
and there, would be used in bad weather or perhaps on ceremonial occasions. The women are dressed in close-fitting bodices
and flounced, bell-shaped skirts. Both sexes alike are represented with remarkably narrow waists, and, by an artistic convention, the unclothed parts of the female figures are generally
painted white, those of the men brown. Of the favorite sports
and amusements in Minoan society we may single out dancing
and bull-baiting.

Exploration, as well as the study of paintings, seal-stones, and
so forth, has taught us much about the religious practices of this
people. Characteristic sacred places, at least from the beginning
of the Middle Minoan period, are rock sanctuaries and votive
caves. Thus, in the extreme east of the island, at Petsofa, there
is a sanctuary where the excavators found a number of human
and animal figurines and also single limbs fashioned in clay.
Clearly the divinity who was believed to haunt this sanctuary
was worshipped for his or her healing powers. Close to Cnossus,
on Mt. Iuktas, there stood another sanctuary, frequented, as the
finds show, throughout the Middle Minoan Age. Again there
existed several votive caves, near Kamares high up on Mt. Ida,
close to Psychro below Mt. Dicte, and at Skoteino, about three
hours from Cnossus in an easterly direction. The first two have
been thoroughly explored, and from the objects found there it
appears that, while the Kamares cave was much frequented in
the Middle Minoan period, but abandoned at the beginning of
Late Minoan I, the Psychro cave does not seem to have attracted
worshippers till the very end of the Middle Minoan period but
enjoyed much esteem in the centuries that followed. We have,
at all events, continuous evidence for mountain and cave worship on the part of the Minoans. Their chief divinity was a
mother goddess; associated with her in the cult was a young
male divinity, a conjunction of deities which recalls similar cults
in Anatolia. In her representations the mother goddess is reg-

ularly flanked or accompanied by beasts, especially wild creatures like lions, pards, snakes, and birds. The shrine of this divinity in the palace at Cnossus contained a large variety of remarkable cult objects, libation bowls and tables, cups and jugs used in sacrifice, a marble cross, and charming faïence panels of domestic animals. Trees and pillars, which we find both on seal impressions, on paintings, and on a painted sarcophagus from Hagia Triada, were important cult objects; so too was the double axe. Such pillars may perhaps be regarded as aniconic symbols of the deity.

Though the material civilization enjoyed by the pre-Hellenic inhabitants of Crete has been revealed in all its profuse and splendid variety, we are almost wholly in ignorance of their political history and institutions. This is chiefly due to the fact that we have no written records to guide us. For the epigraphic material, though fairly abundant, is still undeciphered. There are several kinds of Minoan script; the earliest is pictographic and is known mainly from seal impressions. Its beginnings go back to the last part of the Early Minoan period. While there is much truth in Evans' observation that these pictographs, inasmuch as they represent various tools and objects in common use, animals, plants, and so on, are "an epitome of Minoan civilization," their value, so long as they are unread, is still only partial. From this, the earliest form of Cretan writing, developed an earlier and a later linear script; that is to say, the objects depicted in the picture writing became simplified into conventional signs. There are numerous clay-tablets inscribed with such linear writing. Some are accounts, — Evans has been able to identify some of the numeral signs, — others may be letters or despatches, whose decipherment would without doubt greatly advance our knowledge of topics which even abundant archæological material cannot illuminate.

If, then, we are for the present ignorant of the character of Minoan government, if we can only guess that the ruler of Cnossus was also the overlord of lesser chiefs and cities in other parts of the island, we can be a little more positive about the foreign relations of Crete in the third and the second millennia B.C. The archæological evidence is sufficient to warrant the statement that commercial relations between Egypt and Crete existed continuously.[1] A prehistoric road, running from Cnossus to Phæstus, can still be traced in places. It not only served to link Cnossus with the chief city in southern Crete, but by giving convenient access to the harbors on the south coast afforded a means of transit from the Cretan capital to the African coast which was quicker and safer than an all-sea journey. The relations between Crete and Cyprus, Asia Minor, and Syria, prior to the Late Minoan period, are still extremely obscure; but it is likely that further excavations in those regions may produce evidence showing the existence of such intercourse in the third millennium. It was, however, with some of the Cyclades and with southern Greece that the foreign relations of Crete were closest.

The Cyclades, owing to their smallness and their geographical position, must from very early times have been liable to be influenced by more powerful neighbors. The copious evidence furnished by the remains of three settlements of different dates at Phylakopi in the island of Melos is corroborated by the scantier finds from other islands, notably Paros and Thera. The earliest remains are contemporary with those of the Early Minoan period in Crete. Cretan influence, which seems to have begun not later than the beginning of the Middle Minoan epoch, had reached its maximum before the end of that age, and continued during the greater part of the sixteenth century B.C. It can scarcely be doubted that these islands had come directly under Cretan domination. Some intercourse with the

---

[1] In view of the assertion of some recent scholars that Egypt in her imperial days exercised sovereignty over Crete and other islands in the Aegean, it seems desirable to indicate the more noteworthy archæological data for Egypto–Cretan relations. They cannot be said to warrant such sweeping generalizations. (1) Egyptian stone vases in Early Minoan deposits. (2) Seal stones made in Crete but imitating Egyptian types of Dynasties VI–IX. (3) A Diorite monument of User (Dyn. XII) in a Middle Minoan II deposit at Cnossus. (4) Middle Minoan pottery found on several Egyptian sites (e.g. Abydos and Kahun) with objects of the XIIth Dynasty. (5) Vase-lid with cartouche of the Hyksos king, Khian, found at Cnossus. (6) Late Minoan objects found in Egypt contemporaneous with finds of the early XVIIIth Dynasty. (7) References in Egyptian inscriptions to the people of Keftiu; their general appearance on Egyptian paintings is very similar to the Cretans as known from the Cretan frescoes. (8) Association of Late Minoan III pottery with late XVIIIth Dynasty finds at Amarna.

mainland existed also. It became more intensive by the middle
of the second millennium; and, when (*c.* 1400 B.C.) the power of
the Cretan kings came to an abrupt end and the dominant influence in the eastern Aegean passed to Mycenæ, the islands
were also affected by the changed political conditions. Cretan
importations to the islands became scarce and finally ceased
altogether, but mainland pottery found its way thither in
abundance.

So far the finds of the earlier Bronze Age in southern Greece
have not been very copious, and for the most part they come
from a very restricted geographical area, the Argolid and the
region about the Isthmus of Corinth. The dwellings inhabited
by the people of this age were simple rectangular structures of
sun-dried brick, often on stone foundations. While both plain
and painted pottery has been unearthed in considerable quantities, metal objects are not abundant. Yet they suffice to
show that men were no longer in the Neolithic Age. It is not
till *c.* 1600 B.C., or shortly before, that Cretan influence on the
Greek mainland becomes marked. Its outward manifestation
is a very great advance in arts and crafts. The work of the
native potter, though it does not disappear entirely, is for the
time submerged by the popularity of foreign fabrics, which
are promptly and successfully imitated. If Mycenæan art,
though so close to Minoan, nevertheless developed something
of a character of its own, we must attribute the fact to the
survival, in some degree, of endemic styles of decoration. How
the predominance of Cretan culture in Greece came about is an
obscure problem. Did the kings of Crete introduce their Minoan
culture in southern Greece by conquest, followed by some measure of colonization? Or should we rather postulate a more
gradual process of peaceful infiltration? In the sixteenth century B.C. we find a dynasty ruling at Mycenæ and apparently
exercising control over the whole Argolic peninsula. Contemporaneous with them, influential dynasties were established in
Thebes and Orchomenus in central Greece. Were these Mycenæan princes a ruling caste, racially akin to the lords of Cnossus
and governing a subject population in Greece of different stock?
Or were they of the same race as their subjects, but successful
in imposing on them the more advanced alien culture of Crete

a

b

a. HAGIA TRIADA WITH MT. IDA IN BACKGROUND; *b*. HAGIA TRIADA

Plate 8

b

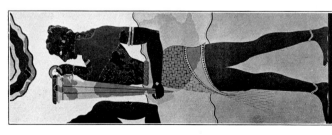

a

a. CUP-BEARER FRESCO AT CNOSSUS;   b. FLYING FISH FRESCO FROM MELOS

Plate 9

the more so as they may for a time have been vassals of Cnossus? Much study and excavation are still needed before these questions, especially the ethnic problems involved, can be solved with even approximate certainty. The historian and the archæologist may well comfort themselves with the dictum of Edward Fitzgerald that the power of suspending judgment is an essential attribute of good scholarship.

At least there is no doubt about the power and prosperity of the sixteenth century rulers of Mycenæ. For the shaft graves in which they were buried were filled with examples of the potter's, the metal-worker's, and the jeweler's skill, rivalling the finest Minoan work. This is especially true of several bronze daggers on which hunting scenes were cunningly inlaid in gold (Plate 12), and of a series of gold masks which covered the faces of the deceased kings. About one hundred years later the kings of Mycenæ — presumably we have to reckon with a new dynasty, though it would be rash to assume also a marked racial difference — were interred not in shaft graves but in domed chambers, to which owing to their shape the name "beehive tombs" has been given. Examples of this type of funeral chamber have also been found, elsewhere than at Mycenæ, over a wide area; this circumstance, coupled with the fact that the same types of pottery and other objects have been discovered in different parts of the Peloponnese, Attica, Bœotia, and Eubœa, makes the assumption of a general hegemony exercised by Mycenæ over southern and central Greece, and by this time also over the Cyclades, extremely probable. The zenith of Mycenæan power was reached in the fourteenth and thirteenth centuries, that is to say, after the downfall of Cnossus and Phæstus. The citadel and palace of Mycenæ were enlarged, and similar building activity took place almost contemporaneously in the dependent stronghold of Tiryns.

The Mycenæan citadel was situated on the side of a hill from the summit of which the lords of Mycenæ could keep a look-out over a great part of the Argolid, northward to Corinth, southward to the Gulf of Nauplia. Massive, so-called Cyclopean, walls, constructed of great limestone blocks, enclosed the palace area, which could be entered by two gates. The chief, now dubbed the Lion Gate, was on the northwest side; it derives its name from the triangular slab, carved in relief with two rampant lions with a sacral pillar between them, which surmounted the lintel of the gate. The lintel itself is a huge block of stone measuring $16 \times 8 \times 3$ feet. The heraldic design of the slab has its counterpart in Minoan and Mycenæan sealstones. There was a subsidiary entrance on the north, near the eastern end of the fortification wall. The best preserved example from this age of fortification and palace construction on the mainland is, however, at Tiryns; for, as a whole, the Mycenæan palace and walls are poorly preserved. The hill at Tiryns contained an upper and a lower citadel. While the latter seems to have been a place of refuge in case of need for the population of the plain, the upper citadel contained a palace. The whole *enceinte* was strongly fortified. The thickness of the walls varies between sixteen and fifty-seven feet. They are strengthened with towers, while on two sides are galleries cut in the rock into which a number of subterranean store-chambers open out. The main entrance was on the east, and the road led up an inclined plane through two pillared gateways into a spacious courtyard. The chief hall of the palace, approached through a vestibule, was of rectangular shape. In the centre was the hearth; the floor was of concrete, while the roof was supported by four wooden pillars. Though these have perished, the stone bases into which they fitted still remain. Supplementary excavations have shown that the walls of the rooms in the palace were extensively decorated with wall-paintings; their character is very similar to that of the frescoes found in Crete.

Two other regions must be briefly noticed to complete our survey of the eastern Mediterranean area. Northern Greece, and the adjacent lands of Macedonia and Thrace, until late were little or not at all affected by the Aegean culture. Exploration of Thessalian sites has proved the existence of a well-developed Neolithic civilization there in the third millennium, which lasted well on into the second. By the seventeenth century B.C. this region had entered the Bronze Age. Its cultural relations so far seem to have been mainly with the North. There has been relatively so little systematic excavation in this area, and scarcely any in Macedonia and Thrace, that it is impossible to reach any adequate historical conclusions.

The influence of Mycenæan culture seems by the fourteenth century to have extended into southern Thessaly, but it was not potent enough to drive out the more primitive local art and pot fabrics. The migrations of peoples, whose arrival coincided with the beginning of the Iron Age, wrought drastic changes which left no portion of Greece untouched.

Troy (Hissarlik), the first pre-Hellenic site to be investigated by Schliemann, stood a short distance inland, but overlooked the eastern entrance to the Hellespont (Dardanelles). Its geographical position laid its inhabitants open to foreign influences from at least two sides — from the uplands of Anatolia and from Europe. Of the remains of nine superimposed settlements at Hissarlik the last three do not concern us here because they belong to the Greek or Græco-Roman periods. The lowest settlement of all (c. 2500 B.C.?) belongs to the Chalcolithic, or to the very beginning of the Bronze Age. The second city was distinguished by a much more advanced culture. It was fortified with walls of sun-baked brick laid on massive stone foundations. Objects of gold, silver, and bronze show that its craftsmen were not greatly inferior to the artists of contemporary Crete. The pottery, too, is well made, but turned by hand. Apparently the potter's wheel was still unknown there towards the end of the third millennium. The third, fourth, and fifth settlements (c. 2100–1500 B.C.?) were very poor; their occupants cannot have exercised any political influence or power. At the same time archæological finds seem to show the existence of some trade connection between Troy, Thrace, and the Danubian basin. The sixth settlement, though small in size, was clearly occupied by a powerful dynasty. The palace that once stood there has gone; but the remains of the fortification walls, made of well-wrought stone and strengthened at intervals by turrets, show that the princes of Troy dwelt in a citadel as strong as were those of the rulers of Mycenæ and Tiryns.

When, after surveying the pre-Hellenic civilization of the Aegean as manifested to us in the archæological remains, we turn to the political history and development of this area in the third and second millennia B.C., we pass from concrete facts to the realm of highly speculative conjecture. In the

third millennium the different regions within the Aegean area
which have been described developed independently, though
we must of course reckon with a certain degree of trade intercourse between them.   By the beginning of the second millennium the more advanced culture of Crete was beginning to
spread very rapidly beyond the limits of the island.   It affected
first the Cyclades and then the Greek mainland; so that, before
the middle of the second millennium, the priest-kings of
Cnossus exercised suzerainty over a considerable empire.   In
other words, not only the cultural but the political influence of
Crete was paramount in the eastern Mediterranean until the catastrophe at the end of the Late Minoan II period (c. 1400 B.C.),
to which reference has already been made.   The nature of
this disaster, in which not only the palaces at Cnossus and
Phæstus were destroyed, but desolation came upon the many
other Cretan towns which had enjoyed such signal prosperity
in the preceding centuries, is obscure.   But the completeness
of the destruction caused makes the conclusion irresistible that
foreign invaders were responsible.   It is most likely that they
came from the Greek mainland; for, though the great palaces
in Crete were not properly rebuilt, their sites and the town
sites also continued to be occupied.   Minoan culture continued;
the pottery and the artistic objects of the third Late Minoan
Age are excellent, even though they lack the brilliance and
costliness which distinguish the productions of previous centuries.   In short, after c. 1400 B.C., if we know nothing of the
political history of Crete, we can see clearly that the cultural
history follows a course closely parallel to that of Greece or the
islands.   Here, as there, the expiring Bronze Age merges into
the early Iron Age.

    The truth is that the number of well-attested historical facts,
or generalizations that are safe because founded on a sufficiency
of archæological material, is regrettably small.   Apart from the
Cretan disaster the following data are of special importance:

    1.   The Egyptian records refer to two occasions on which in-
vaders from over the sea joined in an attack on the Land of the
Nile.   In the assault at the time of Merenptah (cf. p. 107)
the Libyans were reinforced by five different tribes.   Of these
the Ekwesh may perhaps be equated with the Achæans.   Nearly

a

b

BEE–HIVE TOMB AT ORCHOMENUS: *a.* MAIN ENTRANCE
b. ENTRANCE TO INNER CHAMBER

Plate 10

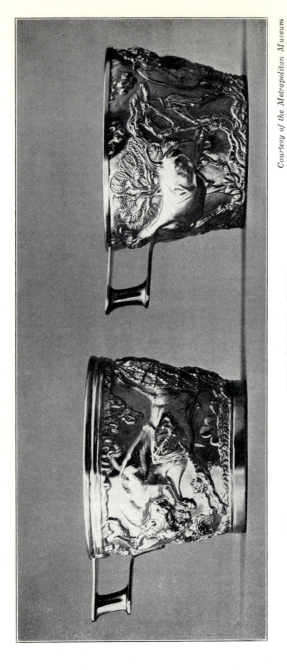

THE VAPHIO CUPS

Plate 11

thirty years later Ramses III (cf. p. 108) was obliged to repel two more formidable invasions. The peoples of the sea formed an important contingent of this formidable horde of enemies.

2. Although, about the end of the twelfth century, the Mycenæan power was overthrown, and Mycenæ, Tiryns, and other sites were burnt, Mycenæan culture lingered on; it was not suddenly extinguished.

3. Greek tradition knew of a war between a Greek host and Troy. Several dates were assigned for that event; the most generally accepted placed the fall of Troy in 1183 B.C. Tradition further speaks of the Achæans as a dominant race or clan in Crete and Greece during the thirteenth century B.C.[1] The invasions of the Dorians into Greece is put fully a century later.

4. The beginning of the Iron Age in Greece can be dated approximately to 1000 B.C.; isolated iron objects are found earlier; in the interior of Anatolia this metal, it would now appear, was known at the beginning of the second millenium. It is, however, probable that the inhabitants of Greece owed their more extended knowledge of it to invaders from central Europe.

5. As far as the pottery is concerned — and there is little other material to work on for the period from 1100–900 B.C. — the two centuries after the downfall of Mycenæ seem to have been an age of great cultural depression. Before its conclusion a new style of pottery, called from the style of its decoration, Geometric, is found over a wide area. But we cannot associate this ware with any particular people or group of immigrants to Greece. It seems to be a development from the more debased form of Late Mycenæan art modified by some foreign influences. Two facts, moreover, are of great significance: although the decorative schemes on Geometric vases are crude and "primitive," on the technical side (well-levigated clay, good paint, etc.) they are excellent (Plate 13a). Secondly, while Mycenæan pottery varies little in character wherever it is found, the Geometric shows a great many variations. This fact is note-

---

[1] The thalassocracy of "Minos," mentioned by Thucydides, is generally interpreted as a maritime empire ruled by an Achæan dynasty in Crete in the thirteenth century. They would presumably be independent of, but on a friendly footing with, the Achæan rulers of Mycenæ.

worthy. It suggests that, after the overthrow of Mycenæ, Greece was broken up into small political and social groups, although their members may have been in many cases of the same stock. Such a condition of affairs would be promoted also by the peculiar geographical features of Greece, and was one which was actually in existence at the beginning of the "historic" period of Greece.

That considerable migrations from central Europe occurred in the second half of the second millennium is beyond dispute, but when and how often is quite uncertain. It has been argued that the Achæan rulers of Mycenæ, who dispossessed an earlier Mycenæan dynasty (that of the shaft-graves?) were in reality a central European body of conquerors. The view is by no means free from difficulties; but they are hardly as great as those encountered by scholars who, accepting later Greek tradition on this point at its face value, see in the Achæans only one of a number of tribes indigenous in Greece. Moreover, though later traditions represent migrations such as the Dorian as a single event, all historical analogies point to the fact that, when a considerable body of nomadic or semi-nomadic peoples are on the move, their infiltration into more distant region is a gradual process. It is thus possible that a further Achæan invasion occurred at a somewhat later date, and resulted in a wider distribution of Achæan political power in the thirteenth century. If that were so, it would not be surprising if the accounts written in a much later age combined into one what were really several migratory movements, prior to the latest with which the name of the Dorians is associated.

That the Greek legends of the Trojan war have within them a kernel of historic fact is very probable. That being admitted, one is tempted to regard the historic event — a war between a group of peoples from the Greek mainland, under the leadership of Mycenæ, and a coalition led by the lord of Troy — as an episode in the larger clash between East and West, which culminated in the overthrow of Hatti and the invasion of Syria.

The latest migratory wave into Greece, the so-called Dorian invasion, seems to have begun about, or soon after, 1100 B.C. The two to three centuries following this date are, in a certain sense, a formative period. For during that time new racial elements found their way into Greece, mainly from the Northwest, which in some cases dispossessed, in others coalesced with, the older population. Many of the mainlanders, deprived of their homes, were driven forth to found communities elsewhere. Thus Crete, the islands of the Archipelago, and the coast of Asia Minor all received their quota of new settlers. These earliest stages in the evolution of the city-states of historic Greece are entirely lost to our view. Whatever the significance of such names, the Greeks of a later time were accustomed to think that the whole body of Hellenes was made up of several large groups, differing one from the other to some extent in customs and speech. The Aeolian group was in occupation of Thessaly and Bœotia, and also of the most northern section of the west coast of Asia Minor, together with adjacent islands like Lesbos. The Ionians were in Attica, in most of the Cyclades, and along the central portion of the Asia Minor littoral, where they thus became the southern neighbors of the Aeolic communities. Finally, the Dorians occupied the greater part of the Peloponnese, Crete, Melos, Thera, and the islands near or off the southwest coast of Asia Minor, and some portion of the mainland lying opposite to these. The distribution of Greek dialects in historic times is in general accord with this grouping.

A review of the Bronze Age in the eastern Mediterranean may fittingly terminate with a brief account of Homeric society. This is not the place for even a short discussion of the numerous problems, archæological, linguistic, and literary, which together make up the "Homeric Question." Even granted that the *Iliad* and *Odyssey*, as they have come down to us, are substantially the work of a single genius, we can do no more than guess at the character of the earlier material utilized by the poet for his great epics. Bards or "Rhapsodes" must have exercised their art at the court of Mycenæan and Minoan chieftains, composing hymns in honor of gods or narrative poems recounting the exploit of a hero. Their choice of subject will often have been dictated by circumstances; that is to say, the most acceptable hero, whose deeds could be extolled in lays, would be the reputed ancestor of the chief whose guest or retainer the minstrel was. It was but a step — though admittedly a great one — to combine in a more intricate narrative a series of exploits of one hero, and to intertwine therewith the fortunes of lesser heroic figures. Thus the short lay developed into the longer epic. That the *Iliad* and *Odyssey* — the only complete heroic epics of Greece that have survived — were composed in the Iron Age is beyond dispute. The probability is that they are not later than *c.* 850 B.C., while their dialect proclaims the home of the poet to have been in Anatolian Ionia. But the society which they portray is in the main that of the late Bronze Age in the Aegean. Nevertheless, there are important features which belong to a later age than that. Such are the use of iron, the practice of disposing of the dead by cremation, not, as was the custom in the Minoan and Mycenæan civilizations, by inhumation, and, in general, the Homeric religion. To use the Homeric poems, as has often been done, in order to reconstruct a picture of early Greek society is only justifiable within certain limits. There was in archaic Greece a number of similarities to, or rather survivals from, the earlier epoch; for example, the likeness of the Spartan to the Homeric monarchy has often been pointed out. But, taken as a whole, these poems, in so far as they depict a uniform civilization, provide us with information which is complementary to the archæological evidence for the latest phase of Mycenæan prosperity and domination.

Homeric society is strongly aristocratic. It is only of the nobles that we get a detailed picture. To the rest of the free population references are sparingly made. They are taken for granted by the poet, as is the institution of slavery. Male and female slaves are found employed on the domains and in the palaces of the great. The title *basileus* (chief or king) is often applied to other nobles besides the king; for instance, in the land of the Phæacians described in the *Odyssey* there are twelve *basileis* in addition to King Alcinous. Thus, the monarch is merely the first among a number of leading chiefs, who are the immediate supporters of the throne and form the nucleus of an aristocratic council, which advises him and may even act as a check on the royal prerogative. Yet, with this limitation, the supremacy of the king is clearly defined. His office is hereditary, and he traces his descent from a divine or heroic ancestor, a fact which adds much to his authority. He combines within himself the function of commander-in-chief in war, judge, and priest. The prestige of Agamemnon in the *Iliad* is so great that even the venerable Nestor, when he gives advice in Agamemnon's council, is very submissive in tone. The economic basis of society is agriculture. The man without land of his own to till, who has to eke out a livelihood by working another's fields, is thought the most wretched of beings, little better than serf or slave. Of trades and crafts we hear little, as is to be expected in a society where the economy is still mainly that of the household. Most of what is needed even on a large domain is produced on the spot, and there is little specialization in callings. Nor are the nobles above doing manual work, if the need arises. Paris of Troy takes a hand in the building of his house, and the Greek Odysseus can make a raft, builds a part of his own palace, and knows how to mow and plow. Thus, when occasionally a specific occupation is named in the poems, it is either a craft which, owing to the exceptional technique required for its exercise, has already passed into the hands of specialists — *e.g.* the calling of the smith and worker in metal — or else it is one of a very limited number of professions, like that of the herald or the leech or the minstrel. The herald, since he acts as the messenger and general amanuensis of the monarch, is a person of some importance. Merchants are rarely mentioned and are most often foreigners, for example, Phœnician traders. So, too, the imported wares referred to here and there are chiefly luxury articles, like purple-dyed stuffs from Sidon. Commerce is carried on by barter, but metallic weights are in use. The two principal occupations of the nobility are hunting and war.

The social and moral ideas are those of a still rude and warlike people, of a society in which a man enjoys little safety outside his own group. Yet society is by no means wholly lawless. Blood-feuds can already be settled by payment of compensation to the relatives of the deceased. The community or its ruler does not interfere except on the demand of both parties to the feud. The sanctity of oaths is great; hospitality to the stranger who takes refuge at the hearth is a sacred duty. Strong, too, are the ties of family, as we should expect in a society that is

strictly patriarchal. Homer's portraits of women — for instance, Helen and Andromache in the *Iliad*, Penelope and
Nausicaa in the *Odyssey* — are not only masterly in themselves, but suggest that women in that age enjoyed a position of more dignity and somewhat more freedom than was
generally the case in classical Greece. But there is also a less
agreeable side to this picture of Homeric society. The stranger,
except where he has sought and received the rights of hospitality
in a particular house, carries his life in his hand among an alien
community. Piracy is an honorable calling, and we may recall
that Aristotle includes it among the occupations practised by
men in a semi-nomadic state. The unhappy lot of the orphan
boy is painted in a few poignant words by the poet. In this
respect it is interesting to note a marked advance in humane
ideas in the poet Hesiod (*c.* 700 B.C.); he decries injury done to
orphans as one of the most serious offenses. Finally, there is
here and there a primitive savagery in the Homeric poems.
We may guess that there was more of it in the material utilized by Homer, but that he has softened most of the brutality
present in earlier lays. We are still left, however, with one example of human sacrifice, Achilles' offering to the dead Patro-
clus. Shocking to Greek even more than to modern notions is
the mutilation of Hector's corpse; and we may wince even at
the stern punishment meted out by Odysseus, after the slaying
of the suitors, to the unfaithful servants in his palace.

The gods and their worship in Homer seem to bear no resemblance to the divinities and cults, so far as we know them,
of Minoan-Mycenæan days. Homeric men created the gods
in their own image. The deities are, as it were, men and women
of superhuman stature and beauty; immortal, all-powerful,
and all-knowing; yet subject to the same pains and passions
as mankind. Zeus, the "father of gods and men" presides in
the assembly of the gods, envisaged by the poet to be situated
on the summit of Mt. Olympus in Thessaly. Though the several
deities have their several spheres of activity or avocations —
Poseidon is god of the sea, Apollo the god of prophecy and
patron of the arts, Ares the god of war — they are subordinate,
though sometimes disobedient, to the will of Zeus. Thus the
Pantheon of Homer is like a large superhuman family. Its

members take some interest in human affairs; they reward
the righteous and punish the evil-doer.   Sometimes their interference is capricious; they harm those who do not deserve
it, or support their favorites among mankind irrespective of
their moral character.   Some of the gods have temples erected
to them by men, or they have sacred places set aside by men,
which they prefer to all others — Zeus at Dodona in Epirus,
Apollo in the Troad and at Delphi.   The Homeric gods became
the gods of Greece, those Olympian deities who were immortalized in the drama and in plastic works of art and were worshipped wherever Hellenes were gathered together.   There were
other elements in Greek religion, the cult of the dead and
hero-worship, of which the former was certainly older than
the Homeric poems. Of such worship and ritual there is scarcely
a trace in the *Iliad* and *Odyssey*.[1]

[1] The following are the approximate dates of the Minoan periods.   It
should be noted that L.M. II is peculiar to Cnossus.   On other Cretan sites
L.M. I passes without break into L.M. III.

E.M. I	3400–3100		M.M. I	2400–2100
E.M. II	3100–2600		M.M. II	2100–1900
E.M. III	2600–2400		M.M. III	1900–1600
		L.M. I	1600–1500	
		L.M. II	1500–1400	
		L.M. III	1400–1100	

CHAPTER VII

SYRIA, PALESTINE, AND THEIR NEIGHBORS,
1200–900 B.C.

> *Now Israel went out against the Philistines to battle, and pitched beside Eben-ezer; and the Philistines pitched in Aphek. And the Philistines put themselves in array against Israel; and when they joined battle, Israel was smitten before the Philistines; and they slew of the army in the field about four thousand men.* — I Samuel, iv, 1–2.

THE second half of the thirteenth century B.C. was a very momentous period in the history of the Near East. The political power of Egypt and of Hatti was declining; new peoples, little heard of before, were emerging into greater influence in Palestine and Syria. In Babylonia, Cassite rulers continued to occupy their precarious throne, their chief anxiety being their northern neighbors of Assyria. The early attempts to advance to the middle Euphrates made by Assyrian kings had, as we have seen, been checked by Shupiluliuma and his successors. But the Assyrian kings of the thirteenth century, especially Shalmaneser I and Tukulti-ninurta, enlarged their kingdom by wars on the North and East; on several occasions they successfully attacked Babylon also. But though more than one Cassite monarch suffered defeat and even deposition at the hands of the hardy northerners, there was not yet any permanent control by Assyria over the Land of Two Rivers. Nevertheless, in spite of a temporary eclipse after the time of Tukulti-ninurta, the Assyrians stand out as the most vigorous of the Near-Eastern peoples at this time.

The most serious threat to Hittite power in the thirteenth century was in the West. Already in Hattushilish III's time a king of Akhkhiawa — the equation with Achæa, Achæans, is tempting but not certainly proven — is heard of as an enemy, and aggression from this quarter apparently continued under Dudkhaliash III. When, about 1200 B.C., the Hittite empire in Asia Minor collapsed, it was before a combined assault of several peoples from the West who overran Asia Minor and flowed over into Syria and Palestine. We can only surmise that the military strength of Hatti had been seriously weakened before this time, and that this process had been accompanied by a certain degree of internal unrest and disintegration. The history of Asia Minor for several centuries after this catastrophe is still one of the unsolved problems. A portion of the Hittite people continued to survive to the eighth century in northern Syria. The capital of this late Hittite principality was at Carchemish on the Euphrates, a site which had for long been one of the southern outposts of Hittite power and civilization.

The western hordes who had destroyed one empire, by their proximity to Egypt threatened another. The Egyptian Pharaoh, Merenptah, who succeeded Ramses II, some twenty years earlier had had to defend his kingdom against foreign attack. The first assault came from his western neighbors of Libya. Infiltration, in some degree, of Libyans into Egypt had probably occurred for centuries past; occasionally Egyptian military intervention on and beyond the border had been necessary. But about 1220 B.C. the Libyans, reinforced by men from overseas — from Crete and perhaps the Greek mainland — attempted a regular invasion of the Land of the Nile. The attack was repulsed by Merenptah, but a possible renewal of the threat from this quarter must have caused him and his successors constant anxiety. In addition, after Merenptah's death (c. 1215 B.C.) several weak rulers occupied the Egyptian throne, and the last twenty years of the XIXth Dynasty seem to have been a period of anarchy at home. This disturbed internal condition offered a favorable opportunity for further assaults on Egypt from the West. These raids, though not so formidable as the invasion of 1220 B.C., nevertheless must have caused much damage to property and some loss of life. The second king of the XXth Dynasty, Ramses III, attempted to cope drastically with what had become a very serious problem. His energetic military reforms were carried out just in time. For now Libyans made common cause with the miscellaneous peoples who had de-

stroyed Hatti and had swarmed into Syria. About 1194 B.C.,
and again two years later, formidable attacks by land and sea
were launched against Egypt. By a supreme effort Ramses III
and his people on both occasions defeated the enemy; the fact
that Egyptian naval strength was greater and better organized
than that of the invaders doubtless accounts to a great extent
for the Egyptian success. Thus was the danger of another
Hyksos occupation narrowly averted. But the days of Egypt
as an imperial power were over. The remaining twenty years
of Ramses' long reign were disturbed by occasional Libyan
raids and by a domestic conspiracy. He was succeeded by a
long line of undistinguished monarchs, all of whom bore the
same name as he. The predominating influence in Near-Eastern
affairs, which Egypt had exercised for so long, passed now to
Asiatic powers; in the end Egypt became, and remained for
centuries, the dependency of first one and then another Asiatic
empire.

Of the peoples of Syria and Palestine, who now emerge into
greater prominence, the more important are the Phœnicians,
the Aramæans, the Hebrews, and the Philistines. The Phœnicians who, if not wholly, were predominantly of Semitic stock,
seem to have been settled along the coast of Syria, northwards
from Mt. Carmel, ever since the first half of the third millennium. Of their history and civilization, more especially in the
earlier period, very little is known. Their settlements were all
maritime, for in that region of Syria the mountains approach
very near to the sea. A race of traders, inhabiting a number
of small independent cities, they appear off and on to have had
commercial relations with Egypt from early times. With the
Egyptian conquest of Syria, Simyra, Byblos, Sidon, and the
rest passed under Egyptian suzerainty. The evidence of
the Amarna letters suggests dissensions amongst the Phœnician
towns themselves; and, indeed, it must have been difficult to
decide which of the two imperial states, Egypt or Hatti, was
preferable as overlord. After the decline and fall of these empires the Phœnician cities entered on a period of much greater
prosperity and influence. Tyre was now (c. 1000 B.C.) the chief
of them. Citium and other sites in Cyprus were settled by
Phœnicians; but their colonial enterprise during the next two

centuries took them above all to the West.   They founded trading-stations along the coast of North Africa, in southern Spain, in Malta, Sicily, Sardinia, and Corsica.   Phœnician or Sidonian merchants are mentioned sundry times in the Homeric poems. But they have left few traces of themselves in the Aegean; even in the western Mediterranean area scarcely any Phœnician finds earlier than the seventh century have so far come to light. It is impossible therefore to form a safe estimate of their trading activities, the extent and importance of which have sometimes been much exaggerated.   Yet so much seems a reasonable assumption: namely, that in the interval between the downfall of the Mycenæan thalassocracy and the age of Greek colonial expansion such carrying trade as may have existed in the eastern Mediterranean was mainly in their hands, and at the same time they continued to be purveyors of such luxury articles as only the East could provide.   In the western Mediterranean things were different, and the Phœnician foundation of Carthage in time built up a powerful maritime empire.

The Aramæans were Semitic nomads who, on their first appearance in history, were in occupation of the desert lands bordering on the Middle Euphrates.   From the sixteenth to the thirteenth centuries sections of these Bedouins filtered through into Syria, while others, crossing the Euphrates, moved on in the direction of the Tigris.   In the twelfth century the Aramæans are again mainly concentrated in the Syrian desert. The check to their expansion northward and westward may have been due partly to the action of the Assyrians; still more it probably resulted from the general advance of foreign tribes from Asia Minor, which has already been noted.   When, in the following century, the Aramæans become more prominent, they are firmly established at important points like Damascus, which gave them control of the great caravan routes from Syria into Mesopotamia.

The Hebrews, too, were originally nomads and racially not very different from the Aramæans.   Before the middle of the second millennium they had entered Canaan from the north. At a time when western Palestine was still securely under Egyptian rule, these Semites must have eked out a bare existence in the hilly regions bordering on the River Jordan.   Some of them,

faced by the prospect of famine, eventually found their way to
the frontiers of Egypt. Here the treatment accorded them was
at first friendly; but later one of the Pharaohs compelled them
to labor as serfs under the lash of Egyptian masters. Ultimately, after a prolonged period of captivity, they were enabled
to leave Egypt. After passing a considerable time in the desert
lands of the Sinai peninsula and the regions east of the Jordan,
the wanderers entered the more fertile country of Palestine.
Unfortunately there is still no kind of unanimity among scholars
about the dates of, and the length of time consumed by, these
movements, which in the Biblical narrative of a later date are
familiar as the Going down into Egypt, the Bondage in Egypt,
and the Exodus. The Jewish historian Josephus, writing in the
first century A.D., brings the appearance of the Hebrews in
Palestine into connection with the expulsion of the Hyksos. On
this hypothesis their entry into Egypt must have occurred at
some time between Dynasties XIII and XVII; the Exodus
would have to be regarded as one episode in the expulsion of
the "shepherd kings." There are, however, serious objections
to so early a date for these migrations of Hebrew tribes, and it
is safer to place the Egyptian sojourn under the later kings of
the XVIIIth Dynasty and the Exodus during, or perhaps at the
end of, the long reign of Ramses II. A well-known inscription
of Merenptah informs us of a rebellion in southern Palestine at
the beginning of that king's rule. Among the insurgents are the
Isirail, whose name must clearly be equated with the Biblical
Israel. From this notice it is obvious that, by the middle of the
thirteenth century, Hebrew tribes had secured a definite foothold in the country west of the Jordan.

Originally nomadic and pastoral in their mode of life, they
were gradually converted to an agricultural and stationary existence. A common interest united them, namely, to make
common cause against the earlier inhabitants of the land,
the Canaanites. Nevertheless, the geographical situation of
the Canaanite cities, which separated the northern from the
southern group of Hebrew tribes, made effective alliance difficult. The struggle must have lasted a good number of years
and was carried on with varying success. In the process the
invaders learnt not a little from their enemies; they became

Plate 12

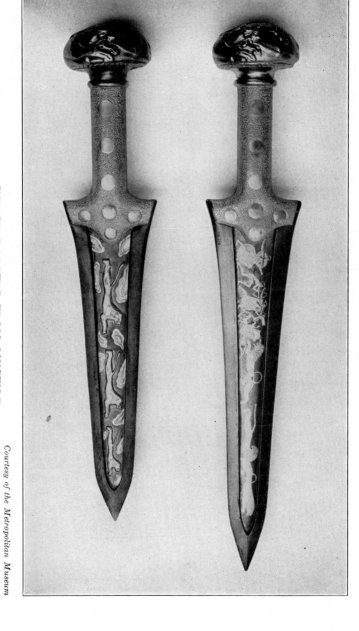

INLAID DAGGERS FROM MYCENÆ

Courtesy of the Metropolitan Museum

habituated to farming operations, to town life, and began to forget the life of the desert, and even paid honor to the gods of Canaan in addition to their own tribal god, Yahweh. At last a great Canaanite alliance was formed and opposed by six of the Hebrew tribes under the leadership of Barak, of the tribe Naphtali. The Song of Deborah (*Judges*, v) is a pæan of victory, commemorating the decisive defeat of the Canaanite army by the Hebrews. "The kings came and fought, then fought the kings of Canaan in Taanach by the waters of Megiddo. They took no gain of money. They fought from Heaven; the stars in their courses fought against Sisera. The river Kishon swept them away, that ancient river, the river Kishon."

Among the foreign peoples who entered Syria and Palestine and threatened Egypt after destroying the Hittite empire were the Philistines (Egypt. *Peleset*). Their appearance and settlement in southern Palestine thus occurred shortly after the time when the Hebrew tribes had finally broken the resistance of their neighbors in Canaan. Before the new and powerful immigrants the Hebrew tribes on the coast were compelled to retire into the hill country.

The racial origin and earlier home of the Philistines are still greatly disputed. The one certain fact about them is that they were a non-Semitic people. That they were Minoan Cretans, as has been suggested by some scholars, is impossible not only on chronological grounds but because the dress and armature of the two peoples were markedly different. On the other hand, local imitations of Mycenæan pottery — commonly called sub-Mycenæan — which have been unearthed in considerable quantities in Philistia, are very similar to wares found over an extended area of the eastern Aegean, namely in eastern Crete, Cyprus, and Caria. There is, moreover, a Hebrew tradition that the Philistines came from Caphtor. The equation Caphtor = Crete is now accepted by a majority of scholars. However, the balance of probability seems to lie with the view that the Philistines came originally from Caria, but that, before joining with other tribes in the attack on Egypt at the beginning of the twelfth century, they had found a temporary home in Crete. Their settlement in the coastal regions of Palestine then followed hard upon their repulse, together with the other attackers, by

Ramses III. In this new home, during the twelfth century, they consolidated their position by force of arms, and formed, in fact, a conquering aristocracy ruling over the earlier Semitic inhabitants of the land. Their success was due not so much to better arms and a more warlike temper as to a greater skill in political and military organization. Like the governing class of Spartans in a later age, the Philistines saw that their own security in the midst of a numerically superior subject population, whose race and customs alike differed from their own, could only be assured by imposing on themselves a strict military régime. The pentapolis of Philistine cities, — Ashdod, Gath, Ashkelon, Ekron, and Gaza, — formed a close political confederation of city-states, each ruled by a despot (*seren*). So long as their power remained unbroken these cities controlled the main highway from Egypt to Syria and beyond, while at Gaza there branched off the main route to the Dead Sea and to Arabia. Furthermore, at the time of their greatest political expansion, when their authority along the coast reached northward beyond Joppa, they were master of all the ports lying south of the Phœnician cities.

How long the Philistines were content to dwell in southwestern Palestine before embarking on a larger career of conquest, is by no means clear. It cannot have been less than fifty years, and was probably as much as a century. In this interval they seem to have become largely assimilated in speech and manners to the Canaanite peoples whom they had subjected on their entry into Philistia. During this period of Philistine consolidation the Israelites had suffered severely at the hands of the Bedouin tribes of Transjordania — Moabites, Ammonites, and Midianites. They were thus much weakened when the Philistines made a bold bid for supremacy over all Palestine. In a single engagement the latter crushed the military resistance of the Israelites, and further broke their spirit by capturing the Ark of the Lord and razing Shiloh. These events occurred in the first quarter of the eleventh century. Then, for about sixty years, Israel was held in subjection by the conquerors, who exacted tribute rigorously and minimized the danger of an Israelite rising by placing garrisons at various strategic points throughout the country.

When, about 1025 B.C., the first attempt to regain national independence was made, it was begun in Transjordania, in the land of Gilead, a region which seems not even to have been a Philistine protectorate. The ringleaders in this struggle were the prophet-priest Samuel and Saul, the Benjaminite ruler of Gilead. Gradually Saul was able to rally many of the Israelites to his standard. He fought with success against the oppressors, until he was finally defeated and killed at the battle of Mt. Gilboa, a little southeast of the historic site of Megiddo. With this disaster ended the first attempt to throw off the Philistine yoke. A second trial of strength was destined to be more successful. For David of Judah, who had first fought for Saul and then, after quarrelling with him, had fled to and come to terms with the Philistines, became, after Saul's death, ruler of Judah, with his capital at Hebron. For a while the northern part of Saul's kingdom formed a separate state under Saul's young son, Ishbaal. The Philistines do not seem to have interfered with the arrangement, seeing rather in the ensuing strife between the northern and southern groups of Israelites a safeguard against renewed aggression on themselves. But, after the assassination of Ishbaal by two of his own officers, David was able to establish an ascendancy over all the tribes and was acclaimed king of all Israel. How long before this momentous event the Philistines may have begun to suspect the loyalty of their vassal we cannot tell. But the unification of Israel under David was followed by a Philistine invasion of Judah. David was hardly prepared for so prompt an attack. Since Hebron was not easily defensible, he retired to the hill fortress of Adullam. From here he harassed the enemy by raids, until such time as he had received reinforcements from the more distant parts of his new kingdom. Then only he ventured on open attack, and in two engagements defeated the Philistine army decisively, forcing his opponents to retire back to Philistia.

The next step in the war of liberation was a sudden attack on Jerusalem, held by the Jebusite allies of the Philistines. Its capture was for several reasons of singular value to David. It was the finest natural stronghold in the country; its strategic position gave David an advantage such as his predecessor had never enjoyed; and it was admirably suited to be the new capital of the united Hebrew kingdom, because it was, as it were, neutral territory. A capital in the old territory of the southern tribes might well have aroused the distrust or dislike of the northern group, who had but recently given their allegiance to the king. Strong in the possession of his new fortress-capital, David now began an offensive war against the Philistines. He invaded Philistia and captured one of its most powerful cities, Gath. These victories finally broke the political and military strength of the late oppressors of Israel. From henceforward the Philistines were confined to the narrow coastal strip of southern Palestine, which had been their first home when they entered the country two centuries before. The solemn installation in Jerusalem of the Ark of the Covenant, which had been recovered from the enemy in the late Philistine war, was now carried out by the king. It was an act of deep significance because it marked out the new political capital to be also the venerated centre of the Jewish faith.

David's career as a conqueror was no less remarkable than his work as the liberator of Israel. Though both the order and the details of the campaigns, which he conducted against his neighbors after the final defeat of the Philistines, are extremely obscure, it is clear that he fought with continuous success against the Moabites and the Ammonites to the east, the Aramæans to the northeast, and the Edomites to the south of his kingdom. Thus, in the end, he was lord of a realm which stretched from the head of the gulf of Akaba to the Lebanon, and which included all Transjordania south of Mount Hermon. The internal organization of this greater Israel was, it would appear, not at all fully carried out by David. Partly this may have resulted from the fact that his skill as an organizer was not equal to his eminence as a conqueror; partly it may have been due to lack of time, since consolidation of newly-won territories is necessarily a slower task than the conquests themselves. But the main reason was probably that the later years of David's reign were clouded by insurrections within his own kingdom and by quarrels within his own family. The former were, it is true, put down, and the disputes about the succession were, to all appearances, settled before the king's death. But when David ended his days, Solomon, his son by Bathsheba and his successor, was faced by a renewal of the intrigues against him, which were only ended by the execution of the principal plotters.

The long reign of Solomon (*c.* 975–935 B.C.) was not remarkable for further conquests; the wars which occurred in this period were without exception defensive. Often, too, the king secured by diplomacy what he could not or would not have effected by force of arms. A raid by an Egyptian army is attested only in a late source, and it may well be doubted if it ever happened. Solomon controlled the trade-routes between Egypt and Phœnicia and Syria. A rising against Solomon's authority in Edom failed; but the king found it politic to fortify Thamar and leave a garrison there to guard the road to the gulf of Akaba. Other cities in different parts of his realm, which Solomon is credited with converting into fortified posts — *e.g.* Hazor, Megiddo, and Beth-Horon — owed their importance partly to their strategic position, partly to their situation relative to important highways of commerce. The Aramæans of Damascus and the neighborhood, after their defeat by David, seem to have been reduced to be tributary vassals of that monarch. In Solomon's time Damascus, under the energetic adventurer, Rezon, probably became again an independent kingdom. With the Phœnician cities Solomon's relations, as had been the case in his father's time, were friendly. To the king of Tyre he conceded certain villages in the north of his kingdom, probably in return for trade facilities; besides this, the two princes concluded an alliance. Although, then, Solomon seems, in the main, to have kept intact the territories bequeathed to him by his predecessor, his internal policy was such that it weakened the resources of his kingdom almost to the point of exhaustion and antagonized a large proportion of his subjects. Thus, on his death, civil war, which culminated in the division of the realm of David and Solomon into the two kingdoms of Israel and Judah, was soon followed by renewed attacks on the part of their neighbors.

The fame of Solomon rests on his work as an administrator and his magnificence as a potentate. It was due to him that the kingdom was administratively organized in a way which recalls the systems in force in Babylonia and in Egypt. The country was partitioned, for purposes of taxation and local government, into twelve regions, corresponding roughly to the geographical divisions of the twelve tribes, but with the addition of the Canaanite cities which had been gradually absorbed into the realm. A royal official or governor was responsible for the administration in each of these provinces. Taxes were heavy; in addition, the king exacted compulsory labor from his subjects in order to carry out the vast building projects for which his reign was especially famous. Judah, being the home-land of the king, was partially exempted from the heavy burdens placed upon the rest of the population. The temple and the royal palace at Jerusalem took thirteen years to build. The whole complex of buildings was erected on the highest part of the hill of Jerusalem, and, being surrounded with a fortification wall, was completely cut off from the city itself, which stood on the lower slopes of the hill. The temple stood at the northern end, the very highest point; though sumptuously constructed of fine stone and cedar wood, its dimensions seem to have been relatively small.[1] It was divided into two unequal parts, of which the smaller inner chamber, the Holy of Holies, was the repository of the Ark of the Covenant. Thus the work, begun by David, of making Jerusalem the religious capital of the Jewish race was carried an important stage further. Jahweh, conceived by earlier generations to be a deity with no fixed abode, who might manifest himself to his people or their chosen leader in a storm-cloud or on a desert mountain-top, has become the god who, ever invisibly present in the temple at Jerusalem, presides over the fortunes of a nation.

To carry out these costly constructions, as well as to satisfy all the magnificent needs of an oriental court, the king was obliged to obtain much raw material and many commodities of great price from distant lands. Lebanon supplied the cedar wood, and it is probable that Phœnician workmen were also imported, to aid in the artistic decoration of temple and palace. Extensive trade was carried on with Syria, Egypt, and the land of Ophir (the Somali coast, the Egyptian Punt?). We are

---

[1] The dimensions of the actual temple building have been estimated at $124 \times 55 \times 52$ feet. (*See* R. A. S. Macalister in *Cambridge Ancient History*, iii, p. 347.)

even told that one of Solomon's vessels joined with Egyptian trading-ships in making the journey to Tarshish (Tartessus) in southern Spain.   Yet it must not be forgotten that this commerce was mainly, if not wholly, devoted to luxury articles.

Of external influences which helped to form the artistic productions of Solomon's age, as well as the elaborate court ceremonial enforced by the monarch, the strongest probably emanated from Egypt.   This may even be true to some extent of the intellectual life of the period.   For instance, though, as a whole, the Book of Proverbs is of later date, it is not unlikely that portions of it go back to Solomonic times.   And in their general form those utterances irresistibly recall collections of moral maxims found in Egypt, like the sayings of Ptahhotep and Amenemhet.   In the account of David's career (*II Samuel*, ix-xx) we possess a historical narrative which is contemporary or almost contemporary with the events that it narrates. That a very high place in the world's historical literature must be assigned to it has been admirably expressed by an eminent historian of the ancient world.   "The account of David," he writes, "shows indubitably by its content that it dates from the time of the actual events, and that the narrator must have been very intimately informed about life at court and the characters and pursuits of the persons portrayed."   Later the same writer observes: "It is astonishing that historical literature of this quality was possible in Israel at that date.   It far surpasses any other known examples of historical composition in the Ancient Orient, the dry official annals of Babylonians, Assyrians, and Egyptians, as well as the stories, akin to fairy-tales, of Egyptian popular literature." [1]

But, though the era of Solomon was characterized by an immense advance in culture on the part of his subjects, though its splendor was such as to form the theme of countless legends in later times, the price paid was too heavy, and Solomon must bear the responsibility of bringing about the undoing of his father's work of political unification.   For, on Solomon's death (*c.* 935 B.C.), the northern tribes petitioned his son and successor, Rehoboam, for alleviation of the heavy burdens imposed by the late king.   Rehoboam, however, made no concessions.

[1] E. Meyer, *Die Israeliten und ihre Nachbarstämme*, pp. 485–486.

The North revolted under the leadership of Jeroboam, who had already in Solomon's time led an insurrection against the monarch's oppressive rule, but had on that occasion failed and been forced to go into exile.   Jeroboam on his return, was crowned king at Shechem.   Hostilities between the two kingdoms of Judah and Israel (or Ephraim) lasted off and on for half a century.   It was not till the time of Omri (c. 887 B.C.) that peace between the two monarchies was definitely established. The southern kingdom was now in a position of dependence on the northern.   In the interval of civil war foreign attacks had added to the general confusion.   An Egyptian raid in the time of Sheshenk (Shishak; c. 930 B.C.) extended as far as Jerusalem; while the northern kingdom had much to fear from the Aramaic kingdom of Damascus.   Omri built himself a new capital at Samaria.   The kingdom which he ruled included all northern Palestine, together with Moab and Ammon in Transjordania. In addition, he exercised suzerainty over the southern kingdom, while he and his son, Ahab, also fostered good relations with Phœnicia.   In the later years of Ahab's kingship a far more formidable enemy than Aramæans or Egyptians first threatened the independence of all Syria and Palestine.   From the middle of the ninth century the political history of the two kingdoms forms but an episode in the fortunes of the Assyrian empire.

CHAPTER VIII

THE ASSYRIAN EMPIRE

> *Over all Egypt I appointed kings, prefects,*
> *governors, grain-inspectors, mayors, and secre-*
> *taries. I instituted regular offerings to Ashur and*
> *the great gods, my lords, for all time. I placed on*
> *them the tribute and taxes of my lordship, regularly*
> *and without fail. A tablet, written in my name, I*
> *caused to be made, and the glory of the bravery of*
> *Ashur, my lord, the mighty deeds which I had*
> *accomplished, under the protection of Ashur, in*
> *my marches, and the victories, the booty of my hands,*
> *thereon I caused to be written, and for the astonished*
> *gaze of all my enemies I set up for future days.*
> — Inscription of Esarhaddon.

1. POLITICAL HISTORY TO THE FALL OF NINEVEH

WHILE paying the fullest tribute of admiration to the men
who, as related in the last chapter, built up a united and powerful kingdom in Palestine, southern Syria, and Transjordania, one
must admit that they could never have succeeded so well, if
during these centuries her greater neighbors had not been reduced to impotence. Egypt could never again hope to rule an
empire; the Hittite power was no more than a fast-dimming
memory of the past; Assyria, save for one brief spell, was a
small kingdom fighting for its existence against its neighbors,
none of whom had sufficient resources to cherish ambitions of
empire. Tiglath-Pileser I, who became king of Assyria c. 1115
and died c. 1102 B.C., conducted campaigns into southern
Armenia, Babylonia, and northern Syria as far as the shores of
the Mediterranean, which made his name feared, and momentarily compelled his conquered enemies to pay him tribute. But
on his death the short-lived Assyrian empire ceased to be.
There follow two centuries of Assyrian history that are all dark

in two senses: dark, because the glory of Assyria was utterly
obscured; dark to us, because of the extreme paucity of the
existing records. It is not till the early years of the ninth
century and the reign of Ashurnasirpal (c. 884–859 B.C.) that
fuller information is again available. From then down to the
destruction of Nineveh in 612 B.C. there exists copious epigraphic material. It reveals the last and greatest period of
Assyrian history as a long, and to the general reader somewhat
wearisome, series of military campaigns.

In the late twelfth, and especially in the eleventh, century
the Aramæan invasions of a large portion of the Fertile Crescent had recommenced with greater intensity than ever before.
Their hold on northern Syria, where they were established in
important centres like Aleppo and Damascus, was very strong.
They were astride the great caravan routes leading from the
Mediterranean and the Euphrates to Assyria and Babylonia.
Southern Mesopotamia was invaded and thereafter largely
peopled by Chaldæan tribes, who seem racially to have been
closely related to the Aramæans. On the northern borders of
Assyria a considerable kingdom became prominent politically
from the end of the ninth century. This kingdom of Van, with
its capital at Tuspas on the eastern shore of Lake Van, is referred to frequently in Assyrian records by the name of Urartu.
At the period of its widest extent it embraced the greater part of
modern Armenia. Though both the origin and the history of
this Vannic people are still extremely obscure — their language
is believed to belong to the Caucasian group — they played a
part of considerable importance in the two centuries during
which Assyria dominated the Near East.

Though he owed something to the work of his immediate
predecessors, it was really Ashurnasirpal who began Assyria's
days of imperial greatness. In his campaigns he advanced
to the borders of Van; westwards he crossed the Euphrates
and reached the Orontes, Lebanon, and ultimately the Mediterranean. His annals relate how the king captured numberless
prisoners and vast quantities of booty, and how he slew in
battle enemies without number. If but a tithe of the record
be true, this monarch surpassed all oriental despots in ferocity
and cruelty; flaying, impaling, and other barbarous methods

of execution were inflicted on his countless foes and captives.[1]
His successor, Shalmaneser III, though apparently less fright-
ful in his methods, was equally tireless as a soldier. In thirty-
five years he is credited with no less than thirty-two expeditions.
Two of his achievements are of most general interest: his intervention in Mesopotamia had the result that Babylon became
for a time a vassal kingdom of Assyria. In northern Syria he
consolidated his father's conquests with some success, but his
first attack on central Syria had no permanent results. At
Karkar in the Orontes valley, a little northwest of Hamath, his
progress was barred by an allied force composed of contingents
from Phœnicia, from Syrian and Aramæan principalities, of
which the chief were Hamath and Damascus, and from the
kingdom of Israel under the leadership of Ahab. Although
Shalmaneser claimed a great victory, it cannot in reality have
been very decisive; otherwise he would hardly have abandoned
his advance southward. He repeated his attacks on several
later occasions; but, beyond exacting tribute from Phœnicia,
he effected nothing permanent. For even his fierce attacks on
Damascus in 842 and 839 B.C. failed in their object of crushing
the Aramæan power. Still, his hold on northern Syria and
eastern Cilicia was secure before his death; and this was an
acquisition of great value, since it gave him the control of the
passes over the Taurus into Asia Minor. As visible token of
his power the king rebuilt the old capital of his country, Ashur,
with great splendor.

Most troublesome were his northern neighbors of Van; for the
most that Shalmaneser was able to effect was to prevent their
incursion into Assyrian territory. A year or two before his
death the aging monarch saw a large part of his work undone.
A rebellion in which one of his sons was involved led to a partition of the empire, and only one-half remained faithful to him.
Another son had to fight for two years before he succeeded in
temporarily reuniting the empire under his sole sway. There
followed a period of internal unrest of more than half a century,

---

[1] Yet the philosophic historian might well ask whether these atrocities
were worse than, for example, the appalling cruelties inflicted on the Báb
and his followers in Persia in 1852. For this terrible persecution see E. G.
Browne, *A Traveller's Narrative Written to Illustrate the Episode of the Báb*
2 (1891), pp. 326 ff.

during which several monarchs occupied the throne. When the Assyrian kingdom itself was disturbed by dynastic disputes, it was inevitable that there should be lack of authority in her dependencies, and the confusion was increased by raids from Urartu. The accession of Tiglath-Pileser III (c. 745 B.C.) brought to the fore a ruler who was able both to stabilize and to enlarge the empire. He gained complete control of Babylonia and reasserted Assyrian sovereignty in southern Syria. He invaded Urartu, and, though he failed to take its capital by storm, he put a stop to the activities of a hostile neighbor for a considerable time. He attacked Syria and Palestine with results more devastating to these countries than any previous Assyrian assaults. To some extent his task must have been facilitated by the practical exhaustion of Israel and its neighbors.

In the interval between Shalmaneser's western expeditions and those of Tiglath-Pileser III there had been little peace in Palestine or Syria. The prince of Damascus, Hazael, reinforced by other Syrian principalities, launched an attack against Israel and Judah soon after 840 B.C. First he conquered the whole of Transjordania; next he invaded the northern kingdom itself; and, finally, he ravaged Judah. It was only by the payment of heavy tribute that the rulers of both kingdoms were able to preserve at least a nominal independence. Under Hazael's successor the hostility of Assyria to her western neighbors was for once of benefit to Palestine, for an expedition of Adad-Nirari III against Damascus laid that kingdom low. The phenomenal recovery of the kingdom of Israel under Jeroboam II (c. 782–743 B.C.), and of Judah under Azariah, falls in the half century when the power of Damascus had been greatly reduced, and Assyria, as we saw, was involved in a turmoil of dynastic and civil dissension. But Jeroboam's work of reconstruction fell to pieces on his death. Faction and rebellion distracted the northern kingdom owing to the assassination of the rightful heir to the throne and to the attempts of several pretenders to seize the royal power for themselves. The most successful of these, Manahem, during his tenure of authority insured the non-interference of Tiglath-Pileser, with whose advent Assyria entered on the last, though most brilliant, stage of her imperial career, by the sending of tribute.

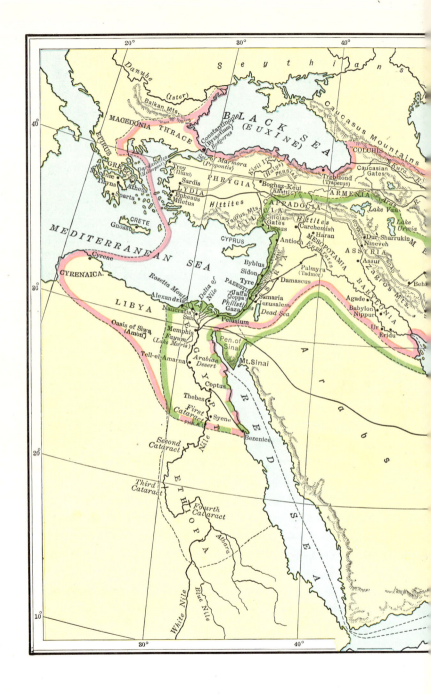

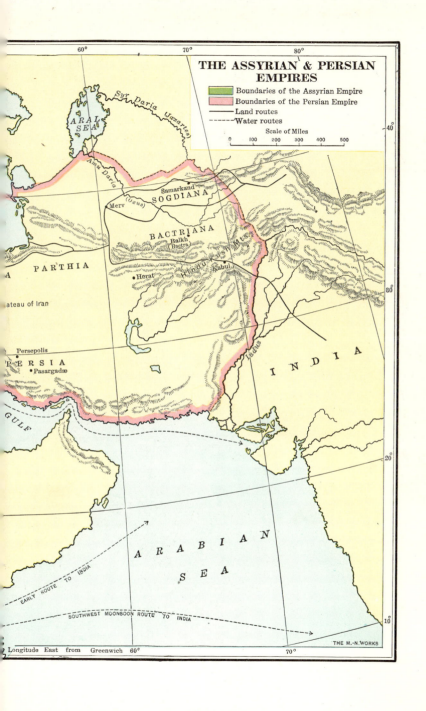

THE ASSYRIAN & PERSIAN
EMPIRES

Boundaries of the Assyrian Empire
Boundaries of the Persian Empire
———— Land routes
- - - - Water routes

Scale of Miles
0   100   200   300   400   500

40°

Syr Daria (Jaxartes)

ARAL
SEA

Amu Daria

(Oxus)

Samarkand
SOGDIANA

Merv

BACTRIANA
Balkh
Bactra

PARTHIA

HINDU-KUSH MTS.

Kabul

30°

Herat

ateau of Iran

Indus

Persepolis

I N D I A

PERSIA
Pasargadæ

20°

GULF

A R A B I A N

EARLY ROUTE TO INDIA

S E A

SOUTHWEST MOONSOON ROUTE TO INDIA

10°

THE M.-N.WORKS

Longitude East from Greenwich 60°   70°

Manahem's son during the two years of his rule followed a similar policy. But he was assassinated by Pekah, son of Remaliah, who himself seized the crown and then adopted a foreign policy which was to prove disastrous to him and to his neighbors also. He formed an alliance with Damascus and other principalities to withstand the aggressions of Tiglath-Pileser, which might be expected when the tribute was no longer forthcoming. The allies sought to draw Judah to their side but without success. Thereupon they invaded the southern kingdom of Ahaz from the north, while the Edomites, who had joined the alliance, entered Judah from the south. In his extremity Ahaz, acting against the advice of the prophet Isaiah, appealed to Assyria for intervention, and sent Tiglath-Pileser gifts and swore fealty to him as his vassal.

Probably in 734 B.C. Assyrian troops appeared west of the Euphrates. Damascus was captured and its population deported. Ahaz made his submission to Tiglath-Pileser in person and was installed as vassal king of Judah. Israel was overrun and would have been completely laid waste, had not its king been murdered by Hoshea, who at once submitted to the Assyrian. As a vassal he was allowed to retain a greatly reduced kingdom, amounting to little more than the hill country of Samaria. All Transjordania was annexed by Tiglath-Pileser, while a large part of the population was deported by him. The Assyrian monarch did not long survive these achievements. Soon after his successor, Shalmaneser V, came to power, Hoshea refused payment of his tribute and submitted only on the appearance of an Assyrian army in the West. When a similar refusal occurred on a second occasion, a belated submission at the eleventh hour was not enough. Israel was invaded by Assyrian hosts and the capital city, Samaria, was besieged. After a heroic defense, lasting three years, it fell. Shalmaneser did not live to see these military operations completed, and it was his successor, Sargon, who in 722 B.C. received the capitulation of the city. According to a Sargonid inscription nearly thirty thousand inhabitants of the northern kingdom were deported by the king. Samaria now became the capital of a new Assyrian province. To repopulate the country, drafts of persons from Syria and Mesopotamia were sent there by the king's

orders. Two years later Sargon decisively defeated a miscellaneous army of Syrians, Palestinians, and Egyptians at Raphia
on the Egyptian border. The Egyptians, in order to prevent an
invasion of their country, sent tribute; the resistance of Syria
and Palestine was shattered; only Judah still remained intact,
but, as before, a vassal or subject ally of Assyria.

Thanks to Sargon's other campaigns to the north, south, and
east of his kingdom, the empire at his death was greater than
any ruled so far by an Assyrian monarch. His successor, Sennacherib, was as active a warrior as the earlier Assyrian kings;
at the same time his numerous campaigns were conducted not
to enlarge the empire bequeathed to him by his father, but to
quell risings, as in Syria and in Babylonia, and to consolidate
his father's conquests. In 681 B.C. he was murdered by an
elder son. His younger son, Esarhaddon, who had been governor of Babylon and marked out by his father for the succession,
had to inaugurate his own reign by suppressing a rebellion
within his kingdom. During his brief rule he kept up the warlike traditions of his line, his most spectacular undertaking
being the invasion of Egypt.

Much of the recurrent unrest in Syria and Palestine, which
necessitated numerous Assyrian expeditions to the west, was
undoubtedly due to the machinations of Egypt. Not strong
enough themselves to build up an imperial power, the Egyptian
kings of the XXVth Dynasty nevertheless could intrigue with
Assyrian vassals in Palestine, Phœnicia, and Syria, with the
object of stirring up rebellion against Assyria, and in the somewhat forlorn hope of undermining the strength of the most
powerful state in the Near East. Already in 700 B.C. Sennacherib had been forced to take energetic action in order to break up
a coalition between Egypt, Tyre, Sidon, and Judah. The last-
named kingdom was at this time ruled by the able and spirited
Hezekiah. Through his rash diplomacy his kingdom suffered
worse than any other state in the anti-Assyrian coalition. Judæan cities were captured by the enemy, and Jerusalem itself
was invested; it would doubtless have succumbed to a siege,
had not Hezekiah found it more politic at this point to tender
his submission. A heavy payment of tribute was imposed on
the rebellious vassal.

Esarhaddon early in his reign had to protect his northern borders against bands of invaders, called by the Greeks, Cimmerians, who, making their way from the Caucasus, overran central Asia Minor to the very frontiers of Assyria. An earlier but less formidable invasion, thirty years before, had been repelled by Sargon. When Esarhaddon by his victory over the Cimmerians had again made the northern part of his kingdom secure, he concentrated all his resources on preparations for an Egyptian expedition. At last in 671 B.C., after preliminary reconnaissances in previous years, he invaded the Land of the Nile. The vanquished Egyptians were compelled to pay tribute, and the ruler, Necho, was forced to become an Assyrian vassal. Two years after this Esarhaddon died. His successor, Ashurbanipal, ruled over Assyria for forty-three years. He continued the war against Egypt begun by his predecessor, with the result that for a few years Egypt became to all intents and purposes an Assyrian province. But in 651 B.C. either because the retention of Egypt within the empire was too costly or because the Assyrian needed all his military strength elsewhere, Psammetichus unhindered threw off his allegiance to Ashurbanipal. He had been accepted by the Egyptians of both Upper and Lower Egypt. Under him, the founder of the XXVIth Dynasty, the entire country was again governed by a single monarch, whereas in the centuries immediately preceding it had happened more than once that two rival monarchs governed in different parts of the country. For a little more than a century Egypt kept her independence, but she was annexed to the Persian empire by Cambyses in 525 B.C.

The wars in Ashurbanipal's time were very numerous. His generals were active in such widely distant areas as Cilicia, where a fresh Cimmerian force was repulsed, and in Elam which, having become a province half a century before, had revolted. This uprising against Assyrian authority was really part of a greater rebellion, stirred up by the brother of the king, who was governor of the Babylonian province. The rebel received support from various quarters of the empire. Hence the suppression of the revolt in Babylonia was necessarily followed by punitive expeditions against the more outlying insurgents. Thus, to cite but one example, Tyre and Akko in Phœnicia were

severely punished for the help which they had given the pretender. Glorious though the reign of Ashurbanipal might seem
to a contemporary, the empire in his day was really far less
secure than it had been in the days of Sargon and Sennacherib.
The number of enemies on the Assyrian borders was growing;
the continuous drain on her man-power was bound in the end
to bring about a collapse. It is significant that Ashurbanipal,
after his Elamite wars, enrolled in his own army large numbers
of the soldiers whom he had just conquered. And Sennacherib
had done the same after his campaigns in Syria. Though doubtless dictated by military necessity, to enroll a late enemy under
his standards was a hazardous experiment for the conqueror.
Only fourteen years after Ashurbanipal's death, Assyria fell
before the joint assault of her enemies from three sides, and her
vast empire was partitioned out between two of her conquerors,
the Medes and the Chaldæans.[1]

2. ASSYRIAN CIVILIZATION

That Assyrian society and culture were more or less slavishly
copied from Babylonia has long been a universally accepted
belief. But here, as in so many other fields of Ancient History,
explorations and study carried on during the last thirty years
have shown that belief to be at best a half-truth. It is still
very uncertain what were the chief influences which moulded
early Assyrian society; but we now know that in some very
noteworthy respects Assyria owed little or nothing to her
southern neighbor. Among recent finds, remains of legal enact-

---

[1] The following are the kings of Assyria from Ashurnasirpal to Ashurbanipal:

Ashurnasirpal	884–859	Tiglath–Pileser III	745–727
Shalmaneser III	859–824	Shalmaneser V	727–722
Shamshi-Adad V	824–811	Sargon	722–705
Adad-Nirari III	811–782	Sennacherib	705–681
Shalmaneser IV	782–772	Esarhaddon	681–669
Ashur-Dan	772–754	Ashurbanipal	669–626
Ashur-Nirari	754–745		

To this list may be added the Queen Regent, Sammu-ramat, who exercised
authority during the first three years of Adad-Nirari III, from 811 to
808 B.C. She is the historic prototype of the semi-mythical queen called in
Greek story Semiramis.

ments, of which the earliest copy belongs to the fourteenth or thirteenth century B.C., occupy a very important place. These juristic fragments are not part of a general body of legal ordinances, like the Semitic and Sumerian codes of Babylonia, but a series of enactments legislating on specific cases. While there is a certain proportion dealing with business contracts, sales, and the tenure of land, the more part is concerned with the position of women, marriage, and widowhood. Perhaps the most striking feature of Assyrian society which has become known through the discovery of this legislation is the levirate marriage. This institution, for whose existence in Babylonia there is so far little or no evidence, was observed also among the Hebrews. Further, these legal documents make it clear that Assyrian society was divided into three groups: a noble or upper class, a middle class including both craftsmen and what we should now call professional men, and a lower class. The organization of the members of the middle class into craft or professional guilds seems also to have been firmly established. Here, then, we have a definite parallel to earlier Babylonian practice. Yet we are not forced to postulate direct imitation on the part of the Assyrian.

The Assyrians were, above all, a warlike people. For their army the kings relied partly on a quasi-professional soldiery, who served for a definite period of time, and partly on a national or citizen militia. We have seen that in the latest period some kings even enrolled their late enemies under their standard. The standing or professional army was probably recruited in the main from the lower class of citizens. But it is not only the fact that the army is more prominent in Assyrian than in other ancient societies, which justifies the statement that Assyria was *par excellence* a military state. For the administration not only of Assyria proper, but of the empire as a whole, was essentially military in character. Yet, in the ruling of their vast territories, the Assyrian monarchs impress one as showing much greater knowledge of the art of government than the kings of Egypt or Babylonia. Unlike these, the later Assyrian kings did not rely wholly or mainly on the loyalty of local chiefs and princes after conquest. Instead, many of the conquered lands were organized as smaller administrative units, ruled by an Assyrian governor who was both civil and military head of the province. He was in constant touch with the king and the king's ministers, and, be it added, the viceroys were kept under close supervision by the ruler. One who was slack or inefficient had little chance of retaining his high office for long.

The towns appear to have enjoyed a certain degree of municipal autonomy; many received charters from the king conferring on the townsfolk privileges that were by no means negligible. Thus, although the town-governor was an imperial official, there was also a council of elders, who could lodge complaints against the governor directly to the sovereign; and, as is known from existing records, they sometimes did so quite successfully. Again, the townspeople were exempt from the *corvée* and, as a general rule, from military service. Thus, in tracing the slow evolution of imperial administration, we are justified in placing the Assyrian system halfway between the still crude methods of Egypt and Babylonia and the more closely knit imperial organization of the Persian empire, with its separation of civil and military authority, devised by the genius of Darius I.

The unfree class, whether agricultural serfs, who were tied to the soil which they cultivated for their masters, or slaves employed in urban centres, was large. Many of them, too, were enrolled in the military forces. Their condition, as in all slave-holding societies, varied immensely, and no generalization about the class as a whole is possible. Slaves in domestic service or employed by their owners in handicrafts — in the latter case they seem often to have worked at a trade independently, though obliged to pay an annual tribute to their owner — perhaps lived a life little different from the lower class of free men. On the other hand, the slaves employed in gangs on the building projects of the monarch and other heavy manual labor no doubt suffered as harsh treatment as did the slaves in the Athenian silver mines or the miserable inmates of the Roman *ergastula*.

Reference has already been made to the spread of the Aramæans during the earlier centuries of Assyrian history. From the ninth century their importance, economically, but not politically, throughout the empire steadily grew. Ashurnasirpal transplanted many of them to Assyria; Mesopotamia also contained large numbers. It is probable that much of the commerce in different parts of the empire eventually came into their hands. While the official language of business, as of diplomacy, continued to be Assyrian, from the eighth century notes and endorsements in the Aramaic language occur on documents, and these rapidly become more common. In the end, though this was not till the close of the fifth century B.C., Aramaic became the *lingua franca* in the Near and Middle East.

The Assyrian kings, with few exceptions, were like other oriental potentates, great builders. Temples, palaces, and sometimes new towns, erected at least in part from the vast spoil taken from the kings' enemies and the tribute wrung from them, were the outward manifestation of imperial power. Thus Sennacherib greatly enlarged the capital, Nineveh. His successor, Esarhaddon, rebuilt Babylon. But it was during the long rule of Ashurbanipal that Assyrian architecture and sculpture in relief reached its artistic zenith. This monarch's name is most famous for the vast library of cuneiform tablets which was collected and housed in Nineveh by the king's orders. In this enlightened work of bringing together and copying the records and literature of the past he was following the example of his predecessors. To cite but two examples, both Sargon and Sennacherib had on a smaller scale made similar collections. The library of Ashurbanipal contained many thousands of clay tablets inscribed with a great variety of subjects — historical annals, oracles and prophecies, mathematics, astronomy, medicine, lexicography and grammar; besides this there was a great quantity of correspondence and official archives. Most of the miscellaneous literature was borrowed from Babylonia. Babylonian poems and legends like the Epic of Gilgamesh (cf. p. 41), the Descent of Ishtar, and the Creation Epic, were copied and edited by Assyrian scholars, and much of this Babylonian literature would to-day be unknown but for the recovery of the Assyrian redactions.

Her science Assyria also derived from those same neighbors; but it is surely creditable to her kings that, immersed almost continuously in the practice of war, they nevertheless gave encouragement to some of their subjects to foster the arts of peace. The careful study of the heavenly bodies had been carried on in Babylonia for many centuries. Though the primary purpose of these observations was to further the pseudo-science of astrology, the foundations of a serious science of astronomy were thus laid also. The length of the solar and the lunar years had been ascertained at a very early date. By the seven so-called planets were meant the sun and moon as well as the five planets known at that date. Observations of the sun, moon, and Venus were recorded, and the twelve signs of the zodiac in the ecliptic were demarcated with approximate accuracy. Finally, much attention was paid to lunar and solar eclipses; again, though the purpose was mainly religious, valuable scientific observations also resulted therefrom.

CHAPTER IX

THE AGE OF GREEK COLONIZATION

A considerable time elapsed before Hellas became finally settled; after a while, however, she recovered tranquillity and began to send out colonies. — Thucydides i, 12 (Jowett's translation).

In the opening chapters of his history Thucydides with a masterly hand sketches in its main lines the development of early Greek society. The general truth of his picture we are not entitled to impugn. At first, we are told, there were constant migrations so that men's life and property were alike insecure. Trade and free intercourse were little known. From the nomadic stage men passed into the pastoral; still later they advanced to an agricultural mode of life. The change from an unstable to a settled existence was momentous. Life became more secure. Among men living a stationary life the ties of family relationship are strong and form the basis of clan and tribal organization. This in turn is at the root of the larger political organisms, whose immediate origin may be attributed to one of two circumstances. Either a dependent population settled round a stronghold which afforded protection in time of need, or a number of village communities amalgamated at a common centre. In either case a rudimentary *polis* (state or city-state) was created. In rapid review Thucydides refers to the sea-empire of Minos, the power of Mycenæ, the Trojan wars, and the ethnic movements which led to the formation of Greek settlements in the islands and on the Anatolian coast. Finally he points out how the geographical features of the country promoted the breaking-up of larger groups of settlers in Greece into much smaller units, which then proceeded to develop independently.

It will be well at this point briefly to touch on the geography of Greece. In proportion to the total area of the country

131

(approximately 45,000 square miles) its seaboard is exceptionally long. The coast-line on the south and east is indented by numerous inlets and bays affording either good, or at least adequate, anchorage for ancient maritime craft. On the west coast harbors are much scarcer, and, especially northward from the mouth of the Corinthian gulf, the coast is rocky and inhospitable save at a few points. The country as a whole is very mountainous, though the highest peaks — with the exception of Mt. Olympus, which rises to a height of 9794 feet — scarcely exceed 8000 feet. The lowland regions are mostly of small extent, being either narrow valleys between the uplands or else coastal strips like Achæa on the southern side of the Gulf of Corinth. The largest plain is that watered by the river Peneios in Thessaly; much smaller, though of considerable fertility, are the upper and lower Messenian plains, the valley of the Eurotas in Laconia, and portions of Bœotia. The regions where cultural advance was slowest — Arcadia and northwestern Greece — are precisely those where the intricacy of the mountain system is such as to make communication both within the area and with the world beyond unusually difficult. At the same time, the very limited resources of those areas retarded the growth of material prosperity. Thus it is only in the fourth century B.C. that the Arcadian cities emerge into some prominence politically, while the northwestern Greeks, especially the Aetolians, did not take a leading part in Greek affairs until the third and second centuries.

The rivers of Greece, though numerous, are, with few exceptions, small and unsuited for navigation. The largest was the Acheloos, which separated Acarnania from Aetolia. It, and some other streams, like the Peneios in Thessaly and the Alpheios and Pamisos in the Peloponnese, could be navigated in ancient times for a short distance from the mouth. But the majority of rivers, including some of the most familiar in Greek literature and story, like the Cephisos, Ilissos, or Eurotas, in the winter and spring, when they are fed by rains or mountain snows, have the character of mountain torrents; in the summer months they are shallow streams or even altogether dry. There is reason to believe that, what is true of the rivers and the climate generally at the present day, was substantially the same

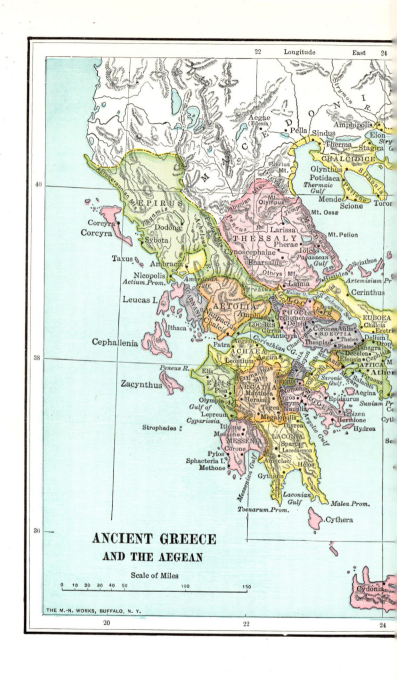

ANCIENT GREECE

AND THE AEGEAN

Scale of Miles

0 10 20 30 40 50   100   150

THE M.-N. WORKS, BUFFALO, N. Y.

in ancient times. It was natural, therefore, that the sea should be the most important highway of communication; and, even from the fifth century B.C. on, when the number of main and subsidiary roads was considerable, the sea continued to be the chief avenue of travel and commerce.

A country in which the amount of land productive enough for self-support was as restricted as in Greece could only maintain a population which in proportion to the square-mileage was small. We shall find in this circumstance a leading cause for colonial expansion. The total number of independent communities in the Hellenic world was very great. Not only is this true of the mainland and western Anatolia, but some of the islands were divided between a number of city-states. Lesbos contained six independent cities and Rhodes three; even small islands, like Amorgos and Ceos, were the home of several autonomous communities. A few of these states, as early as the seventh century, were already politically more powerful, or economically more prosperous, than their neighbors. Such were Sparta, Argos, and Corinth in the Peloponnese; the island of Aegina, Chalcis and Eretria in Eubœa; islands in the Archipelago, like Naxos, Paros, Lesbos, Chios, and Samos; and cities like Miletus, Ephesus, and Phocæa on the coast of Asia Minor. The development of Athens was slower, and till the sixth century she was only a state of the second rank.

The growth of a state in which the political and social life was centred in a city was slow. The fact that the city-state was the ubiquitous form of Greek political community from the sixth century B.C. onwards must not make us forget that the city, which ended by being virtually synonymous with the state, was at first only a convenient centre for the transaction of affairs by groups of villages or clans. At the dawn of the Hellenic period government in the Hellenic states seems to have been uniformly monarchic; but the power of the king was already on the decline. The landed nobility, the heads of the influential families, formed the king's advisory council; in the end they became so powerful that they refused to leave the sole direction of government to a single head of the state who, whether his office was elective or hereditary, ruled for life. In some cases the change from monarchy to aristocracy — that is, rule by the heads of the leading families — resulted abruptly from the deposition or murder of the king. In others a more gradual and peaceful evolution took its course. The king was forced to acquiesce in the limitation of his powers through the appointment from the nobility of one or more magistrates, who took over some of the duties hitherto carried out by the monarch. In such instances the name of king in the end survives only as the title of a magistrate. In some states the monarchy disappeared as early as the beginning of the eighth century B.C.; elsewhere it lingered on into the seventh or even the sixth century. In Sparta kingship, under a peculiar form and subjected to very definite limitations, survived as long as Sparta herself could claim to be an independent state.

The bulk of the population did not benefit by such constitutional change. On the contrary, whereas a single ruler, even if his first obligation and desire was to satisfy the nobles, would find it expedient to keep his subjects as a whole contented, and with this end in view to avoid unduly arbitrary acts, a ruling minority, whether they owed their authority to ancient lineage (aristocracy) or to a virtual monopoly of wealth (oligarchy), provided they were at one among themselves, could more readily govern in the interests of one class only, their own. Except in the case of Sparta and Athens, whose early history will be separately considered, information about the earlier constitutional development of the Greek *poleis* is very meagre in quantity and very poor in quality. It is a cause for bitter regret that of the one hundred and fifty-eight constitutions described by Aristotle, only one, his account of the Athenian constitution, is extant. But there was at all events one means of averting political revolution and relieving economic distress which among the more advanced communities of the Hellenic world was of almost universal application, namely colonization. It was a remedy for present ills which, though often fraught with peril for the colonizers, was productive of tremendous consequences for the Hellenic race.

Nowhere is the danger of reconstructing an important phase of Ancient History with a mind prepossessed by phenomena familiar in modern societies, and of attributing similar causes and a similar line of development to it, more apparent than in most current accounts of Greek colonization. It cannot be too strongly emphasized at the outset that only in a strictly limited sense was the colonial expansion of the eighth, seventh, and sixth centuries B.C. due to an economic cause. The early development of the Greek *polis* operated to the advantage of a minority of land-owners. The growth of the population as a whole, coupled with the fact that the ruling aristocracies suffered more heavily in time of war, and that their numbers steadily declined, produced a condition of affairs in many communities which might at any moment give rise to revolution. Territorially the average city-state was exceedingly small; and, even if the ruling class were thoroughly benevolent, it would be impossible for it to provide land for all the citizens, once the population had increased beyond a certain limit. Thus relief was found when a body of the poor and landless left their native place to found a settlement elsewhere. In their newly chosen home the first and most important business was the "dividing up of the land." Those who till then had been landless and citizens in little more than name, now became the land-owning burgesses of a new *polis*.

Insofar as one can ascertain the forces leading to Greek colonial enterprise, one may say that, inasmuch as colonization was certainly encouraged by the ruling classes of the old Greek cities, and successful new foundations, provided they remained, as was generally the case, on good terms with the parent city, added to her influence and prestige, the causes were political; insofar as the land-hunger of the poorer classes was satisfied by the sending out of a colony, economic reasons were operative. But, to see in the desire for commercial expansion a primary cause of colonization, to attribute to city-states like Miletus and Corinth, which sent many of their citizens forth to found new *poleis* elsewhere, a commercial or trade policy, is not only to invert the true order of events, but to misread the ancient evidence, and to interpret this aspect of the political and social development of archaic Greece in the light of modern colonial foundations. That the presence of many new city-states in the more outlying parts of the Mediterranean or on the Black Sea ultimately led to an increase of trade, and to a more intensive interchange of commodities, no one would attempt to deny.

But this was purely a secondary development; and, moreover, the extent of the commercial intercourse existing in the Hellenic world of the sixth century B.C. has, without doubt, been much exaggerated.

There is a fundamental difference between a Greek and a modern colony. The latter always remains politically dependent on the mother-country, though the degree of dependence may vary; the Greek colony (*apoikia*), on the contrary, once it had been founded, became an independent city-state, whose members ceased to be citizens of the community which they had left. The subsequent relations between mother- and daughter-city were, in the majority of cases, friendly. Often agreements of various kinds existed between the two, which tended to make their relation closer than would have been the case between two states which had never been connected. The institutions adopted by the settlers in the newly founded community were, as was natural, most often modelled on those under which they had grown up in their former home. The same religious cults and festivals, the same calendar and month-names, with which they had been familiar since their childhood, were commonly transplanted by them to the colony. But however great the friendship for the mother-city, however close the moral and religious ties might be, the *apoikia* was a new and sovereign city-state, owing no political allegiance to the parent city.

It is instructive to note that the states which were most active in sending out bands of their citizens as colonists were situated in regions where the possibility of territorial expansion was very slight. In Miletus, Corinth, Megara, Chalcis, Eretria, and Phocæa, to mention only the more important, the geographical area of the *polis* was so limited that there was no solution other than emigration for a serious political and economic problem. For we must bear in mind that the Greek city-state was essentially an agricultural state, and that the ownership or occupancy of land, however restricted in amount, was almost inseparable from full citizenship. We shall have occasion to remark hereafter how, even much later than the age of colonization, commerce and trade, in Athens and elsewhere, were mainly in the hands of the non-citizen population.

The regions to which from the late eighth century groups of

settlers from the old city-states of Greece and the Asia Minor littoral chiefly found their way were in the West and the Northeast. Sicily and southern Italy, the Thracian coast, the shores of the Sea of Marmora and of the Black Sea, afforded land to the landless and ample opportunity for enjoying all the privileges of citizenship of which the colonists had been partially or wholly deprived at home. The colonists went out from the mother city under the guidance of an official founder (*oikistes*) to whom, in the first place, the task of organizing the new settlement was entrusted. We have no means of knowing of how large a body of persons an *apoikia* was generally composed. It must have varied greatly; for the number was not fixed, as was the case with the Roman and Latin colonies founded by Rome several centuries later. It is regrettable, too, that there are few data from which to judge of the relations normally existing between the colonists and the earlier inhabitants of the region occupied. Obviously no one generalization would be in place, bearing in mind the differences between the various natives with whom Greek colonists came into contact, and the circumstances under which a new foundation was made. It is probable, however, that in many cases the colonists were secured in their possession only after a good deal of fighting; probable, too, that disasters, like that which befell an Athenian colony sent to Ennea Hodoi *c.* 464 B.C., occurred from time to time in the earlier period of colonization.

Almost invariably the new Greek cities were on or close to the coast. Even if the immediate vicinity was soon made safe, there might be continued peril from the aborigines of the interior. Thracian tribes, like the Triballoi, appear to have been a constant menace to the Greek cities on the coast, raiding them with varying sucess at intervals. Similarly, the Lucanians in southern Italy from time to time attacked Greek settlements like Thurioi. Thucydides, in his sketch of early Sicilian history (vi, 2–3), makes it clear that many of the Greek colonists in that island had to fight and dispossess the natives before they could establish their cities. Save in the case of the colonies on the Black Sea, the remains of whose material culture seem to make it plain that the population by the fourth century B.C. was only half Hellenic, the new Greek cities kept their Greek charac-

ter for centuries. Intermarriage with natives, and the conse-
quent fusion of races, was probably small in extent. The native
rarely attained citizen status in the Greek communities; probably their position usually approximated that of resident
aliens in the older cities of Greece; for few colonies, so far
as we can tell, went as far as Heraclea Pontica, whose citizens
reduced a neighboring tribe to serfdom.

The Ionian city of Miletus surpassed all others in the number
of her colonies. From the very fragmentary information at
our disposal more than forty city-states can still be designated
as Milesian foundations. The total number may have been
nearly double that figure. With few exceptions, these colonies
were on the Black Sea; for example, Odessus, Olbia, Panti-
capæum, Theodosia, and, above all, Sinope, whose earliest
history as a Greek *polis* appears to go back to the middle of the
eighth century, while a subsidiary colony went there about a
hundred years later. Nearer home were such Milesian colonies
as Cyzicus, Proconnesus, and Scepsis. In these three settlements it is clear that Greek communities had already been
established for some time before they were strengthened by
these accessions of settlers from Miletus. Most of the Milesian
colonies were founded in the seventh century; but in very few
instances can we affix even an approximate date. Early in
the same century (*c.* 685 B.C.) the mainland state of Megara
sent out a body of colonists who settled at Chalcedon, at the
southern end of the Bosphorus and on the Asiatic side. Seventeen years afterward a second Megarian colony was established
opposite to Chalcedon on the European side. The site of Byzantium is unsurpassed in the Mediterranean for its natural
advantages. Yet the city in classical times was troubled occasionally by the Thracian tribes of the interior. Hence we
need not be surprised that its occupation took place only after
the Chalcedonians had for some years surveyed the scene from
the security of the Asiatic shore.

If Miletus acquired almost a monopoly of territory suitable
for occupation on the shores of the Euxine, the city of Chalcis
in Eubœa was no less active in Thrace during the seventh
century. The rivalry existing at home between Chalcis and
her neighbor, Eretria, extended also to their colonial founda-

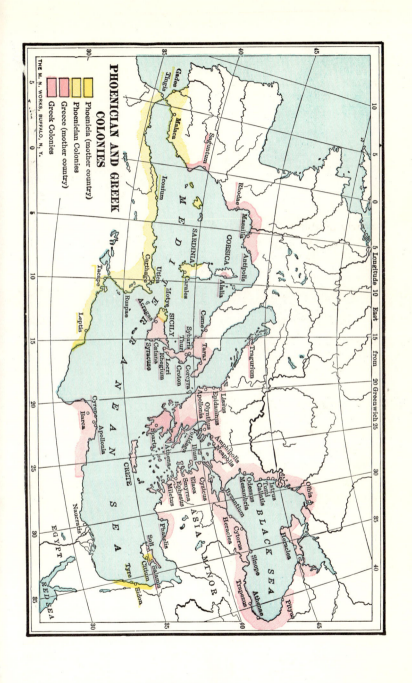

PHOENICIAN AND GREEK
COLONIES

Phoenicia (mother country)
Phoenician Colonies
Greece (mother country)
Greek Colonies

THE M. N. WORKS, BUFFALO, N. Y.

tions. Thus, though Chalcidic cities on the Thracian coast were more numerous, several of the most flourishing *poleis* in this region at a later date were foundations of Eretria (Methone, Mende, Scione), or of other cities, like Paros (Thasos) or Corinth (Potidæa). The colonizing activities of Chalcis were, however, not confined to the northern Aegean. Almost a century earlier, that is to say, in the late eighth century, many of her superfluous citizens had begun to voyage to the West and found fresh homes at Cyme and Neapolis on the southwestern coast of Italy, and at Naxos in Sicily. For about a hundred years the periodic migration of Chalcidians westward continued, and many of the Greek settlements, which in the fifth and fourth centuries played an important part in the western Mediterranean, were daughter cities of the Euboic *polis;* to wit, Catana, Leontini, Himera in Sicily, and also Zancle, which, with Rhegium on the Italian side, guarded the straits between the island and the mainland.

Among the colonizing cities of the Greek mainland Corinth was easily first in achievement; indeed, in the extent and thoroughness of her colonial policy, she was surpassed by Miletus alone. The Corinthian colonies were to be found at various points along the route from the Gulf of Corinth to southern Italy and Sicily. Some eight are known to have stood on the northwest coast of Greece, from Oiniadæ to distant Epidamnus; chief, however, of these western Greek settlements was the island colony of Corcyra. In Sicily the Corinthians found that they had been largely forestalled by Chalcis. Yet, of the three or four Corinthian colonies in that island, one, Syracuse, was destined to become the premier Greek city in the western Mediterranean.

Though space forbids the enumeration of all the Greek cities responsible for the founding of colonies, there is one other which deserves special mention, Phocæa, the most northerly of the twelve Ionian cities. Information about its history is most scanty; yet there are sufficient indications that the Phocæans in the seventh and early sixth centuries were an extremely prosperous community. Herodotus (i, 163 ff.) tells us how Phocæan sailors had found their way westward as far as Tartessus in southern Spain, with whose king they had then established friendly relations. The familiarity with the western Mediterranean thus acquired was in due course utilized for colonizing purposes. For, although the earliest Phocæan colony of which we have any record was at Lampsacus on the Sea of Marmora, — the traditional date of the foundation is 654 B.C., — the most famous *apoikia* sent out by the Ionian city was Massilia in distant Gaul (*c.* 600 B.C.). Half a century later when Phocæa herself was reduced by the Persians, a large part of her population, rather than live as subjects of an oriental power, emigrated to the West. Their efforts to secure a permanent foothold at Alalia in Corsica were frustrated by the hostility of the Etruscans. Ultimately they found a more permanent resting place at Elea in southern Italy. Closely connected with the foundation of Massilia was the gradual establishment of more than a dozen small city-states scattered along the coast to the east and west of Massilia herself. This group of Phocæo-Massiliot *poleis* maintained its independence and prosperity for many years, in spite of the hostility of the more powerful maritime states of Etruria and Carthage.

CHAPTER X

THE GREEK STATES TO THE END OF THE SIXTH CENTURY

> *For the real difference between democracy and oligarchy is poverty and wealth. Wherever men rule by reason of their wealth, whether they be few or many, that is an oligarchy, and where the poor rule, that is democracy. But as a fact the rich are few and the poor many; for few are well-to-do, whereas freedom is enjoyed by all, and wealth and freedom are the grounds on which the oligarchic and democratic parties respectively claim power in the state.* — Aristotle, *Politics*, iii, 8 (Jowett's translation).

1. SPARTA AND CRETE

ALTHOUGH such ancient testimony as we possess points to the fact that Dorian Argos was at the end of the ninth and the beginning of the eighth century the leading state in the Peloponnese, she did not retain that position long. The character of the ancient sources and the eventual issue of a long political struggle justify us in focussing our attention first on Sparta of all the Peloponnesian states. There is a certain epic interest in the tireless energy of her citizens, which made her before the end of the sixth century the premier military state in Hellas and the head of a powerful though loosely knit confederacy; something also to admire in the relentless logic, by which the entire social and economic life of a community was subordinated to what began by being a military necessity and ended by becoming a political ideal.

Only in recent years, especially since systematic excavations have been carried out at Sparta and in its vicinity, has the contrast become clear between early Sparta and the Sparta familiar from the pages of Herodotus, Thucydides, and Plutarch. In that earlier period — the eighth and seventh centuries —

her general development was not markedly different from that of many other city-states. The phenomenon of a mixed population, consisting of a dependent or serf majority dominated by a ruling minority, who alone are in the enjoyment of civic rights, can be paralleled elsewhere, for example, in Crete and in Thessaly. The excavations at Sparta have shown that for fully a century and a half (from the end of the eighth century to *c.* 550 B.C.) the arts and crafts flourished as notably in Laconia as in any other part of the Hellenic world. Laconian pottery, both in technique and artistic design, can hold its own with the best contemporary products of Miletus, Samos, or Corinth. Architects and sculptors, who were active in this age at Sparta and at neighboring Amyclæ, even if they were foreigners not citizens, exercised their art at the invitation of Sparta's rulers. The designs of some of the artistic products of Laconia, notably certain ivory plaques representing the Spartan goddess Artemis Orthia, suggest Anatolian influences. This, coupled with the distribution of Laconian pottery (cf. Plate 14), and sporadic evidence from literary sources like Herodotus, prove that, whatever the extent and character of early Greek trade and commerce as a whole, Laconia at least performed its share. The "splendid isolation," which we associate with the Spartan state of the fifth century, was not yet.

In this earlier period, then, we must picture Sparta as one of the more powerful Peloponnesian states, gradually extending her territory and her influence, till either her aggressions or her growth in power brought her into conflict with formidable neighbors, especially Argos. The city of Sparta, formed, we are told, by the union of five adjacent villages, was the chief political unit in the valley of the Eurotas. Beginning with the conquest of the two promontories of Tænarum and Malea as well as the neighboring island of Cythera, the Spartans next turned their attention to the fertile regions lying west of Mt. Taygetus. The conquest of this region, Messenia, seems to have been completed by the end of the eighth century. The conquered populations of Laconia and Messenia were not uniformly treated. That part of them which was needed to cultivate the land occupied by the Spartan citizen body was reduced to serfdom. The others (*perioikoi*) were left personally free,

Plate 13

a

GEOMETRIC VASE OF DIPYLON STYLE

b

ARCHAIC GREEK VASE
(So-called Melian Amphora)

THE ARCESILAS CUP

Showing King Arcesilas of Cyrene superintending the weighing of silphium on shipboard

Plate 14

but politically powerless. Thus in the enlarged Lacedæmonian
state there were three elements of the population. The ruling
class of citizens (Spartiatæ), who numerically did not comprise
more than a tenth of the total inhabitants,[1] and the *perioikoi,*
together compose the Lacedæmonians in the nomenclature
used by the Greek historians. The *perioikoi* were numerous;
they lived in communities of their own, occupying one hundred
small unfortified towns. Some few of them were peasants;
but the majority appear to have been engaged in industry and
trade. Left largely to themselves, though under general Spartiate supervision, they owed as their one obligation to their
overlords the performance of military service. Their general
condition was very tolerable. They had a monopoly of trade
and commerce, which was some compensation for the absence of
political privileges. In this respect their position resembled
in a general way that of the resident alien population of other
Greek states, notably Athens. Only when Sparta was engaged
in prolonged warfare — for instance during the last quarter
of the fifth century — did the *perioikoi* suffer serious incon-
venience or even hardship, owing to the prolonged interruption
caused to their professional and commercial occupations.

Far different was the condition of the serfs (Helots). It was
they who cultivated the land for their Spartiate masters. A
certain number was assigned to each lot (*klaros*), which provided each citizen and his family with the necessities of life.
The Helots and their families lived on these farmsteads. In
the earlier period they were obliged to hand over one-half
of all their produce to their master. From the sixth century
onward they paid a fixed amount in kind annually; but we
cannot tell whether, when averaged over a number of years,
this was a more or a less severe exaction than the other. The
power of the Spartiate master over his Helots was limited, since
he could neither sell them, nor liberate them, nor put them to
death. The ownership, and therefore the disposal, of the serf
population were vested in the state, that is in the citizen body

---

[1] Later, *e.g.* in the fourth century, the proportion of Spartiatæ to the
total population was even smaller. Though we have not the data from
which to estimate the population of Lacedæmon at any given period,
evidence for the steady decline of the citizen body is consistent and conclusive.

as a whole and its executive officers. The removal of Helots from one farm to another, or from agricultural work to perform military service, was likewise at the discretion of the government.

Since the primary purpose of the conquest of Messenia had been to acquire more land for the growing body of Spartiatæ, the greater part of her population after defeat was reduced to serfdom. Thus the Spartans acquired land for the landless citizens without having recourse to the all but universal remedy at this period for over-population, namely, colonization. For the solitary foundation of a Lacedæmonian colony at Taras in southern Italy (c. 705) was due to political causes — a domestic revolution whose genesis and progress are alike obscure. The oppressed Messenians did not acquiesce in their fate without a further struggle. About half a century after the Spartan conquest of Messenia (soon after 650 B.C.) the Messenians rose in revolt. It would appear that it took the Spartans many years before they finally broke the resistance of their neighbors. Nor could they have succeeded in this, had not the *perioikoi* remained loyal to them throughout. Even so the length and exhaustive nature of the late war, joined with the realization that a large serf population would always be a potential danger, unless exceptional measures for the security of the state were taken, led the Spartans to remodel their military and social organization.

The communistic military state, with its iron system of education for the young, and its regimentation of children and adults alike, suspicious of all foreigners, and indifferent or hostile to all that made up the amenities of life in other Greek states, that state which we think of as characteristically "Spartan," seems primarily to have been a product of the fifty years following the suppression of the Messenian revolt. Yet it is inconceivable that so well-organized a system could have been perfected in so short a time, had not its main features already been in existence before, and Sparta's social and political organization been in its general character essentially the same in earlier centuries, but much less rigidly enforced. The ancient evidence, though confused and sometimes contradictory, nevertheless bears out our contention; while the extreme diver-

gence of opinion among modern scholars about such topics
as the origin and date of the Spartan constitution, or the reforms attributed to a lawgiver, Lycurgus, whom some would
accept as a historical person, and others elevate to the dignity
of a hero or depress to the humbler status of a wolf-totem,
illustrate the difficulty or even impossibility of separating what
is early from what is late. The system now to be described
was firmly established by the middle of the sixth century,
and remained practically unchanged till the last half of the
third.

Life in and for the community of citizens was the duty of the
Spartiate, and from his birth he was trained under state
supervision to become and to remain an efficient member of a
military aristocracy. After birth children were inspected by
the heads of the tribe, and, if sickly, were exposed in a ravine
of Mt. Taygetus. Until they had completed their seventh
year Spartan boys were reared at home; but after that the
state took charge of their education. They were organized
in troops according to age and were put under the supervision
of the oldest and most efficient of the *eirenes*, youths between
fourteen and twenty. The troops messed, slept, and trained
together. Similar arrangements applied to the *eirenes* as a
whole. The training, which gradually increased in severity
as the boys grew older, was almost wholly physical; athletics,
gymnastic and quasi-military exercises, hunting, coupled with
strenuous and often harsh discipline, scanty clothing, and ex-
posure to all weathers, were calculated to produce a well-developed and hardy young manhood. The supreme test of stoic
fortitude was undergone by those youths who, as competitors
for the honor of being acclaimed "altar-victor," submitted to
the ceremonial flagellation carried out annually at the altar of
Artemis Orthia. So severe was the ordeal that occasionally
contestants died under it.[1] At twenty the Spartan youth
began his proper military training. His life was passed in the
barrack and in camp; and, although there were some few
privileges enjoyed by men over thirty, the communal military
life continued for all citizens up to the age of sixty. The men
ate together in messes (*syssitia*, *phiditia*), fifteen to a mess, to

[1] The rite is commonly explained as a substitute for human sacrifice.

which each member was required to contribute a fixed amount of barley, oil, and so forth, derived from the lot assigned to him by the state and cultivated for him by Helots. Failure to make the fixed contribution brought with it partial loss of civic status and exclusion from the *syssition*. Spartan girls, though living in their homes, received a training analogous to that of the boys. The physical beauty of Spartan women, and the comparative independence which they enjoyed in contrast to woman's position in other Greek communities, are noted by the Greek writers.

Of intellectual training and pursuits among Sparta's citizens we hear very little. Memorization of parts of the Homeric poems or of the martial lyrics of Tyrtæus, learning and performance of Alcman's choral odes, — for early Sparta could boast of two lyric poets, — were scarcely sufficient mental exercise to counterbalance the incessant physical and military activity, and we are not surprised that even an admirer of many Spartan institutions, like Aristotle, condemns Spartan education as altogether too one-sided.

The constitution under which the Spartans lived had features which struck contemporary and later Greek observers as peculiar and archaic. Officially at the head of the government were two kings. The monarchy was hereditary in two royal families, the Agiadæ and Eurypontidæ, between whose representatives there commonly existed much rivalry. This, so far from being confined to their personal relations, at times reacted very decidedly on public affairs. Their functions and privileges in early times much resembled those of a Homeric *basileus*. They were supported in their duties by a council (*gerusia*) of twenty-eight elders. These were elected by the citizen body from those of their number who had completed their sixtieth year, and who offered themselves as candidates for the office. Once elected, the elders served in the *gerusia* for life. This council, besides collaborating with the kings and magistrates in the general business of government, owed a good deal of its power to the fact that it acted also in a judicial capacity. Before it were tried serious criminal offenses, condemnation for which rendered the accused liable to loss of civic rights, banishment, or even death. The assembly, composed of all citizens over twenty, was at Sparta named the *apella*, and was supposed to meet monthly at the time of the full moon.   In early days it was summoned by the kings, who also presided at its regular meetings, and who could call extraordinary ones in case of any public emergency. The *apella* never developed into an influential deliberative body. Its members seem practically to have been restricted to listening to such measures as were laid before them by the *gerusia* or the magistrates, and to voting thereon.   Questions of war and peace, treaties and alliances, disputes over the succession to the kingship, when such arose, and new laws, were submitted to the vote of the *apella*.   But the strength of the magistracy and of the *gerusia* deprived this theoretical sovereignty of the people of most of its actual power.   Nor did the *apella* act in a judicial capacity.   In short, its most important function was that it elected in each year the magistrates, called ephors.

The origin of the ephorate, which, owing to the aforenamed method of election, Aristotle justifiably calls the democratic element in the Spartan constitution, is as obscure as that of the dual monarchy.   The official list of ephors, we are told, went back to the middle of the eighth century (754–753 B.C.).   That there were from the first five such officials is improbable.   For that number is almost certainly connected with the redistribution into five tribes, in place of an earlier three, which did not take place till after the second Messenian war.   One thing at least is clear, that the election by the citizens of magistrates holding office for one year, even though their duties and influence were at first very restricted, represents a very definite curtailment of the regal authority.   The great development in the powers of this magisterial college dates from the middle of the sixth century; — Chilon, ephor in 556 B.C., is reputed to have been the first to raise the office to equal power with that of the kings.   The powers of the monarch were gradually limited in every direction, though on occasion a strong man, like King Cleomenes I, might defy the ephoral college.   The ephors superseded the kings as presiding officers in the *gerusia* and the *apella*; they decided all civil suits save two types, the decisions in which now constituted the sole remnant of what must once have been the extensive judicial powers of the kings.   In the criminal cases brought before the *gerusia* the ephors initiated the prosecution;

in doing this they were but giving effect to one element in the general supervision or censorial power that they exercised over the entire citizen body. But it was not only in the internal government of the Lacedæmonian state that the ephors were supreme; they, too, guided the foreign policy of Sparta, negotiated with the representatives of other states, and even wielded considerable influence in the conduct of war. For, though the commandership-in-chief of the army was normally entrusted to one of the kings, it became customary for two members of the ephoral college to accompany the monarch on his campaigns. So, also, they issued instructions to military and naval commanders in charge of Spartan contingents, doing this on their own responsibility, or after consultation with the *gerusia*, and sometimes at least after ratification by the *apella*.

The Lacedæmonian army consisted of five Spartan regiments, corresponding to the five tribes, and of regiments of *perioikoi*. The Helots at first served only as soldier-servants to their masters in the field. But from the last third of the fifth century they were increasingly used as fighting troops. As a reward for this service they received their liberty; they then formed a separate class in the Spartan state, called *neodamodeis*, and a separate corps in the army.

The constitution and social organization of Sparta find their nearest parallel in the Dorian *poleis* of Crete; indeed it is hardly open to doubt that, when the Spartans at the beginning of the sixth century introduced sweeping reforms in their social system, they copied or adapted much from the practices of their traditional kinsmen in that island. Thus, agricultural work in Crete was carried on by a serf population resembling the Helots of Laconia and Messenia. The education of Cretan boys was very similar to the Spartan training, though perhaps not quite so rigorous. The Spartan *syssitia* have their parallel in the Cretan men's messes, called *andreia*. Considerable similarities also existed between the constitutions of Sparta and of the Cretan cities. But monarchy seems to have been abolished early in Crete, and the government was mainly in the hands of ten magistrates (*kosmoi*), who were elected annually from among a limited number of families. Thus the government of these *poleis* was more closely aristocratic than that of Sparta. In the Hel-

lenic period these Cretan states, though they sometimes fought
among themselves, seem to have played little part in the
political history of the greater Hellenic world — a striking
contrast to pre-Hellenic days, when the rulers of the island
were for centuries the most powerful princes in the Mediterranean. That the conservatism of Cretan institutions was not
untempered by progressive ideas is the thought suggested by
the laws inscribed on stone that have been recovered by excavation at Gortyn in southern Crete. Some fragments seem
to belong to the early sixth century, but the bulk of what
remains is probably not earlier than *c.* 450 (Plate 18*a*). Nevertheless much that these fifth-century laws contain is considerably older; for there are various references to earlier
enactments, making it clear that these laws are not so much
a code as a series of revisions of previous legislation. The
surviving ordinances are concerned primarily with inheritance,
adoption, marriage and divorce, the position of slaves, and
debt. Substantial fragments on legal procedure are also preserved. Of criminal law there is only a small portion; this,
as also some matters connected with prosecution and evidence,
still bears an archaic, almost a primitive, character. On the
other hand, parts of the private law are more advanced than
what is found, for instance, in contemporary Athens. Thus,
at Gortyn women enjoyed more freedom. Their property did
not pass to the husband on marriage; he had the use of it but
could not dispose of it. In inheritances the real estate and
cattle passed to the sons, but the rest of the property was
proportionately divided so that each son received two shares,
each daughter one.

To return to Sparta: so far we have considered only the
growth of the Lacedæmonian state and the characteristic institutions of Sparta as they were in the days of her greatness.
But, in the process of advancing her political power in the
seventh and sixth centuries, Sparta had been by no means
wholly successful. Her earlier conflicts with Argos had generally ended in defeat. For Argos, after a temporary decline
in the late eighth century, enjoyed another brief period as the
leading state in the Peloponnese, or even in Greece, during
the first half of the seventh. This appears to have been the

time when she was ruled by King Pheidon, whose influence or authority extended beyond the Argolid to Corinth, Aegina, and Megara. The efforts of the Spartans at this time to expand westwards of Laconia were brought to nothing by their crushing defeat at the hands of the Argives in the battle of Hysiæ (*c.* 669 B.C.). It was more than a hundred years before the Spartans successfully retaliated on their old rivals, and, by defeating an Argive force, secured for themselves control over the district called Thyreatis (*c.* 546 B.C.). Long before this, however, Argive influence in Greece had waned. In particular she was outshone in prosperity by her neighbor, Corinth, and her territory no longer embraced the whole Argolic peninsula. Sparta, before her triumph over Argos in the middle of the sixth century, had attempted the military conquest of Arcadia on her northern frontier; but the venture did not succeed. The acquisition of Thyreatis was some compensation for her failure in the north. Moreover, we can dimly descry a marked change in Spartan policy after this date. What she failed to do by force of arms she at least in part effected by diplomacy. The process by which a league of Peloponnesian states under Spartan leadership was formed in the second half of the sixth century is as obscure as its inner organization and the obligations of its members. We know that there was no permanent council of the league. When need for concerted action arose, the Spartans summoned representatives with full powers from each of the league-members. The league session was usually held at Sparta. If another city desired to bring about joint action, it addressed itself in the first place to the Spartans. If they approved, then it was they who issued a general invitation to all the constituent members. The procedure in 432 is related in some detail by Thucydides.[1] The Corinthians lodged complaints against Athens at Sparta. Their representatives, and some from Athens who were in Sparta on other business, were afforded the opportunity of stating their respective cases before the Spartan *apella*. The vote of this assembly was for hostilities against Athens. Thereupon Sparta summoned envoys from all her allied cities. Thus the effective head and executive of the league was the Spartan government, or, in other words, the

[1] Thucydides i, 66–88; 118–125.

board of ephors.   In the field each contingent of allies was under
its own commander; but the supreme command to which all
were subordinated was vested in one of the Spartan kings.
From the middle of the fifth century, moreover, the Spartans
appointed one of their own officers to each of the allied divisions.
These did not supersede the generals of the allies, but coöperated with and advised them.   But, although this confederacy
may have been a loosely knit aggregation of independent city-
states, without even a rudimentary federal constitution, it was
effectively held together, partly by the military prestige of
Sparta, partly because the various Peloponnesian cities realized
the advantages to be derived from such solidarity as was insured by membership in the league, unaccompanied as these
benefits were by any loss of autonomy on the part of the members.

2. The Age of Tyrants

There is a general similarity in the political, constitutional,
and economic evolution through which the many Greek *poleis,*
other than Sparta and the cities of Crete, passed in the archaic
period (*c.* 800–500 B.C.), because the conditions of life, in spite
of local variations, were in a general way the same.   We have
already considered one of the most noteworthy, and in its
effects most far-reaching, developments of this age, namely,
colonization.   Internally both the older Greek cities and many
of their daughter colonies progressed on similar lines.   The
ruling aristocracies governed only in the interests of their class.
The mass of the people, though citizens in name, exercised
no political influence.   Yet a peasant population is long-
suffering and even content, so long as it can earn or produce
sufficient for its daily needs.   Only when its livelihood is in
danger, does it turn for help to the governing class; and, if no
help is forthcoming, it will in the last resort rise against its
rulers.

We cannot tell whether the majority of those who tilled the
soil for the aristocratic land-owners were free tenant farmers,
or were from the first in some degree dependents.   Even if
they were free, their difficulties in most parts of the Hellenic
world were great.   There was no soil there to compare for fer-

tility with the rich acres of Mesopotamia or the Nile valley, and the margin of profit from the operation of a small farm can never have been ample. The tithes, too, which they must pay to the owners were heavy. For example, the Attic peasants before the Solonian reforms were paying the landed nobility one-sixth of their annual produce. Thus one bad season might be sufficient to put a man in debt. In his difficulty he would turn for help to his landlord, or, if he were a freehold farmer, to the owner of a large estate. In either case, by contracting a debt, even if he were free before, he came into the power of a member of the aristocracy. In the last instance the persons of the debtor and of his family were the security for loans. For it is probable that the enslavement for debt, which is definitely attested in early Athens and in early Rome, was in reality a general practice at this time. Moreover, in disputes there was no written law to which the debtor could appeal, if his treatment seemed unjust or harsh. Customary law there was; but it was handed down orally from generation to generation of the ruling class. There was little hope of bare equity, not to speak of forbearance for the debtor, while the governing families, to which his creditors belonged, were both the keepers and the interpreters of unwritten law. It is not surprising, then, that in many communities, when the people finally rebelled against their governors, their first constructive act was to choose some man, eminent for fair-dealing and common sense, as a lawgiver. Of such legislators Pittacus at Mitylene in Lesbos was one; apart from his work of codifying already existent customary law and framing new enactments to secure juster treatment for all the citizen body, he appears to have exercised a benevolent dictatorship for ten years (c. 585–575 B.C.). The laws of Gortyn, as we have seen, refer to previous legislation or to a code of early date. Among the Greeks of the West we hear of lawgivers like Zaleucus at Locri (c. 650 B.C.) and Charondas at Catana (c. 500 B.C.?). It has sometimes been doubted whether these men, and other early lawgivers whose names have come down to us, were really historical personages. The matter is really immaterial; what is important, and at the same time not open doubt, is the general striving of the Greeks, as a first step towards more constitu-

tional government, to get the law or customary procedure of
their respective city-states committed to writing.

The people's task of carrying through a successful revolution
against aristocratic misrule was often facilitated by disunion
among the rulers. The efforts of one or two aristocratic families
to exert a dominating influence in the state might antagonize
other members of the governing class. In that case the way
lay open for an understanding between some less influential
aristocrat and the people, whose cause he undertook to champion in return for their support in overthrowing what was now
the common enemy of their interests. Echoes of these various
class struggles are not rare in the fragmentary poetry of the
seventh and sixth centuries. "The people's chiefs," cries
Solon,[1] "are rich by trusting to deeds of injustice, and they
steal and rob from this source and that, sparing neither the
treasure of the gods nor of the state." Theognis of Megara,
whose sympathies were with the oligarchy and whose poetry
abounds in allusions to class war in his native city, with
graphic touch compares it to the storm-tossed, captainless ship,
a metaphor that had already been used by Alcæus in railing
at a would-be tyrant.[2]

Had I wealth, Simonides, I should not feel the distress that I now
feel in the company of the good. Now, while I perceive it, it has passed
from me; but poverty makes me voiceless, though I know better than
many that we are borne along, having lost our shining sails, from the
Melian sea through the murky night. The men refuse to bale; the
sea washes over both sides. To judge by what they are doing, scarce
may any man be saved. They have set aside the good steersman who
with knowledge was on the watch. By force they are seizing the goods,
discipline is at an end, power is no longer fairly divided. The most
menial of the crew command, bad men lord it over the good. I fear
a wave will suck down the ship.

At Corinth in the early part of the seventh century Cypselus,
with the support of the people (*demos*), drove out the ruling
clan of the Bacchiadæ, and governed the city as an irresponsible
ruler. Almost contemporaneously the neighboring state of
Sicyon passed under the control of Orthagoras who, unlike

---

[1] Solon, *Fragment* 4.
[2] Theognis, *Lines* 667–682. For Alcæus, see below, page 195.

other such autocrats, was said to be of quite humble origin. Some twenty years later (*c.* 635 B.C.) we find Theagenes in power at Megara. In many of the Greek cities of Anatolia or of Southern Italy and Sicily, such absolute rulers rose and fell, though often little more than their names have been transmitted to us. Thus, in Samos the landed aristocracy was seemingly overthrown for a time by a despot. An oligarchic reaction followed, and then further civil strife, until the reins of government were firmly taken over in the middle of the sixth century by Polycrates. So, too, at Miletus during the seventh and sixth centuries periods of Tyrant rule alternated with oligarchy and internal warfare. Of a Sicilian Tyrant it is recorded that he disarmed the wealthy and the knights. At Ephesus the power which a Tyrant, Pythagoras, brought to an end was apparently concentrated in the hands of one clan, the Basilidæ, a situation similar to that existing in Corinth before the advent of Cypselus. But it is impossible to distinguish the precise circumstances which in each case led up to the overthrow of aristocracy and the emergence of an absolute ruler. Nor did these changes all come about at precisely the same time; for, generally speaking, this stage in Greek constitutional development came later in the West than in Greece and Anatolia.

To this type of irresponsible monarchy, then, the Greeks gave the name of *tyrannis*. The derivation of the word and of its fellow, *tyrannos*, that is, Tyrant, is uncertain; but the institution itself has certain clearly marked characteristics. The Tyrant was an irresponsible and absolute ruler; generally he owed his position to popular support or even election, and the first Tyrants in different cities often continued to rely for their position on the goodwill of their subjects. Yet, in the last resort, the Tyrant's power rested on force, and very generally he had a body-guard of mercenaries.[1] The first Tyrant was usually not the last, but the founder of a line. Cypselus of Corinth was succeeded by his son, Periander; Orthagoras of

[1] Many Tyrants were thoroughly benevolent rulers, *e.g.* Peisistratus. The evil connotation of the English word "tyrant" is absent from the Greek word, at all events in the earlier period. The essential notion underlying the word "tyrannos" is that of a monarch, absolute and irresponsible.

Sicyon is overshadowed by his magnificent grandson, Cleisthenes; the sceptre of Peisistratus passed to his two sons, Hipparchus and Hippias. The importance of the age of Tyrants in Greek history is beyond measure great. In the political sphere it marks the end of the oppressive rule exercised by the old aristocracies of birth. Now for the first time all classes of the population begin to be treated alike, and a majority can claim to be citizens in fact, not merely in name. A city might owe her complete autonomy to a Tyrant, as Sicyon did after Cleisthenes had freed her from the political control of Argos. Inter-state relations might also be improved by treaty or by intermarriage. Cleisthenes married his daughter, Agariste, to an Athenian aristocrat, Megacles. The son born of this union was Cleisthenes, the reformer. Periander of Corinth maintained friendly relations with the ruler of Miletus, and doubtless with other despots. Peisistratus, as we shall see, concluded several valuable alliances with other Greek states. In later pages it will appear how these absolute rulers also furthered economic, artistic, and intellectual development in the Hellenic world.

CHAPTER XI

THE GREEK STATES TO THE END OF THE SIXTH CENTURY

In a bough of myrtle will I bear my sword, even like Harmodius and Aristogeiton, when the twain slew the tyrant and made Athens a city of equitable laws for all.

Dear Harmodius, thou art not dead at all, but men say thou dwellest in the islands of the blest, where tarries swift-footed Achilles, where they tell is Tydeus' son, goodly Diomede. — From an anonymous Greek drinking-song (*Anthologia lyrica, scol. 7 and 8*).

1. ATHENS

THOUGH in the case of Athens references in later Greek writers to her earliest history are somewhat more abundant than to other Hellenic states, with the possible exception of Sparta; though, in addition, we are in the fortunate position of having in Aristotle's *Constitution of Athens* a single survivor from a large number of similar monographs compiled by him on other Greek constitutions, we can nevertheless discern only dimly that the early development of Athens was similar to that of the majority of *poleis*. That Attica had been occupied in Mycenæan times is proved by archæological finds from the Athenian Acropolis and half a dozen other Attic sites. According to later Athenian tradition the inhabitants of this little tract of Greece, with an area of approximately 1000 square miles, were *autochthones*, that is to say, indigenous. Thucydides (i, 2) maintains that the country was little affected in the period of the migrations. Compared with other parts of Greece Attica was probably little disturbed, and these generalizations may be accepted as in the main correct. There were at first a number of diminutive states in Attica, which were gradually amalgamated to form one state with Athens, whose geographical position near the sea and possession of a natural stronghold, the Acropolis, must from the beginning have given her a superior position in Attica. This unification (*synoikismos*) continued to be commemorated at Athens in later centuries by an annual festival called the *synoikia*. The latest Attic community to be incorporated was Eleusis (*c.* 700 B.C.?). One result of this gradual process was that territorially the city-state of Athens, as distinct from the city itself, was conterminous with Attica, and therefore considerably larger than the majority of Greek states.

The government was at first monarchic; but step by step the nobles encroached upon or limited the royal power. This diminution in the regal authority was effected in two ways. On the one hand, the monarchy from being hereditary became elective; on the other hand, its tenure was limited first to ten years (*c.* middle of the eighth century?), and finally to one year (*c.* 683 B.C.?). The duties of the office, too, were drastically curtailed, the conduct of military affairs being assigned to the polemarch (*polemarchos*) and the most important magisterial functions to the *archon eponymos*. Though the title king (*basileus*) continued to survive, the holder became merely an annually elected magistrate, whose duties were mainly concerned with religion. As elsewhere, so at Athens, the early kings without doubt were supported by an advisory council of clan-heads or nobles. But the oldest council of which we hear was the council of the Areopagus, composed of ex-magistrates. Since the last-named were chosen exclusively from the noble families, this council was at that time purely aristocratic. To the three senior magistrates — archon, basileus, and polemarch — there were added in the seventh century six thesmothetæ; somewhat later it became usual to refer to these nine officials as the nine archons. According to Aristotle the thesmothetæ were appointed "that they might publicly record all legal decisions and act as guardians of them with a view to determining the issues between litigants." [1] This means that the writing down of hitherto unwritten law, which in many other states was performed by, or at least attributed to, a single lawgiver, was in Athens entrusted to a small group of officials. It was only much later, with the development of Athenian democracy and the growth of judicial business, that the thesmo-

[1] Aristotle, *Constitution of Athens* 3.

thetae were charged with the presidency in certain kinds of law prosecutions, thus becoming judges in place of what they had been before, recorders and guardians of the law in close coöperation with the council of the Areopagus.

The civic population of Attica was divided into various groups of uncertain origin. We hear of a number of brotherhoods (*phratriai*), which in the religious sphere alone retained some importance in later historic times, of four tribes (*phylai*), each containing several *phratriai*, and of clans (*gene*). It would appear that the entire citizen body was included in the tribes and brotherhoods, but that membership in the clans was restricted to the nobility, or, in other words, to the wealthier land-owners. It was this class which had gradually effected the abolition of the monarchy, and had arrogated all power in the state to itself, with the usual result that the rest of the population were citizens in name rather than in fact. The institution of the four tribes should perhaps be brought into connection with the military reforms of the seventh century, to which reference will be made hereafter. The general economic distress toward the end of the seventh century was so great that a considerable part of the rural population seemed little better than serfs. "Thereafter, it chanced," says Aristotle, "that there was civil strife between the nobles and the people. For in various other respects the constitution was all in favor of the few, and, in particular, the poor with their wives and families were in servitude to the rich. These poor were called *pelatai* and *hectemoroi* (sixth-part men). In accordance with this tithe (*i.e.* of one-sixth) they worked the lands of the rich. Moreover, the whole land was in the hands of the few. If the *hectemoroi* failed to pay this tithe, they and their children were liable to be sold into slavery. Furthermore, to the time of Solon, all loans were on the security of the debtor's person. Solon was the first champion of the people. For the mass of the people slavery was the hardest and most intolerable of the ordinances of the constitution. Not but what they chafed at other grievances; for, broadly speaking, they had no privileges." [1]

Of an earlier lawgiver, Draco (*c.* 621 B.C.), we really know very little that is definite. He appears to have been the first

---

[1] Aristotle, *Constitution of Athens* 2.

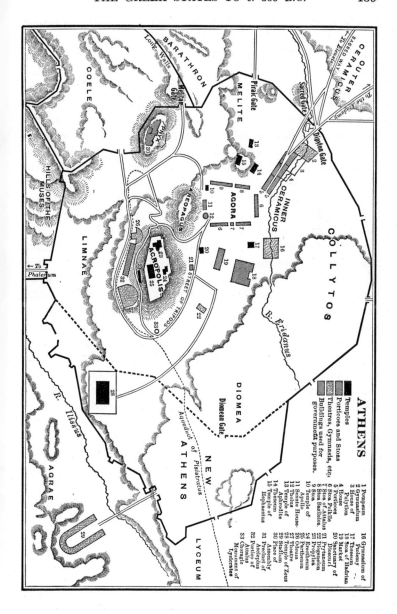

ATHENS

	Temples
	Porticoes and Stoas
	Theatres, Gymnasia, etc.
	Buildings used for governmental purposes.

1 Pompeum
2 Gymnasium
3 House of
4 House
5 Porticoes
6 Stoa Pœcile
7 Stoa of Attalus
8 Stoa Basileios.
9 Stoa
10 Temple of
11 Temple of
12 Apollo
13 Tholus
14 Senate House.
15 Tholos
16 Temple of
17 Temple of
18 Temple of Hephaestus

16 Gymnasium of Ptolemy
17 Theseum
18 Stoa of Hadrian
19 Market
20 Sanctuary of Dionysos
21 Prytaneum
22 Diogeneion
23 Propylæa
24 Erechtheum
25 Parthenon
26 Odeum
27 Theatre
28 Temple of Zeus
29 Stadium
30 Place of Assembly
31 Precinct of Aesculapius
32 Portico of Attalus
33 Choregic Monument of Lysicrates

legislator at Athens to formulate a written code of laws, thus presumably going beyond what was already being done by the thesmothetæ. But the only parts of his work that are to some extent known are those enactments which abolished the old blood-feuds and established a regular procedure for the trial of homicide. Though the Draconian reforms were doubtless of benefit in furthering order and security in Attica, they did nothing to remedy the serious economic evils to which Aristotle bears witness. Apparently in the seventh century it had been found expedient to classify the civic population according to the property which they owned. As was the case with the so-called Servian organization at Rome, so here the primary purpose of the classification was military. In both cases the individual was required to supply his own equipment. The *hippeis* (horsemen) belonged to the wealthiest or ruling class; the *zeugitai* (teamsmen?) were sufficiently well-to-do to serve as heavy-armed infantry in time of war; finally the *thetes* (workers for hire?) made up the poorest part of the civic body. Some of these last may have served as light-armed troops; but in general they were at this time exempt from military service, save perhaps in a great national emergency. Although this classification was in the nature of a concession by the ruling class to the populace, who from the mere fact that they bore arms were bound to exercise more influence in political affairs than before, the real power and the magistracies were still under the exclusive control of the richest class. Such military classification of the citizen body, for which we have some precise information only in the case of Athens, must have been widely adopted throughout the Hellenic world during the course of the seventh century. There is no reason to doubt the truth of Aristotle's statement that in the early Greek *polis* the chief fighting body was the cavalry of the nobility.

The earliest government which existed after the overthrow of the kingly power grew up out of the warrior class, and was originally taken from the knights; for strength and superiority in war at that time depended on cavalry; indeed, without discipline, infantry are useless, and in ancient times there was no military knowledge or tactics, and therefore the strength of armies lay in their cavalry.[1]

---

[1] Aristotle, *Politics* vi (iv), 1297b16 ff. (Jowett's translation).

A greater abundance of metal, lowering the cost of iron and bronze, and more skill in working them, coupled with the discovery that a solid formation of foot soldiers, protected by heavy body armor and armed with spear and sword, could effectively stop a charge of mounted troops, ended by bringing about a drastic change in the methods of warfare. The brunt of the fighting henceforward was carried on by massed formation (phalanx) of heavy-armed citizen troops. This is in strong contrast to the Homeric battles, which usually resolve themselves into a series of single combats between the nobles of either party. The skirmishing of their respective followers, with little or no defensive armor, is of quite secondary importance. Yet even in Homer companies of heavy-armed infantry are not unknown:

As when a man builds the wall of a high house with close-set stones, to avoid the might of the winds, so close were arrayed the helmets and bossy shields, and shield pressed on shield, helm on helm, and man on man, and the horse-hair crests on the bright helmet-ridges touched each other when they nodded, so close they stood by each other.[1]

Doubtless the change everywhere was very gradual; the Spartan phalanx organization, for instance, was probably not finally perfected till after the Second Messenian War. But the change was none the less revolutionary in its results.

The first serious attempt to bring about a more equitable government at Athens, and particularly to arrest the gradual reduction to bondage of the small-farmer class, was made by Solon. Let us hear his own words:[2]

As for me, regarding the objects for which I brought the people together, you ask why I stopped before I had achieved those objects? To those most excellent measures the great mother of the Olympian gods, black Earth, shall in the just fulness of time bear witness, even she whom once I freed from the boundary stones that encumbered her all about. She who before was enslaved is now free. To Athens, our divinely founded country, I restored many who had been sold, some unjustly, some according to the law, and others who through hard necessity were in exile, who no longer spoke the Attic tongue, as would

[1] Homer, *Iliad* 16, 210 ff. (translated by Lang, Leaf, and Myers).
[2] Solon, *Fragment* 32.

befall men wandering far afield.   Then those who suffered cruel slavery
here on the spot, trembling at their masters' ways, I liberated.   These
things I performed by the might of law, joining together force and right,
and I fulfilled my promises.

In 594 B.C. Solon became *archon eponymos* and, to carry out the
work of reform, was given extraordinary powers.   It is curious
that so little is known about the details of Solon's first and most
drastic measure of reform, the *seisachtheia* or "shaking-off of
burdens."   As the name itself shows, it effected the cancellation of outstanding debts.   So radical a step could only be
justified by the exceptional conditions which needed to be
remedied.   Closely connected with this measure, and perhaps
a part of it, was the absolute prohibition for all future time
of enslavement for debt.   Thus, whatever their earlier status
may have been, the *hectemoroi* were converted by Solon into
tenant farmers.   They continued to pay, as before, one-sixth
of what they produced to the owners, but, being included in
the lowest of the census classes, benefited with the rest of the
thetes by the constitutional reforms of Solon.   For he amended
the earlier three-fold division of the citizen body by separating
the wealthiest men in the community from the rest of the
hippeis.   The minimum rating of each class was assessed in
natural produce — grain, oil, and wine.   To the first class
belonged those whose returns amounted to not less than five
hundred measures, its members being known henceforward as
pentakosiomedimnoi.   For the *hippeis* the minimum was three
hundred measures, for the *zeugitai* one hundred and fifty, which
was later changed to two hundred.   The rest, whose income
was less than this, made up the class of *thetes*.

Political privileges were graduated in an analogous way.
The archons were elected from the first two classes, certain
financial officials from the first alone.   A number of minor
magistracies could be held by *zeugitai*, and these were also
eligible for the new council of four hundred (*bule*), instituted by
Solon.   The *thetes* were excluded from all these offices, but they
were members of the citizen assembly (*ecclesia*).   The *bule* —
one hundred councillors were annually chosen from each tribe
— being recruited from three out of the four census classes, had
a much more democratic character than the old aristocratic

Areopagus, which continued to be composed of ex-archons. We know little of the functions of the *bule* at this period beyond the fact that it helped the magistrates in a general advisory capacity. The powers of the *ecclesia*, too, which now elected the magistrates, were confined to certain matters affecting the community as a whole, for example, the ratification of declarations of peace and war, or the bestowal of the citizenship on foreigners, besides the elective functions already named.

The most striking innovation introduced by Solon was the institution of the *heliaia*. It was, as Aristotle remarked, the most essentially democratic part of the Solonian constitution. The *heliaia* was a court of justice in which the decisions rested with a jury, and adult male citizens over thirty years of age from all four classes were eligible to act as the jurors. It is probable that at first there was but one court, and that its duties were confined to hearing appeals from magisterial sentences. The increase in the number of courts, and the wide extension of their judicial powers, were a development of the following century. Nevertheless, by giving to the citizen body as a whole, whether acting in a political capacity (*ecclesia*) or in a judicial one (*heliaia*), the ultimate decision in certain cases, Solon fully merited the title, "first champion of the people." He had securely laid the foundations on which was built up the advanced democratic constitution of the fifth and fourth centuries.

An Athenian of the age of Pericles or Demosthenes might refer to Solon only with reverent admiration; to his contemporaries Solon's reforms were too essentially a compromise to bring about prolonged peace and harmony in Attica. The newly enfranchised part of the population resented the privileges which wealth and descent conferred on their more fortunate fellow-citizens; the old aristocracy of birth and the richest class were angry that they had been deprived of the exclusive control of the government. On the whole, the middle class benefited most by the reformer's work, and so they were the most contented. After his period of office Solon left Athens and was away for many years. When at last he came back to his home, he took no further part in Athenian political life. For more than a quarter of a century after Solon's archonship

Attica was the scene of factional disputes, which threatened to undo all the good done by the reformer. We hear of three groups, "the men of the plain," "the men of the shore," and "the men of the uplands," whose feuds distracted the land with civil war. Yet we cannot be sure of the rival interests that these factions represented.[1]

To wide-spread unrest at home were added the further distress and burden of a foreign war. Athens may have been engaged in war with her neighbor, Megara, before Solon's time; she certainly fought with her shortly before 560 B.C. The main cause of hostilities was the possession of the island of Salamis, which had been in Megarian hands and was now acquired by Athens, after she had seized Megara's port of Nisæa, and thereby forced her rival to cede the island. The Athenian through whose energy and initiative these successes were won was Peisistratus, a young man of aristocratic birth. With the help of a body-guard, assigned to him by the vote of the people because of an attempt on his life by an assassin, and with the general support of the faction of the uplands, Peisistratus made himself master of Athens. But his position as Tyrant was not yet secure. After a brief period of rule he was forced to go into exile owing to the powerful coalition brought against him by the leaders of the two other factions, who sunk their own differences to unite in a common cause. Megacles, a member of the influential family of the Alcmæonidæ and leader of the "men of the sea-shore," was the most formidable of Peisistratus' opponents. The Tyrant's departure was the signal for a renewal of civil war, and was shortly followed by a fresh struggle with Megara, in which the Athenians lost their late conquests. In the distressful state of the country Peisistratus saw an opportunity for recovering the power he had lost. His wealth, derived largely from successful exploitation of silver mines in Thrace, he used to enlist a numerous body of mercenaries. With these he landed in Attica and was

[1] A facile generalization, now very popular, would equate the "men of the shore" with the great mercantile class whose interests clashed with those of the "men of the plain," who represent the landed proprietors. Unfortunately there is no justification for assuming the existence of mercantile magnates in Attica at this period; moreover, Aristotle expressly says of the "men of the shore" that they were agriculturists.

immediately joined by many of his old supporters.   With this mixed force he defeated his political opponents utterly and again secured the Tyranny, exercising it till his death (*c.* 546–528 B.C.).[1]

When Aristotle characterized the rule of Peisistratus as more democratic than tyrannical, he meant that Peisistratus' arbitrary power was exercised for the good of the majority of his subjects, and that he did not abolish the existing constitution. His political opponents, members of the nobility of birth and wealth, were compelled to go into banishment.   In some cases at least their property was confiscated; the land so acquired was parcelled out into small farmsteads.   These the Tyrant allotted to the poorest class of citizens.   The *hectemoroi* disappeared, and the small cultivators, new or old, became free-hold farmers.   All had to pay to the ruler a tax of one-tenth, or, according to another account, one-twentieth;   even if the larger sum be correct, the difference between one-tenth and the earlier tithe of one-sixth paid by the *hectemoroi* represented a considerable relief to the small cultivator.   We are further told that Peisistratus advanced small capital sums to the new farmers, so as to give them a start and enable them to lay in the necessary stock.   He made no attempt to change or abrogate the Solonian constitution; at the most he insured that the important magistracies were, as far as possible, held by his kinsmen or by reliable supporters of his régime.   That, even so, his position rested directly on force could not be disguised; for the Acropolis was garrisoned by his mercenaries.

In his foreign policy Peisistratus aimed at cementing good relations with important foreign states, for example, with Sparta and the princes of Thessaly.   Whether he won back Salamis from Megara, or whether the island only became permanently Athenian twenty years after his death, is a moot point.   At all events the island had been recovered before the end of the sixth century.   But that part of the Tyrant's policy which had the most far-reaching effect was his promotion of colonial enterprises.   Sigeum on the Asiatic side of the Dardanelles was won by the Athenians, after a good deal of fighting with neighboring

[1] For a different version, which tries to reconcile the contradictory and in part fantastic stories about Peisistratus in the Greek writers and accepts the story that the Tyrant was twice exiled, cf. *Cambridge Ancient History*, iv, pp. 61 ff.

states, like Mytilene and Lampsacus, who feared that their own
interests were being threatened.   At the same time, Miltiades,
member of an old Athenian family and once at least the political
opponent of Peisistratus, led a colony to the Thracian Chersonese (Gallipoli).   It has been suggested, not without some probability, that the islands of Lemnos and Imbros were first brought
under Athenian control at this time.   Apart from the immediate
benefit accruing to the Athenian settlers in this region, the occupation of these geographically important sites was of great value
at a time when Athens was already looking to some extent to
foreign grain to feed her population.   Indeed, an ordinance forbidding the export of Attic grain is attributed to Solon.

On Peisistratus' death his sons, Hippias and Hipparchus, seem
to have adhered closely to their father's policy for a number of
years.   At last, however, a conspiracy, not due to general discontent but arising out of a private quarrel, was instigated by
two Athenians, Harmodius and Aristogeiton.   Hipparchus was
killed, but his brother escaped the danger; while of the two ringleaders, Harmodius was slain outright and his companion was
subsequently executed (c. 514 B.C.).   Hippias' government now
became more despotic, and his harshness, coupled perhaps
with a growing desire for political freedom on the part of his
subjects, brought about a general revolt against the Tyrant four
years later.   But Hippias was clearly in a strong position, as is
proved by the fact that the Athenians only succeeded in ousting
him with the help of a Lacedæmonian contingent.   The intervention of Sparta was due to the diplomacy of the exiled Athenian family of the Alcmæonidæ.   They had won great influence
with the priests at Delphi, where they had rebuilt Apollo's temple, largely from their own resources.   The vaticinations of a
grateful oracle were insistent in calling on Sparta, now the leading military state in Greece, to rid Athens of her Tyrant.
Hippias was allowed to leave Attica with his family, and retired
to Sigeum, which he held for a number of years as a vassal of
Persia.   His departure was followed by a renewal of party strife
in Attica.   After four years of civil unrest, Cleisthenes, son of
Megacles, the erstwhile opponent of Peisistratus, and now head
of the Alcmæonid family, with sufficient popular support overcame his political rivals led by Isagoras.

Instead of taking advantage of his strength, he introduced a series of reforms and amended the Athenian constitution, so that the Athenians after his day lived under a stable government for nearly two centuries, and, save for two brief episodes, had no direct experience of the civil dissension (*stasis*), which sapped the strength and was the curse of many other Greek states. Cleisthenes' primary task was to devise means for abolishing the local interests and the power of the Eupatrid families, which had made possible the sixth-century factions of the shore, the plain, and the uplands, and in a different form had been responsible for the recent civil war. The old four tribes were abolished and the free population of Attica was redistributed on a territorial basis into ten tribes. Each *phyle* contained three *trittyes*, each of which was situated in a different part of Attica; each *trittys*, again, was made up of several smaller units — townships or rural districts — called demes (*demoi*). The total number of demes was originally one hundred; but it was gradually increased after Cleisthenes' time, so that, by the fourth century, there were not less than one hundred and fifty. Artificial as this rearrangement of Attica and her population seems in the too brief descriptions that have come down to us from ancient times, the work of the reformer endured, and was, as results showed, eminently practical. The long-standing family feuds and rivalries of clans ceased, because the new geographical distribution cut right across the old groups. Moreover, a new element was introduced into the citizen population by the enfranchisement of persons of only partial Athenian descent. Resident foreigners had lived in Attica since Solon's time at least, and their number had steadily increased, because their economic value to the state had been recognized by Peisistratus and his successors. Doubtless there had been intermarriage with Athenians, and it was the descendants of such unions whom Cleisthenes could now add to the civic body, when citizenship no longer depended on membership of phratries. Very possibly he enfranchised some resident aliens, with no Athenian blood in their veins, as well. It was, at all events, a far more liberal policy than that followed by the Athenian democracy fifty years later. The new tribes had approximately equal influence in the assembly (in which the town dwellers naturally had an advantage over the farmers who resided at a distance from the capital), because a deme in each tribe was situated in or near Athens. The new demotic division of the civic body formed the basis for military organization, taxation, and so forth. The lists of the demesmen that were compiled, and hereafter carefully kept up to date, furnished the material from which the census list of citizens was drawn up. The adjective derived from the name of the deme now formed part of the official name of every Athenian citizen.[1] Youths were admitted into their father's deme on the completion of their eighteenth year, after their legitimacy had been attested on oath by the parent. Admission to the deme was tantamount to attaining one's majority and full civic status.

Of no less importance were the constitutional changes introduced by Cleisthenes. The council of four hundred was enlarged to one of five hundred members to correspond more conveniently to the new tribal division. Fifty councillors were hereafter chosen by lot from each tribe. Moreover, the *thetes* or fourth class in the Solonian classification now became eligible to be councillors. Indeed, one of the most decided steps in the direction of more democratic government was this innovation of Cleisthenes. Just as Solon's reforms had extended more political privileges to the middle class (*zeugitai*) so Cleisthenes' reconstruction of the council added considerably to the influence and political responsibility of the poorest class of citizens. To facilitate the transaction of administrative business the *bule* was divided into ten committees or prytanies, each of which for a tenth part of the year shouldered the main burden of the council's work. While competent to decide minor questions on their own initiative, the prytanies had to refer all major questions to the decision of the whole council. The old magistracies were left untouched by Cleisthenes, and the archonship continued to be open only to members of the first and second census classes, with which likewise the reformer did not interfere. But the political power of the old magistracies rapidly declined and passed partly to the council, partly to a board of ten officials (*strategoi*) which, if not actually instituted by Cleisthenes, came into being very soon after his time. As their name, *strategoi*

---

[1] E.g. *Isokrates Theodoru Erchieus*, Isocrates, son of Theodorus, of the deme Erchia.

(generals), shows, these persons were originally appointed to command the military detachments raised from each of the tribes. They naturally very soon took over the general military and naval administration, sharing these duties for some years with the polemarch. The *strategoi* were annually elected, one from each tribe, and continued to be elected after other magistracies were regularly filled by lot. Within half a century they had become the chief executive magistrates in the Athenian state.[1] In conclusion we must refer to the curious institution of ostracism, which some have attributed to Cleisthenes and which at any rate was in operation very soon after his time. Once a year the members of the *ecclesia*, after so deciding at a previous meeting, came together socially to record a vote against any citizen who might be regarded as dangerous to the state and whose banishment was therefore desirable. Not less than six thousand votes altogether must be cast for the proceedings to be valid. The person who received the largest number of votes — these were scribbled on pieces of potsherd (*ostraka*) from which the proceeding derives its name — was forced to go into honorable exile for ten years. His property was not confiscated, and he was reinstated in all his civic rights on his return. In origin this institution was doubtless intended to be a safeguard against any attempted renewal of Tyranny at Athens. But in the recorded instances of its use — the earliest was in 487 — it was the leaders of the political parties in the *ecclesia* who were liable to be sacrificed to party rivalry. So far from being generally beneficial in its effects, the institution sometimes resulted in the temporary loss to Athens of one of her ablest men.

2. The Economic Development of Greece

The economic development of Greece in the earlier period is a topic fraught with difficulties. The literary evidence is of the scantiest, and the archæological is scattered and often not easy to interpret. We have seen that in Homer household economy was the rule. Specialization is confined to a very few occupa-

[1] For the further development of Athenian political institutions see below Chapter XIX.

tions; maritime trade is mentioned in connection with the traffic in luxury articles carried on by Sidonian, that is to say, Phœnician, traders. In Hesiod, who describes the fertile region, Bœotia, we find economic and social conditions that in many ways resemble those depicted in the Homeric poems. But there are some notable differences, too. Not only is the division between rich and poor more marked in the *Works and Days*, but it is clear from the language used that many of the poor had become dependent on the wealthy through indebtedness. The chief difference in the later poem, however, lies in the more frequent mention of commerce, which is carried on not by foreigners, like Phœnicians, but by the poorer class of Bœotian. The occasion of it is either to dispose of surplus farm produce or else sheer necessity.

When thou wouldst turn thy foolish soul to trafficking, to escape debts and joyless hunger, I will show thee the measures of the surging sea, though I have no skill of seafaring or of ships.[1]

But in an equitably governed community, where the land provides enough for all there will be no need of seafaring.[2]

The problem of economic life in archaic Greece has been further complicated by a large number of modern writers who reconstruct the economic history of Greece during this and later ages in terms of nineteenth and twentieth-century "big business." To do this they are obliged to read into the sporadic allusions found in Greek writers meanings which the text does not warrant, and to deduce from the archæological data conclusions which, at the best, are highly hypothetical, and which often are no more than wild conjectures. The result of this method can only be that the impressiveness of their admittedly fascinating picture of Greek trade and commerce is in inverse proportion to its historical veracity. We may begin with certain incontrovertible facts, which must never be forgotten in any discussion of the subject, and which show at the outset that deductions based on economic conditions existing in the modern world are in the highest degree fallacious.

Commerce in the Greek world was mainly carried on by sea. With the small sailing vessels of that day communications were

[1] Hesiod, *Works and Days* (transl. by A. W. Mair), l. 646 ff.
[2] *Ibid.*, l. 236.

necessarily very slow. A speed of four and a half to five knots an hour was considered a fair rate of progress. It was only warships that were propelled by a large number of rowers that could move a good deal faster, at least over short stretches. But merchantmen regularly relied on canvas. Again, the risks involved in conveyance by sea were infinitely more serious than now. The rates of interest on loans, which now seem exorbitantly high, are eloquent proof of this contention. Moreover, the winter months were, in general, a closed season, and maritime trade, like naval and military operations, was limited to seven, or at the most eight, months in the year (March to October). Even as late as the fourth century the methods of banking and transacting business were, as we can see clearly from the Private Orations of the Attic Orators, extremely primitive. It must be admitted that such conditions as are implied by these acknowledged facts were not favorable to the development of industry on a large scale, or to the creation of mercantile magnates. There is, in truth, a vast difference between the significance of the political and the economic life of the Greeks. The Greek *polis*, tiny though it was in comparison with the nation-state of more modern times, was in the fifth and fourth centuries a most highly developed organism. The political practice of Greek statesmen, and the political philosophy of Greek thinkers who, even when portraying an ideal Utopia, never forgot the reality of actual institutions familiar to them, convey a lesson of abiding value for all time. But their economic theory and practice, even on the most favorable estimate, were still in their infancy when the *polis* had passed its prime, and when its old age was cut short by the successful ambitions of Philip and Alexander of Macedon.

In the archaic period, with which we are here concerned, two facts stand out: Greek states were predominantly agricultural, and production was very largely governed by the economy of the household. Trade by barter or payment in weight of metal was general to the beginning of the seventh century, and this method continued in many regions for very many years after the introduction of coinage. The comparative scarcity of gold and silver in the Aegean area would greatly retard

the general adoption of an invaluable aid to commercial intercourse.[1]   It is doubtful whether the Lydians or the Ionian
Greeks deserve the credit of the momentous invention; for
there is little ascertainable difference in date between the
earliest coins known from these two regions.   Their example
was followed by the people of Aegina, then by Corinth, Chalcis,
Eretria, and thereafter, more slowly, by other mainland and
island states.   Before long the Greeks of the West also followed
suit.   Solon is credited with changing the weight standard of
the Athenian currency from that used by Aegina to the lighter
standard favored by Corinth and the cities of Eubœa.   We
can hardly doubt that the Athenians benefited by the change,
which simplified trade relations with Corinth, their neighbors
of Eubœa, and the Greek cities of the islands and Anatolia,
where the lighter standard was also in use.[2]   The same reformer,
it may be mentioned in this connection, also prevailed on his
countrymen to adopt a new system of weights and measures
in place of the old Peloponnesian, so-called Pheidonian, standard
which had hitherto been used in Attica.

The adoption of metallic currencies greatly facilitated and
thereby also stimulated trade.   On the other hand, where so
many independent communities minted their own issues and
these were not only not all on the same standard, but, what
was more vital, differed in the purity of their metal, the full
benefit of the new invention was not always achieved or
maintained.   At a later date the currency of Athens is specifically mentioned as one which, in contrast to the mintages
of other cities, which hardly circulated — except at a loss —
outside the particular localities in which they were issued,
was readily accepted everywhere.   The reason for this was
simple.   The Athenians did not allow their tetradrachms to

[1] Siphnos was very prosperous in the sixth century owing to her gold
and silver mines.   Later the mines became exhausted and the prosperity
of the island declined.   Thasos and the coastal regions of Thrace lying
opposite the island were rich in both metals.   The mines at Laurium in
Attica began to be worked in the sixth century, but were not more intensively exploited till the fifth.

[2] The Aeginetan two-drachm piece (didrachm) weighed 193 grains
(12.3 grams); the Euboic didrachm weighed only 135 grains (8.4 grams).
This was the silver standard.   The gold standard was universally 130–
135 grains for the gold stater.   The normal ratio of gold to silver was 1:13.

deteriorate in quality and did not, as many Greek governments seem to have done from time to time, tamper with their coinage in order temporarily to improve their revenues. It was a piece of sharp practice which brought its own punishment. The earliest coins are of electrum, a natural alloy of gold and silver, and some of the Asiatic Greeks continued to strike electrum currency to the beginning of the fifth century. Broadly speaking, however, gold generally superseded the alloy in the cities of Asia Minor and some of the islands, while silver was universally used in the mainland states and in the West.

The only industry of this age about which, thanks to excavation, and the durable character of the objects, we can form a fairly clear picture is the ceramic. The number of decorated wares of the archaic period is considerable; both in fabric and decoration they are of great merit. The place of manufacture is often doubtful, although the more notable and popular kinds have been assigned by archæologists with greater or less certainty to particular regions. One type of ware, long wrongly described as Rhodian, has thus with much probability been classed as Milesian, another as Samian; Corinthian ware, too, is found over a very wide area, as is another class of vases commonly called proto-Corinthian, though these are probably not a Corinthian but a Sicyonian fabric. We have seen that in Laconia also during the seventh and sixth centuries the potter's art flourished. In these and other centres there must have dwelt many craftsmen, each of whom made his own wares in his own workshop, assisted by his sons and perhaps an apprentice and a slave or two. The political and social status of these men and of craftsmen engaged in the manufacture of other articles is difficult to determine. Many of them at this time seem to have belonged to the poorest class of citizens; but we have noted that in Laconia and Messenia such occupations were left to the *perioikoi*, while in sixth-century Athens, Greeks from other cities began to settle permanently, and rapidly increased in number. Of two well-known potters working in Athens in the second half of the century, Amasis and Exekias, the former certainly, the latter probably, was a resident alien. But long before their time Solon, in order to attract foreign craftsmen to Attica, is said to have promised them the citizenship. Nothing, too, is more striking than the frequency with which artists and artisans were requisitioned from outside by this or that state. We have already observed how this happened at Sparta. Polycrates, the Tyrant of Samos, to attract workmen from other cities, offered very high wages, and the famous water-conduit in Samos was constructed by a Megarian engineer.[1] The physician, Democedes, to whom Herodotus alludes, was a native of Croton, but practised his art in Athens, Aegina, Samos, and even in Persian territory.[2] Among the artisans engaged in building the sixth-century temple of Artemis at Ephesus were Samians and natives of Crete; and indeed we find Cretan craftsmen mentioned in various other localities. We cannot doubt but that the unstable political conditions throughout the Hellenic area were responsible for a large floating population, composed of men who were "city-less" in the sense that they lacked the privileges of full citizenship in their own *polis* and sought a livelihood elsewhere, as chance or good prospects lured them. In the light of this explanation certain lines of Solon gain a fresh significance. The conditions portrayed demonstrate with great clearness the economic instability prevalent in his day.

If a man be needy and the toils of poverty constrain him he thinks he will acquire much wealth in any way he can. Many are the men and many the aims of their striving. One roams o'er the fishy sea in ships, yearning to bring home gains, driven on by relentless winds, sparing his life not a whit. Another, cleaving the fruitful earth serves for a year the owners of the curved plough. Another, skilled in the works of Athene and Hephaistos, master of many crafts, brings together a livelihood with his hands. Another, taught gifts by the Muses of Olympus, has learnt the measure of fair wisdom. Another has been made a seer by the lord Apollo who works from afar and who knows the ill that comes from afar upon men, the ill that even the gods attend on; for the decrees of Fate assuredly no omen or sacrifice shall avert. Others possess the craft of Paion, the skilled in many drugs, even the physicians, and no assured end to their task is theirs.[3]

It is a varied gallery of itinerant traders, artisans, day-laborers, minstrels, prophets, and leeches that the poet brings before us, and no more.

[1] Herodotus iii, 60.   [2] *Ibid.* iii, 125; 131.
[3] Solon, *Fragment* 13 (M. L. W. Laistner, *Greek Economics*, pp. 2–3).

The excellence of Attic clay for pottery, the proximity of copper mines in Eubœa, which furnished the raw material for the metal workers, or the exceptionally favorable geographical situation of cities like Corinth or Byzantium, which made them important marts for the exchange of commodities, may serve as instances of natural advantages such as would attract workers from other parts of Greece. Where a particular variety of pottery is found over a wide area, it is not safe to assume that it all emanated from a single centre. There may have been many cases where the potter and not his wares emigrated to a new home in which he might hope more successfully to practise the craft than in the city of his birth from which excessive competition or political oppression had driven him.

The use of slave labor, whether in the home or in the workshop, was probably very restricted in this age. The traffic in non-Hellenic slaves began to develop in the sixth century, and in the following century assumed much greater proportions. While, however, there is a danger of exaggerating the extent of this institution, especially in the earlier period, there can be no doubt that some slaves had been kept by the wealthier classes from earliest Greek times, just as was the case in the society portrayed in the Homeric poems. Apart from other evidence, the custom of enslaving insolvent debtors, which has been noticed above, offers clear proof of the prevalence of the institution.

The commerce between different regions in the Aegean, and from there to the Black sea, Egypt, and the western Greeks was partly carried on in the interests of the food-supply — for with the growth of city-states many of them ceased to be wholly self-supporting — partly in what may be broadly classed as luxury articles, such as decorated pottery, metal-work of various kinds, or the finer sorts of textiles. There must also have been a good deal of trade in raw materials, metal ores, timber for ship-building, perhaps also woollen yarn from those regions like Miletus in the East and southern Italy in the West, where sheep-rearing was practised greatly in excess of what was needed for local consumption. The governments of the states derived their profit from these enterprises indirectly. They imposed taxes on imports and exports, and often harbor dues as well. A city like Corinth, being a great centre of exchange, would secure a large revenue in this way. That her wealthy governing class engaged directly in commerce is not only not proved, but in the highest degree unlikely. These persons sold the excess of the produce from their estates and invested the capital which they accumulated from the land in loans to merchants or in carrying out contracts for their government. It is significant that Herodotus, after having observed that the exercise of a craft or trade was regarded as not honorable, that is to say, incompatible with free citizenship, by the Egyptians, from whom the Greeks took over this attitude, and by other non-Hellenic peoples, states that of all the Hellenes the Corinthians looked down least on those engaged in such occupations.[1] The reasonable interpretation of the statement is that the Corinthian attitude, though more liberal in a general way, did not differ basically from that of other Greeks.

It will be apparent from the foregoing remarks that we still know little that can be called certain about Greek economic life in the archaic period. Doubtless further excavations, especially along the Asia Minor littoral and in some of the more outlying parts of the Hellenic world, will help to unravel some of the numerous outstanding problems and to fill in some of the worst gaps in our knowledge. But it is questionable whether it will ever be possible to trace the continuous growth of Greek commerce and industry in the earlier period as we can now, in spite of many obscurities, follow up the political and constitutional evolution of the Greek city-state.

[1] Herodotus ii, 167.

CHAPTER XII

RELIGIOUS INSTITUTIONS AND ART IN THE ARCHAIC PERIOD

> *For many and great are the reasons which hinder us from doing this, even though we should desire. . . . Then, secondly, there is the bond of Hellenic race, by which we are of one blood and of one speech, the common temples of the gods and the common sacrifices, the manners of life which are the same for all; to these it would not be well that the Athenians should become traitors.* — Herodotus, viii, 144 (Macaulay's translation).

THE previous chapter, being mainly concerned with political history and institutions, necessarily stressed the absence of political unity in archaic Greece. There were independent city-states without number, and constant fighting between them. Nevertheless, if politically the Greeks were and remained incurably particularistic, they were also conscious of being all alike members of the Hellenic race, and this consciousness found its expression and its perpetuation in some of their most noteworthy religious institutions. The Greek word *barbaros*, should, down to the end of the fourth century B.C., be rendered in English by "non-Hellenic." For it was applied to all non-Greek races, — to the highly cultured peoples of Egypt or Persia as well as to the uncouth nomads of Scythia or the wild hillsmen of Thrace and the Anatolian uplands. Only from the Hellenistic period onward, when "Hellenic" signified community in culture rather than in race, can *barbaros* justifiably be translated "barbarian." The citation from Herodotus which heads this chapter is taken from the reply made by the Athenians to the Spartans when the latter were afraid that Athens might make a voluntary submission to Persia in 479 B.C. We are justified in thinking that the statement, put into the mouth of the Athenians by the historian, presents the general belief entertained by the Greeks in the fifth century. That the attendance at common sanctuaries of great antiquity, and the periodic celebration of common religious festivals, were prime factors in insuring the essential homogeneity of the Hellenes is beyond dispute.

From very early times there existed in different regions of the Greek world leagues of cities, which were originally formed for a religious purpose. Representatives from a group of *poleis* met periodically at some sanctuary for the joint worship of a common protecting deity. Thus, there was a league of seven cities — four in the Argolid, Aegina, Athens, and Bœotian Orchomenus — whose meeting place was the shrine of Poseidon in the little island of Calaureia off the Argolic peninsula. At Cape Samikon in Triphylia a number of communities in that part of the Peloponnese joined together from time to time in the common worship of the same divinity. Similar religious confederations existed in Bœotia, at Delos, in Thessaly, and in Asia Minor.[1] The best known, and in every way the most important of all, was the Great Amphictiony of twelve tribes which met twice a year, in the spring in the shrine of Demeter at Anthela near Thermopylæ, and in the autumn in Apollo's sanctuary at Delphi. The fact that the members of this league were tribes, not city-states, shows the great antiquity of what was in origin a religious confederation, though, from the sixth century B.C. onward, it at different times exerted considerable political influence.[2] At the deliberations of the Amphictionic league each race or tribe had two votes, so that, in theory, even at a time when Sparta or Athens were the leading states in Greece, these two city-states were only a part of the Dorians and Ionians respectively. In practice, of course, the powerful states largely determined the voting of the tribes to which they belonged, and sometimes that of others as well.

Delphi, the autumn meeting-place of the Amphictiony, was a very ancient cult centre (Cf. Plate 15). It is mentioned in the

[1] The Pan-Ionian confederacy of twelve Ionian cities, whose meeting place was the sanctuary of Poseidon at Mycale, is held by some scholars to be political *in origin*.

[2] Such leagues existed partly for the mutual protection of the members and therefore served some political purpose from the first. This is shown by the wording of the Amphictionic oath, which even in the fourth century B.C. was still quaintly archaic. No member should destroy a city whose people were also members, or cut off their water supply in peace or war.

Homeric poems, being famed already for its riches, while its oracle is consulted by Agamemnon. Literary tradition points to the fact that the worship of the god Apollo was superimposed on an earlier cult of the Earth goddess. Delphi was the most famous oracular seat in the Greek world, and, in spite of occasional vicissitudes, continued to exist down to the later years of the fourth century A.D. Even older, it would seem, was the oracle at Dodona in Epirus, where the shrine was sacred to Zeus and Dione. It also, and "its priests with unwashed feet who couch on the ground" (*Iliad* 16,233), are named by Homer. These two mantic cult-centres surpassed all others in importance. For, though there were many other oracles — among the most notable was that of Apollo at Branchidæ near Miletus — the influence of these was, in general, only local. Dodona, and especially Delphi, were Panhellenic in their appeal and authority. Both oracles were extensively consulted by private persons on all manner of topics, and there can be no doubt that they exerted a weighty influence on human life, and that their advice was seriously regarded by the average Greek. The Delphic oracle, besides, at times wielded great political power. States sought the guidance of the god on matters of policy, and many tales were current about the oracular responses which often allowed of two interpretations. How deeply the oracle's counsel was valued in the earlier period is shown by the regular custom of seeking its advice before sending out a colony. It was not merely asked to approve the colonizing expedition projected by the mother-city, but often indicated the founder's name and the site on which the new settlement should be established.

The sanctuary, which attracted worshippers from every quarter of the Hellenic world, was gradually enriched by dedications and treasure given by pious devotees, by grateful recipients of Apollo's counsel, and by states who took a pride in embellishing this most national of all Hellenic holy places. Even foreign princes who, like Crœsus of Lydia, admired and were to a great extent imbued with Greek culture, lavished gifts on Delphi. Thus, in time, the temple and its precincts became a veritable museum of art, a show-place unrivalled save by Olympia, the hallowed spot on which were held the oldest and the most celebrated of the Greek athletic festivals (Cf. Plate 17).

The importance of the national Games as a unifying force, and their influence on Greek life and manners, were profound. The celebration at Olympia was traditionally two centuries older than the other three national festivals, held respectively• at Delphi, the Isthmus of Corinth, and Nemea in the Argolid.[1] The Olympian and Pythian Games took place every four years, the Isthmian and Nemean every other year. The rules governing the athletic competitions, which, it must be remembered, were held in honor of a god — Zeus at Olympia and Nemea, Apollo at Delphi, Poseidon at the Isthmus — and were essentially sacred institutions, were extremely strict. Some further details about the Olympian festival will serve to illustrate this side of Greek civilization somewhat more fully. The competitors were required to be of pure Greek descent and of unblemished life. Those who, for one reason or another, were not in possession of the full civic rights of their state were ineligible. A long period of training (ten months) was also obligatory. There were separate athletic competitions for boys. Women, with the exception of the priestess of Demeter, were excluded from the celebration, but there was a separate festival for them, the Heræa, at Olympia. The Games took place at the time of the first full moon after the summer solstice, and during their celebration a sacred truce binding on all Hellenes was proclaimed. From the fifth century B.C., if not slightly earlier, the festival attained a far wider significance; it became an immense national Greek assembly, at which the various states vied with one another in providing magnificent equipment for their official delegates. The rewards of the victors at the Games were of the simplest kind, but states rewarded those of their citizens who were successful with high and substantial honors.[2] Thus, at Athens an Olympic victor on his return home was escorted, clad in purple and drawn by white steeds, into the city through a breach made in the city

[1] The traditional date of the first Olympian festival was 776 B.C. The dates recorded for the others were: Pythian festival at Delphi, 586; Isthmia, 582; Nemea, 573. It is probable that before these dates local celebrations had occurred from time to time at the respective sanctuaries.

[2] At Olympia the victor was crowned with a wreath of wild olive. At the Pythia the wreath was first of oak leaves, later of bay leaves. The Isthmian crown was made of wild celery in earlier years, later of pine; while the Nemean was of wild celery.

walls. He received the privilege of dining in the Prytaneum for life as the guest of the state, and a monetary gift as well. It would be quite erroneous to regard such treatment as a mere manifestation of the worship of athleticism. These demonstrations were inspired by strong religious feeling, by an implicit belief that the victor was a special favorite of the gods, and — on the principle of *mens sana in corpore sano* — qualified to perform the highest services for his country, in fact the nearest human approach to the perfect man. It was only from the end of the fifth century that undue specialization began to ruin the old spirit of the Games, and the athletes who competed tended to become more and more a special class, men of brawn with second-rate brains.

The athletic festivals, with their encouragement of the finest physical development of the human form, exerted a powerful and abiding influence on Greek art. They were also an inspiration to Greek literature, above all to the greatest of Greece's lyric poets, Pindar. Let us, in fine, hear the praise bestowed on the Olympian festival by one of the finest of the fourth-century writers. Even if we allow for some idealization, the claim he makes remains fundamentally true. "The men," says Isocrates (*Panegyricus*, 43), "who founded these festival assemblies deserve our praise. By them we are enabled to make truce with each other and interrupt existing enmities and then forgather together in one centre. Thereafter we join in common prayers and sacrifices and recall that we are all of the same kindred. In the future we are more kindly disposed to each other, and renew old guest friendships and form new ones, and that sojourn is of value to competitors and non-competitors alike."

It is probable that the despots of the sixth century did much to further the development and enlarge the scope of these national festivals. To Peisistratus belongs the credit of reconstituting several Attic festivals and religious celebrations in such a way that, within a century, they had ceased to be of merely local interest and were attended by visitors from all parts of the Greek world. The worship at Eleusis of the two goddesses, Demeter and her daughter, Kore (Persephone), with whom were associated several lesser male deities or heroes, was of great antiquity. The earliest literary reference to this

cult is in the seventh-century Hymn to Demeter; its inclusion
in the Athenian state religion is at least as old as Solon's time.
The celebrations took place every year, but it was probably
Peisistratus who instituted more elaborate ceremonies, to take
place every four years. The chief religious offices in connection
with the cult were hereditary in certain families. The general
superintendence of the festival was entrusted to the archon
basileus and four other officials. If we include all preliminaries,
the entire celebration, which took place in the autumn, lasted
eight or nine days. The culminating ceremonies, a solemn
procession from Athens to Eleusis and the performance of the
Mysteries, occurred on the last two days. The initiated were
vowed to strict silence about what they had seen and done,
and there is much uncertainty about the nature of the mystic
rites on the last day. Apparently certain sacred objects were
shown to the *mystai*, who also witnessed a religio-dramatic
performance dealing with the grief of Demeter at the loss of
her daughter and her joy when reunited with Kore. The up-
lifting effect on the worshippers is too well attested by the
best classical writers to be doubted. Unlike the ordinary formal
ceremonies of the state religion, the Mysteries satisfied man's
emotional and spiritual craving and held out to him the hope
of happiness after death. All Greeks, provided they were un-
tainted by any religious pollution, might participate in the
festival and, after the needful period of probation, become
initiated. Thus the Eleusinian Mysteries became one of the
important Panhellenic cults.

In the first month of the Attic year, corresponding to part of
July and August, it had been the custom from early times to
celebrate at Athens a festival in honor of the goddess Athena,
Guardian of the City (Polias), which lasted from six to nine
days. It was due to the initiative of Peisistratus that in the
third year of every Olympiad the celebrations were conducted
on a more magnificent scale. This four-yearly festival was
known thereafter as the Greater Panathenæa. There were
gymnastic and equestrian contests; the Pyrrhic war dance,
supposed to have been introduced from Laconia in the time of
Solon or Peisistratus, was performed by troops of armed men,
the successful team being rewarded with the prize of an ox; the

"muster of men" was another team competition, in which the best-looking and fittest men from each tribe paraded. From Peisistratic days there was also a musical contest between rhapsodists who recited portions of the Homeric poems; other musical competitions were added in the following century. The prize in the athletic events was a large amphora filled with olive oil, and a garland of olive leaves. Innumerable specimens of these Panathenaic amphoræ, varying in date from the sixth century to the Hellenistic period, have survived and now adorn the museums of Europe and America (Plate 16a). The shape of the vases and the decoration are more or less constant. One side was adorned with a figure of Athena in full armor, the other with a picture of, or allusion to, the competition for which the vase was won. The outstanding ceremony of the Greater Panathenæa was a solemn procession from the city of Athens to the Acropolis, in which both citizens and resident aliens took part. A robe (*peplos*), spread sail fashion on a ship's mast fixed on rollers, was conducted to the foot of the citadel and then carried up to the temple of the goddess on the Acropolis, where it was solemnly dedicated to Athena. A great sacrifice was also performed on an altar in front of the temple. A regatta at Peiræus, in which crews from each tribe competed, formed the after-celebration. The Panathenaic procession is known not merely from literary sources, but is plastically represented on the frieze which ran round the cella wall of the Parthenon, the new temple to Athena on the Acropolis built in the Periclean age.[1]

The worship of Dionysus, god of the vine, with its strongly emotional and even orgiastic celebrations, was well established among the rural population of Attica by the seventh century. In the time of Peisistratus no less than three festivals in honor of this deity took place each year, the Lenæa in January, the Rural Dionysia in December, and the Greater Dionysia in Athens itself during March. Of these three the last was either newly instituted or else completely reorganized by the Tyrant.[2]

[1] See below, page 382, and Plates 24, 25, and 26.

[2] The festival which at Athens became the Greater Dionysia is said to have been transferred by Peisistratus from Eleutheræ to his capital. This new celebration may, however, have been superimposed on an older Dionysiac festival in Athens. This is not the place to enter into the numer-

By his action the worship of Dionysus became a part of the
state religion of Athens. More momentous, however, was
the stimulus which the institution of this festival gave to the
development of the Attic drama. The singing of choral songs
in honor of the god, accompanied by ritual dances, had long
been customary. A dramatic element was introduced into
the performance only when the choirs were occasionally interrupted by a dialogue between the leader of the chorus and
another, who at first may well have been the poet himself.
Tradition makes Thespis the "father of tragedy" and the
first victor in a dramatic contest held at Athens in 534–533 B.C.
But for fifty years after that date nothing is known of the
scope and character of the dramatic performances held at the
Greater Dionysia. Only from the time of the Persian wars
can the history of Attic drama be clearly traced.

The Age of Tyrants corresponded to the century and a half
which was the formative period of Greek art, the age when
Greek lyric poetry all but reached its zenith, the age in which
implicit belief in the old polytheistic religion and the mythologies and cosmogonies of earlier centuries was succeeded by
scepticism and the spirit of inquiry on the part of a few bold
speculators. The patronage of absolute rulers and their desire
to beautify their cities acted as a powerful stimulus to artistic
achievement. At Corinth and in other centres the despots
erected temples and public buildings at great expense. Poets
and artists, whose creative work could shed lustre on, or help
to give distinction to, the city in which they found a temporary
or a permanent home, were welcomed by the Tyrants. As
usual, our information is fullest for Athens. Peisistratus rebuilt the temple of Athena on the Acropolis and constructed
the earliest initiation hall (*Telesterion*) at Eleusis over the site
of an older sanctuary. Both structures were fated to be destroyed by the Persians in 480–479 B.C. He also began to
build a temple at Athens in honor of Zeus Olympios; but it
was not completed by him and his sons, and remained a fragment for many centuries. The poets Anacreon and Simonides

---

ous problems connected with the origin of tragedy and comedy. The
reader interested in these questions is referred to the works enumerated
in the Bibliography.

were honored guests at the court of Hippias and Hipparchus, while Peisistratus' zeal on behalf of religion has already been noted.

In the cultural evolution of the Hellenic race the Greeks of Asia Minor can justly claim to have been pioneers in every field. Early examples of Ionian art, moreover, like the ivories and other *objets d'art* found below the sixth-century temple of Artemis at Ephesus and belonging to the late eighth and early seventh centuries, show very plainly the study of non-Hellenic, that is to say, Eastern, prototypes by Ionian artists and craftsmen. Similar oriental influence can also be observed in mainland products, such as the ivory plaques from Sparta, or the decorative designs of Corinthian, and, to a less extent, of Laconian pottery. The earliest Greek sculptures in the round, however, and the earliest Doric architecture, seem to owe more to Egyptian models. Yet it was not long before the individuality of the Hellenic artist in either sphere asserted itself, and totally new art forms were evolved.

Though private dwelling-houses were at this time, and remained for centuries, of the simplest character, more stable and impressive edifices in honor of the gods were erected. Of the nature and appearance of other public buildings in this age we can, in the absence of remains, form no accurate estimate. The two styles of architecture known as Doric and Ionic developed contemporaneously. The former may be called Western, the latter Eastern, in this sense: In Sicily and Magna Græcia the Ionic order was rarely met with, while in Asia Minor the Doric was equally unpopular. In Greece both styles coexisted, but, judging by the extant remains, the Doric order was in much greater favor. The earliest shrines were small rectangular structures fronted with a vestibule, the entablature, roof, and pillars, where these were employed, being of wood. A great advance was reached when larger temples began to be set up and the rectangular building (cella) itself was surrounded by pillars, thus forming a continuous ambulatory (peristyle) round the outside of the cella. Wooden pillars were replaced by columns of limestone or marble, and finally the whole upper structure also was built of stone. In the remains of early Doric temples like the Heræum at Olympia (seventh century; *see* Plate 17*a*) and the old temple at Corinth (sixth century) and some early examples in Sicily, perfect symmetry of all the columns is still absent, and the individual columns are too short and heavy and generally of a clumsy appearance. The triangular gables formed by the ends of the roof at the short sides of the temple, *i.e.* at the east and west ends, were often decorated with sculptures. Fragments of such pedimental groups which once adorned temples on the Athenian Acropolis of the pre-Peisistratic and Peisistratic ages, though their execution is still crude, show considerable skill in their arrangement, so as to fit into a triangular space. One depicts Heracles doing battle with the Hydra, while his charioteer, Iolaus, stands by with the chariot. Another shows the same hero and the Old Man of the sea in one half of the pediment and in the other half a bearded figure of benevolent aspect having three bodies ending in long snaky coils which taper off into the corner of the gable. Yet another group contained amongst other figures a realistic portrayal of a lioness devouring a bull. Of somewhat later date was a presentation in marble of Athena standing in triumph over a prostrate giant whom she has transfixed; on either side some male figures are approaching towards the conqueress, the corners of the pediment being filled by two recumbent giants. The effect for the spectator, who would necessarily contemplate the pediments from some distance off, was heightened by a lavish use of color both on the sculpture and on the architectural details of the entablature. The colors also disguised the poor material used for most of these groups; the crudity of the pigments would be more effective from afar than delicate tints. The custom of using coloration freely on statues and on buildings continued in the finest period of Greek art.

While the general plan of Ionic temples was very similar to that of the Doric, the columns rested on bases instead of directly on the stylobate, were of slenderer proportions, and were crowned with a volute capital in place of the plain Doric capital. The decoration of the entablature was also characterized by somewhat greater elaboration of detail, the architrave being surmounted by a continuous frieze instead of by a succession of separate plain or sculptured slabs (metopes) separated by triglyphs, as was the case in a Doric temple. The decoration

a

b

DELPHI: *a*. Temple of Apollo; *b*. Colonnade of the Athenians with Polygonal Wall behind

Plate 15

b

THE FRANÇOIS VASE

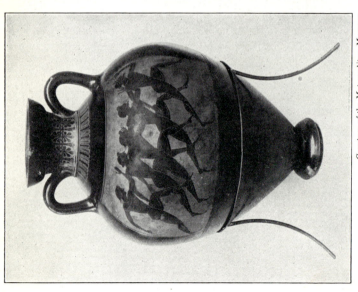

Courtesy of the Metropolitan Museum

a

PANATHENAIC AMPHORA (A Footrace)

Plate 16

of the lowest drums of columns, and of their bases, with sculptures in high relief, which is found in the sixth- and again in the fourth-century temple of Artemis at Ephesus, was an unusual addition to the plastic decoration of a temple. Such ornamentation was indeed in questionable taste and was not generally adopted.

Specimens of archaic sculpture in the round and in relief are much more numerous than examples of early architecture. There is a very great variety in the detail of the statues, and their number is so considerable that all stages in artistic development are represented, from the crudest figure, in which little more than the head and extremities are indicated, the torso being flat or round, but hardly suggesting the human form, to statues of the end of the sixth or the beginning of the fifth century, in which the artist has attained almost complete mastery in portraying free movement and life-like expression, and in reproducing all with anatomical exactness. The two chief types are nude male and draped female figures, both represented in a standing attitude. To the former the name "Apollo" has rather arbitrarily been given. Statues of this class have been found in various districts and their main characteristics are the same. The man is entirely nude and stands with hands and arms glued stiffly to his sides; only at the elbows are the arms free from the body. The left leg is always advanced a little way in front of the right. The facial expression is fixed, the man staring straight in front of him. The eyes are prominent, the inner corners being well marked, while both lids are rather accentuated. The mouth is usually curved slightly upwards, the result being an expressionless grin which has been dubbed "the archaic smile." In matters of detail, of course, there are many differences. Sometimes the torso is slender, sometimes square and thickset; and some are technically superior to others. It is easier, because of the abundant material available, to trace a continuous evolution of an art form in the case of the draped female figures. In the earliest examples the lower half of the statue is little more than a shapeless block, square or round. On the upper part of the torso the breasts are roughly indicated. The position is stiff and erect with feet close together and arms pressed to the sides. The expression of the

face, as in the male statues, is a staring half smile. In more
developed examples the left leg is advanced and the arms also
receive more life-like treatment, since one is often folded across
the breast and perhaps clasping some object, or else the lower
arm is extended so as to be quite free. The drapery, too, is
instructive; at first a shapeless lump, it is later on studied more
carefully by the artist, so that the folds are represented and an
attempt is even made to indicate the human figure beneath.
A whole series of draped female figures was recovered on the
Athenian Acropolis. They may have been votive offerings set
up by the worshippers of Athena and were overthrown when
Athens was sacked by the Persians in 480. These "maidens,"
or, as more facetious persons have dubbed them, "aunts," illustrate every stage of artistic development, from the most
primitive to the completely naturalistic, both in the treatment
of the draperies, which are extremely complicated on the latest
statues, and of the face. On one of the most beautiful and most
recent in date the upper lip is straight; the "archaic smile"
has given place to a look of wistful sadness. Most of these
statues were made in several pieces. The effect of the carefully
chiselled draperies was further enhanced by decorative patterns
applied in paint.

A third class of archaic statue represented persons seated and
draped. A series of these lined the sacred way that led from
Miletus to the temple of Apollo at Branchidæ. They were
above life size and portrayed male and female dedicators of
offerings to the god. A more advanced technique is exhibited
by the statue of Athena dedicated on the Athenian Acropolis
by one Callias and made by Endoios. The goddess, robed and
wearing her ægis, has her arms raised and free from the elbows.
The right leg is bare to the knee, the right foot being not flat
on the ground but resting on the toes. Reliefs also afford a
valuable indication of the rapid progress of Greek art in these
earlier centuries. We cannot here mention more than a very
few examples. From Laconia come several funerary or "hero"
reliefs. Their technique is peculiar, for they were cut in parallel
flat planes, of which there might be as many as five. The best
known of them, now in the Berlin Museum, shows the dead
man and his wife seated and facing right. They are approached

from the right by two worshippers carrying offerings. These
are on a much smaller scale than the heroized dead. On some
metopes from a sixth century temple at Selinus in Sicily the
unknown artist has essayed, not wholly without success, to
depict several ambitious subjects from mythology, for instance,
Perseus slaying Medusa and Europa riding on the bull. A
little later in date and noticeably more advanced in technique
and design are the remains of a frieze from the Treasury of the
Sicyonians at Delphi and of metopes from the Athenian Treasury in the same holy place. In spite of errors in perspective, occasional stiffness in grouping, and the same wooden expression
that is found on the faces of the statues, there is a greater freedom in the general treatment of the various reliefs than in that
of contemporary sculpture in the round.

The extant examples of early Greek sculpture are almost
exclusively in stone. The earliest pedimental figures from the
Athenian Acropolis are in soft poros; limestone was occasionally
used, but in the majority of cases the material is marble. Of
this there were in the Aegean area a good many varieties, but
the most popular were that from the island of Paros and that
quarried on Mt. Pentelicus in Attica.

The invention of hollow-casting in bronze made possible the
creation of life-size statues in this substance. Though very
few bronze figures — other than small statuettes — have survived from antiquity, there is abundant evidence to show that
in the archaic period certain artists or schools of artists employed metal in preference to stone. The islands of Samos and
Chios both produced noted artists in the sixth century. The
art was handed down from father to son, and in the case of one
Chiote family we have the names of artists belonging to four
successive generations. This family of sculptors worked exclusively in marble; their contemporaries and, we may say,
rivals in Samos specialized in bronze-casting. In the centuries
that follow bronze was the favorite material for single statues
in the round.

Finally, in the seventh and especially in the sixth century
the art of vase-painting made astonishing strides. Different
localities produced different styles of decoration, the most artistically striking development being perhaps found in the vases

made by potters resident in Athens. The true black-figure
style of painting belongs to the age of Peisistratus and his sons.
The body of the vase was red, the color of the fine clay from
Cape Colias intensified by the addition of red ochre. The
design was in a lustrous black varnish, purple and white being
used sparingly as accessory colors. The shapes and the subjects represented were exceedingly varied. A fine early example
is the handsome crater, signed by the potter Ergotimos and the
painter Klitias, which is now at Florence (Plate 16b). There
are no less than five friezes of ornamentation on this masterpiece of ceramic art besides the decorative panels on the handles
and the decoration on the foot of the vase. The best known
craftsmen at Athens in the second half of the sixth century were
Exekias, Amasis — the former probably, the latter certainly, a
foreigner — and Nicosthenes. The last named was an artist
of the transition period, who, besides his black-figure vases,
also experimented in white designs on a black ground and in the
red-figure technique that reached its full development in the
following century. He even combined the black figure and red
figure on one and the same vase, choosing one for the interior
and the other for the exterior ornamentation.

CHAPTER XIII

LITERATURE AND THOUGHT IN THE ARCHAIC PERIOD

> *Let us pour libation to the Muses, daughters*
> *of Memory, and to their lord, Leto's son.* — Ter-
> pander, *Fragment* 3.

THE rise and spread of Greek literature would hardly have
been possible but for the invention of the alphabet. It is uncertain at what date the Greeks first became acquainted with
the Phœnician alphabet; but once they had been familiarized
with the Semitic symbols, they rapidly adapted them to the
needs of their own tongue. Some superfluous consonantal signs
they used to express the vowels, which in Phœnician, as in other
Semitic languages, were not written, and they also added four
new letters to the alphabet. No extant Greek inscriptions are
demonstrably older than the latter part of the seventh century,
but the beginning of Greek writing is likely to be at least a
hundred years earlier. Moreover, the invention spread to all
parts of the Hellenic world, and local differences in the forms,
and sometimes in the value, of individual letters arose. We
can in fact distinguish two main groups, an eastern and a
western. The former includes the cities of the seaboard of
Asia Minor and the Aegean islands, the latter the communities
of northern Greece and of the Peloponnesus. Athens, Corinth
and her colonies, Argos, and some other states of central Greece
occupy an intermediate position between those two extremes.
In addition there were minor variations in the usage of different
members of each group, which disappeared but slowly. The
Ionians were once again in the van of progress. Their letters
proved to be best adapted for all purposes, and, ultimately, the
Ionic alphabet was universally employed, although uniformity
was not finally achieved till the middle of the fourth century.

We have no means of knowing when the Homeric poems were

first committed to writing; but, whether handed down orally or set down in the new script, they found many imitators. Save for a few fragments these lesser poems of the epic cycle have disappeared. But a group of shorter poems, written in hexameter verse, the so-called *Homeric Hymns*, has survived. They are hymns in honor of certain gods, Apollo, Demeter, Hermes, and so on, but they are not all of the same date. The earliest may go back to the end of the eighth century, others do not antedate the sixth, showing how long the epic tradition lasted even after other and more popular forms of poetry had been created. The Greeks of the classical period were wont to associate with the name of Homer that of Hesiod. He lived at Ascra in Bœotia at the end of the eighth or the beginning of the seventh century. Of three works that have come down to us under his name, the *Works and Days* is certainly, the *Theogony* probably, a genuine work of the poet. The *Shield of Heracles* is a composition of later date and inferior merit. While the *Theogony* is a history of the creation of the world and of the gods, which the Greeks of later centuries regarded together with the Homeric poems as canonical, the *Works and Days* is a didactic epic, which is very loosely knit together and really falls into two unequal parts. The first and shorter section briefly traces the five ages of man, the longer portion depicts farm life in Bœotia, and provides many practical instructions for the farmer together with a goodly list of ill-omened actions which he should sedulously avoid. A short citation from the poem, which is written in hexameters, will help to illustrate its practical good sense and rustic tones:

But when the House Carrier (*i.e.* the snail) crawls up the plants from the ground, fleeing from the Pleiades, then is it no longer seasonable to dig about the vines, but rather to sharpen sickles and arouse the thralls, and to fly shady seats and sleep toward the dawn, in the season of harvest when the sun parcheth the skin. In that season must thou busy thee to lead the harvest home, rising up in the morning that thy livelihood may be secure. . . . But what time the artichoke bloometh and the chattering cicala sitting on a tree poureth his shrill song from beneath his wings incessantly in the season of weary summer, then are goats fattest and wine best, women most wanton and men most weak, since Sirios parcheth head and knee and the skin is dry for heat.[1]

[1] *Works and Days* (transl. by A. W. Mair), ll. 571 ff.

Experiments in iambic and elegiac verse must have been made at a very early date, for by the seventh century both had been developed to a high degree of excellence. Little, if at all, later in date are various lyric metres. The poems composed in these were all intended to be sung to the accompaniment of the lyre. Thus a great quantity of poetry, much of it doubtless of first-rate quality, was put out in the two centuries preceding the Persian wars; but, save for a miserable remnant of citations preserved in later Greek writers, slightly augmented in recent years by the recovery of some additional fragments in Egyptian *papyri*, all this body of literature has been lost. Of the nature of the music which accompanied the lyric compositions we are entirely ignorant. Again the eastern Greeks were intellectually in advance of their mainland kinsmen. Archilochus of Paros (*c.* 650 B.C.) served as a mercenary soldier and spent some part of his life in Thasos before finally returning to his native island. He composed elegiac poetry in which he depicted episodes of his own life, and hymns to the gods which he wrote in the iambic, not the epic, metre. But he was most famous for his bitter lampoons and satire in iambics on some of his contemporaries, above all, on a well-to-do citizen of Paros, Lycambes, and his daughters, one of whom the poet had unsuccessfully wooed. In this last genre of poetry, satiric verse, Archilochus had his imitators and successors, notably Semonides of Amorgos and Hipponax of Clazomenæ, but none of them seems to have been his equal either in power or in diction. The contempt in which these poets, and for that matter Hesiod also, speak of the female sex suggests that under Ionian influence the position of women in some parts of the Greek world had changed considerably since Homeric days.

Elegiac poetry had many exponents: Callinus of Ephesus (*c.* 650 B.C.) and his contemporary, Tyrtæus of Sparta, Mimnermus of Colophon in the next generation, and the Athenian Solon, and Theognis of Megara in the sixth century. Judging by the surviving fragments, we can see that any of a large variety of subjects was regarded as suitable for treatment in this verse form. Callinus called on his countrymen to perform deeds of prowess against the Cimmerian invaders. Tyrtæus similarly strove to fire the Spartan warriors to utmost valor against the Messenians. Solon used the elegy to express his philosophy of life and particularly voiced therein his reflections on the politically troubled times during which he lived. Thus, after enumerating existing evils, he concludes:[1]

This is the warning my heart bids me give the men of Athens: bad laws bring ills innumerable upon a city, but good laws display all things in good order and in their proper place and simultaneously lay shackles on the unjust. They make rough places smooth, check greed, blot out insolence, and cause the growing flowers of guilt to wither. They make straight crooked customs, quell deeds of arrogance and end deeds of faction. They end the wrath that comes of grievous strife, and under their sway all things are rightly and prudently ordered among men.

Mimnermus and Theognis sing of love and friendship, seek to instil moral maxims, and, like Solon, express their views on contemporary affairs. Early lyric poetry is especially associated with the island of Lesbos. Here Terpander (c. 650) is said to have founded a school of lyric bards. But it is in the first half of the next century that the two most famous singers of this island flourished, Alcæus and Sappho. The former was deeply implicated in the political disturbances in the island which led finally to the appointment of Pittacus as legislator and quasi-dictator for ten years. Alcæus, with other recalcitrant members of the Lesbian aristocracy, was compelled to go into exile; nor did he mince his words when he wrote:[2]

With one voice they have set up the base-born Pittacus to be tyrant of their spiritless and ill-starred country, shouting his praise by their thousands.

His contemporary, Sappho, also suffered banishment with her relatives for a space, but eventually a general amnesty enabled the political exiles to return to Mytilene. Alcæus' poems appear to have dealt with a great variety of themes — his political fortunes, his wanderings, love, and the joys of the wine-cup.

Let us drink; why wait for the lamp-lighting? the day has but a finger's breadth to go. Take down the great cups, beloved friend, from

[1] Solon, *Fragment* 4. The translation is taken from M. L. W. Laistner, *Greek Economics*, p. 2.
[2] Alcæus, *Fragment* 160, in J. M. Edmonds, *Lyra Graeca* i, p. 419.

a

b

OLYMPIA: *a*. Temple of Hera; *b*. Temple of Zeus

Plate 17

the cupboard; for the son of Semele and Zeus gave wine to make us forget our cares. Pour bumpers in a mixture of one and two, and let cup chase cup around hotfoot.[1]

He had an unrivalled gift of vivid description, as can be seen from one of the longer extant fragments: [2]

I cannot tell the lie of the wind; one wave rolls from this quarter, another from that, and we are carried in the midst with the black ship, labouring in an exceeding great storm. The water is up to the mast-hole, the sail lets daylight through with the great rents that are in it, and the halyards are working loose.

A late writer in quoting these lines informs us that in them there is a hidden warning to Alcæus' countrymen against a potential tyrant. Sappho's lyrics covered a more restricted field of subjects. She composed a number of wedding hymns (*epithalamia*) of which but a few lines have survived; but her most famous poems were inspired by personal passion for the girl pupils whom she instructed in dance and song. Her best known stanzas, in the metre named after her, have been turned into English Sapphics by John Addington Symonds with singular felicity:

Peer of Gods he seemeth to me, the blissful
Man who sits and gazes at thee before him,
Close beside thee sits, and in silence hears thee
    Silverly speaking,

Laughing love's low laughter. Oh this, this only
Stirs the troubled heart in my breast to tremble!
For should I but see thee a little moment,
    Straight is my voice hushed;

Yea, my tongue is broken, and through and through me
'Neath the flesh impalpable fire runs tingling;
Nothing see mine eyes, and a noise of roaring
    Waves in my ear sounds;

Sweat runs down in rivers, a tremor seizes
All my limbs, and paler than grass in autumn,
Caught by pains of menacing death, I falter,
    Lost in the love-trance.

[1] *Fragment* 163 (*op. cit.* p. 421).   [2] *Fragment* 37 (*op. cit.* p. 345).

The ancient critic, to whose fortunate habit of citation we owe the preservation of these passionate verses, comments as follows: [1]

Are you not amazed how at one instant she summons, as though they were all alien from herself and dispersed, soul, body, ears, tongue, eyes, colour? Uniting contradictions, she is, at one and the same time, hot and cold, in her senses and out of her mind, for she is either terrified or at the point of death. The effect desired is that not one passion only should be seen in her, but a concourse of the passions. All such things occur in the case of lovers, but it is, as I said, the selection of the most striking of them and their combination into a single whole that has produced the singular excellence of the passage.

To modern readers the remains, scanty though they be, of Alcæus and Sappho have always had a special appeal, because they are pervaded with the poets' personal feelings and experiences. Added to this dominantly subjective tone — a thing rare in Greek poetry, at least before the Hellenistic age — is the simple beauty of the language and the subtle rhythm of the lines, qualities which no translation — even one so good as Symonds' — can adequately reproduce.

Among the writers of choral lyrics the best known was Alcman. Though not a Spartan by birth — he is said to have come from Lydia — Alcman spent most of his adult life in Laconia and wrote his poems in the Doric dialect. His hymns, of which only one substantial fragment remains, were composed to be sung antiphonally by two groups of girl singers at religious celebrations. Their content was partly mythological, partly in praise of the leaders of the choirs. We may conclude this brief sketch of early Greek poets with a reference to Stesichorus. Unlike the other poets already named, he came from the far West, from Himera in northern Sicily. He was in every sense an innovator. Several ancient critics — amongst them the author of the treatise, *On the Sublime*, and Quintilian — coupled his name with Homer's, doubtless because he was the first who sought to use lyric poetry as a medium for long narratives dealing with heroic and mythological subjects. Although not enough of his verse has been preserved to permit a proper estimate of his poetic powers, and although he does not seem to have found any direct imitators, he probably exerted an

---

[1] [Longinus], *On the Sublime* 10, 3 (W. Rhys Roberts' translation).

indirect influence on lyric poets of the next generation, like Pindar and Bacchylides, in whose epinician odes stories from Greek mythology have a regular place.

Great as was the cultural progress of the Hellenes during the sixth century, as manifested in their art and poetic literature, those hundred years witnessed a yet greater achievement, revolutionary in character, — no less than the birth of science and philosophical speculation. Once more it was certainly Greeks of Ionia who first took the tremendous step — for such indeed it was — of setting aside the mythologies and crude cosmogonies of the poets and the more esoteric doctrines concerning the creation of the world, the gods, and mankind, held by the adherents of a mystery religion, like Orphism, and of setting man's reason in the place of faith.[1]

The first bold speculator whose name has been recorded as questioning the received explanations of the Universe was Thales of Miletus. Ancients and moderns alike have justly regarded him as the father of philosophy and science. We know little of his life beyond the fact that he was an influential statesman in his native city, and that he had become familiar with the astronomy of the Egyptians and Chaldæans. Whether he acquired his knowledge by travelling himself to these regions we do not know, nor is it necessary to assume that he did. For the settlement of Greeks at Naucratis, made in the seventh century with the good-will of the Egyptian monarch, had stimulated intercourse between the land of the Nile and the Aegean cities; while the lore of the Middle East could readily reach the West through Lydia. Making the best use of what he had learnt, Thales, we are informed, foretold a solar eclipse which occurred in 585 B.C. Had he done nothing more than make the mathematical and astronomical lore of the Orient

---

[1] The adherents of the Orphic sect seem to have been found in all parts of the Hellenic world. They had a sacred literature of their own, chiefly of a prophetic character. Their cult was untrammelled by the limitations imposed on the official religion of the city-state. The central doctrine of their system was the belief in the immortality of the soul. The sufferings of earthly life are a punishment for transgressions committed in an earlier existence and the soul suffers many reincarnations. But the hope of final redemption was held out to those who lived an ascetic and morally pure life, and were strict observers of the ritual prescribed to the initiates.

his own, his accomplishment would have been noteworthy and doubtless influential in that age. But his real and epoch-making achievement was that he was not content merely to record observed phenomena of nature, but that he deduced therefrom the general conclusion that all nature is subject to fixed laws, and asked himself the question, "What is the world made of?" In more philosophical terms, he was the first to inquire into the material cause of the Universe. That his solution of the problem was crude, namely, that water was the primordial substance, is of secondary importance. It was he who began the process of rational inquiry, which subsequent speculators carried many stages farther and to more scientific conclusions. Thales does not seem to have committed anything to writing, but he had at least one eminent disciple, Anaximander. He not only propounded a less simple but more profound explanation than his master of the growth of the physical Universe, deriving all four "elements" from a primordial mist or vapor, which he called "the Unlimited," but he interested himself in geography and was reputed to have constructed the first map of the world. Anaximenes, a younger contemporary of Anaximander, in one sense returned to the earlier position of Thales, inasmuch as he found the original substance in one of the "elements," air. In reality, however, his rationalism was more marked than that of either of his predecessors, since he explained the genesis of the other three "elements," and of the heavenly bodies, from air by condensation and rarefaction, such as he could observe in his actual experience.

In the meantime a new line of inquiry and explanation had been begun by two Ionian Greeks, who, toward the end of the sixth century, had found their way to the West. Pythagoras of Samos left his native land in or soon after 530 B.C., perhaps for political reasons — Samos being then ruled by the Tyrant Polycrates — and emigrated to Croton in southern Italy. Primarily he was a mathematician; but to the world at large he was more familiar as an educator and the founder of a semi-philosophical, semi-religious brotherhood, whose members were vowed to secrecy and to an ascetic life not unlike the followers of Orphism. Indeed, Pythagoras borrowed some of his religious teaching, including the doctrine of transmigration of souls, from this source. He has the distinction of being the first to propound that the earth is not flat but a sphere, and to evolve a doctrine which came very near to being the heliocentric theory of the Universe. The sun, moon, and planets, including the earth itself, are endowed with motion, he taught, and revolve around a central fire. This part of Pythagoras' teaching remained without influence, partly because so bold a generalization could not hold its own against the less lofty but more intelligible tenets of the Ionian school, mainly, however, because Pythagoras himself sought a solution for everything in mathematics, that is to say in numbers, to which he assigned a mystical significance. Even so, both his mathematical discoveries — *e.g.* the theory of progressions which he applied also successfully to acoustics, discovering that the length of a taut string stands in a fixed relation to the pitch of the tone emitted when the string is struck — and his philosophico-religious doctrines exerted a profound influence on later philosophers.

His contemporary, Xenophanes of Colophon, found a new home at Elea in southern Italy, though much of his life seems to have been spent in travel. He was not so much a philosopher as a poet and moralist, who in his verse criticized severely the anthropomorphic and anthropopathic religion of his countrymen, and preached a monotheistic belief in "one God, greater than any god or man, unlike man in form or thought, directing all things without labor by the thought of his mind, ever staying in the same place motionless."

Though Xenophanes is generally described as the founder of the Eleatic school of philosophy, its real founder was his pupil, Parmenides. He constructed an elaborate philosophical system in which he differentiated between Being, or a universal element of nature, which alone can be the object of knowledge, and an infinite plurality of modifications which can only be the object of opinion. His difficult but important metaphysical doctrines he expounded in a long hexameter poem of which some fragments alone survive. Finally we may mention Heracleitus of Ephesus who, though he probably did not die till *c.* 475 B.C., in a philosophical sense belongs essentially to the previous generation. He was a more thorough sceptic than any of the thinkers already named. In contrast to Pythagoras, or Parmenides, or, for that matter, to the Ionian physicists, he insisted that not Being but Becoming was the ultimate reality of the Universe. The world is constantly dying, he maintained, and constantly being reborn, and above all there is Reason (*logos*) which rules it, which "guides all things through all things"; he refers to this also as Fire, because that is the purest form in which this divine life is perceptible to human eyes or senses. Heracleitus' teaching, though for many years it did not perhaps win many adherents — his uncompromising and hostile attitude to other speculators and systems, and the obscurity of his own writings had much to do with this neglect — exercised a profound influence at the beginning of the third century B.C. on the early Stoics.

The thinkers whom we have considered, when they committed their tenets to writing at all, did so in verse. It was not until the latter part of the sixth century that prose compositions were attempted by the Anatolian and the mainland Greeks. The earliest prose writers were compilers of genealogies and chroniclers like Pherecydes of Athens(?) and Acusilaus of Argos. They dealt with the epic stories of various heroes to whom the historic Greeks traced back their descent, gathered together and compared local traditions, and drew up genealogies. Their treatment exhibited a certain degree of rational criticism and their antiquarian researches prepared the way for the historical writing of the next generation. The most interesting of these authors was, however, Hecatæus of Miletus. His date is fixed by the fact that he advised his fellow Milesians against undertaking the Ionian revolt in 499 B.C. Hecatæus' scientific interest was in geography. He improved the map of Anaximander, and wrote a long explanatory work about it. Nor did he confine himself strictly to geographical data. He occasionally added information about the customs and mode of life of peoples in different parts of the world; at other times he included useful *data* about the *flora* and *fauna* of particular regions. Hecatæus also composed a genealogical work in which he exercised more criticism than his predecessors in this field; but it was far less influential than the other compilation, which Herodotus half a century later did not disdain to use with some freedom for his history.

CHAPTER XIV

THE NEAR AND MIDDLE EAST IN THE SIXTH CENTURY B.C.

> *Darius the King says: Under the protection of
> Ahura Mazda, these are the countries which do
> that which I place on them as commands; countries
> which muster here; Persia, Media, and other lands
> and other tongues; the mountains and the level
> country of this side of the sea and the other side
> of the sea, of this side of the desert land and of
> the other side of the desert land. All that I have
> done I have accomplished under the protection of
> Ahura Mazda. May Ahura Mazda, together with
> all the gods, protect me and my rule.* — Inscrip-
> tion of Darius at Persepolis.

THE downfall of Assyria resulted from a hostile coalition
formed against her by her neighbors. To keep secure hold of
Babylonia was a problem which many Assyrian kings had
found difficult, not because its population was unruly, but
because the ruler of Babylon, whether independent or a provincial governor appointed by the Assyrian monarch, was in a
strong position, if he wished, to dispute Assyrian supremacy
in the Land of the Two Rivers. Babylon had suffered cruelly
more than once; most severe was her punishment when captured
and sacked by Sennacherib. In Ashurbanipal's reign it was
the disaffection of his brother, the governor of Babylon, which
brought about the most serious threat to his authority that
Ashurbanipal had to face. During the last quarter of the
seventh century Babylonia was independent. Its one-time
governor, Nabopolassar, had himself proclaimed independent
king of Babylon in 625 B.C., and he seems to have been a man
whose ability was not unworthy of his ambition. The Assyrian
king was too harassed on his northern and eastern borders, and
his kingdom too weakened by internal dissensions, to bring the
disloyal governor to order.

Little is known of these eastern neighbors of Assyria, the Medes. They were an Indo-European people who had migrated apparently from Scythia (*i.e.* southern Russia) into Armenia. Finding the kingdom of Van too strong to be occupied or over-run, they had borne off to the southeast, to find a home on the western side of the Iranian plateau. The date of their settle-ment in that region can only be guessed. It probably occurred about 1000 B.C. At this time, and for many years to come, the Medes were a pastoral people. There were, we are told, six tribes, each containing a number of smaller groups or clans. While the régime of the family and clan was strictly patriarchal, there was evidently no more developed system of political organization. The clans seem to have lived more or less inde-pendently; sometimes, too, they warred among themselves. But, in the face of a foreign foe or invader, the Median tribes stood together to repel the common enemy of them all. In the Assyrian annals there are occasional references to this people and to the attacks of Assyrian kings. In a record of Shalmaneser III two peoples are named who may, with great probability, be identified as the Medes and their southern neighbors, the Persians. The last named were akin in race and speech to the Medes. They had probably migrated southward from northern Khorasan, ultimately to find a home in southern Iran (the region corresponding approximately to the modern Persian province of Fars). Separated from Assyria only by the Zagros mountains and, as it were, sitting astride the main highway from Mesopotamia into Iran and beyond, the Medes were naturally brought into contact with their Semitic neighbors earlier than were their kinsmen of the southern plateau. The Assyrian king, Shamshi-Adad IV, invaded Media and com-pelled its inhabitants to pay tribute. Further Assyrian ex-peditions into Media are mentioned in the Assyrian records during the eighth century, in the time of Adad-Nirari and Tig-lath-Pileser III. The latter's task of subduing the Medes seems to have been facilitated by the disunion of the Median tribes among themselves, contrary to their usual solidarity. The con-queror claims to have brought back many prisoners and quanti-ties of spoil in the shape of horses and cattle.

Yet another incursion is recorded in Esarhaddon's time, but

this does not seem to have seriously interrupted the process of unification, which was now going on in Media, and which was an essential prerequisite for future imperial greatness. According to the legendary account, this development dates from the time when one of the clan or tribal chiefs, Deioces, was unanimously accepted as head of all the Medes and assumed the royal name and style.[1] He reigned for fifty-three years (c. 708–655 B.C.) and made of the Medes a united people. He fixed his capital at Ecbatana (Hamadan) in the heart of the Zagros hills. It was a strong natural fortress, on the very summit of which stood the royal palace. In royal ceremonial and doubtless, too, in the more important task of government, the Median kings found their model in the Assyrian state. Deioces, by scrupulously punctual payments of the tribute, is said to have warded off possibly hostile attentions from his overlord. Thus he was left to carry out the work of building up the Median state undisturbed. His successor, Phraortes (c. 655–633), followed a similar policy toward Assyria, which was ruled at this time by its last great king, Ashurbanipal. Thus he met with no interference when he set out to conquer his southern neighbors, the Persians. When finally he was rash enough to try his strength against Assyria, he was killed in battle and his army was heavily defeated.

With the next Median king we are on firmer historical ground. Cyaxares, profiting, if the traditional account of his predecessor's death be correct, by that disastrous experience, strove to reform his military machine. The old system of the Medes, under which each clan chief furnished contingents to the king when called upon, did not produce a fighting force that was a match for a highly trained and largely professional army like the Assyrian. Cyaxares succeeded in reorganizing his military resources on the Assyrian model, and at the same time improved the armature of his men. Special care was taken to train the cavalry thoroughly, so that it became the strongest arm of the service.

The situation of Assyria was now becoming desperate, and even an alliance with king Psammetichus of Egypt only helped

---

[1] In accordance with the usual practice, the Greek forms of these names, for which Herodotus is our main authority, have been kept throughout.

to check for a time Nabopolassar's advance to the Middle Euphrates. Hordes of Scythians had in the meantime overrun eastern Asia Minor and increased the peril of the Assyrian kingdom. At first the Assyrian king was able to come to terms with the northern invaders, even to the point of receiving them as allies against his enemies. But, at the critical moment, the Scythians forsook him. For, in 614 B.C., Cyaxares entered Assyria, and, though his attack on Nineveh failed, he succeeded in taking Ashur and levelled it to the ground. Nabopolassar and he now formed a close alliance, a political and military union cemented by the marriage of Cyaxares' granddaughter to the son of Nabopolassar. In 612 a grand assault on Nineveh was made. Enemies from three sides joined in the attack, for Cyaxares had won a diplomatic triumph by bringing the Scythians over to his side. Nineveh was taken and destroyed; the Assyrian empire was at an end. A remnant of the Assyrian troops escaped to Harran where, supported to some extent by Egypt, they held on for a few years. The Egyptian king for some little while had nursed the ambition of regaining control over Syria; for, since the last years of Ashurbanipal, Assyrian overlordship there had become quite ineffective. Nor would Assyria, allied now with Egypt against her numerous enemies, put any check on Egyptian ambitions. The efforts of Nabopolassar to recreate a Babylonian empire, on the other hand, would be a far more serious obstacle to Egyptian plans. Psammetichus of Egypt died c. 610 B.C.; the Babylonian forces were now commanded by Nebuchadrezzar, the son of the aged Nabopolassar, who succeeded his father as king in 605. The war in and about Harran seems to have dragged on till 605. In that year Nebuchadrezzar inflicted a crushing defeat on the Egyptian host at Carchemish on the Euphrates. Thus were the hopes of political aggrandizement, cherished by the Egyptian king, finally shattered. Syria was annexed to Babylonia, while the kingdom of Assyria was incorporated in the Median empire. The Medes, after their triumph at Nineveh, appear to have attacked their Scythian allies, and either put them to the sword or driven them from the country.

Although all Syria and Palestine were necessarily affected by these momentous happenings, the fate of the kingdom of Judah was specially poignant. The king, Josiah, had reigned over that land for many years. At first, like his predecessors, he was a vassal of Assyria; but his religious reforms, completed by 622, had also a political significance. For, by cleansing the temple of Jerusalem and then other parts of his kingdom from Assyrian and other foreign gods and rites, he was in effect throwing off his allegiance to his overlord. The annexation of Samaria followed; finally came the wholesale execution of the priests of Baal. For a few years the kingdom remained unmolested. But when in 609 B.C. an Egyptian army moved to the aid of the hard-pressed remnant of the Assyrian forces, Necho II found his way barred at Megiddo by the army of Josiah. Whether Josiah took this step because he had definitely allied himself to Nabopolassar, or merely from hostility to Assyria and her ally, Egypt, is not clear. In any case, without support from outside, he had undertaken a hopeless task. In a brief engagement the Judæan army was utterly beaten and the king himself was slain. His elder son succeeded him, owing his position to the favor of Necho; but he was an oppressive despot who tried to undo his father's religious reforms. The result was that his subjects were split into two religious factions, and the military strength of a small kingdom, recently weakened by foreign attack, was still further exhausted by intestinal strife. Soon after Necho's defeat at Carchemish all Syria and Palestine were annexed by the Babylonian monarch. Thus Jehoiakim of Judah, too, was forced to submit and pay tribute. After three years of vassalage, he, in 599, revolted against Nebuchadrezzar; but death overtook him before the Babylonian army appeared at the gates of Jerusalem. His young successor, to save his capital from utter destruction, surrendered himself to the invader. For many years he languished in prison, while of his subjects some eight thousand with their families were deported to Babylon. The unhappy Jehoiachin's uncle, who ruled under the name of Zedekiah, was installed by Nebuchadrezzar as his vassal. During the next ten years the situation remained outwardly unchanged. But the influence of the nationalists, egged on by priests and prophets, grew stronger, and, what was more, it was now hoped that Egyptian support might be won to counterbalance the might of Babylon. Thus, when Judah once more rebelled, a terrible punishment came upon her.

Nebuchadrezzar defeated an Egyptian army, but he made no effort to attempt the annexation of that country. His bitterest anger was reserved for Judah. In 586 B.C. Jerusalem was stormed, its temple and its palace were levelled to the ground, its inhabitants slaughtered or deported, and the kingdom of Judah was no more. From that day Palestine was always controlled by a foreign power, and no independent Jewish state was able to establish or maintain itself there.

The destruction of Judah was but one episode in Nebuchadrezzar's victorious career. He had defeated the forces of Egypt more than once, and had dealt no less drastically with Egypt's Phœnician allies. At his death in 562 his empire, including, besides Babylonia proper down to the Persian Gulf, the Euphrates valley as far as the Taurus, Syria, and Palestine to the borders of Egypt, seemed built on stable foundations. In addition, during his lifetime, relations with Media continued uniformly good. That all his territory fell a prey to a new conqueror twenty-four years later was due to the feebleness of his successors and to dynastic disputes, and, consequently, to periodic revolutions in different parts of the realm.

It was not only the Babylonian king who had enlarged his empire after the downfall of Assyria. The Mede had during the early years of the sixth century advanced his authority northwestward until, by c. 590 B.C., the furthest frontier of his realm was the river Halys. Thereby he was brought into direct touch with the powerful kingdom of Lydia. The hostilities which ensued between the two states may have lasted some five years, for the last recorded engagement between the two occurred in 585 B.C. The war ended in a stalemate. Since it had been impossible to reach a decision by force of arms, Cyaxares of Media and Alyattes of Lydia came to terms. The Halys remained the boundary between the two kingdoms, and a marriage alliance between the two royal houses was the beginning of friendly relations which continued between the two states for the next thirty-five years. The political history of the interior of Asia Minor for several centuries after the destruction of Hatti is still almost unknown. No considerable power existed in Anatolia during the centuries in which its coast-line became dotted with Hellenic settlements, whose cultural progress and political development were more rapid than those of the states on the Greek mainland.

A Phrygian kingdom existed in Asia Minor in the ninth and eighth centuries, but such importance as it may have had declined in the seventh before the might of neighboring Lydia. The growth of Lydia into a first-class power was not unattended by set-backs. Invasions by Northerners, whom the Greeks called Cimmerians, devastated the country more than once and compelled the kings of Lydia to sue for help from Assyria. In return they were constrained to become the vassals of the Assyrian monarch.[1] Great uncertainty still surrounds the nature of the Lydian race and language. Archæological remains have shown that the Lydians had by the beginning of the sixth century attained to a high degree of civilization, and that their material culture had been considerably influenced by that of the Ionian Greeks. Whether they are rightly credited with the invention of coinage or not, their kings were certainly among the earliest rulers to issue a metallic currency. In the forty years following their war with the Medes the Lydians, secure on their eastern frontier by treaty, followed an aggressive policy in the West. The Greek cities of the coast were forced to submit to Lydian overlordship and to pay tribute to the Lydian king. The name of Crœsus, who was destined to be the last Lydian monarch, and who was far more Hellenized than any of his predecessors, became proverbial for magnificence and wealth.

During these years of Lydian power in the West, the Median empire was ruled by Astyages. The reputed splendor of his court and the despotism, not unmixed with harshness, of his rule, seem to stamp him as a typical Oriental potentate. His fate was not less characteristic of the East. On the appearance of a rival, many of Astyages' subjects revolted and went over to the former, and the Median king suffered defeat and deposition. His conqueror and successor was not a Mede but a Persian. Cyrus styled himself king of Anshan, a region corresponding to that part of Elam in which lay the ancient city of Susa. This was now Cyrus' capital, and became in time the capital and administrative centre of the Persian empire. After a successful war which lasted several years Cyrus had vanquished

[1] Cf. p. 125 above.

Astyages (c. 549 B.C.), and followed this by occupying the
Median capital, Ecbatana. The inhabitants of the Medo-
Persian empire seem to have been little affected by what appears
essentially to have been a dynastic struggle, from which the
Persian prince emerged victorious. It was not long before the
new ruler showed that he was a man of boundless military
ambition and ability. The friendly relations which had existed
for nearly forty years between Media and Lydia did not satisfy
him. Crœsus seems to have realized that a change of dynasty
among his eastern neighbors might become a danger to his
own kingdom. He went so far as to take the offensive by invading Cappadocia, and, after a siege, captured the fortress of
Pteria. At the same time he concluded alliances with the
rulers of Babylonia and Egypt, and entered into friendly relations with Sparta. But he underrated the genius and strategy
of his opponent. Cyrus attacked Lydia before the normal
campaigning season had begun, thus taking Crœsus by surprise
and preventing him from receiving help from his allies. A
battle fought close to Sardes was followed by the siege of that
city and by its capitulation soon after. The fate of Crœsus is
uncertain, but he ceased to rule and Lydia became a part
of the Persian dominions. But, whatever his actual end
may have been, the downfall of this wealthy and powerful
ruler seems to have captured the Greek imagination. Several
legends about him gained currency, even as the swift change
in his life from prosperity to wretchedness might form a
theme for moralists. What, however, is most remarkable, is
that his supposed self-immolation on the funeral pyre and
the quenching of the flames by the miraculous intervention
of Heaven occur as a subject in art and literature, from which
historical personages and events were almost invariably excluded. A red-figure vase depicts the king seated on his pyre
to which an attendant is in the act of applying a torch. The
poet Bacchylides in one of his odes tells the story in graphic
lines: [1]

He caused a pyre to be built in front of his courtyard with walls of
bronze; he mounted thereon with his true wife and his daughters with

---

[1] Bacchylides, *Epinician Ode* 3, 31–63. The translation is by R. C. Jebb.

beauteous locks, who wailed inconsolably; and, lifting up his hands to
the high heaven, he cried aloud: — 'O thou Spirit of surpassing might,
where is the gratitude of the gods? Where is the divine son of Leto?
The house of Alyattes is falling; . . . the gold-fraught tide of Pactolus
runs red with blood; women are ruthlessly led captive from the well-
built halls. What once was hateful is welcome; 'tis sweetest to die.'
So spake he, and bade a softly-stepping attendant kindle the wooden
pile. The maidens shrieked, and threw up their hands to their mother;
for the violent death which is foreseen is to mortals the most bitter.
But when the bright strength of the dread fire began to rush abroad,
Zeus brought a dark rain-cloud above it, and began to quench the
yellow flame. Nothing is past belief that is wrought by the care of the
gods. Then Delos-born Apollo carried the old man to the Hyper-
boreans, with his daughters of slender ankle, and there gave him rest,
in requital of his piety; because of all mortals he had sent the largest
gifts to divine Pytho.

Thus the god of Delphi proved grateful in the end!

The Greek cities — Miletus alone had previously come to
terms with Cyrus — soon found that the end of Lydia did not
mean the recovery of their political independence. In fact they
merely received a new overlord, although a number of them only
submitted after several years of fighting against the generals of
Cyrus. Samos alone maintained her independence somewhat
longer, and, under her Tyrant, Polycrates, became for a few
years the foremost maritime state in the Aegean. But, when
her ruler fell into Persian hands (c. 524 B.C.), she too was forced
to pay tribute to the Great King.

While Cyrus' officers were thus advancing the authority of
their master to the shores of the Mediterranean, he himself was
engaged in campaigns of conquest, which seem to have taken
him to the shores of the Caspian Sea, to the River Jaxartes in the
northeast, where he erected fortresses which were still in existence in the time of Alexander the Great, and to the frontiers of
India. Of these warlike enterprises we know almost nothing.
The nearer neighbor of Persia, once the ally of Media, he
did not attack for six years after the fall of Sardes. At last,
in 540 B.C., he invaded the kingdom of Babylonia, his main
objective being Babylon itself. The capture of the capital
and the annexation of Mesopotamia cost the conqueror a comparatively small effort. For the people of the land were thoroughly dissatisfied with their ruler, Nabonidus, the last of the

Chaldæan dynasty, and were ready to welcome the Persian king as their master. In 539 B.C. Cyrus was able to take Babylon; hereafter the Chaldæan empire, including Mesopotamia, Syria, Phœnicia, and Palestine, was incorporated in the Persian. Cyrus lived for another ten years, but of his acts and policy during that period we are ignorant, save in a few particulars. He was extremely tolerant, permitting his various subjects to practise their national religions without molestation. He allowed a colony of Jews, hitherto in captivity, to return to Jerusalem and rebuild their temple, and he at the same time gave back to them the gold and silver vessels which had been carried away from there by Nebuchadrezzar. The organization of the vast Persian empire into provinces, and the administrative system devised for their government, which shed glory on the reign and name of Darius I, may well have been projected and perhaps begun by Cyrus. He fell fighting in 529 B.C., but the ancient writers disagree about the enemy against whom this last and fatal campaign was directed.

His son, Cambyses, who succeeded him as ruler of a vast realm, seems to have been associated with his father on the throne during the last years of Cyrus' life. His cruelty and caprice were perhaps due to a diseased body, for he appears to have been an epileptic. The one outstanding event of his short reign (529–522 B.C.) was the subjugation of Egypt. The inclusion of Phœnicia in the Persian empire, which was one of the results of Cyrus' conquests, was now and hereafter of great military as well as of economic value. For in the attack on Egypt the coöperation of the Phœnician fleet was of first-rate importance, while in the future it would be a matter of grave concern to the Greeks of the Aegean that this formidable navy obeyed the behests of the great oriental despot who was soon to plan their subjection. The Egyptian war was begun in 526 B.C. and successfully carried through in the next year. Thus the land of the Pharaohs enriched the Persian empire by another province of boundless resources. But during Cambyses' absence a serious rebellion against his authority was staged in Media. The king, after three years in Egypt, started to return to the centre of government, but on the way, for reasons that are unexplained, he committed suicide. The Median, Gaumata, who had begun the revolt against the late king, ruled for a few months and was then assassinated by a small band of Persian nobles led by Darius. He, though he was descended from another branch of the royal house, could claim to be the legitimate heir of Cambyses, since the latter had left no issue. The death of Gaumata was, however, followed by insurrections in various districts of the empire, and by the emergence of sundry pretenders to the throne. It took Darius several years before he had suppressed all opposition and his sole authority was acknowledged throughout the empire of Cyrus and Cambyses. If Cyrus justly ranks as one of the world's foremost conquerors, Darius is no less entitled to be regarded as one of the world's great administrators. The system of imperial administration and provincial government perfected by him marked an immense advance on earlier practice, whether in Egypt, Babylonia, or Assyria, and, in spite of imperfections, endured for nearly two hundred years, in fact, as long as the Persian empire itself.

The Medes and Persians had for centuries come under the cultural influence of their neighbors in Assyria and Babylonia. Their scribes in time had taken over the cuneiform script, and had adapted it to the needs of the Persian language. It is in this Persian cuneiform that the great inscriptions of the Persian kings were written, the most famous being carved on the sheer rock of Behistun. Persian architecture and sculpture, as illustrated, for example, by the remains at Pasargadæ, Susa, and Persepolis, are primarily indebted to Assyrian models. Thus, as we should expect, the Persian imperial administration is in the first instance copied from Assyrian practice. Darius, however, was able to achieve a unity in diversity within his empire, which went far beyond anything found in earlier empires. Many of his innovations were of first-rate importance. Civil and military authority in the provinces was to some extent divided. The central government, that is to say, the king, exercised a close supervision over his subordinates. This was made possible by the greatly improved communications between different regions of the far-flung empire. Of the good roads constructed by the king's orders the best known is the Royal Road described by Herodotus. It ran from Sardes and Ephesus in Asia Minor to Susa, a distance of nearly 1500 miles. Postingstations were placed at intervals of about fourteen miles (four parasangs), and an imperial post was maintained for the swift transmission of royal despatches and rescripts from the capital to the satrapies. The total number of provinces or satrapies was, according to Herodotus, twenty; in the Persian inscriptions the total is slightly larger. The difference must be due to the subdivision of several of the remotest and most extensive provinces, which the Greek writer regarded as single administrative units. The civil head of the province was the satrap or viceroy. In addition, there were in each satrapy a secretary and a military commander who was in general charge of all the military garrisons in that province. These two personages were, to a great extent, independent of the viceroy, for they were directly responsible to the Great King himself. The duties of the secretary consisted in part in keeping watch on the satrap and reporting on his conduct to the king. Besides this there was a more general system of surveillance over the empire. The "Eyes and Ears of the King" were, in effect, travelling inspectors — usually they were members of the royal family — who each year, accompanied by military escorts, visited especially the more outlying satrapies, and then reported on their general condition to their master. Officials with somewhat analogous duties had been periodically sent into Syria by the rulers of the XVIIIth Dynasty in Egypt. If military operations in a satrapy were called for, the satrap also acted as the military head of the province. But, since the military commander, who must technically have been the satrap's subordinate, acted under the direct orders of the king, in practice the military authority of the viceroy was not unrestricted.

The inhabitants of the empire were treated with much toleration. Many were allowed a great measure of local self-government, and there was no interference with their religions, customs, and social institutions. Their one major obligation was punctual payment of the tribute, imposed on them partly in kind, partly in money. While the total amount payable by each province was assessed at Susa, its timely collection and transmission to the capital counted as one of the chief duties of the satrap. Persis, or Persia proper, being the king's own country, was exempt from regular taxation. The performance of military service, to which all subjects of the king were liable, rarely bore heavily on all parts of the empire at the same time. The finest part of the army was recruited from Persia and Media; and the detachments raised in time of war in other parts of the empire were usually commanded by officers of Persian or Median stock. The raising of the required levies in a given satrapy devolved upon the viceroy. The two chief weaknesses in this provincial system were the danger that the satraps might become too independent, and the occasional difficulty of obtaining coöperation between neighboring viceroys in face of a common foe. We shall have occasion later to note cases of satraps who went so far as to intrigue with their master's foes in order to bring about the discomfiture or even downfall of a rival governor.

Reference has been made to the general tolerance in matters of religion shown by Cyrus and Darius and their successors. Even in Media and Persia there was much variety in religious practice. The mass of the people there practised a nature worship in which the adoration of the four "elements," fire, earth, air, and water, played the most important part. The Median clan of the Magi observed a special ritual of their own which was of great antiquity but whose form at the time of the Achæmenid kings is unknown. For that part of the Persian sacred book, the *Avesta*, which deals with ritual, belongs to a much later date when there had in all probability been some fusion of the Magian religion with the teaching of Zoroaster. The date at which this teacher and prophet lived is much disputed; according to the most generally accepted view he flourished in the seventh century B.C. While his teaching was in the main ethical, he also preached a monotheistic belief in a supreme god, Ahura-Mazda. The worship of this divinity was older than the prophet, so that Zoroaster's doctrine was the exaltation of Ahura-Mazda to the exclusion of other deities. We have no means of knowing how wide-spread Zoroaster's influence was in the earlier period of Persian history. Darius in his inscriptions describes himself as standing under the protection of Ahura-Mazda, but later kings of the line associated other deities with the supreme god. Again, the general tolerance of the Persian rulers toward the gods of their subject races was scarcely compatible with strict Zoroastrian belief. The evidence available seems to show that Zoroastrianism did not become the dominant or state religion in Persia till many centuries after this time.[1]

Darius' early military expeditions had as their purpose the reëstablishment of his authority throughout the empire which he had inherited. His first attempt at adding to his dominions was an expedition into Scythia, that portion of Europe which lay north of the Danube and abutted on the western and north-western shores of the Black Sea. Although the traditional date for this undertaking is 512 B.C., it may actually have taken place a year or two before. Its purpose and the course it took are shrouded in mystery. The fleet which accompanied and transported the large military force led by the king in person, was drawn from the Greek cities of Asia Minor. Darius, having left his naval detachment on the Danube, advanced with his army into the unknown interior and seems to have been gone for a good many months. He was finally forced to retreat back to the Danube and suffered considerable losses on the way. The proposal of one of the Greek naval commanders to his fellow Greeks, to sail away and leave Darius to his fate, was defeated by the rest, notably by the Tyrant of Miletus, Histiæus. Although the Scythian expedition was a complete failure, one of Darius' best officers was detailed to effect the conquest of Thrace. As a result of his operations all the coast from Byzantium to the mouth of the River Strymon was forced to submit to Persia. Another officer effected the conquest of Lemnos and Imbros. The newly acquired territories together formed a new satrapy, the twenty-first according to Herodotus' reckoning.

[1] Thus, in a very recent work, *La Perse antique et la civilisation iranienne*, by the late Clément Huart (Paris, 1925), the discussion of Zoroaster and his work is not introduced till the third section of the book where the author deals with the Sassanian period of Persian history. This began in 224 A.D.

CHAPTER XV

THE AGE OF THE PERSIAN WARS

Land of the East, thou mournest for the host,
Bereft of all thy sons, alas the day!
For them whom Xerxes led hath Xerxes lost —
Xerxes who wrecked the fleet, and flung our hopes
away!

How came it that Darius once controlled,
And without scathe, the army of the bow,
Loved by the folk of Susa, wise and bold?
Now is the land-force lost, the shipmen sunk below.

—Aeschylus, *Persæ*, 548–557 (Morshead's translation).

THE first quarter of the fifth century, judged by the political issues which were then decided, was one of three or four supremely critical epochs in the history of the world. Though it is generally as easy as it is misleading to speculate on what might have happened if a series of interdependent episodes had had an outcome different from the actual one, it is indisputable that a Persian victory over the European Greeks, followed, as it would have been, by a Persian suzerainty over Hellas, would have materially checked or altered the progress of Greek civilization to which all subsequent western civilizations owe so much.

Darius I, though his real greatness was as an administrator, was sufficiently like his predecessors to wish to essay the rôle of conqueror. It was only to the westward that he could satisfy his military ambition. His first European venture was, as we saw, a failure, although it was followed by the annexation of Thrace. How soon he would have tried to renew his operations in the ordinary course of events we cannot tell. Actually, the preliminary round in the struggle between East and West began in 499 with a revolt of the Greek subjects of the Great King in Asia Minor. Both the causes and the course of the Ionian Revolt, as it is called, are very obscure, because Herodotus, who

215

is practically our only informant of this episode, has, partly owing to his own political prejudices, partly on account of the sources used by him, written a very unsatisfactory narrative of it. The restlessness of the Greek cities of Asia Minor, which ended in rebellion against their overlord, must have existed for a number of years before 499. Resentment at being tributaries of an oriental power, dissatisfaction at being — as most of the Ionian cities then were — ruled by Tyrants, elation at Darius' failure in Scythia, were some of the factors which influenced the minds of the Asiatic Greeks. The episodes cited by the Greek historian as the causes of the revolt merely precipitated the outbreak of hostilities.

It will be remembered that one of the Greek commanders who accompanied Darius on the Scythian expedition was Histiæus, Tyrant of Miletus. Some years later Histiæus was summoned to the Persian court at Susa for reasons that are not very clear. His place in Miletus was taken by his son-in-law, Aristagoras. The latter proposed to the Persian governor of the province of Lydia, Artaphernes, a military and naval expedition to the Cyclades, which, if successful, would bring Naxos and probably some other islands under his, and so, indirectly, under Persian, control. The Great King's permission for the undertaking was given, but the attempt to take Naxos failed. Thus Aristagoras was compelled to return to Asia Minor without achieving his object. His failure he judged — no doubt rightly — would bring upon him the anger of Artaphernes and punishment from Darius. Hence, on his return to Miletus, he worked to bring about a general revolt of the Greeks against Persia. As a proof of his genuine patriotism for Hellenic liberty he abdicated from his Tyranny. The readiness with which, besides Miletus, the other cities fell in with the proposal to rebel is sufficient proof that discontent had been steadily growing for some time. The Tyrants of the other *poleis* abdicated or were forcibly deposed.

Aristagoras, realizing how formidable was the undertaking to which all alike were now committed, went to Greece in the hope of winning substantial support from their kinsmen on the mainland. His application to Sparta for military assistance was refused. Athens promised and soon after sent twenty war

vessels to help the insurgents, while the city of Eretria in
Euboea despatched five. The material help which Aristagoras
thus obtained in Greece was slight enough; we may guess that
the moral effect on the Ionians of getting some outside support
was considerably greater. Once the revolt was an accomplished
fact, the brunt of the fighting on the Persian side fell on the satrap of Lydia. But Artaphernes seems to have had only a small
detachment of troops at his disposal, and some weeks would
elapse before the needed reinforcements from neighboring satrapies could arrive. His intended objective was Miletus, the
centre of the Greek rising, but his projected offensive was forestalled by the confederates, who began operations by boldly
marching to Sardes (498 B.C.). The citadel there held out,
although the city itself fell into Greek hands; but the allies were
deprived of the fruits of their success by a fire which broke out
accidentally and spread so rapidly that they were forced to
evacuate Sardes. This was followed by their retirement to the
coast, probably because they got wind of the near approach of
Persian reinforcements.

The destruction of Sardes had important and immediate consequences. The Eretrian and Athenian squadrons returned
home, though whether from a genuine belief that their help
would now no longer be required, or because of a change of
policy toward Persia on the part of those two cities, is not clear.[1]
Any depression which this retirement might ordinarily have
caused among the allies was submerged in the exhilaration which
they felt at the general rally to their cause on the part of the
Thracian, Propontic, and Carian communities, and even Cyprus. In spite of the vastly greater resources of the Persian
empire, the allies, for the most part, held their own well in the
first and second years of the war; and they might have effected
much more, but for their lack of unity, which became more

[1] Much has been made of the fact that one Hipparchus, a member
of the Peisistratid family, was elected senior archon at Athens for 496–495.
This is supposed to denote that the influence of a pro-Persian party was
in the ascendant. This assumes, however, something of which we have
no proof save Aristotle's vague statement (*Const. of Ath.* 22, 4) and the
fact that Hipparchus was ostracized in 487, that the sympathies of this
man on account of his descent were pro-Tyrannic, and therefore pro-
Persian.

marked as the revolt progressed. Cyprus, it is true, was recovered by Persia in 497, but this success was counterbalanced
by a severe defeat inflicted on a Persian army by the Carians.
The disunion of the Greeks and their lack of a clear objective
were especially palpable in 496–5. Nor was Histiæus, who had
been sent to the West by Darius to act as mediator, able to
help on a peaceful settlement. His interview with Artaphernes
was so unsatisfactory that he went over openly to the allied
cause and made his escape to Chios. His efforts to return to
Miletus were equally futile, though his knowledge of Persian
organization and tactics might have been of great service to the
Greeks. In the end, with some ships obtained at Lesbos, he
lived a semi-piratical life for two years. Ultimately he was
caught and put to death by the satrap of Lydia. At last, in
494, the Persians began a new and serious offensive. A large
fleet blockaded Miletus, while Artaphernes simultaneously despatched an army to invest that city from the land side. At
this juncture the confederates mustered all their naval strength
— according to Herodotus it amounted to 353 vessels. At the
crisis, when the Persian fleet attacked, jealousy and treachery,
which may have been the result of earlier Persian intrigues,
did their work more effectively than the naval manœuvres of
the enemy. Though the navy of Chios and other confederates
more than held their own in the battle of Lade — a small
island outside the harbor of Miletus — the fleets of Samos
and Lesbos deserted at a critical moment. With the utter
defeat of the Greeks ended all hopes of the ultimate success
of the Greek cause. Miletus was captured a few months later,
and then the remaining allies — including Caria and the cities
of the Propontis and Thrace — were compelled to return to
their Persian allegiance. The punishment of Miletus was severe;
for a large part of her population was deported and much of the
city utterly destroyed. Some of the other cities were similarly
treated. After these rigorous measures the Great King reverted
to his traditional policy of toleration. There seems to have
been no appreciable increase in the tribute imposed on the
Greeks, and, save in two instances, Tyrannies were finally
abolished and democratic governments were set up in the Greek
poleis by Darius' orders. It was a remarkable example of

broad-mindedness on the part of an oriental despot who would be least in sympathy with any form of popular government.

Of the various operations which followed the battle of Lade and the fall of Miletus the latest was the recovery of Thrace by Mardonius in 492. Macedonia, too, acknowledged the authority of the Great King, and the Persian commander did his work thoroughly, though not without some mishaps. His army suffered losses at the hands of Thracian tribesmen, while a great part of his fleet was wrecked in a storm off the promontory of Athos. This last disaster necessitated extensive repairs to the fleet, and brought about a delay of eighteen months before the Great King sent out an expedition to chastise the two cities, Athens and Eretria, that had assisted his rebellious subjects.

Meanwhile, during the past fifteen years, the political situation in Greece had undergone some changes. Sparta (c. 494 B.C.) and her hereditary rival and enemy, Argos, had once more gone to war, and the Spartan king, Cleomenes, inflicted a crushing defeat on the Argives at Sepeia near Tiryns. Argos lost so many of her men that she was crippled for a generation or more, while Spartan military predominance in the Peloponnese and beyond was hereafter more marked than ever before. At Athens the democratic government ushered in by Cleisthenes' reforms functioned satisfactorily, though not without considerable rivalry between the leaders of the chief political parties. But, little as we know of the internal history of Athens at this date, it is at least clear that differences were settled constitutionally in the assembly, not by recourse to violence as in the preceding century. Truly Cleisthenes had done his work well! In 493–492 the senior archon was Themistocles, perhaps the greatest statesman ever produced by Athens. In his year of office he began those plans for the naval expansion of Athens which he was only able to complete a decade later, by beginning the fortification of Peiræus, five miles southwest of Athens. Thereby Athens acquired a first-rate harbor in place of the open bay of Phalerum which had mainly served her purpose in earlier years.[1]

[1] Early in 493 the historical drama, *The Capture of Miletus*, by the poet Phrynichus was produced at the Dionysiac festival. The audience was so overcome and contrite at having left their kinsmen in the lurch that Phrynichus was prosecuted and fined for reminding the Athenians of

The Persian operations in Thrace compelled the Athenian, Miltiades, Tyrant of the Thracian Chersonese and nephew of the elder man of the same name who led the first Athenian settlement to that district, to flee. He made his way to Athens in 493, and in the following years attained to great influence in his native city. This was partly due to his wealth, partly because he was a member of one of the old Athenian families; above all, however, his familiarity with Persian methods of warfare marked him out as the best leader that Athens could have at a time when she was expecting punitive reprisals from Darius. The preponderating influence of Miltiades in 491–490 for the time being forced Themistocles and his naval policy into the background. In the critical year 490, when the Persian fleet, commanded by Artaphernes the younger, son of the former Lydian satrap, and Datis, an experienced Median officer, sailed across the Aegean, Miltiades was one of the ten *strategoi* at Athens. The official commander-in-chief was at this date still the polemarch, who in 490 was Callimachus. Whatever the method by which it was effected — and the question is much disputed — it seems clear that the success of the Athenian military operations was due to Miltiades. Though they must have been generally aware of the impending danger, the Athenians were in doubt as to the precise plan of campaign which the Persians would adopt. Hence it was only when the latter had reached Eubœa that the proper measures for the defense of Attica could be decided and that an urgent message for help was sent to Sparta. That the Spartan government promised to send a military force as soon as the moon was full is the statement of Herodotus. Even if no religious scruples delayed their action, at least ten days would be needed for the necessary mobilization of the Peloponnesian troops and their march to Attica.

The Persian commanders, who were accompanied by the ex-Tyrant of Athens, Hippias, now a man of advanced years, after crossing the Aegean forced the submission of Carystus in south-

---

their misfortunes. The suggestion of J. Beloch (*Griechische Geschichte*, ii, 1, p. 16, note 3), which is further elaborated by E. M. Walker (*Cambridge Ancient History*, iv, p. 172), that the play was "political propaganda" for Themistocles' policy is ingenious but based on nothing but conjectures, some of which are very improbable.

ern Eubœa and then sailed up the straits to Eretria. The city
held out for six days, but was then betrayed to the enemy by
pro-Persian citizens and traitors. From Eretria the Persian
fleet sailed south along the Attic coast to the bay of Marathon,
guided thither by Hippias. Here a large part of the military
force was disembarked. In the meantime the Athenians had
passed a decree proposed by Miltiades authorizing the effective
military strength of Athens to march out and block the Persian advance, instead of remaining in the city and standing a
siege. So the Athenian army marched to Marathon, where they
were joined by a small band of men from Platæa, a little Bœotian
city which had been in alliance with Athens for some years. Together they encamped near the mouth of a narrow valley which
led out into the centre of the plain of Marathon (Plate 18b).
The Persian troops who had landed were camped at the northern
end of the plain and may have numbered about 20,000. The
Greek force was not more than half that number strong. Datis
delayed for several days before ordering his men to march by the
coast road to Athens, while the fleet would sail round Cape
Sunium and so to the bay of Phalerum. From their position in
the valley of Vrana, Miltiades and Callimachus could narrowly
observe the movements of the enemy. Delay was of advantage
to them since each day brought the promised Peloponnesian
help nearer. At last the Persian general, probably because he
had learnt that the Spartans were approaching, gave the order
to advance. The Athenian commanders ordered an attack on
the enemy as they approached the mouth of the Vrana valley.
The Greek hoplites, when they had come within range of the
Persian archers, pressed forward at a quick march and tackled
the enemy at close quarters. The Athenian centre had a hard
time against the Persian troops opposed to it, but the right and
left wings carried all before them, and then, having routed the
Persian wings, came to their comrades' rescue and closed in on
the Persian centre, all but annihilating it. Nearly all the Persian vessels got safely away, but the military casualties were
heavy; for, not only had most of the centre been wiped out, but
a good many fleeing soldiers perished in the marsh at the
northern end of the plain. Herodotus tells us that 6,400 Persians lost their lives at Marathon, while only 192 Athenians

were killed on that day. In view of the character of the engagement the figures are not improbable.[1]

Miltiades at once led his men back to Athens, realizing that
the enemy had sailed for Phalerum and would try to surprise the
capital. Also, though we cannot be sure how true the stories
current in later times were, there are grounds for believing that
Athens contained some disaffected citizens. If they succeeded
in their treasonable designs, Athens might yet share the fate
of Eretria. When Datis and Artaphernes reached the bay of
Phalerum they found the Athenian army encamped by the city
walls. Thereupon they abandoned the attempt at conquest and
sailed back to Asia. Great as was the victory at Marathon and
notable as were its results, its importance has sometimes been
exaggerated. Even the victorious Athenians were fully aware
that the Persian danger had been only temporarily averted, and
that, after Marathon, Darius would more than ever plan to
rehabilitate his military renown and impose his authority on
European Greece. Nevertheless the recent campaign had
weighty consequences at Athens. It ended for good any possibility that Tyranny would be restored there, and it gave the
Athenians and indirectly other Greeks confidence, as they realized that Persians were not invincible, and that at close quarters
the heavy-armed Greek foot-soldier could more than hold his

[1] Reference must here be made to the brilliant reconstruction of the
campaign essayed by J. A. R. Munro (*Cambridge Ancient History*, vol. iv,
228–252), even though it does not appear so far to have won general
acceptance. In addition to putting the expedition of Datis and Artaphernes
in 491, that is, one year earlier than the traditional date, Munro would
make the whole course of the operations leading up to Marathon hinge on
the Persian siege of Eretria and the failure of the Athenians to send timely
aid. The army which marched from Athens under Miltiades and Callimachus had as its objective the relief of the Eubœan city. But on its
march towards Chalcis news was brought to the commanders that Datis
was forestalling such a move by landing a part of the Persian forces in the
Bay of Marathon. Hereupon the Athenians changed their plan and bore
off to the east, occupying the valley of Vrana that led down to the Mara-
thonian plain. The signal by flashing a shield, to which Herodotus refers,
Munro interprets as a signal by disaffected Athenians not to the defeated
Datis, but to Artaphernes moving with his fleet across from Eretria; and
he accepts the view, some time current in Athens, that the Alcmæonidæ
were responsible for the attempted Medism. It may be added that the
latest investigator to marshal the evidence about the Alcmæonidæ arrives
at no certain conclusion. See P. Cloché in *Revue des études anciennes*,
1928, pp. 269 ff.

a

b

a. GORTYN, GREAT INSCRIPTION CONTAINING LAW-CODE; *b.* PART OF
   THE PLAIN OF MARATHON (MT. PENTELICUS IN BACKGROUND)
Plate 18

own against even greatly superior numbers of oriental troops. Further, this achievement must have greatly enhanced the prestige of Athens in the eyes of other Greek states.

Three years later the Great King began preparations for a new and larger European expedition, but they were interrupted by a rebellion in Egypt. Toward the end of 486 Darius died, and five more years elapsed before his successor, Xerxes, steeled himself to carry out his father's plans. During this interval or respite the clash of political parties at Athens seems to have been very intense. Miltiades, the hero of 490, died in the next year under a cloud.[1] Recourse was had to ostracism almost every year, and several prominent citizens were in this way removed temporarily from the political arena. The two most influential men were Aristeides and Themistocles. The former, though a patriot of the finest type and universally respected for his personal integrity, was content to allow Athens to develop on traditional lines and was averse to the daring innovations urged by Themistocles. But the ascendancy of the latter was so great that in 483 Aristeides was ostracized. Four years before, an important change had been made in the Athenian constitution. The archonship ceased to be an elective office and was hereafter filled by lot. The polemarch at the same time was deprived of his military functions, and his duties were confined to judicial decisions in certain classes of civil litigation. The result was that the importance of the archons rapidly declined, and the board of *strategoi* became the chief executive of Athens. Moreover, the presiding *strategos* was elected from the whole body of the Athenian citizens, the others being chosen from the tribes. In practice, if not in theory, his authority seems to have been greater than that of his colleagues. Reëlection at the end of the year of office was permitted and could be repeated indefinitely.

In 488 B.C. Athens had become involved in a war with her neighbor, Aegina, — a war which from the nature of the case was purely naval. The mismanagement of it strengthened the hands of Themistocles, who was not at that time in office. But several

---

[1] The expedition which Miltiades led to Paros, with the purpose of winning over that island which owed allegiance to Persia, was a fiasco. He was arraigned on his return to Athens and condemned to pay a heavy fine. But he died shortly afterwards from the effects of a wound contracted on the expedition. Cimon discharged his father's debt.

years elapsed before he finally prevailed on his countrymen to embark on a program of naval building which was far in excess of what was needed to worst the Aeginetans and was intended to make Athens the first maritime state in Greece, putting her at the same time in a far stronger position when the Persian attack on Greece should be renewed. At last, in 482, Themistocles succeeded in carrying a decree which authorized the building of two hundred war vessels. The Athenian treasury had at that time a large surplus, which was now used for naval purposes, because the silver mines at Laurium had become unusually productive owing to the recent discovery of very rich veins of ore. Thus Themistocles with his pertinacity and farsightedness persuaded the Athenians to make a tremendous effort in the two years before Xerxes' attack, and to begin a career of maritime expansion which made Athens mistress of the eastern Mediterranean for more than half a century.

The new Persian king does not appear to have been over anxious to carry out his father's plans for the conquest of Hellas, but the influence of the queen mother, Atossa, and of his counsellors, among whom was Mardonius, carried the day. By 482 the expedition had been planned, and the following year was taken up with preparations on a vast scale. It was proposed to enter Greece by Thrace and Macedonia, the fleet meanwhile sailing along the coast and keeping in close touch with the army. A bridge of boats moored together was built across the Hellespont, a canal was cut through the end of the Athos promontory — it was nearly a mile and a half long — so as to avoid the dangerous circumnavigation, stores of supplies were set up at various points along the land route, and orders were despatched to all the satrapies to furnish contingents of troops for the undertaking. Thus, by the winter of 481, a large host had assembled in Asia Minor. The army which actually set out for Europe early in the following spring may have numbered 100,000 to 150,000 men; the total naval force perhaps amounted to upward of 500 vessels.[1]

[1] No one accepts the impossible figures given by Herodotus, two and a half million fighting men and 1207 ships. The conjectures of the moderns are multitudinous, but anything like certainty is impossible. For discussions of the problem and different estimates cf. J. Beloch, *Griechische Geschichte*, ii, 2, pp. 61–81; *Cambridge Ancient History*, iv, pp. 271–276; Sir F. Maurice in *Journal of Hellenic Studies* 50 (1930), pp. 210–235.

These vast preparations could not in any case remain unknown in Greece, but the Persian king made known his intentions before by sending, in the winter of 481, envoys to various Greek city-states demanding their submission.   A congress of representatives from the Greek states had already been held in the autumn at the Isthmus of Corinth.   A Hellenic league was formed under Spartan leadership; differences, like the quarrel between Aegina and Athens, were sunk in face of the common danger; reprisals were voted in advance against any Greeks who "medized," that is to say, voluntarily submitted to Persia; and defense measures were discussed.   In spite of all, Argos and some other communities remained neutral, and the loyalty to the Greek cause of many parts of northern and central Greece was not above suspicion.   Though we have no certain information about the strength of the confederate forces by land and sea, they cannot have been much more than half those of the enemy, perhaps 60,000 to 70,000 men in the army and a fleet of a little over 300 ships.   Strategy therefore demanded that the Greeks should remain on the defensive, until they could engage by land or sea in a position where natural advantages would to some extent counterbalance numerical inferiority.   The three main defensive positions against an army from the northeast were the vale of Tempe in Thessaly, the pass of Thermopylæ, and the Isthmus of Corinth, the last and strongest line of defense.   But to concentrate on this from the beginning meant abandoning all northern and central Greece, and might mean the defection of Athens with her powerful navy.   Thessaly could not be held save by a combined Greek force, most of whose members would have been fighting far from their own homes.   Tempe, though the natural gateway into Greece from the northeast, was not the only pass which an army of invaders could use.   Thus, though a military detachment was sent to Thessaly early in 480, its commanders found that the Thessalians as a whole were unwilling to fight.   The expeditionary force therefore made its way back to the Isthmus, and the Thessalians on the Great King's approach submitted. The Persian host had left Sardes in the spring, and reached Therma in Macedonia toward the end of July.   By the middle of August the army had passed through Thessaly and come to the western end of Thermopylæ, while the fleet, after encountering a severe storm off Cape Sepias, which wrecked or drove on shore a large number of vessels, finally anchored at the mouth of the Gulf of Pagasæ.

Meanwhile the Greek fleet, over 300 strong, had proceeded to the northern end of Eubœa, where it moored off Cape Artemisium in order to bar the progress of the enemy's navy. On land it had been decided to defend the pass of Thermopylæ. A small Peloponnesian army was reinforced by contingents from Phocis, Locris, and Bœotia; the whole force, which may have numbered 10,000 men and was commanded by the Spartan king, Leonidas, occupied the pass with the purpose of delaying the advance of the Persian host until the Greek fleet had fought a decisive action by sea. In short, the land operations were subordinated to the naval, and there can be little doubt that the master mind on the Greek side was Themistocles, although the supreme command on both elements was in Spartan hands. Xerxes, whose original plan was a combined attack by land and sea on the pass, found his calculations upset by the storm which damaged and temporarily disorganized his fleet, and by the strength of the Greek naval preparations. After some days, he decided to force the pass with his army alone, but his direct attacks were beaten off for two days. In the evening of the second day a Persian detachment, guided by a renegade Greek, was despatched by a mountain pass to attack the Greeks in the rear. Even this manœuvre might have been defeated by the Greeks, if the Phocian contingent, which had been detailed to guard against this very danger, had not allowed itself to be surprised, and then fled in panic. When the Greek army in the pass found the Persians in possession of the surrounding hills they were seized with dismay, and some tried to escape before it was too late. The Spartan king and 300 Spartiates fell fighting in the pass to a man. The total Greek losses in the three days' fighting and the pursuit on the third day are said to have been as high as 4,000 men. Leonidas and his Spartans on that day won undying glory for the heroism of their death. The poet Simonides eulogized their deeds in simple but moving lines:

Of them that fell at Thermopylæ the fortune is noble and fair is their fate. Their burial place is an altar, in place of libation cups they have remembrance, and their wine is praise. Neither decay nor Time, the all-tamer, shall make such a burial dark. This shrine of good men hath chosen the fair fame of Greece as its guardian. Leonidas, Sparta's king, is witness hereof, he who has left behind him the great ornament of valor and eternal fame.[1]

Yet, sentiment apart, the disaster might probably have been avoided, if the Spartan king had been a really able commander as well as a brave soldier.

The allied fleet had in the meantime, after some preliminary skirmishes, been engaged in a naval battle with the enemy. But, although the Greeks held their own, they were unable to force a decision, and both sides suffered severe casualties. When the news reached them that the enemy had seized the pass, the Greek naval commanders at once decided to retire to the Saronic Gulf and the Straits of Salamis, whence they could defend the approach to the Isthmus of Corinth, and at the same time afford protection to the non-combatant population of Attica, if and when they evacuated the country. For Xerxes' success at Thermopylæ meant that all Greece north of the Isthmus of Corinth lay open to him. Hence Themistocles prevailed upon the Athenians to put their whole trust in their navy. The women and children and those too old to fight, together with such personal property as could be moved, were transported to Salamis, Aegina, and the Argolid. In the three weeks following the action at Thermopylæ the Persian army passed through Phocis and Bœotia into Attica, which was thoroughly laid waste, and the buildings on the Athenian Acropolis were burnt in revenge for the destruction of Sardes. The Persian fleet had sailed along the Attic coast and took up its position in the Bay of Phalerum. The confederate Greeks were now divided in their counsels. One part urged the retirement of the fleet to the Isthmus, where they would be in close touch with the army. The Athenians, Aeginetans, and Megarians demanded the defense of the Salaminian straits. Themistocles, as commander-in-chief of the Athenian squadron, in addition urged the strategic advantages of this position, and his advice prevailed. The narrow waters be-

---

[1] Simonides, *Fragment* 4 (Bergk).

tween the island and the mainland would give an advantage
to the Greek vessels, which were numerically inferir, and
Xerxes would not wish to risk a naval engagement save in
more open waters.   An early decision was, nevertheless, imperative, because the season was getting late and the commis-
sariat problem with so large an armada must have been extremely difficult.   But Themistocles, with the cognizance of the
other commanders, also had recourse to a stratagem.   The bare
facts, which were later embroidered into one of many pictur-
esque tales that circulated about the great Athenian, would
seem to be that Themistocles sent a confidential servant to
Xerxes, informing him that the Greek fleet was about to withdraw to the Isthmus, and advising him to block all the channels
forthwith.   The king believed the story and that night (September 22, 480 B.C.?) ordered his fleet to move, with the object
of taking the enemy by surprise at dawn on the next morning.
The move was successful, and early next day the Persian ships,
having entered the straits and ranged themselves parallel to
the Attic coast, bore down upon the enemy.   The battle was
begun by the Phœnician fleet, which formed the right wing
of the Persian navy, and was opposed to the Athenians, who
were on the Greek left.   The latter succeeded in forcing back
their opponents, whose fresh manœuvres, as they were carried
toward the Persian centre, not only threw their own line into
disarray but the central squadron as well.   The Greeks pressed
home their advantage, bearing down on the disorganized Persian lines to drive them out of the straits.   In the confusion
that ensued many Persian ships collided among themselves;
others that escaped for the moment were subsequently caught
and rammed by the Aeginetans on the Greek right.   At the
end of the day the sea was strewn with wrecks and dead.
Thus does the Persian messenger describe the crucial fight in
the play of Aeschylus, who himself was serving with the Athenian forces: [1]

> . . . And first
> One Grecian bark plunged straight, and sheared away
> Bowsprit and stem of a Phœnician ship.
> And then each galley on some other's prow

---

[1] Aeschylus, *Persians*, ll. 409 ff. (E. D. A. Morshead's translation).

Came crashing in. Awhile our stream of ships
Held onward, till within the narrowing creek
Our jostling vessels were together driven,
And none could aid another; each on each
Drave hard their brazen beaks, or brake away
The oar-banks of each other, stem to stern,
While the Greek galleys, with no lack of skill,
Hemmed them and battered in their sides, and soon
The hulls rolled over, and the sea was hid,
Crowded with wrecks and butchery of men.

The Persian vessels that escaped retired to Phalerum. What percentage of the whole fleet was destroyed we cannot tell, but probably not more than a third. Xerxes, however, decided to attempt no further operations that year, and after a few days gave orders for a general retirement. The damaged fleet was sent back to Asia, while the army retired the way it had come. In Thessaly the king left a strong army of occupation in command of Mardonius, whereas he himself returned to Asia Minor with the rest. The rigor of the Thracian climate in the late autumn caused his men much hardship and was responsible for many deaths.

Early in the following spring military operations began afresh. The Greek leaders, who were now more confident, were prepared to abandon their defensive position at the Isthmus and to risk an open engagement with Mardonius. A confederate Greek fleet, a little over 100 strong, was sent off to the Cyclades to guard the islands and keep watch for any Persian fleet that might try to sail across the Aegean. Mardonius, on the other hand, tried to detach the Athenians from the Greek alliance by generous promises, but without success. Knowing that he could not force the Greek defense at the Isthmus without naval collaboration, he nevertheless marched into Bœotia, in the hope of drawing out the Greek army to give him battle, and of overawing the Athenians by his proximity to Attica. Unable to defend their country without assistance, — and the Peloponnesian mobilization was not yet complete, — the Athenians once more evacuated Attica, refusing Mardonius' second offer of terms as they had refused the first. And so their country was ravaged again within twelve months. Mardonius'

movements had been rapid and had taken the confederate army
unawares.   The Spartan king and commander-in-chief, Pausanias, however, sent an advance detachment to Megara with
all speed to reinforce the town garrison.   The help arrived just
in time.   Mardonius, rather than waste time over a siege which
was not essential to his plans, or risk an open engagement in
Attica, which in any case was too desolate to afford food for
his army, retired to Bœotia.   There he encamped near Platæa
on a site best adapted for his tactical plans when the enemy
should appear.   The central Greek states, Bœotians, Phocians,
and Locrians, had submitted voluntarily to him, and their
military contingents were enrolled on his side.

The Peloponnesian army now moved from the Isthmus,
being joined on its way to Bœotia by Megarian and Athenian
detachments.   The total strength of the Greeks was perhaps
60,000 men; Mardonius' army, including his compulsory allies
from northern and central Greece, was only slightly more
numerous.   Tactical moves and counter-moves on the part of
the two hosts, and occasional skirmishes between small groups,
went on for nearly a fortnight before Mardonius, thinking to
take advantage of the Greek divisions, when in changing their
position early one morning they had been thrown into some
disorder, gave the signal for a general attack.   The battle raged
for many hours, but in the end the heavy-armed Greek
infantry carried the day as it had done eleven years before at Marathon; and, when Mardonius himself was killed,
the Persian centre finally broke and ran.   The Persian second-
in-command, Artabazus, under cover of the cavalry managed to
rally a good part of his army and to effect an orderly retreat
into Thessaly, and so back to Asia.   But the Persian camp was
stormed by the Greeks, and immense quantities of booty were
taken by them.   An attack on Thebes followed; after three
weeks' siege the city was compelled to capitulate.   The leaders
of the pro-Persian party were subsequently executed and the
league of Bœotian cities, which had existed under the head-
ship of Thebes since the middle of the sixth century, was dis-
banded.   An interesting memorial of the victory at Platæa
survives to the present day.   From the Persian spoil captured
by the Greeks a tithe was set apart for Apollo.   This was

used to erect at Delphi a golden tripod resting on a tall column of bronze made in the form of three closely intertwined snakes. Pausanias had this inscription placed on the dedication:

> Pausanias, as general of the Greeks, after he had destroyed the army of the Medes, dedicated this monument to Phœbus.

It was not long before these lines, owing to protests against such arrogance, were erased. Instead the names of thirty-one states, whose contingents fought at Platæa or at Salamis, were engraved on the column. The gold tripod was removed by the Phocians during the Sacred War in the middle of the fourth century; but the serpent column remained at Delphi till it was carried off to Constantinople by Constantine I. There it still stands in the Hippodrome (At meidan).

The allied fleet, whose headquarters were at Delos, had in the interval seen no sign of the Persian navy. During the summer the admiral-in-charge received an urgent invitation from the islanders of Chios and Samos to cross to Asia Minor, since on his appearance the Asiatic Greeks would rise in general revolt against their overlord. The chances of a notable success seemed good, and the Greek fleet sailed from Delos to Asia Minor. On news of its approach a Persian naval squadron lying off Samos retired to the neighboring mainland coast at Mycale. Here the Persians landed, beached their ships, and formed an entrenched camp; and here, in the last days of August or the first days of September, 479 B.C., they were attacked and defeated by the Greeks. The Persian ships were burnt, probably by the Persians themselves, when they saw that their position was hopeless. After this stirring success the victors proceeded to the Hellespont and invested Sestos, which commanded the straits and was held by a strong Persian garrison. The siege was prolonged into the late autumn. The Peloponnesian part of the allied force returned home before the end, leaving the Athenians, supported by their newly liberated Ionian allies, to carry on. At last the place capitulated, and with the capture of this important strategic point the Greek operations of 479 came to an end. Truly it had been a memorable year. For had not the oriental invader been driven out of Greece, while a second victory, that at Mycale, had brought about the liberation of the Asiatic Greeks after they had been subjects of a foreign power for nearly a century?

Simultaneously with the epic conflict between Persians and Greeks in Hellas and Asia Minor there occurred events in the western Mediterranean which no less decisively insured the freedom from foreign control of the Sicilian and Italian Greeks. Of the political history, during the seventh and sixth centuries, of the numerous Greek cities founded during the age of colonization very little is known. Their general constitutional development, their social and economic conditions, seem to have been very similar to what is already familiar from Greece and Anatolia. Till the second half of the sixth century the Greek *poleis* in Sicily generally lived at peace with one another, although certain cities were more powerful than the rest. Thus, Acragas under her brutal Tyrant, Phalaris, enjoyed a brief period during which her political influence in the island surpassed that of any other city (*c.* 570–555 B.C.). It was fortunate for the western Greeks that they warred so little among themselves at this period, since they had strong neighbors to whom the growing prosperity of the Hellenic communities seemed a challenge and a menace. In Italy the chief power was the Etruscan kingdom; but we have no evidence that the Etruscans tried at any time to interfere with the Greeks of Magna Græcia, though at the height of their power they controlled Campania and a good part of the western coast southward from their own territory.

Very different was the attitude of Carthage. This city had originally been founded by Phœnicians from Tyre (*c.* 800 B.C.). Before this Phœnician emigrants and traders had occupied a number of sites on the northern coast of Africa and in southern Spain, but none of them attained to the importance of Carthage. Before the middle of the sixth century she was undisputed mistress in all this region, having extended her control over all Phœnician settlements in the western Mediterranean and secured three towns or trading stations in northwestern Sicily, — Motya, Solus, and Panormus. That, in these circumstances, the Carthaginians would sooner or later try to restrict the growth of the western Greeks, who might become political and commercial rivals, was obvious. From the scanty sources

available it would appear that Greek cities were at war with
Carthaginians on two or three occasions during the sixth
century. More fully attested is the naval battle in 535 B.C., at
which the Phocæans of Alalia in Corsica fought against the
allied navies of Carthage and Etruria. Alalia was subsequently
abandoned by the Greek settlers and passed under Etruscan
domination. The Carthaginians a few years later conquered
all the coast-lands of Sardinia, though they failed, or perhaps
did not seriously attempt, to subdue the natives in the interior.
The most serious check to Carthage was a naval defeat inflicted
on her by the Greeks of Massilia (c. 530 B.C.?). The two states
thereafter concluded a treaty delimiting the regions in which
each was to exercise political control without interference from
the other.

The last years of the sixth century and the early years of
the fifth were a time when numerous Tyrants attained to power
in Sicily and southern Italy. The kind of conditions which
brought about these changes can to some extent be illustrated
from the case of Syracuse. Here, until the end of the sixth
century, the landed proprietors (gamoroi), who were the descendants of the original colonists, exercised a narrow and oppressive oligarchic rule. Their land was tilled for them by a serf
population composed mainly of Sicilian aborigines (Sicels).
The free citizen population (damos) was made up of small
proprietary farmers, craftsmen, and traders. But, since magistrates and officials were exclusively chosen from among the
gamoroi, and a citizen assembly, if it existed, had no powers,
the members of the damos had few if any political rights.
Doubtless similar conditions were to be found elsewhere in
Sicily and Italy, and in due course brought about revolution
and Tyranny.

In the early years of the fifth century the most powerful
of these despots were Anaxilas of Rhegium, Hippocrates of
Gela, and Theron of Acragas. The ablest of these was Hippocrates, who extended his sway over at least four cities besides
his own. On his death (c. 485 B.C.) he was succeeded by Gelon,
who had served with distinction in the late Tyrant's army.
At the invitation of some of Syracuse's oppressed population
who were in revolt against their masters, Gelon interfered in

the affairs of that city by armed force, and having occupied it made himself Tyrant there, leaving his brother Hiero to govern Gela. Gelon next greatly enlarged Syracuse, strengthened it with new fortifications, and built great docks in the harbor to accommodate his nascent navy. By marrying the daughter of Theron, Tyrant of Acragas, who was also master of Himera in northern Sicily, he brought about close and friendly relations with the despot who, next to Gelon himself, was the most powerful ruler in the island. That other Greek cities viewed this situation with alarm is not surprising, and it is probable that Carthage also foresaw the possible loss of her Sicilian dependencies. Hence a clash between her and Gelon was only a matter of time. That it came already in 480 was due to an appeal from Himera to Carthage to interfere on her behalf in Sicilian affairs. Anaxilas also entered into friendly relations with the Semitic power.

In the summer of 480 therefore a large Carthaginian expedition sailed for northern Sicily and invested Himera, which was strongly fortified and held by Theron himself. He, on the approach of the Punic forces, sent an urgent message for support to the Tyrant of Syracuse. Gelon with a large army — it is said to have amounted to 55,000 men all told — marched to the relief of his father-in-law, and outside the walls of Himera engaged the Carthaginian forces (September ? 480 B.C.). He inflicted a crushing defeat on the invaders, and then dictated terms to them by which they were obliged to pay a heavy indemnity, but were left in possession of their cities in the northwest of the island. That Gelon's great victory coincided in point of time with the Greek victory over Xerxes at Salamis led later Greek writers to assume that Carthage had attacked the western Greeks at the suggestion or request of the Persian monarch. But in Herodotus there is no hint of such a Perso-Punic understanding, and Carthaginian interests in Sicily, coupled with the invitation extended by Himera, are quite sufficient to account for the Punic invasion. That it was actually undertaken in 480, and that the fight at Himera occurred about the same time as the battle of Salamis, was a coincidence.

Gelon's prestige in Sicily and beyond, and his popularity in Syracuse, were immensely enhanced by his victorious campaign.

But within two years he died and was succeeded by his brother Hiero, since his own son was an infant. The twelve years of Hiero's reign (478–466 B.C.) were notable for their magnificence and for the prosperity of Syracuse. The city was adorned with fine public buildings, paid for out of the spoils of Himera. The despot attracted to his court the most distinguished poets of the day, among others, Simonides, Aeschylus, and Pindar. The last-named celebrated Hiero's victories in the chariot races at Olympia and Delphi in more than one fine epinician ode. It is in one of these that he refers to Gelon's victory at Himera:

From Salamis shall I essay to win for my reward the favour of the Athenians, but at Sparta I shall tell of the battle before Cithæron, those battles twain in which the Medes with curved bows suffered sorely; but, by the well-watered bank of the river Himeras, (I shall win reward) by paying my tribute of song to the sons of Deinomenes, — the song of praise, which they won by their valour, while their foemen were fore-spent.[1]

Politically Hiero's greatest triumph was a naval victory which he won in 476 over the Etruscans off Cumæ. Thereby he saved Cumæ — reputed to be the oldest Greek settlement in the West — from foreign domination.

Truly it may be said that by the end of the first quarter of the fifth century Hellenism had emerged triumphant throughout the whole Mediterranean area.

[1] Pindar, *Pythian Odes*, 1, 75–80 (J. E. Sandys' translation). Of the extant odes of Pindar the first Olympian and the first three Pythian were written for Hiero. The second Pythian, however, celebrates a victory not at the Pythian games but at the Iolæa at Thebes.

CHAPTER XVI

THE RISE AND DECLINE OF THE ATHENIAN EMPIRE

> *To maintain our rights against equals, to be politic with superiors, and to be moderate with inferiors, is the path of safety.* — Thucydides v, 111 (Jowett's translation).

1. FROM 478 TO 431 B.C.

WITH the repulse of Xerxes and Mardonius the relations between Hellenes and Persians entered on a new phase. The Greeks of Asia Minor and the adjacent islands had for the moment recovered their political independence; to keep it they needed more strength than their own unaided resources could give them. The interest of Sparta and the other Peloponnesian states in the cause of the Anatolian *poleis* was at best lukewarm; but in 478 a small confederate fleet under the command of Pausanias did cruise in the Aegean, and, after bringing about the defection from Persia of several islands lying off the Carian coast, and of a part of Cyprus, expelled the Persian garrison from Byzantium. Pausanias' arrogant conduct, however, gave offense to the allies serving under his command and the Spartan government was obliged to recall him. The Asiatic Greeks, who in 478 had joined Pausanias' squadron, now turned to Athens and invited her to put herself at the head of a maritime confederacy which should serve a twofold purpose. It would insure that the cities lately under Persian suzerainty would not relapse into their former position of subjects to an oriental despot, and it would make possible offensive operations against Xerxes, with the object of freeing all those Hellenic communities which were still under his domination.

The general organization of the league, the conclusion of agreements between Athens and her new allies, the definition or assessment of the military, naval, or financial obligations to be

undertaken by the constituent members, were by common consent entrusted to Aristeides, who in 478 was in charge of the
Athenian detachment serving under Pausanias. Delos, Apollo's
sacred island and the seat of an old religious confederation, was
chosen as the meeting place of the new league; the temple of the
god was designated as the treasury in which the confederate
funds should be stored. Each member undertook to make a
certain contribution annually, its amount and character being
fixed by Aristeides and graduated according to the resources of
the particular city. From the first there were two classes of
members. Some states — for instance, Chios, Lesbos, Samos,
Naxos, and Thasos — had substantial navies of their own.
These, or a part of them, they bound themselves to put at the
disposal of the league as required. But the greater number of
poleis were much smaller, owning no naval forces to speak of,
and they met their liabilities to the confederacy by paying an
annual tribute (*phoros*) in money into the federal chest. The
funds thus accumulated would be used partly to defray the cost
of upkeep of the allied navy, partly to finance the expeditions
undertaken by the league. How far these smaller cities were
required to furnish contingents of men to act as rowers or fighters
is quite uncertain. Each city was free and independent, and
through its representatives voted at the federal congress in
Delos, the principle followed being apparently one city one vote,
irrespective of its importance or power. The executive was from
the beginning left to Athens, that is to say, the chief command
was exercised by Athenian admirals, and the financial business,
collection of the tribute, and so forth, was under the control of
ten *Hellenotamiai*, who were Athenians elected by the Athenian
ecclesia. The total sum which was annually collected from the
allies according to Aristeides' assessment was, so Thucydides
states (i, 96), 460 talents ($552,000 = £110,500). Epigraphic
evidence, however, shows that this amount was not exceeded
thirty-five or forty years later, when the membership roll of the
league was far larger than in the first ten years of its existence.
Hence it is likely that the amount collected in the early period
was considerably less, and that Thucydides' figure is only appropriate to the years after *c.* 454 B.C.

Themistocles' statesmanship for fifteen years had so moulded

the destinies of Athens that this maritime league under Athenian leadership may be called the direct outcome of his policy.
It was he also who, in the years immediately following the war
with Xerxes, persuaded the Athenians to rebuild the fortifications of Athens in spite of the protests of the Spartan government. For the head of the Peloponnesian league was to some
extent suspicious of Athens' growth in power, and loath to see
Athenians turn their city into a fortress of the first rank. This
accomplished, Themistocles carried through the work first
begun in 493–492 B.C., — the fortification of Peiræus and of the
two smaller harbors of Zea and Munychia, adjacent to it.
The total length of these walls was approximately seven and a
half miles. Each of the harbors was protected on the sea side
by strong moles. Athens now possessed a port and naval
base worthy of the head of a great maritime confederacy, and
before long Peiræus became the foremost commercial mart in
the eastern Mediterranean. Twenty years later, in 457, the
Athenians took a further and very necessary step. Hitherto,
had an invader attacked Athens, he could have cut off the
capital completely from its port. To prevent any such possibility in time of war the Athenians constructed two "Long
Walls," one connecting Athens with Peiræus, the other with
Phalerum.[1] The fortification of the two cities was the last
important public service performed by Themistocles for his
country. In the next few years his influence steadily declined,
as that of Cimon, son of Miltiades, mainly through his military
successes, grew. One leading feature of Cimon's foreign policy
was the maintenance of good relations with Sparta and the
Peloponnesian league, whereas Themistocles, after his diplomatic duel with the Spartan government in 478 concerning the
fortification of Athens, was consistently hostile to that state.
At last, in 471 or 470, recourse was had to ostracism, and Themistocles was forced to go into exile. After some years of residence
at Argos, where he seems to have been actively engaged in
anti-Spartan propaganda, he was compromised by revelations

[1] In 445 a second Peiræus wall, parallel to the first, was built and the
wall from Athens to Phalerum was allowed to fall into disuse. Between
the two Peiræus walls, the "North Wall" and the "Middle Wall," ran a
high road connecting the city with its port.

made by Pausanias before his death.   The latter had been
actively intriguing with Persia, and Themistocles seems to
have been aware of some at least of Pausanias' designs.   The
Athenian was summoned to his native city to stand his trial
for high treason; but, whatever the degree of his guilt or innocence may have been, he took no risks.   He left Argos,
and, after several years of moving from place to place in
Greece, he finally made his way to Asia Minor.   From there
he went as a political refugee to the Persian capital and was
well received by the new king, Artaxerxes I, who had succeeded Xerxes in 464.   He was established regent of Magnesia-
on-the-Mæander, and lived there till his death about a dozen
years later.   With regard to the later years of Themistocles'
career the ancient evidence is too conflicting to justify us in
passing judgment on it.   The sentimentalist may shed a tear
that the victor of Salamis ended his days as a dependent of
Persia;   the dispassionate student of history will remember
Themistocles' inestimable services to Athens and to Greece,
and will be content to accept the éloge of Thucydides:

For Themistocles was a man whose natural force was unmistake-
able; this was the quality for which he was distinguished above all
other men; from his own native acuteness, and without any study
either before or at the time, he was the ablest judge of the course to be
pursued in a sudden emergency, and could best divine what was likely
to happen in the remotest future.   Whatever he had in hand he had
the power of explaining to others, and even where he had no experience
he was quite competent to form a sufficient judgment; no one could
foresee with equal clearness the good and evil event which was hidden
in the future.   In a word, Themistocles by natural power of mind and
with the least preparation was of all men the best able to extemporize
the right thing to be done.[1]

The development of the maritime confederacy, so auspiciously
initiated in 478–477 B.C., and the imperial position thereafter won
by Athens, were, above all, the work of Cimon, who in 476 had
become head of the naval forces of Athens and thereby admiral-
in-chief of the allied fleet, a position which he retained for fifteen years.   His first success was the capture of Eion at the
mouth of the Strymon river.   The place owed its importance
to its proximity to the mines of Mt. Pangæus and was still

---

[1] Thucydides i, 138 (Jowett's translation).

held by a Persian garrison. In the next few years Scyros was seized, its inhabitants were expelled, and the island was colonized by Athenian settlers. Carystus in southern Euboea was compelled to become a member of the confederacy (c. 470 B.C.). A year or two later the Athenians did not hesitate to use coercion against Naxos. The islanders desired to sever their connection with the league, which, so far as we can tell, they were entitled to do under the original terms of the alliance. But the retirement of so strong a member from the confederacy might easily have been followed by other secessions, and the maritime empire which Athens and Cimon were building up step by step would very soon have collapsed. Hence the Athenians chose to interpret the action of Naxos as a revolt, and laid siege to the island (469 or 467 B.C.). When they capitulated, the Naxians ceased to be wholly autonomous: their fleet was impounded by Athens, and they became her tribute-paying subject allies. Whether Athens, on the basis of the original treaty by which Naxos had joined the league, was able to put forward any legal justification for her use of compulsion or not, is not known, nor is it of any material importance. What mattered was that her action at Naxos, and the coercion she had used to make Carystus a league-member, made it clear to all the world that she was not content to be head of a voluntary confederacy, but was aiming at its conversion into an Athenian empire. In 465 the Thasians, undeterred by the fate of Naxos, indicated their intention to retire from the league. It was the prospect of an Athenian colony coming to settle at the "Nine Ways" (the site of the later Amphipolis), a few miles inland from Eion, in order to exploit the natural wealth of the district, — lumber and mines, — which, we may suppose, was the main cause of the quarrel between the island and Athens. The colony of 10,000 actually set out and reached its destination in 464; but, shortly after, the settlers were attacked and all but wiped out by Thracian tribes of the interior. Thasos meanwhile had been blockaded by the Athenians, and after two years the islanders, having applied in vain to Sparta for help, surrendered. Thasos, like Naxos, became a subject ally; her fortifications were razed and her navy confiscated; in addition, she was forced to give up certain dependencies on the mainland opposite to Thasos and all interest that she had hitherto held in the Pangæus mines.

While the relations between Athens and her allies were thus undergoing a gradual change, the original purpose of the league was not forgotten. There were still substantial districts within the Aegean area which owed allegiance to Persia. To deprive the Great King of these subjects, and to include them in the maritime confederacy, were the objects of a strong expedition, composed of two hundred Athenian and allied vessels, that set sail under Cimon's command in the spring of 468. Caria and Lycia were the objective; systematically the communities there were won over, many of them joining the Greek alliance readily as soon as Cimon appeared. Others were held by Persian garrisons and had to be reduced by force. The most formidable resistance might have been shown by Dorian Phaselis. Her interests were largely commercial, and much of her trade was with Syria and other regions subject to Persia. But friendly relations had also existed for some time between her and Chios, and it was owing to the intermediation of the Chians that Phaselis agreed to surrender to Cimon. Meanwhile the Persian government sent military and naval forces to Pamphylia to protect or recover the towns threatened by the allies. Before the end of the summer Cimon had inflicted a double defeat on the enemy by the River Eurymedon, and then captured an additional squadron of eighty vessels which was on its way to reinforce the Persian main fleet. This campaign was Cimon's greatest achievement; its effect was to leave the navy of Athens and her allies in undisputed control of all the Aegean as far as Cyprus, and to confine the Persian navy to the narrow waters between that island and the Syrian coast.

While the Delian confederacy was thus carrying out its aims, and was at the same time passing more and more under Athenian control, the Spartan government was faced with a succession of problems. Important members of the Peloponnesian league were showing signs of discontent with Spartan leadership. One of the Arcadian cities, Tegea, allied herself with Argos, and Sparta was forced to undertake a campaign against these allies. A little later a more general rising of all the Arcadian cities, except Mantinea, against Spartan authority again necessitated military action. In both these wars the efficiency and discipline of the Spartan troops carried the day. Yet, that Sparta's position as head of the league was after this more unchallenged than ever before was partly due to the half-hearted attitude of Argos, and to the fact that at Athens, thanks to the strength of the Cimonian party, a philo-Laconian policy was the order of the day. In 464 a disaster befell Sparta, which, if her authority in the league had not been firmly re-established a few years before, might have led to her political extinction. A violent earthquake shook Laconia, causing great destruction and loss of life. The oppressed and dis-contented Helot population of Messenia saw an opportunity for turning on their masters. They revolted *en masse* and were even joined by some Pericœcic communities. An attack on the city of Sparta failed, and the Helots were decisively defeated in the field. They now took refuge on Mount Ithome, which already in the seventh century had served as a rallying point for the Messenians. The siege of this stronghold was long and difficult; besides, as Thucydides tells us, the Spartans were not adept at operations of this kind. They accordingly summoned the help of their allies, including Athens, which, it must be remembered, was still a member of the Hellenic confederation formed in 481 B.C. When this request for aid came before the Athenian assembly, a heated debate seems to have ensued. Cimon, true to the view that he had consistently advocated, that Sparta and Athens should stand shoulder to shoulder as the leaders of Greece, urged that an expeditionary force be sent to Laconia without delay. The anti-Laconian party at Athens was also that party which desired to bring about a more complete democratic régime at home, and abroad to enforce more ruthlessly the authority of Athens in the Delian league. What may thus be called the democratic party was also the imperialist party, whose program could only be opposed to a policy of alliance and friendship with Sparta. Its leader at this time was Ephialtes, a man of whose career we know practically nothing, but whose great ability is not open to doubt. On this occasion, however, he and his party were not yet strong enough to defeat the supporters of Cimon. The

relief expedition to Sparta was approved and started out forthwith, with Cimon himself in charge. It proved to be the only
time that Cimon's military genius failed him; for what reason
we do not know. Even he could not bring the Messenians to
capitulate, and, eventually, the Spartan government took the
drastic step of curtly dismissing the Athenian force. This
action, if it was a serious error of judgment on the part of the
Spartan ephors, also reacted very strongly on the political
situation at Athens, and on Cimon's own career. Ephialtes'
party gained the upper hand, and, within a year of his return
from Ithome, Cimon was ostracized, the alliance between
Athens and Sparta was regarded as at an end, and the Athenians, by way of direct challenge to the head of the Peloponnesian
league, contracted alliances with Argos and with Thessaly. A
few months later, that is, before the end of 461, Ephialtes was
murdered, probably by a member of one of the oligarchic clubs
whose methods of political warfare were as crude as their influence on affairs at this time was small.

His successor as head of the democratic party was Pericles,
who in the next few years carried through to the end the
sweeping constitutional reforms begun by Ephialtes.[1] Athens'
most famous statesman was the son of Xanthippus, the admiral of the Athenian squadron which fought at Mycale; on
his mother's side he was a member of the Alcmæonid clan, being
in fact the great nephew of Cleisthenes. The finest speaker
of his age, he was in temper and bearing an aristocrat rather
than a popular leader. Withal he was reserved in manner,
frugal in his private life, the friend of artists and philosophers. Though, from time to time, called upon in the performance of his office as *strategos* to take charge of military or
naval expeditions, his ability in that character was little more
than mediocre. The foreign and domestic policy of Athens
for the next thirty years was, with one brief exception, the
policy of Pericles; for more than half that period his authority
was often challenged. For twelve years preceding the outbreak of the great Peloponnesian war he was in effect the benevolent autocrat of Athens.

The unfortunate disagreement with Sparta in 461 made hos-

_____
[1] See p. 331 below.

tilities between Athens and some of the Peloponnesian states inevitable. The Spartan government, it is true, was not anxious to force the issue; but Athens, by cutting herself off from the Hellenic confederation, gave a handle to Corinth and Aegina, both of whom were jealous of her growth as a maritime power. In 460 Athens concluded an alliance with her neighbor, Megara, then involved in a quarrel with Corinth; this agreement meant war between Athens and the Isthmus city. The so-called first Peloponnesian war continued at intervals from 459 to 445. An Athenian victory over the Corinthian and Aeginetan navies in 458 was followed by the siege of Aegina, which capitulated in 457. The city-state that had so long been the proud rival of Athens was then enrolled as a tributary subject in the confederacy; with her independence she lost her navy. The successes of Athens brought the Peloponnesian league as a whole into the field against her. In 457 a Peloponnesian army was despatched to Bœotia to restore the Bœotian league with Thebes at its head, and thus create a more formidable and potentially hostile neighbor to Athens on her northern frontier. The Athenians replied by sending an army across Cithæron, which engaged the enemy at Tanagra but suffered defeat. The Peloponnesians, instead of following up their victory, and especially securing the position of Thebes, returned home. Before the end of the campaigning season the Athenians entered Bœotia a second time, defeated a Bœotian army decisively at Oenophyta, and compelled the Bœotian cities to join the Athenian alliance. Their neighbors of Phocis had already done so voluntarily, and, under pressure, the Locrians followed suit.

Thus, in 456, Athens was mistress of central Greece as far as the pass of Thermopylæ. By concluding treaties with most of the cities of Achæa her influence extended also into the Peloponnese, and, by 455, she controlled a valuable naval base on the northern shore of the Corinthian Gulf. For in 455 the revolted Messenian Helots had at last surrendered to the Spartans, on condition that they be allowed to emigrate from the country. With the help of Athens the exiles were settled at Naupactus which had lately been wrested from the Locrians. The value of this place to a power like Athens was obvious, as it commanded the entrance to the Gulf of Corinth, and that at a time when,

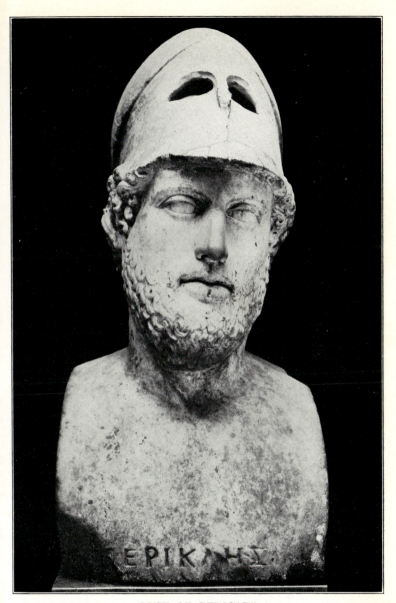

BUST OF PERICLES

Plate 19

through her close alliance with Megara, Athens also controlled the Megarian port of Pagæ, as well as Nisæa on the Saronic Gulf. In 454 Athens seemed to emphasize her imperial position by transferring the treasury of the league from Delos to Athens. That the Delian confederacy was in reality a league no longer, but had become an Athenian empire must have been clear to many as far back as 461. But the removal of the treasury, and the dedication thereafter of one-sixtieth of the annual tribute to Athena, the patron goddess of Athens, was interpreted by enemies as an act of imperial arrogance, and may have caused heartburning to some of her allies as well. It is not improbable that there was a more practical and immediate reason why the change was made in 454.

Five years before this the Athenians had equipped a large naval expedition, and sent it to Cyprus to free the whole of that island from Persian control. When the two hundred Athenian and allied vessels had already set out, a request for active support reached the Athenians from Inaros, a Libyan prince, who was the ring leader of an Egyptian insurrection against Persia. To damage Persian interests by helping to bring about the loss of one of her richest provinces seemed a dazzling prospect to the Athenians. A part of the Cypriote fleet was detached and ordered to proceed to Egypt to coöperate with the insurgents. For several years all went well, but the arrival of large reinforcements from Persia altered the situation. The rebellion was crushed, and the Athenian expedition, together with a relief force of fifty vessels sent out in 454, was wiped out almost to a man.[1] The loss of ninety or a hundred vessels with all their crews and fighting men was a serious blow to Athens; it also caused a temporary weakening of her naval control in the Aegean, and the removal of the Delian treasury may have been due to the fear that Persia might follow up her late success by sending a naval squadron to raid the Cyclades.

After 455 the war in Greece languished for some years. The

[1] That only a portion of the Cypriote fleet — forty or fifty vessels — was despatched to Egypt in 459, and that the Athenian expedition to Egypt was not as great a disaster as suggested by Thucydides, has been demonstrated convincingly by M. Cary in *Classical Quarterly*, vii (1913), 198, and by F. E. Adcock in the *Proceedings of the Cambridge Philological Society* for 1926. Their conclusions have here been adopted.

failure of the Egyptian enterprise made the Athenians anxious, when they had had time to make good their losses, to retaliate on Persia. But a fresh expedition on a larger scale could only be undertaken if Athens were free from the danger of being attacked at home. In other words, if the war against Persia was to be continued, Athens must come to an accommodation with Sparta. In 451 Cimon's period of exile came to an end and he returned to Athens. The political situation there was such as to restore him at once to a position of authority; and for two years — the only occasion in his long career — Pericles, in modern parlance, led an opposition minority. Through Cimon's efforts a five years' truce was concluded between Sparta and Athens, the latter abandoning her alliance with Argos. The Argives for their part signed a thirty years' treaty with Sparta. In the following spring (450) the second part of Cimon's program was carried out. A fleet of two hundred Athenian and allied vessels under his command sailed for Cyprus. After capturing some minor places he laid siege to Citium; but in 449 the great commander died, the victim of an epidemic which also attacked many of his troops. The siege was abandoned, but before leaving these eastern waters the Athenian fleet attacked the Persian off Cypriote Salamis and won a striking victory. No less than one hundred enemy ships were taken, and the disaster of 454 was amply avenged.

With Cimon's death Pericles' ascendancy in the Athenian *ecclesia* was quickly reëstablished. One of his first acts was to send an embassy to Susa to come to terms with the Great King. An agreement was reached after both sides had made substantial concessions. Athens undertook to interfere no more in Egypt or Cyprus, both countries being acknowledged as Persian dependencies. The Persian king bound himself to send no warships into the Aegean and to abstain from attack on the Greek cities of Asia Minor. While not formally renouncing his authority over those who had once been his subjects, he acquiesced in the situation that had existed in Ionia and Aeolis since 478, and in Caria since the Eurymedon campaign. The friendly, or at least peaceful, relations between the two powers endured for nearly forty years.

In Greece, on the other hand, the truce concluded in the

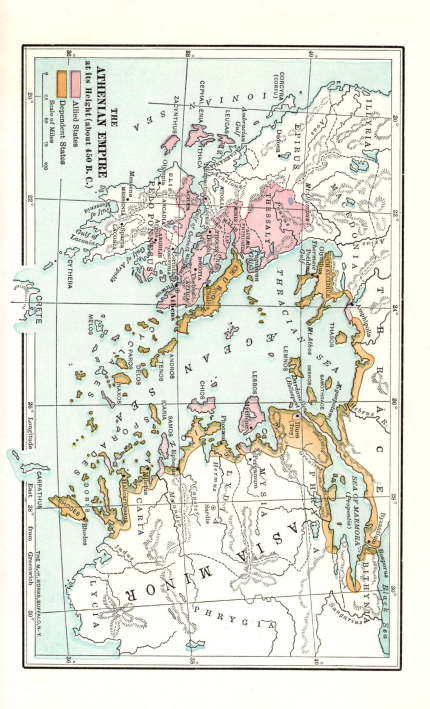

THE
ATHENIAN EMPIRE
at its Height (about 450 B. C.)

Dependent States
Allied States

Scale of Miles
0 25 50 75 100

CORCYRA
(CORFU)

CEPHALLENIA
ZACYNTHUS

E P I R U S

Dodona

Ambracian
Gulf

LEUCAS
ITHACA
ACARNANIA
Achelous
AETOLIA
OZOLIAN LOCRIS
Naupactus

I O N I A N
S E A

Messene
MESSENIA
Pylos
Gulf of
Messenia

PELOPONNESUS
ELIS
Olympia
ARCADIA
Mantinea
Sparta
LACONIA
Gulf of
Laconia

ARGOLIS
Argos
Gulf of Argos
CYTHERA

CRETE

Messenia

MELOS
Melos

CARPATHUS

RHODES
Rhodes

LYCIA

THESSALY
Pharsalus
Mt. Olympus
Olympus
Thermaic
Gulf

MACEDONIA

ILLYRIA
Axios

Mt. Athos
CHALCIDICE

Amphipolis
THASOS

T H R A C E
Hebrus

THRACIAN SEA

IMBROS
SAMOTHRACE
LEMNOS

A E G E A N   S E A

MALIS
Thermopylae
DORIS
PHTHIOTIS
PHTHIOTIS
ACHAEA
Delphi
BOEOTIA
Thebes
Chalcis
Athens
Megara
Corinth
Piraeus

ANDROS
TENOS
DELOS
PAROS
NAXOS
ICARIA
SAMOS

CHIOS

LESBOS
Mytilene

Ilium
(Troy)
Dardanelles
(Hellespont)

Phocaea
Ephesus
Miletus
CARIA
Halicarnassus
DORIS

Hermus
Sardis
Cayster
Maeander
LYDIA
Pergamum
MYSIA

SEA OF MARMORA
(Propontis)

Byzantium
Bosporus
BITHYNIA
Sangarius
Black Sea

P H R Y G I A

A S I A   M I N O R

Indus

20°   22°   24°   26°   28°   30°

20° Longitude 26° East 28° from 30° Greenwich

36°   38°   40°

THE M. N. WORKS, BUFFALO, N. Y.

winter of 451–450 was not fated to last for the whole period. Pericles, it is true, was at first pacific. In 448 he invited all the states of Greece and the Greeks of the islands and Asia Minor to attend a Hellenic congress at Athens, to discuss various matters of interest to all, primarily the restoration of buildings and temples destroyed during the Persian wars. The magnificent project failed because of the opposition of the Peloponnesian states, and especially of Sparta. Nor can the last named state be blamed for her refusal; acceptance would have been equivalent to acknowledging herself second in importance to Athens among Greek states. A dispute about the control of Delphi in the next year led to a renewal of hostilities and a general movement against the Athenian land-empire. The Bœotian cities, led by oligarchic exiles, became actively hostile, and at Coronea their army inflicted a decisive defeat on an Athenian contingent sent to repress what the Athenians, apparently against Pericles' advice, were pleased to believe was only a slight revolt against their authority. It proved a costly and disastrous error; for many Athenians had been captured by the enemy, and, in order to ransom them, Athens was obliged to renounce all control over Bœotia. The loss of Bœotia was followed by the defection of Phocis and Locris, in which again the Athenians could only acquiesce. The Bœotian league from this time became more formidable than ever before, and Thebes once more became its acknowledged head. The constitutions of the cities that made up the league appear to have been oligarchic without exception.

In the summer of 446 Athens was hit in a more vital quarter. Eubœa revolted, and Pericles himself took charge of the operations needed to reduce the islanders to obedience. But now a strong Peloponnesian army passed the Isthmus, Megara rebelled against Athens, its citizens massacred the Athenian garrison in their city, and in a few weeks a hostile army was encamped on Attic soil. At this critical moment Pericles needed all his diplomatic skill to avert disaster. He opened negotiations with the Spartan king, Pleistoanax, who was in command of the Peloponnesian army, and, being prepared to make heavy concessions, prevailed on the king and his advisor, Cleandridas, to withdraw from Attica. The provisional agreement reached

by the generals in the field was in the winter following ratified
by their respective governments. By the terms of the treaty,
which was made for thirty years, Athens acknowledged the
independence of Megara, withdrew from the Megarian harbors
of Pagæ and Nisæa, abandoned her alliances with Achæa, in
fact, gave up all that she had won in Greece during the past
fifteen years, save only Naupactus and Aegina. The last-
named was to recover her full autonomy, while remaining a
member of the Athenian empire; but this provision of the
treaty was subsequently ignored by Athens, and the position
of the Aeginetans remained unchanged. Sparta and her allies,
on their part, formally acknowledged the maritime empire of
Athens. Disputes arising between members of the two leagues,
the Athenian and the Peloponnesian, were to be submitted
hereafter to arbitration. When this danger to Athens was
over Pericles returned to Eubœa — the threat to Attica in the
previous year had obliged him temporarily to give up the recovery of the island — and quickly reëstablished Athenian
authority there. A part of the population of Chalcis was expelled; the inhabitants of Histiæa were altogether evicted, and
their town, rather later named Oreus, became a settlement of
Athenian cleruchs; other communities were punished by a
partial loss of their territories.

Pericles' policy of making Athens a great land power, as
well as maintaining herself as the first naval power of Greece,
had ended in failure. Her position in 445 was, territorially
speaking, no better than in 461 (if we except the cases of Aegina
and Naupactus); she had, however, expended large sums and
lost many men in what proved to be very ephemeral successes.
It is due to Pericles to observe that he showed his statesmanship
in rectifying his mistake before it was too late, and in effecting
a settlement in 445 which, though in one way a humiliation to
Athenian pride, left her naval empire intact and recognized by
the rest of Greece.

In this empire there were now only three states — Lesbos,
Chios, and Samos — which were completely sovereign, with
their own navies. The rest were all dependent on Athens to a
greater or less extent, and all paid tribute. From 443 the empire, to facilitate the collection of *phoros*, was divided into five

tribute areas, — Thrace, Hellespont, the islands, Ionia, and Caria. Five years later (438), as the size of the Carian region had been reduced by the defection of some communities there, and the Athenians did not think it worth while to attempt their recovery by coercion, the remaining part of Caria was united with Ionia to form one district. The allies, apart from the three independent states, whatever form their government had previously taken, had been compelled by Athens to adopt democratic constitutions. All alike were in numerous cases subject to the jurisdiction of the Athenian law-courts, which tried serious criminal offenses in which members of an allied state were involved, as well as certain types of civil cases, especially commercial litigation. There are no adequate grounds for believing that the treatment received by citizens of allied states was not as a rule equitable. For the statement of the soured oligarchic writer, who in the last quarter of the fifth century composed a treatise on the Athenian constitution, need not be taken too seriously, when he observes that the citizen of an allied state "must needs behave as suppliant in the court of law, and clasp the hands of the jurors as they enter. Hence the allies feel more and more that their relation to the Athenians is that of slaves to masters." Still, it must be admitted that, inasmuch as this subordination to the Athenian *dicasteria* was a concrete and palpable proof of partial loss of independence, it was a cause of discontent among the allies. Another of their grievances was that Pericles and the Athenians after 454 did not hesitate to use part of the tribute money purely in their own interest, for example, for the beautification of Athens by temples and public buildings. Such resentment is perfectly intelligible, although Pericles could fairly reply that it was due to Athenian energy and initiative that the eastern Mediterranean had been made safe for all who dwelt on its shores — neither Persians nor pirates any longer threatened the peaceful Greek merchant vessel; and that the security thus enjoyed by all members of the empire had resulted in a great increase in their material prosperity.

That the assessment of tribute was, with very few exceptions, carried out by Athens was another cause of complaint; yet, as the executive had been from the first in Athenian hands, and by general consent the original assessment had been entrusted to an Athenian, Aristeides, Athens in her imperial days could not be expected to relinquish a prerogative that she had exercised when only head of a league. And the complaint would only have been justified, if she had greatly and arbitrarily increased the amounts which each member was liable to pay. But we know that no appreciable increase in the *phoros* was imposed before 425. The most serious, and the most justified, grievance of the allies is to be found in the establishment of the Athenian cleruchies. The cleruchy (*kleruchia*) was a body of settlers, sent to some district outside Attica but subject to Athens, who retained all the rights and privileges of their Athenian citizenship. While following their ordinary vocations they also formed, in effect, an Athenian garrison in dependent territory; the fact that they continued to be Athenian citizens marked them out as a privileged group in those communities where they were settled side by side with the earlier inhabitants. Settlements of this kind were essentially different in character from Greek colonies, which, once they had been founded, became independent political organisms, and their citizens ceased to enjoy the civic rights of the city-state from which they had emigrated. The earliest Athenian cleruchy was sent out before the end of the sixth century; fifty years later such bodies of Athenians were established in Lemnos, Imbros, Scyros, Chalcis, and some other places. The cleruchy could, in the economic sphere, serve the same purpose as a colony, though differing from it in character. In other words, it was a means of providing for poor citizens of an over-populated city-state.

The second period of Pericles' government in Athens was noteworthy for extensive "colonial" activity. Between 450 and 437 numerous cleruchies were sent out, for instance, to Eubœa (Histiæa), Andros, Naxos, and the Thracian Chersonese. A body of Athenians, in about 443, proceeded to Brea in Thrace. This settlement, the site of which is unknown, was a colony, not a cleruchy. But for the chance discovery of an inscription recording certain regulations for this *apoikia*, we should not know of its existence. Another colony, destined to play a more prominent part in Greek affairs, was that founded at the "Nine Ways" in 437. The earlier attempt to colonize this site had, as we have seen, ended in disaster; but now, under the name of Amphipolis, the new city flourished greatly and soon overshadowed most of the other Greek communities in Thrace. The Hellenic colony which was planted at Thurii in southern Italy was made up of citizens from various *poleis*, a goodly quota being Athenians.

In 440 an event occurred which, but for the energetic action of Pericles, might have seriously disturbed the stability of the empire. Samos and Miletus became involved in a dispute, in which Athens sided with Miletus. After some preliminaries, including an attempt of the Athenians to replace an oligarchic by a democratic constitution in Samos, the island openly seceded from Athens; her example was followed by Byzantium. After a siege lasting eight months, starvation in Samos did the work which the Athenian siege engines were unable to do, and the Samians capitulated. They were treated as the Naxians and Thasians had been a quarter of a century before. Byzantium, doubtless realizing the hopelessness of a single-handed conflict, hastened to return to her allegiance. It may have been partly to settle outstanding questions in this vitally important spot, commanding the entrance to the Black Sea, but it was especially to promote Athenian interests in a more general way, that Pericles, probably in 437, sailed with a large fleet to the Propontis and the Euxine. Athenian settlers were established in several districts bordering on one or other of those seas; but perhaps the most valuable result of this voyage was a friendly agreement signed between Athens and Spartocus, ruler of the Cimmerian Bosporus (Crimea). This prince and his successors granted Athens certain commercial privileges affecting the export of grain, which were of inestimable value to a city-state now importing more than half the wheat necessary for feeding her population.

Thus Pericles did his utmost to strengthen the Athenian empire and to widen the field of Athenian influence. In this direction his achievement, in contrast to his disastrous efforts to create and maintain a land empire, were not only eminently successful and beneficial at the time, but of lasting effect.

2. The Peloponnesian War, 431–404 b.c.

In spite of all, it was not many years after the agreement had been signed between the Peloponnesian states and Athens before ominous signs began to appear that the peace would be broken long before the expiration of the treaty. It is not easy to apportion blame to, or to determine the responsibility of, either side for the prolonged struggle known as the great Peloponnesian war. It is probably true to say that Pericles was mainly responsible for bringing about an open rupture in the particular year 432–431; it would be grossly unjust to attribute the war simply to his imperial ambitions. He foresaw that Athens would inevitably be involved very soon in a great fight with her Peloponnesian neighbors. Being convinced of what was bound to occur in any case within a very few years, he may have forced the issue at the last because, if Athens had to go to war, he wished her to do so at a time and under circumstances that were favorable to her, and above all, while he himself was still alive and able to guide her destinies. In the *History* of Thucydides we have a full and masterly account of the struggle from 431 to 411, and the historian, who analyzes the preliminaries to the war with a great wealth of detail, is careful to distinguish those events which immediately preceded the rupture, and were thus the immediate reasons for the war, from the real, though less tangible, causes that lay deep down in the character of Greek city-states and of the two groups of combatants.

However great the advantages derived by the subjects of Athens from their membership in her maritime empire, neither they nor the rest of Greece could forget that they had lost that possession which was dearest to the Greek heart, political autonomy. Nor, when the Spartans, in going to war, claimed that they did so in order to liberate the Greeks from enslavement by Athens, were they conscious hypocrites. That they failed thirty years later to be true to their earlier professions, and were then far worse oppressors of Hellenic liberty than ever the Athenians had been, proves only that their leaders when power was in their grasp did not know how to use it. In 432 Sparta hesitated to go to war; it was other members of the Peloponnesian league who had to use all their influence with

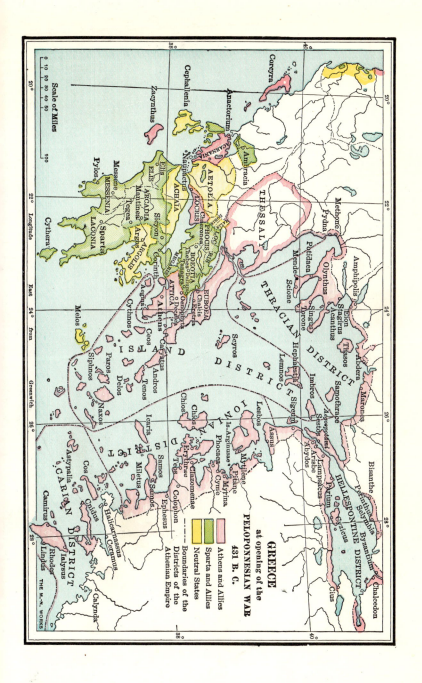

GREECE
at the opening of the
PELOPONNESIAN WAR
431 B. C.

Athens and Allies
Sparta and Allies
Neutral States
Boundaries of the
Districts of the
Athenian Empire

Scale of Miles
0 10 20 30 40 50
100

the head of the league to take the final step. Corinth especially was bitterly hostile to Athens, partly because she was filled with jealousy of the state whose naval power had far outstripped her own, partly through exasperation at the events of 435–432 in which her interests suffered seriously.[1] There were, in fact, two incidents which had ended in open conflict between Corinthians and Athenian troops, though both were in outlying parts of the Hellenic world. Corinth in 435 was involved in a quarrel with the powerful island-state of Corcyra, which had originally been a Corinthian colony. The latter, after some initial successes, found herself in a position of dangerous isolation; in her difficulty she appealed to Athens for alliance and help. After a lengthy debate the Athenian *ecclesia* acceded to the Corcyræan request. Before the end of the summer of 433 the presence of Athenian vessels in Corcyræan waters had deprived Corinth of a victory over her daughter-city. The Corinthian government was naturally annoyed; a few months later their annoyance was increased to exasperation. The city of Potidæa in Chalcidice was also a Corinthian colony, and her relations with the mother-city were closer than usual, since her chief magistrates came to her annually from Corinth. But Potidæa had been a member of the Athenian empire for some time, and had recently had her tribute considerably increased. Relying on the support of Corinth and of the Macedonian king, Perdiccas, who looked with disfavor on Athenian expansion in Thrace, and was himself scheming to bring about a general revolt among the Athenian allies in Thrace, the Potidæans prepared to revolt. The Athenians, learning what was in the wind, delivered an ultimatum. When their demands were not met, an Athenian squadron was sent off to bring the recalcitrant ally to order. Corinth despatched an officer with a body of irregulars to help her daughter-city in her need, and this force succeeded in reaching Potidæa before the Athenian blockade had become fully effective. The Corinthians now

[1] Yet, when Samos in 440 appealed to the Peloponnesian league for help against Athens, it was Corinth who urged non-intervention. This was of course only five years after the conclusion of the thirty years' peace; also the Corinthians may well have felt that it was undesirable, as it certainly was against the terms of the peace, to interfere in what was a domestic quarrel within the large Athenian family.

exerted themselves to make Sparta and the Peloponnesian league proclaim war on Athens.

Some months before the representatives of the league had convened at Sparta, Pericles had prevailed upon the Athenians to take a step which would either hasten on a war which he already regarded as inevitable, or else would so intimidate the enemies of Athens that they would fail to rally to the support of Corinth. In the summer of 432 the Athenian assembly passed a decree excluding the Megarians from all the markets and harbors of the Athenian empire. It is true that the Athenians at this date had several legitimate grievances against their neighbor; nor had they forgotten the defection of Megara in 446 and the slaughter of the Athenian garrison. Nevertheless, the decree, which meant the economic ruin and the semi-starvation of Megara, was far more than a punitive measure inflicted by Athens on an offending neighbor; it was a challenge to the enemies of Athens as a whole, a demonstration of what Athenian control of the eastern Aegean could do.

At the Peloponnesian congress, held in the autumn of 432, the Spartan government was won over by the war party in its own city and in the league. A majority of the league voted for war, but the winter months were still spent in diplomatic exchanges. Had Athens been prepared to make some concessions, it is doubtful whether Sparta would have finally broken off negotiations. Though the first fighting occurred in the early spring of 431 with a surprise attack by the Bœotians on Athens' ally, Platæa, general hostilities did not open till the end of May. Virtually all Greeks save those of the far West were involved in the struggle that now began. The enemies of Athens comprised all the Peloponnesian states, except Argos, and most of the Achæan cities, which remained neutral; Megara, Bœotia, Phocis, and Locris in central Greece; and, in the Northwest, Leucas, Anactorium, and Ambracia, all of which were in close and friendly relations with Corinth. Athens, in addition to her subjects and her two independent allies, Lesbos and Chios, had on her side Corcyra, Zacynthus, most of Acarnania, Naupactus, and Platæa. As regards the "sinews of war" she was in an infinitely stronger position than her enemies. A reserve of 6000 talents lay on the Athenian Acropolis, and there was a large and regular income each year from the tribute of her subjects. The opponents of Athens commanded no such resources; and, though the suggestion was put forward by Corinth that the treasures of Olympia and Delphi be used by them to finance the war, the religious sentiments of a majority of her allies were evidently opposed to such sacrilege, since the suggestion was never adopted. Nor did they succeed in their efforts to enlist the active support of Persia in the fight against Athens.

Pericles' plan of campaign was, briefly, to evacuate Attica and bring all the population inside the walls of Athens and Peiræus, leaving the enemy to do such material damage in the country as they could. For the Athenian food-supply was safe as long as the Athenians controlled the sea. Her naval strength Athens must use to harry the coasts of the enemy, and, so far as possible, to carry out an economic blockade of the Peloponnese. At all costs a military engagement must be avoided; for the Peloponnesian army outnumbered the Athenian field-force by more than two to one. It is a proof of Pericles' tremendous hold on his countrymen that he prevailed on them to abandon farms and homes, and crowd into the city, and that, later, when they knew the foe was ravaging and burning crops, vineyards, and oliveyards, he was able to restrain them from rushing out to fight. The invasions of Attica by a Peloponnesian army were at first almost annual occurrences. The Athenians attacked the Megarid and Argolid more than once, but these expeditions were subordinate to the naval operations undertaken over a wider area.

The first serious blow suffered by the Athenians was not inflicted by the enemy. In the early summer of 430, when the Peloponnesian army for the second time had invaded Attica, an epidemic which had already ravaged many parts of the Persian empire reached Peiræus and Athens. In spite of the careful and detailed description of the symptoms and progress of this plague, which Thucydides, who was himself a victim, has left us, it has not been possible for medical experts to identify it with any disease now known. But there is no doubt about its deadly character, especially when, through overcrowding, indifferent housing, and bad sanitation, the conditions were so favorable to the spread of contagion. The death rate was very high, the situation in the city being made worse by the fact that many of the dead had to be left unburied. The worst phase of the pestilence was in 430–429, but there was a recurrence in 427, and cases continued to occur for a further two years before the disease had entirely spent its force. The total death-roll in these years is said to have been no less than a third of the population; for in 430 the infection had been carried to the besieging force at Potidæa by a supplementary detachment of troops sent from Athens to expedite operations against the rebellious communities of Chalcidice. The physical illness of the citizens was not the worst part of the visitation. The misery all around them, the uncertainty of existence caused by the knowledge that though they were alive one day they might be dead the next, slackened the moral fibre of the Athenians and brought out their worst passions and a readiness to commit any excess. "Knowing not what would become of them, they disregarded all the ordinances of gods and men."[1] Seeking for a scapegoat, they found him in the statesman who had been responsible for massing them in the city and had prevented them from going out against the enemy.

In 430 Pericles was indicted for misappropriation of public funds. He was found guilty, — no doubt quite unjustly — fined, and deposed from his high office. Yet in a few months, in the early spring of 429, the Athenians had repented of their action, and Pericles was reëlected to the office of *strategos*. Before the end of that year the great statesman died, and there was no one to replace him. Thucydides, in his appraisal of Pericles' character and abilities (ii, 65), expressly stresses the unrivalled authority which, by his personality and force of character, his personal integrity, and his knowledge of mass psychology, he had been able to exercise over the Athenians. Although the general policy which he had laid down for them at the beginning of the war was to a great extent followed for the next eight years, there was no single man to guide the ship of state. Party warfare succeeded the Periclean autocracy, and for a space the two outstanding politicians at Athens were Nicias and Cleon. The former was a rich land-owner; he had

[1] Thucydides, ii, 52.

the backing of the wealthy class, on whom a great part of the expenses of the war devolved, and of the farming population. The peace party or moderates, whichever we call them, though no less patriotic than their political opponents, on the one hand proceeded, as far as possible, along Periclean lines, on the other they counselled moderation toward the allies; and, if a suitable opportunity for making peace should present itself, they were prepared to make concessions to save the prolongation of the war. Cleon was a man of very different type and antecedents. Whether the "tanner" had actually practised his craft himself or merely owned some slaves, from the profit of whose leather work he derived an income, we do not know; at all events he sprang from the proletariat, and to it he looked for support when his native ability brought him to the front as a politician. His regular supporters were those on whom the burden of war lay least heavily, and who either immediately or in the near future could derive some profit from it.

For several years after Pericles' death neither group of combatants could boast of any striking successes. Had her enemies possessed a commander of genius, Athens, weakened as she was by the plague, might have been forced to come to terms within the first five years of the war. Potidæa at last surrendered in the late autumn of 430; the operations had cost Athens dearly both in men and money. So, for the present at least, she abandoned the attempt to recover completely her grip on Chalcidice. On the other hand, the Peloponnesian efforts to detach the Athenian allies in northwestern Greece, and to deprive Athens of her base on the Corinthian Gulf at Naupactus, failed miserably, partly owing to the incompetence of the Peloponnesian commanders, partly through the skill of the Athenian, Phormio, who won two notable naval victories in the Corinthian Gulf against greatly superior forces. Athens' little ally, Platæa, was assaulted by a Peloponnesian army in 429 — the year in which the plague made an attack on Attica unsafe for any invader — but without success; the active siege was, however, changed to a blockade. At last in 427, after a part of the garrison had managed to escape to Athens, the rest of the Platæans were forced to surrender, and, after a trial which was a mockery of justice, were put to death. The help which Athens had prom-

ised her ally had never come, but there were, from the Athenian
point of view, extenuating circumstances. She probably had
not the men available to risk a battle in the open with the Peloponnesian army, and only a clear victory could have saved her
besieged friends. For, before the end of 428, Mitylene, the
chief city in Lesbos, had revolted, and all the lesser cities in the
island, except Methymna, followed suit. The Athenians needed
all their resources to punish a defection which, if neglected,
might easily have become the signal for a general rising of her
allies against her. In the summer of the next year, shortly
before the fall of Platæa, Mitylene capitulated. Cleon persuaded the Athenians to visit their utmost fury on the unhappy
city, and to put to death all the adult males and enslave the
women and children. Fortunately more moderate counsels prevailed on the day after this decision had been made by the assembly, and the order for this mass execution was countermanded
in time. Even so a thousand of the chief men of Lesbos were
executed. The land of the Lesbians was confiscated and handed
over to 3000 Athenian settlers, to whom the former owners who
continued to cultivate the land were obliged to pay a heavy
tithe. Costly as the operations had been — and in order to
meet her immediate needs Athens for the first recorded time
levied a property tax on the wealthier citizens and denizens —
they seem to have had a generally salutary effect on the
members of the Athenian empire. Before the end of 427 the
Athenians for the first time cast their eyes to the far West. In
the autumn of that year, and again in 425, they sent small
squadrons to Sicily to help their allies there against the growing
and aggressive power of Syracuse.

The period of Tyrant-rule, through which all Sicily had passed
in the early part of the century, had come to an end c. 465.
Everywhere despots were deposed and a period of civil war
followed. The older Sicel population for a brief spell was organized by one, Ducetius, and made its influence strongly felt;
but its power collapsed as quickly as it had arisen. By c. 445
general peace at last reigned again in the island, and the leading
position among the Sicilian cities was by common consent accorded to Syracuse. In the early part of the Peloponnesian war
Syracusan statesmen were showing a disposition to change that

leadership into a more definite sovereignty, the result being a renewal of warfare in the island.

There were at least three communities in the far West which had had treaty relations with Athens for some time. Segesta had concluded an alliance with Athens in 453, Leontini and Rhegium had done the same somewhat later, and their treaties had been renewed in 433–432. Although the Athenian operations of 427–424 in Sicily did not lead to any substantial results, they did make the Athenians more familiar with that country. The venture had been urged on by Cleon and the war party, whose aims were frankly imperialistic in the worst sense. It may have prevented coöperation between the Dorian cities of the island, like Syracuse, and the Peloponnesian league. By 424 the Sicilians had settled their differences among themselves after a pan-Sicilian congress at Gela. The Athenian commanders, in face of this development, could do nothing but withdraw from the island. A disappointed Athenian assembly, on their return to Athens, fined one and exiled the other.

Meantime neither side in the main theatre of war had been able to win any substantial advantage. The most noteworthy operation was the Athenian capture of Pylos on the west coast of Messenia, which gave them a serviceable base from which to harry Spartan territory. A further blow was dealt to Sparta by the Athenian seizure and occupation of the island of Cythera. The capture of Pylos, moreover, had other than military results. The Athenians had taken 292 Lacedæmonian prisoners, of whom 120 were full Spartan citizens. The fact that these were in Athenian hands prevented the Peloponnesians from continuing their annual invasions of Attica, since an exasperated Athenian assembly might have retaliated by putting the prisoners to death. Again, Cleon had won all the credit, which more properly belonged to the Athenian commander, Demosthenes, for the successful conclusion of the Pylos campaign, and for the moment his ascendancy in Athens was so great that he carried through a measure for the drastic reassessment of the tribute payable by the subjects of Athens. The actual sum now assessed against them was nearly 1000 talents. That the action of the Athenians was unpopular in the empire we cannot doubt; on the other hand, there was some justification for raising the *phoros*, because most of the cities had greatly advanced in wealth and prosperity during the past half century. In some instances, where the resources of a city had not increased, no additional tribute was imposed, or the amount previously fixed was actually reduced.

In the next three years, 424–422, the tide began to turn against Athens. An attempted surprise attack on Bœotia failed through the incompetence of the Athenian generals, and the Athenians suffered a severe defeat at Delium. The Spartan commander, Brasidas, who had already performed some notable acts in the war, at the head of a small contingent made his way with much secrecy to Thrace. There, with great diplomatic skill, he sowed disaffection among the subjects of Athens. He made himself master of Amphipolis, and the loss of this city, quickly followed as it was by the secession of other Chalcidic communities, was one of the severest blows that Athens had suffered so far. The Athenian efforts to oust Brasidas and, above all, to recover Amphipolis failed; finally, in an engagement fought near that city in 422, Brasidas and Cleon, who was in charge of the Athenian operations, were both killed. The death of Cleon was a blessing for Athens. It removed the one dominant man of the war party at Athens, and the moderates, led by Nicias, were able to convince their war-weary countrymen of the need of coming to terms with the enemy. The Spartan government, too, at this time was disappointed that the Peloponnesians had been unable to make any permanent impression on the strength of Athens, and so was pacifically inclined. In the spring of 421, after preliminary negotiations during the winter, a peace was concluded between the chief combatants.

For Sparta to conclude peace with the Athenians was one thing; to ensure that the terms of the agreement would be accepted by all her allies was another, and proved to be impossible. So for three or four years Greece witnessed a tangle of diplomatic moves and counter-moves, agreements and counter-agreements, at the end of which Sparta had reasserted her authority in the Peloponnesian league, while Athens was in a more isolated position in Greece than before. The events of 421–416 can here be only very briefly touched upon. Inability on the part of Sparta to persuade the Bœotians, Corinth, and some other states to agree to the peace of Nicias for a moment led to the break-up of the Peloponnesian league. To counterbalance its loss of influence with some of the most powerful allies, the Spartan government made approaches to Athens and contracted a defensive alliance with the late enemy. But a change in the Spartan ephorate and in the political leadership at Athens made this understanding inoperative almost at once. On the expiry of the thirty years' truce, concluded between Sparta and Argos in 451, the Athenians allied themselves to Argos. Sparta settled her differences with the Bœotian league and Corinth, but the alliance between Athens and Argos was enlarged to include two Peloponnesian states, Elis and Mantinea, each of whom had a quarrel of her own with Sparta. It was not till 418 that the general peace was again broken in Greece. An attack by Argos on Epidaurus, a member of the Peloponnesian league, led to Spartan intervention. In the summer of that year a Lacedæmonian army, reinforced by contingents from Tegea and other Arcadian cities who were loyal to Sparta, decisively defeated an allied force of Argives, Mantineans, and Athenians close to the city of Mantinea. The result of this Spartan victory was to restore to its former solidarity the Peloponnesian league, and to reëstablish completely the hegemony of Sparta. Argos was compelled to form a new alliance with her victor, and the Athenians found themselves deserted by their recently found friends in the Peloponnese. The calculations of the Spartans respecting Argos were, however, upset by a revolution in that city in 417, as the result of which a democratic government took the place of the former oligarchy. The several efforts of the Spartans to get the Argive oligarchs restored to power were unsuccessful but meant that the two states were intermittently at war for several years. The Athenian-Argive alliance, on the other hand, had been renewed for a period of fifty years in 417.

At Athens the interval between the peace of Nicias and the sailing of the expedition to Sicily in 415 had served to bring to the political front a young rival to Nicias for the control of the assembly and of Athenian policy. Alcibiades, the nephew and ward of Pericles, having completed his thirtieth year, was in 420 elected to the office of *strategos*. For the remainder of the war he was to be the evil genius of Athens. Handsome, endowed with a great personal fascination and exceptional intellectual gifts, he was indulgently forgiven by the Athenians for the vagaries and occasional ostentation of his private life, while the war party saw in him the makings of a brilliant leader working for their advantage. Yet his whole career shows that he lacked stability and character, that personal ambition, not the interest of his country, was the motive power of his political conduct. First and last he was a self-seeking politician; to put him, as some modern writers have been inclined to do, in the same class as a Pericles or a Themistocles is an insult to the memory of those men and to the critical faculty of the modern student of Athenian history. It was Alcibiades who was responsible for the various *rapprochements* with Argos and the break-down of the more friendly relations between Sparta and Athens. His policy did not go unchallenged, for the influence of Nicias was still very strong; and, just as he had brought about the peace of 421, so he continued to desire peace with Sparta. Finally in 417 recourse was had to the obsolescent expedient of ostracism. The result was farcical, inasmuch as the adverse vote of the assembly pronounced the decree of exile against Hyperbolus, a politician of the stamp of Cleon, but without his ability, who had been prominent in the counsels of the war party for some years. It is not unlikely that this outcome was the result of an understanding between Alcibiades and Nicias, brought about by the persuasive tongue of the younger man because he had cause to fear for his own position.[1]

In 416, at Alcibiades' instigation, the Athenians committed a shocking act of injustice. The island of Melos, a reputed Dorian colony, was, though one of the Cyclades, not a tribute-paying member of the Athenian empire. The Athenians had made earlier but unavailing efforts to press the Melians into alliance with themselves. Now they delivered an ultimatum,

---

[1] After the case of Hyperbolus ostracism seems to have been entirely abandoned at Athens. In 417 it had proved quite useless for the purpose for which it was originally intended.

and, when their demands were opposed, besieged the island. On its capture they killed off the adult males and sold the women and children as slaves. Then they sent a body of Athenian settlers to the island. Such harsh treatment, however deplorable, was by the usage of the time condoned by public opinion in the case of revolted allies or even active combatants in the war. So to act toward a small neutral state nothing but the most brutal cynicism could justify.

With the war virtually at a standstill in Greece the minds of the Athenians were once more filled with ambitions of conquest in Sicily. The arrival, in the late autumn of 416, of an embassy from their old ally, Segesta, provided an excuse, if one was needed, for despatching an Athenian expedition to the West. The peaceful settlement of Sicily reached by the congress at Gela in 424 had lasted very few years. Syracuse had attacked and destroyed Leontini, and then, at the request of Selinus, she had intervened in a quarrel between that city and Segesta. The Segestan envoys at Athens promised that their city would provide the Athenians with funds to carry on operations in Sicily on their behalf. The Athenian assembly, with surprising caution, did not commit itself at once, but sent representatives to the West to investigate on the spot the financial strength of their ally. When they returned to Athens a few months later they brought with them a substantial sum in cash and a promise of more to come. The renewed deliberations of the *ecclesia* showed that there was a great majority in favor of the enterprise. The spokesman of this majority was Alcibiades, who saw in an expedition, which he hoped to lead himself, a magnificent opportunity of furthering his own ambitions and satisfying his lust for power. Thus the timely and urgent counsel of Nicias against the proposed undertaking was set aside; when, at a second meeting of the assembly, he tried to deflect the Athenians from their purpose by representing that the force which they intended to send was quite inadequate, they were so far from being deterred that they voted a much larger armament. The command was entrusted to Alcibiades, Lamachus — an experienced soldier but without political experience or influence — and Nicias. The appointment of so ill-matched a trio to act jointly in the conduct of a difficult war was the first of several vital errors committed by the Athenians. Preparations were now pushed on with speed and with the determination that men, ships, and equipment should all be of the best. Almost the entire population was carried away with a boundless enthusiasm which Plutarch describes graphically when he writes, "that the young men in the wrestling schools and the older men sitting in their workshops or in the lounges of the gymnasia drew outline maps of Sicily and the details of the sea surrounding the island and the harbors and places on the side of the island facing Africa." [1] The total force of Athenians, strengthened by some of their allies, amounted to 134 ships of war, 130 smaller vessels for taking supplies, 5100 heavy and 1300 light-armed troops, and 30 cavalry. Since the normal complement of a trireme was 200, the total personnel of the expedition was more than 27,000 men.

An act of sacrilege cast a certain gloom over Athens shortly before the fleet was due to sail. In one night almost all the busts of Hermes, which adorned numerous shrines and also the vestibules of dwelling-houses in the city, were hacked and mutilated by impious hands. A wanton act of this kind aroused all the latent superstitions of the masses. An oligarchic revolution was feared by many, and the almost hysterical condition of the people gave ample scope for informers and occasion for numerous investigations and prosecutions. The political enemies of Alcibiades exploited the situation for their own ends. Information was laid about other sacrilegious acts which had taken place in the past, especially a mock celebration in a private house of the Eleusinian Mysteries, in which Alcibiades was supposed to have taken part. The latter wanted an immediate trial, but his enemies managed to get it deferred, so that it could take place when the soldiers and sailors with whom he was a favorite were no longer in Athens. To postpone the sailing of the expedition was impossible, and Alcibiades was therefore forced to depart for Sicily with a prosecution on what might well be a capital charge hanging over him. The armada left Athens before the end of June, 415; after a review at Corcyra it proceeded in three divisions to Italian

[1] Plutarch, *Nicias*, 12.

and Sicilian waters. At Rhegium three scout vessels, which had been sent on in advance to Segesta, rejoined the main fleet, bringing with them the unwelcome news that the Segestans had deceived the Athenians when they promised ample financial aid, and that only thirty talents were available. The council of war that was now held by the three commanders showed that a radical difference existed between them regarding the best plan of campaign. Nicias wished to confine the operations to assisting Athens' ally, by moving at once against Selinus; Lamachus urged an immediate attack against the real enemy, Syracuse; Alcibiades, whose proposal carried the day, argued that they should, before beginning active operations, try to win as many allies in the island as possible. Thus precious time was lost at the outset. When the Athenians arrived at Catana they were met by the state trireme *Salaminia* which had been sent to bring Alcibiades home to stand his trial. Allowed to return in his own ship, Alcibiades escaped from his escort, made his way to the Peloponnese, and finally reached Sparta, quite ready to play traitor to his country. The responsibility for the mutilation of the Hermæ was supposedly brought home to members of the oligarchic clubs.

Nicias, after this, ill-advisedly continued to follow Alcibiades' plan of action, with the result that a serious attack on Syracuse was not made till the spring of 414. In consequence the Syracusans had ample time to make preparations against the danger that threatened them, and, above all, they were able to communicate with their mother-city, Corinth. Through her good offices the Spartan government was persuaded to send a Lacedæmonian officer, Gylippus, to take charge of the small relief expedition equipped by Corinth, and of the general defense of Syracuse when he reached Sicily.

The Athenian operations against Syracuse started auspiciously; for, owing to the enemy's negligence, the Athenians were able to get control of the hill, Euryalus, and the high plateau, Epipolæ, which overlooked and commanded the city. The object of the Athenians was now to cut off Syracuse entirely from the land side, by constructing a wall running approximately north and south across the peninsula on which the city was built. Their opponents sought to prevent this by building counter-walls at right angles to the Athenian works and so to hinder them from completing their plan. Twice the Syracusans were defeated, and their constructions captured and demolished. On the second occasion the Athenians suffered a severe loss in the death of their best officer, Lamachus. Before the northern end of the Athenian wall had been carried to the sea, and thereby completed, Gylippus, who had landed in northern Sicily by this time and had there collected a considerable body of auxiliaries from Himera and other cities, had managed to elude the vigilance of the Athenians and had made his way into Syracuse. The unaccountable negligence of Nicias in failing adequately to guard the ascent to Euryalus, thus allowing Gylippus to slip through and past the Athenian lines, cost the Athenians dear. Nicias had, it is true, reason for believing that the Syracusans were on the point of surrendering to him on conditions; yet this was no excuse for relaxing the siege operations or for gross military negligence.

The arrival of Gylippus, which occurred in the nick of time, marks the turning point of the Syracusan fortunes. The citizens were heartened by his presence, by the realization that they were not forgotten by their friends in Greece, and by the arrival of much needed reinforcements. Gylippus, for his part, took infinite pains to improve the discipline and efficiency of the Syracusan army. The third counter-wall was now successfully built after they had driven back the attacking Athenians, who were thus prevented from completing the blockade of the city. By the autumn of 414 the Athenians were strictly on the defensive and thoroughly disheartened besides. Their losses from fighting and sickness had been considerable, and Nicias, who was himself suffering from an organic disease, was desirous of abandoning the whole enterprise. Fearing to do this on his own responsibility, he sent an urgent despatch to Athens in which he put two alternatives to the council and the assembly: either to allow the withdrawal of his troops or to send a large body of reinforcements. In case the second course should be adopted he asked to be relieved of his command. But the assembly were not yet convinced that the situation in Sicily could not be retrieved. A fresh armament was voted, which, before it reached Syracuse, totalled 73 triremes, 5000 hoplites, and 3000 miscellaneous light-armed troops. The command was intrusted to Demosthenes and Eurymedon; yet Nicias was not superseded, but instructed to coöperate with his new colleagues. A small advance reinforcement was sent off under Eurymedon as soon as possible; the second expedition did not sail till the spring and reached Syracuse in July, 413.

The winter months had been a period of military inactivity in Sicily; but, when the campaigning season of 413 began, it became more than ever clear how invaluable to the Syracusans the presence of Gylippus was. At his instigation they reorganized their naval forces and equipment with the hope of successfully attacking the Athenian fleet in the harbor when opportunity offered. Without the destruction of their navy the Athenians could not be completely crushed, and a means of escape remained open to them. Both by land and sea the advantage, in spite of some set-backs, rested with the Syracusans, and, when at last the second Athenian expedition arrived, it was not a moment too soon. On the previous day the enemy had won a notable victory in the harbor, and the position of Nicias and his men was well-nigh desperate. Demosthenes urged on his colleague the necessity of an immediate offensive, with the object of destroying or capturing the Syracusan counter-wall. This done, it would be possible to shut in the city completely. But for a direct assault by day conditions were unfavorable; the enemy were too strong and too well disciplined. Hence a night attack was planned by way of Euryalus. All went well at first on the critical evening; but, once well on the plateau, when the alarm had been given and the fighting had become general, the advance Athenian force pressed on too far, and, being met by a fresh detachment of the enemy, was pushed back in disorder, and the main body of their men was thrown into confusion. The Syracusans drove home their advantage and the whole Athenian army was thrown back with very heavy loss — perhaps as much as 2000 men. The sequel to this disastrous failure Demosthenes foresaw would be a new and energetic offensive by the Syracusans; he therefore urged immediate departure on his colleagues. Once more Nicias could not steel himself to take decisive action; also, he still appears to have entertained hopes that the philo-Athenian party in Syracuse — how large it was we do not know — might play into his hands. For three weeks the Athenians remained on the watch, yet inactive, during which time Gylippus had secured additional help in Sicily, and some overdue reinforcements from Greece also arrived at last. In view of this even Nicias could hesitate no longer. On August 27th, 413, the retirement from Syracuse was to be undertaken; in the evening, however, when all was ready, a total eclipse of the moon occurred. The soothsayers protested that nothing could be done until twenty-seven days had elapsed. Was the advice mere folly, or were there traitors among the Athenian interpreters of celestial phenomena? We do not know; but Nicias, religious or superstitious, whichever we choose to call him, obeyed their advice.

Gylippus had quickly learnt of the intended retirement of the enemy and of the consequences of the eclipse. He thus laid his plans for cutting off the Athenian retirement by land, at the same time staking his hopes on the successful issue of a grand assault on the Athenian fleet. In their first naval engagement the Syracusans drove the Athenian vessels on shore; though they had suffered severe casualties themselves, they were once more masters of their own harbor. They at once closed its entrance with warships and other craft securely anchored together, anticipating that their opponents, as soon as they had effected the most necessary repairs to their vessels, would try to escape by sea. In this they calculated correctly. When the Athenians tried to make good their escape they were defeated and driven back to shore with heavy loss. Their commanders wished to make a second attempt to break through with their remaining sixty triremes; but now the crews refused to embark, and there was nothing left but to retreat by land. For six days they retired, dogged by the enemy. At last the two divisions in which the army was marching got separated. Demosthenes' was the first to be surrounded and forced to surrender on the seventh day, to the number of 6000. On the eighth day the army of Nicias was overwhelmed as it was desperately trying to fight its way across the Assinarus river. The official captives on this occasion numbered 1000, but many Athenians had been privately taken prisoner by Syracusans. To the survivors the Syracusans were merciless. Nicias and Demosthenes were executed, an ignominy spared to Eurymedon, who had fallen in an engagement before the final retreat. The other captives were imprisoned in stone quarries near Syracuse where most of them perished after many weeks of untold suffering. Truly, the people of Melos had been heavily avenged!

The catastrophe in Sicily, a disaster to a Greek state of hitherto unparalleled magnitude, her enemies believed would be followed by the immediate collapse of Athens. In holding out instead for another eight years against a most formidable coalition of opponents, the Athenians showed indomitable courage and resourcefulness; but this would have availed them little if they had not been helped by the crass incompetence of their enemies' higher command. In Greece, active hostilities between Athens and Sparta had been reopened by the spring of 413. King Agis with a Peloponnesian army invaded Attica; he seized and fortified Decelea, and having sent part of his troops back remained in occupation there with the rest. Decelea on the slopes of Mt. Parnes was situated about a dozen miles from Athens and a like distance from the Attic-Bœotian frontier; it was a position from which the whole of northern Attica, and especially the land route from Athens to Oropus and Eubœa, could be controlled. Moreover, as Thucydides observes (vii, 27), the Athenians had in the past suffered only from temporary invasions of Attica; now they were for the rest of the war to have an enemy force permanently within their frontiers. Raids in different parts of Attica became frequent, cattle and flocks were destroyed, more than 20,000 slaves deserted; later on it became impossible properly to work the silver mines at Laurium. In fact, the population of Attica was compelled to reside continuously in the capital, which became like an armed camp in a perpetual state of siege. Yet, while she had command of the sea, Athens could not be starved into submission. After the disaster in Sicily the possibility or need of crushing Athens on her own element was borne in upon her foes, and during the winter months, 413–412, they engaged in great naval preparations. That same interval of six months' virtual suspension of fighting was the salvation of the Athenians. It enabled them to take stock of

their resources and to effect such changes and reforms in administration as seemed called for by the exigencies of their situation.
The first need was money, since the treasury was exhausted.
To increase the tribute would have been too dangerous a measure when the subjects of the empire were already restive and
disposed to revolt. The *phoros* was therefore abolished and the
Athenians calculated that they would get a safer as well as a
larger income by imposing a 5% tax on all imports and exports
throughout the empire. It is regrettable that we are ignorant
of the details of this financial experiment; nor do we know the
total sum forthcoming in any year. The fact that the Athenians
were able to carry on the war so long is sufficient proof that their
calculations in 413 were approximately correct.

The war party at Athens was deemed responsible for the
Sicilian catastrophe, and suffered eclipse. To put the executive
in more responsible hands the assembly voted the appointment
of ten commissioners (*probuloi*), who took over many of the
most important functions of the Council of Five Hundred, for
example, the direction of finance and the superintendence of
naval construction. At the elections for the *strategia* held early
in 412 several of the newly elected officers were men of marked
oligarchic sympathies, another sign that the disasters suffered
by the Athenians, when the government was in the hands of
advanced democrats, were producing a strong reaction against
the extremer forms of democracy.

Meanwhile, the anti-Athenian coalition was steadily growing.
The Syracusans sent a naval squadron to join the Peloponnesian navy. Many of the Athenian subjects or allies in Ionia
were intriguing with the enemy, and in 412 many of them openly
revolted. Of these the chief was Chios; the secession of this
powerful state was a very severe blow to the Athenians, who
now used the reserve fund of 1000 talents, which had been set
aside for a naval emergency at the beginning of the war, in order
to increase their ship-building. One consequence of the revolt
of Ionia and the coöperation of the Peloponnesian fleet with
Athens' late subjects was that the main theatre of the war was
transferred to the eastern Aegean. An additional reason for
this is to be found in the intervention of Persia in Greek affairs
at this date. The occasion for reasserting his authority over the

Anatolian Greeks seemed to Darius II to have come, and his two satraps in western Asia Minor were given a free hand to assist the enemies of Athens. Unfortunately for the interests of the Great King, Tissaphernes and Pharnabazus, under the influence of personal jealousy or ambition, did not collaborate; but each worked only to recover the Greek cities in the vicinity of his own satrapy. It was with Tissaphernes that the Spartans first came to an understanding; from him they now secured funds, without which they could hardly have carried on the war over so wide an area.

The operations in the Aegean during 412 and 411 were indecisive in character. Though Athens failed to recover any appreciable part of what she had lost, she inflicted much loss on her opponents and prevented them from carrying out any combined movements against her. This achievement was the more noteworthy because the year 411 saw an oligarchic revolution in Athens itself. By the beginning of that year the Athenians had lost all Ionia save only the island of Samos, which remained staunchly loyal to them and now became the headquarters for Athenian operations in the Aegean. Many of the leading men in the Athenian fleet were disposed to favor a constitutional change at Athens. In communication with the influential members of the oligarchic clubs at Athens — the most prominent was Antiphon, by profession a writer of law-court speeches and a man who combined great legal knowledge with a remarkable gift for organization and intrigue — the Athenian oligarchs at Samos had also got in touch with Alcibiades. Undoubtedly some of the energetic measures taken by the Spartans in 413 and 412 had been due to his astute advice. But a quarrel with King Agis made it advisable for Alcibiades to leave Sparta, which he did by joining the Peloponnesian fleet destined to help the revolted Chians. His real aim was to bring about his own recall to his native country; to pave the way for this, he now made his way to the satrap Tissaphernes and began to intrigue against Sparta, as he had previously intrigued against Athens. To the Athenian oligarchs at Samos he sent communications promising Persian support for Athens, provided an oligarchy were set up there. When the point of negotiating with the satrap himself was reached, the oligarchs found that Alcibiades had promised more than he could perform, and almost immediately afterward Tissaphernes made a fresh agreement with Sparta. But the oligarchs at Samos had no intention of dropping their plans for a revolution at Athens, and, indeed, matters there had gone too far.

There were many responsible and moderate-minded citizens who wished to see a considerable modification of the democratic régime which had prevailed in recent years. Hence the actual revolution, though it was preceded by some assassinations and terrorization, for which the extreme section of the oligarchs was responsible, was effected with comparative ease and little disturbance. A council of Four Hundred was elected, ostensibly as a provisional government, until such time as a proper constitution could be drawn up, in which full citizen rights would be limited to 5000 persons, able to perform civic and military duties at their own expense, in other words, the wealthy and middle classes. The Four Hundred, or at least the extreme part of that body, once in power, aimed to keep it, by ignoring or postponing the nomination of the 5000. But there were reasons why their régime was doomed to failure almost from the beginning, quite apart from the exasperation caused by their excesses when in power. In the first place, there was no unanimity among the Four Hundred themselves, but they were divided into two factions. One of these was composed of extremists, led by Antiphon, and two men who had once been democrats, Peisander and Phrynichus; the other, whose leading spirit was Theramenes, was genuinely desirous of establishing the "limited democracy" of the 5000.

Secondly, the oligarchs had gravely miscalculated the sentiments of the Athenian military and naval forces stationed at Samos. Knowing that the leading officers were sympathetic, they anticipated that the rank and file would accept without demur the constitutional changes effected at home. Herein they were utterly mistaken; for the troops deposed their oligarchic commanders and elected others in their place, chief among them being Thrasybulus and Thrasyllus. They followed up this decided and practical expression of their views by what was, in the circumstances, an astute move. They recalled

Alcibiades and appointed him their chief *strategos*. Although his fresh attempts to bring about a rupture between Tissaphernes and Sparta failed, it was his influence which, for the time being, reconciled the Athenians at Samos to the proposed moderate democracy of Theramenes. This knowledge strengthened Theramenes' hands, and he and his adherents succeeded in deposing the Four Hundred after four months' misrule at home and failure abroad. For their peace overtures to Sparta had been rejected and their inefficient government had encouraged Euboea to revolt. The direction of affairs now passed into the hands of approximately nine thousand citizens, all, in fact, who belonged to the first, second, and third Solonian classes. This limited democracy remained in power for seven months. Of the extreme members of the Four Hundred some escaped, others, among them Antiphon, paid for their short-lived tenure of authority with their life.

In the spring of 410 the Athenian fleet commanded by Alcibiades annihilated the Peloponnesian fleet off Cyzicus. This striking success produced a strong political reaction at home. The old democratic constitution by which every citizen was a member of the sovereign *ecclesia* was restored. It was unfortunate that the leading position in that assembly was grasped by the demagogue Cleophon. For, whereas he appears to have been a man of great ability, his war policy was similar to that of Cleon, allowing for the altered circumstances of Athens. Like Cleon he was an able financier, but resolved to prosecute the war at all costs. Thus, through his influence, the Athenians more than once — for instance, after the battle of Cyzicus — rejected offers of peace made by their opponents. The operations which culminated in the Athenian naval victory in 410 had followed hard upon the successful efforts of their enemies to bring the Athenian subjects in the Propontis and the Hellespontine region to revolt. In spite of great efforts on the part of Alcibiades, who was still in command of the Athenian forces, few of these places were recovered during the next two years. His greatest success was the recovery of Byzantium before the end of 408. Early in the following spring, after eight years' absence from his native city, he returned to Athens, where he was received with enthusiasm and elected chief *strategos* for the ensuing year. His triumph, this time through no fault of his own, was to be short-lived. The Great King, dissatisfied with the dilatory conduct of his satraps, decided on stronger measures to recover his hold on the coast lands of Asia Minor. He sent his younger son, Cyrus, to the West to take complete charge of Persian operations and to coöperate closely with Sparta. At Athens the unfortunate experiences of 411 had embittered the people, once they were again in full control of the government, and made them suspicious of all who had, or were believed to have, sympathy for oligarchy or indeed anything short of extreme democracy. In consequence there were many unjust prosecutions before the popular jury courts, and much corruption; the class of professional informers, who had long been an unsavory element in Athenian society, did a thriving business; worst of all, the Athenian people on more than one occasion during the last years of the war showed a lamentable lack of confidence in, and even injustice to, their leaders. Of this popular caprice Alcibiades was a conspicuous victim. In the late summer he proceeded to the Aegean in charge of the Athenian forces, in order to continue the task of winning back as many as possible of the revolted subjects of Athens.

The arrival of Cyrus in the West coincided with the appointment to the Spartan chief command of Lysander. This man's earlier history is quite obscure, but he was probably the ablest person whom Sparta produced during the whole course of the war. Though as a commander he may not have been quite the equal of Brasidas or Gylippus, he was, what in a Spartan was a singularly rare gift, an adept diplomat and the very person to succeed in his relations with an oriental prince. Helped by Persian gold, Lysander quickly established an ascendancy over the cities of Ionia and enlarged his fleet of seventy vessels to ninety, their headquarters being at Ephesus. Here, in the early spring of 406, he defeated the Athenian fleet which was stationed at Notium and under the command of Antiochus during the temporary absence of Alcibiades. The latter had warned his subordinate to avoid an open engagement, but his orders were disobeyed. Though the defeat was not especially heavy, Antiochus had lost fifteen triremes, while the responsibility for the reverse fell on Alcibiades. At the elections held at Athens shortly afterward for next year's *strategia*, popular resentment against Alcibiades was so intense that he was not reappointed. He did not risk a return to Athens but withdrew to Thrace, where, realizing some time before that he might one day need a place of refuge, he had acquired two castles.

It was a Spartan rule that the office of admiral-in-chief could not be held for more than one year. Hence in 406 Lysander was succeeded by another officer, Callicratidas. The change was unwelcome to Cyrus and probably prolonged the war by a year. In the early autumn of 406 was fought a naval battle between the Peloponnesians and the Athenians in which the numbers engaged — 150 Athenian against 120 Peloponnesian ships — were greater than in any sea-fight so far known between Greeks. To make the effort of equipping so large a number of triremes and manning them, the Athenians had been forced to melt down the silver plate in their temples and to press into service on ship-board every available man, including denizens and even slaves. The engagement near the Arginusæ islands, between Lesbos and the mainland, ended in a striking Athenian victory, and the Peloponnesians lost more than half their fleet with the crews. The Athenian losses in the battle were only twenty-five ships. Twelve of these were still afloat, but badly disabled. After the fight the sea became rough and the Athenian commanders — eight out of the ten *strategoi* of the year — failed or were unable to rescue the crews struggling in the water. Something like 2000 sailors perished in this way after the battle. When news reached Athens about the battle, jubilation at the victory was mingled with rage at what was regarded as the criminal negligence of the admirals. All eight were impeached, but only six actually stood their trial, the other two deeming it wiser to go into voluntary exile. The proceedings at the trial were in the highest degree irregular, and the unhappy men were condemned to death on a single vote, in direct violation of constitutional law. This flagrant piece of injustice the Athenian people followed up by a no less flagrant piece of folly. Overwhelmed by the disaster at Arginusæ, the Spartan government once more made peace proposals; but the Athenians rejected the enemy's overtures, being swayed by Cleophon, "who appeared in the assembly drunk and wearing his breastplate, and prevented peace being made, declaring that he would never accept peace unless the Lacedæmonians abandoned their claims on all the cities allied with them." [1]

The urgent representations of Cyrus and of many of the Ionian Greeks now led the Spartans to reappoint Lysander, technically in a subordinate office, actually in charge of operations. The reconstruction of the Peloponnesian fleet after the catastrophe of the previous year, and even with generous financial aid from Persia, took time. The summer was therefore well advanced before Lysander began operations in the Aegean. With the object of striking Athens in her most vulnerable point, the Hellespont and approach to the Black Sea, whence she derived her food supply, he attacked and captured Lampsacus. The Athenians who had been renewing their offensive against Chios, at once followed the enemy and took up their position in the straits at Aegospotami on the European side, opposite to Lampsacus.[2] For several days they tried to draw out Lysander to give battle, but in vain. Then they became less vigilant, and on the fifth day most of the crews went on land for foraging and other purposes. Suddenly Lysander swooped down upon the Athenians before they could get their ships into battle array, or even before many of the crews had had time to get on board. Of the 180 Athenian vessels only twenty made good their escape. Of the crews of the others many got away to Sestos and the Chersonese, but, even so, several thousand were taken prisoner. Those who were Athenians were subsequently put to death.

It was the end for Athens. She had neither men, money, nor fleet with which to continue the struggle. The very few cities which she still retained of her once mighty empire went over to, or were taken by, the enemy. Samos alone remained

---

[1] Aristotle, *Constitution of Athens*, 34 (Kenyon's translation).

[2] Alcibiades on this occasion came from his castles in Thrace and advised the Athenians to take up safer anchorage at Sestos. His well-meant and well-founded counsel was ignored. In 404, when Sparta was rounding up Athenian exiles everywhere, Alcibiades fled to Pharnabazus. The satrap, on the demand of Lysander, executed him.

faithful to the end, and, in gratitude, the Athenians conferred their franchise on all the islanders. When the news of the disaster in the Hellespont reached Athens, horror and desperation seized the citizens. We cannot do better than transcribe the famous passage in Xenophon who lived through those awful days. Though he did not write his *Hellenic History* till many years later, the memory of Athens' agony after Aegospotami must still have been vividly present to his mind.

It was night when the *Paralus* reached Athens with her evil tidings, on receipt of which a bitter wail of woe broke forth. From Peiræus, following the line of the Long Walls up to the heart of the city it swept and swelled, as each man to his neighbor passed on the news. On that night no man slept. There was mourning and sorrow for those that were lost, but lamentation for the dead was merged in even deeper sorrow for themselves, as they pictured the evils they were about to suffer, the like of which they had themselves inflicted on the men of Melos, who were colonists of the Lacedæmonians, when they mastered them by siege; or on the men of Histiæa; on Scione and Torone; on the Aeginetans, and many another Hellenic city.[1]

The energy of desperation seized the Athenians. Every preparation for standing a siege was made, and with many there still lingered a faint hope that the enemy might grant peace on terms. Soon a Peloponnesian army entered Attica under the command of King Pausanias and joined forces with King Agis and his garrison from Decelea. Shortly after Lysander sailed into the Saronic Gulf, and Athens and Peiræus were thus completely invested by land and sea. During the winter months only the fleet continued the blockade, since the Spartans had no intention of attempting a difficult and costly assault when in a few months famine would do its work. Efforts were made by the Athenians, through Theramenes, to persuade Lysander not to proceed to extremes, but the Spartan rejected any proposal short of unconditional surrender. When a congress of Peloponnesian states and their allies met in the spring there were some who urged the complete destruction of Athens. The chief advocates of this ferocity were the Corinthians and Bœotians, but to such a course Sparta would not assent. The terms imposed on Athens were as severe as they could be, consistently with

---

[1] Xenophon, *Hellenica* II, ii, 3 (Dakyns' translation).

leaving her an autonomous state. Starved into surrender, the Athenians had needs to accept the destruction of their Long Walls and the fortifications of Peiræus, the loss of their fleet, save only twelve vessels, the loss of the few remaining dependencies left to them outside Attica, including Lemnos, Imbros, and Scyros, and the recall of their political exiles. Lysander, having received the formal surrender of Athens, sailed to Samos and, after two to three months' siege, compelled the islanders to capitulate. Then he intervened once more in Athenian affairs. Bitter struggles had begun at Athens, since Theramenes and other oligarchs deemed the time ripe for instituting an oligarchic régime in the city. With the support of Lysander, who threatened dire penalties if the government at Athens were not reconstituted on the lines proposed by Theramenes, — which he could do with an appearance of legality because the Athenians had not completed the demolition of their walls and had therefore broken the terms of the peace, — the democratic constitution was abolished and the direction of affairs put into the hands of thirty persons, all of whom were oligarchs, though, as the sequel showed, of very different views and aims.

CHAPTER XVII

THE POLITICAL HISTORY OF GREECE TO THE DEATH OF PHILIP II

> *Yet all the faults committed by the Spartans in those thirty years, and by our ancestors in the seventy, are less than the wrongs which, in thirteen incomplete years that Philip has been uppermost, he has inflicted on the Greeks; nay they are scarcely a fraction of these, as may be easily shown in a few words.* — Demosthenes, *Third Philippic*, 25 (Kennedy's translation).

1. THE EMPIRES OF SPARTA AND THEBES

IT is regrettable that the few contemporary sources which we possess for the early years of the fourth century are, where Sparta is concerned, not free from bias. Xenophon, the admirer of her polity and institutions, is frankly enthusiastic for Sparta and her king, Agesilaus.[1] Isocrates, on the other hand, who does not hesitate to criticize his fellow Athenians, under the influence partly of the memories of his youth and earlier manhood, partly of his political theories, is always inclined to depict Spartan policy and conduct in the most sombre colors. Hence, while we sorely miss some dispassionate and profound delineator of the short-lived Spartan and Theban hegemonies, who might rank with the historian of the Athenian empire, Thucydides, we must seek for a mean between the extremes of partisanship and enmity. Even thus, the verdict will be against Sparta. Granted the shortcomings and misuse of power, of which Athens as an imperial state was guilty in the fifth century, were frequent, granted too that many of the complaints made against her by her allies were justified, it still remains true that the Athenian empire was a work of constructive statesmanship,

---

[1] It is only in the last section of his *Hellenic History* that Xenophon gives the impression of having to some extent lost faith in Sparta, and even allows himself to make adverse criticisms (*e.g.* V, iii, 27 — V, iv, 1).

and an effort to bring at least a part of the Hellenic world into closer coöperation. Even if it was of most benefit to Athens herself, it also promoted the prosperity of all the other cities, great and small. In 404 Sparta had a great opportunity of shouldering the burden of empire fairly, and of promoting political harmony and union among the Hellenic states on a wider basis than ever Athens had succeeded in doing; but her failure, and the political decline which followed it, were far more complete than the Athenians'. In truth, Sparta's traditions and narrow military régime fitted her neither to inaugurate a true federal organization, like the leagues which arose elsewhere in Greece in the third century, nor yet to lead and knit together into a looser confederacy a multitude of scattered maritime communities. Finally, the statesman who had brought the Peloponnesian war to a successful conclusion, was of the stuff of which Tyrants were made, and was influenced solely by motives of personal ambition. In the communities that had lately belonged to the Athenian empire oligarchies were uniformly established by the action of Lysander, in many cases only after brutal scenes of violence and bloodshed. Had the Spartans in 404 adhered to the professions made by Spartan leaders at the beginning of the Peloponnesian war, they would have tried to adapt and enlarge the Peloponnesian League to include the late empire of their beaten foe. Actually Lysander's methods were those of unqualified tyranny and terrorization through the small oligarchic Boards of Ten (*decarchies*) which he set up in the different Aegean communities. Their system of government, or rather misgovernment, was similar to that of the Thirty at Athens, and often they were, like the Thirty, supported and abetted in their misrule by Spartan garrisons commanded by a Spartan commander (*harmostes*).

Another important factor in the general political situation, which developed in the decade after Aegospotami, is to be found in the attitude of Sparta to her allies. We have already seen how, when she had concluded a truce with Athens in 421, she took little cognizance of her allies' interests. In 405–404, when she had emerged triumphant from the war, her treatment of her confederates, without whose help she could not have beaten Athens, was even more cavalier. In general, the Peloponnesian

a

b

a. FORTRESS OF PHYLE; *b*. FOURTH-CENTURY FORTIFICATION WALL
NEAR PEIRÆUS

Plate 20

states were still too overawed by her military prestige to turn against her.   A few years later some of them were emboldened to take up arms against the head of the league when involved in renewed warfare with Persia.   The Bœotians were more daring.   The unsatisfactory peace of 405–404 quickly reacted on the state of political parties in Bœotia, and anti-Spartan leaders seem to have predominated in the Bœotian league.   At all events, in spite of a Spartan prohibition, the Bœotians gave a friendly welcome to Thrasybulus and a number of other political exiles, who had fled from Athens at the installation of the Thirty.   The misrule of this oligarchy, which endured for eight months, was far more noxious than that of the Four Hundred had been in 411.   Theramenes again represented the moderate element, but now he had no outside support, and a majority of his colleagues sided with the extremist, Critias.   For the first few weeks of their government they sought to give an appearance of legality to all their acts; but soon, on a specious pretext, they applied to Sparta for a harmost and garrison.   Once these were established in the Acropolis the extremists began a systematic persecution of wealthy citizens and resident aliens, in order, after killing them off, to seize their property.   The roll of citizens was restricted to 3000 only, instead of to all able to serve as hoplites.   The others were disfranchised, and could be put to death without trial.   These high-handed measures were strongly opposed by Theramenes, but he was overruled.   Then Critias, fearing his continued influence and opposition, struck his name off the civic list and had him executed.   How lacking in any semblance of justice, indeed how monstrous, the régime of the Thirty was, can still be read in the vivid pages of Lysias.   Two of his longest extant speeches were composed when the democratic government had been restored, the one against Eratosthenes, once a member of the Thirty, the other against Agoratus, long a low informer in the pay of the oligarchs.   Even if we allow for the vehemence and *ex parte* presentation of the advocate, who had himself suffered under the late misrule, the following passage, one of many, presents a harrowing picture: [1]

So these persons, men of Athens, lost their lives through information laid by Agoratus.   When the Thirty had removed them, you are fully

[1] Lysias, *Orat.* 13, 43–49.

aware, I think, of the many misfortunes that befell the city thereafter; and for all of them this fellow, by doing those persons to death, bore the blame. Now I am sorry to remind you of the calamities that overtook Athens, but, gentlemen of the jury, I must do so at this point, so that you may know how exceedingly appropriate it is for you to pity Agoratus! You know the character and the number of the citizens carried off from Salamis, and the manner of their utter destruction by the Thirty. You know how many Eleusinians suffered this undoing. You also recollect our own people here who because of private enmities were marched off to jail. And they, who had done the city no ill, were forced to die by the most shameful, the most infamous, of deaths. Some left behind them aged parents, who were hoping to be supported in their declining years by their own sons, and to be buried by them when the end came; others left behind them sisters unmarried, others young children who were yet in need of much care. What will be their thoughts, do you suppose, gentlemen of the jury, about the defendant here, how would they vote, if it were to rest with them, seeing that by him they have been robbed of what was dearest to them? Furthermore, you remember how the city's walls were pulled down, the ships handed over to the enemy, the arsenals demolished; how the Lacedæmonians held our acropolis, and the entire power of our city was laid low, so that she was no different from the tiniest city. In addition to all this, you lost your private property, and in the end with one sweep you were thrust forth from your native land by the Thirty. Those good citizens envisaged those dangers, gentlemen of the jury, and refused to agree to the peace. You, Agoratus, caused their death when they wished to help the city, by giving information that they were plotting against our democracy, and you are the cause of all the ills that have come upon the city. Remember therefore, each one of you, your individual misfortunes and those of the body politic, and punish the author thereof.

The friendly disposition of Thebes to the Athenian refugees was providential. With her help Thrasybulus and some seventy companions entered Attica and in the late autumn of 404 seized the fortress of Phyle (Plate 20*a*) on the slopes of Mt. Parnes. The efforts of the Thirty to dislodge them failed, as did an attack by the Spartan garrison in Athens. Gradually more and more men flocked to the standard of the liberator. At last, when his force numbered about 1000, Thrasybulus one night led them to Peiræus and occupied the hill of Munychia. Here he was welcomed by the inhabitants, many of whom joined him. With this augmented army he defeated an attack by the Thirty and their supporters. Critias was killed fighting, and his removal greatly weakened the authority of the Thirty. The assembly of the 3000 deposed them and appointed a board of Ten to take their place. One or two of the Thirty were reëlected, but the rest fled to Eleusis. Although the executive at Athens was thus changed, an agreement with the democrats at Peiræus was not reached. The latter, though unable to occupy the city, reduced the oligarchs to such straits by the summer of 403 that these appealed to Sparta to intervene. For the moment Lysander's influence there predominated, and military and naval forces were despatched to crush the democratic faction in Peiræus. But there was not wanting a large number of persons at Sparta who had been viewing Lysander's career, his inordinate ambition, and his utterly ruthless methods, with alarm and disapproval. These opponents of Lysander now gained the upper hand. He was superseded, and the settlement of Athenian affairs was intrusted to King Pausanias. Through him and a board of fifteen commissioners, who were sent from Sparta for this express purpose, a peaceful agreement was arranged. A general amnesty was proclaimed from which only the surviving members of the Thirty and Ten, and a few of their immediate subordinates in Athens and Peiræus were excluded. Eleusis was to form a separate city-state, to which any Athenians — that is to say, those with oligarchic sympathies — could withdraw within a specified time-limit. With the constitution now to be set up at Athens the Spartan commission did not interfere. Hence the full democracy, in which all citizens had political rights, was restored. Two years later Eleusis was reincorporated in the Athenian state without any opposition from Sparta.

Meantime the Lysandrean régime had broken down generally in the Aegean area. The decarchies were abolished and the cities allowed to restore their "ancestral constitutions." But the most difficult problem confronting the Spartan government was the nature of its future relations with Persia. In return for the aid which the Great King had given in the last years of the Peloponnesian war he expected the formal cession of all the Asiatic Greek cities. In reality, after 405, Sparta had made peace with Athens without consulting Persia, and still retained her hold on the Hellespontine region, though Ionia had been

ceded to Cyrus. In the same year Darius II died and was
succeeded by his eldest son, who ruled under the name of
Artaxerxes II. The queen mother, Parysatis, however, had
intrigued to secure the succession for her younger son, Cyrus.
Foiled in his attempt to obtain the throne on his father's
death, Cyrus now plotted to attain his goal by force. In 401
his preparations were completed, and he set out from Asia
Minor at the head of a large army, composed partly of Greek
mercenaries, partly of oriental troops. In the summer Cyrus'
host, numbering nearly 13,000 Greeks, about as many orientals,
and 2600 cavalry, engaged a somewhat greater army of Artaxerxes at Cunaxa, about eighty miles north of Babylon. Though
the Greek hoplites routed the Persians opposed to them, the
Persian commander, Tissaphernes, retrieved the day for Artaxerxes with his cavalry. In the last stage of the fighting, moreover, Cyrus himself was killed, so that the Greek portion of his
army was left without a leader or a purpose. At first they were
granted a truce to leave the country, and were escorted up the
Tigris as far as the Greater Zab by Tissaphernes. The Persian
satrap stood high in the confidence of his master and had been
a bitter enemy of Cyrus and Parysatis. He now treacherously
seized the Greek officers in command of Cyrus' mercenaries and
had them put to death. The troops, however, elected other
commanders from among themselves. Under these leaders they
pushed on, trusting ultimately to get back to Greece and to
their homes. Encountering tremendous hardships, caused partly
by the severity of the climate, in part by the attacks of the wild
hill tribes through whose territory they passed, they made their
way through the heart of the Armenian highlands. Several
times they badly lost their way through the ignorance or treachery of native guides, so that weeks passed before they ultimately reached Trapezus on the Black Sea. Among the Greek
officers who led the retreat was the Athenian Xenophon, whose
Anabasis gives a graphic account of Cyrus' expedition and the
subsequent adventures of the Greek mercenaries.

By 400 relations between Sparta and Persia had become very
strained. Though giving no official support to Cyrus, the
Spartan government had facilitated his recruitment of Greek
mercenaries; it had also failed to carry out all the terms of the

agreement between the two states. Moreover, some of the Greek cities which had reverted under Persian, that is to say, under Cyrus', control in 405, had regained their independence when that prince set out for the Middle East. Above all, in 400 Tissaphernes was once again installed as satrap of both Caria and Lydia; his relations with Sparta had never been very harmonious. When he proceeded to attempt the recovery of some of the lately revolted Greek communities in his satrapy, these appealed to Sparta for aid. Rather than abandon the Asiatic Greeks entirely to a foreign power, the Spartans sent an expeditionary force to Asia Minor, primarily to the relief of Cyme, which was being attacked by the satrap. By this action Sparta actively renewed hostilities with Persia, and, with some intervals, the two states were at war for the next fourteen years.

Sparta's most substantial successes were won by her King Agesilaus in 396 and 395; but his military career in Asia Minor was cut short by political developments in Greece, which forced his government to recall him. The anti-Spartan coalition between Corinth, Argos, Thebes, and Athens, which had come into being by 395, was in the first place the result of the genuine discontent of Sparta's allies with the treatment they had received at the end of the Peloponnesian war. It was strengthened by Persian diplomacy and Persian gold distributed by a Greek agent of the satrap Pharnabazus. The influence of this Persian governor had steadily increased as that of Tissaphernes declined, — the latter was deposed in 395 and subsequently executed, thanks to the implacable hostility of the queen mother, — and he had been largely instrumental in procuring an admiral's commission in the Persian fleet for the exiled Athenian commander, Conon. The earlier operations of the Persian navy in the Aegean (396–395) were not greatly successful, although a democratic revolution at Rhodes, followed by the island's secession from Sparta, was a symptom of the waning loyalty of Sparta's allies, which the presence of a powerful rival might, as in this case, change into open defection. In the summer of 394, however, the Persian fleet completely crushed the Peloponnesian naval force commanded by Agesilaus' brother, Peisander, in an engagement off Cnidus. This victory, which in effect ended Sparta's hegemony in the Aegean and left the Persian navy mistress of that sea, was due partly to the skill of Conon and the large number of Greeks who were included in the crews of the Persian vessels, partly to the doubtful loyalty, and, at the crucial moment, the defection of that part of Peisander's force which had been recruited from the maritime allies of Sparta. It was Sparta's punishment for a decade of misgovernment and oppression.

In 393, after a general cruise in Aegean waters, which completed the break-up of Sparta's maritime empire, the Persian fleet returned home. But, with Pharnabazus' permission, Conon with a naval detachment sailed to Athens, from which he had been a voluntary exile since 405, and where he was now rapturously received. The Athenians, emboldened by their new alliance with Corinth, Argos, and Thebes, had begun to reconstruct their fortifications. Conon now used his men and the funds he had received from Pharnabazus to complete the building of the Long Walls. In the next three or four years Athens began in a small way to rehabilitate herself as a naval power. She recovered Lemnos, Imbros, and Scyros, and she concluded alliances with a number of island states and cities in Asia Minor. These efforts turned out to be premature; for Sparta, after an abortive attempt to make peace with Persia, which was followed by renewed hostilities, at last effected a more permanent settlement. It ended the war with Persia and also the so-called Corinthian war on the Greek mainland, which Sparta and the anti-Spartan coalition had been carrying on during the past eight years without decisive results on either side. But, although it was Sparta who through her envoy, Antalcidas, initiated the peace, it was Artaxerxes II who dictated the terms. In the winter of 387 the satrap of Lydia, Tiribazus, called a congress of Greek representatives at Sardes. To them the behests of the Great King were solemnly read. Early in 386 the King's Peace, or Peace of Antalcidas, was subscribed to by all the Hellenic states. By its terms the Greeks of Asia Minor and Cyprus reverted under Persian suzerainty; the other Greek states were to be independent, and alliances like those recently contracted by Athens, or even the

Bœotian League in which Theban authority predominated, were to be given up.

The King's Peace, and Sparta's rôle in bringing it about, have been severely censured by ancient and modern observers alike. And, undoubtedly, in one sense it was a calamitous confession of failure in the larger problems of political organization that, just a century after the Persian wars, the Asiatic Greeks should be allowed to revert once more under the Persian yoke. If much of the blame for the ignominious peace of 386 rests with Sparta, some of it also must be assigned to the opponents of Lacedæmon on the mainland, who had not hesitated to attack her when all her resources were needed in Asia Minor, and to accept Persian gold. The Asiatic Greeks themselves we cannot justly censure. They had had severe burdens placed upon them by Athens when she was mistress of the seas; they had suffered heavier exactions from Sparta, and more ruthless interference with their autonomy and systems of government. Small wonder if they at last concluded that materially they would be no worse off — perhaps better — when their main obligation was to pay an annual tribute to the Great King. And, though it was a hardship to be required to supply troops from time to time to an overlord, it was assuredly no novelty for them to be bound by such military liabilities.

The adverse effects of the Peace were more patent in Greece itself and in the Aegean area outside the Great King's jurisdiction. If, before 387, Sparta had, under the blighting influence of Lysander, grossly misused her authority in the Aegean, she now, under the guidance of her king, Agesilaus, and with the pretext of strictly enforcing the terms of the Peace, interfered in the most high-handed manner with the liberties of autonomous states. Thus in the Peloponnese she dealt harshly with the cities of Mantinea (385) and Phlius (379); in Thrace she intervened with a military force, at the request of one or two cities which were unwilling to join the league of Greek city-states — the so-called Chalcidic league that had grown up since the last half of the fifth century under the leadership of Olynthus. This intervention was not restricted to safeguarding the autonomy of two insignificant *poleis* in Chalcidice. The ascendancy of Olynthus in the league was as marked as that of Thebes in the Bœotian confederacy before 387 or after 371, and this circumstance gave the Spartans a pretext for using force to break up the confederation as being contrary to the terms of the King's Peace (379). In this action they seem to have received some support from King Amyntas of Macedonia. From an inscription we know that a few years before he had made a treaty with the League for their mutual protection and advantage. A late writer (Diodorus 14, 92; 15, 19), probably using a fourth-century source, states that the king gave up some territory to Olynthus in return for promised help against the Illyrians. The Olynthians, however, did not fulfil their part of the bargain, and the king was temporarily driven from his throne by his troublesome neighbors on the northwest. When he recovered the monarchy, his anger against Olynthus led him to side with Sparta. But the most flagrant act of violence, committed by a Spartan officer, Phœbidas, and subsequently condoned by the Spartan government on the advice of Agesilaus, occurred in 382. Phœbidas, who was in charge of a detachment destined for Chalcidice, when passing through Bœotia was approached by members of the oligarchic faction in Thebes. Although Sparta and Thebes were at peace, he fell in with the treacherous plan laid before him and seized the citadel of Thebes, the Cadmeia. This act, the failure of the Spartan government to punish Phœbidas and give redress to Thebes, followed by the cynical retention of the Cadmeia, damaged Sparta's prestige immensely and outraged the sense of right even of her admirers.[1] For the moment her authority throughout Greece was greater than it had ever been. There is a certain poetic justice in the fact that the state which Sparta had most deeply wronged, within little more than a decade destroyed Sparta's predominant position in Hellas.

It was fortunate for Thebes that at this crisis in her history she produced two men of markedly different character, but both of sterling ability and devotion to their country. The one, Pelopidas, with a number of Theban exiles who had found a temporary home in Athens, carried through a successful plot in the winter of 379. The pro-Spartan oligarchs in Thebes were overthrown, the Spartan garrison driven out, and Thebes regained

[1] Cf. the note on page 279 above.

her liberty.   The other Theban, Epaminondas, though not involved in this conspiracy, became, in the anxious years that followed, the chief guide of Thebes' policy and the builder of her short-lived empire.   In 378 her position was very precarious. Her action produced open war between herself and Sparta, and Sparta's position in central Greece was strong because she had placed garrisons in several of the Bœotian cities. In their rather isolated condition the Thebans sought an Athenian alliance.   At Athens there was an influential party opposed to a rupture with Sparta; but their hesitation was changed to indignation when a Spartan officer, Sphodrias, who was in command of the Lacedæmonian garrison at Thespiæ, in the early spring of 378 and, apparently on his own responsibility, made a raid into Attica by night with a view to seizing Peiræus.   His attempt failed as it deserved to do; its immediate political consequence was a Theban-Athenian alliance concluded in the summer of the same year.

In 378 and 377 Peloponnesian armies invaded Bœotia and ravaged the territory of Thebes.   But, as the Thebans remained within their walls, Agesilaus was unable to make any impression on the enemy beyond the material damage done to fields and crops.   Another projected invasion in 376, commanded by the other Spartan king, Cleombrotus, for reasons that are obscure, was abandoned before the Lacedæmonians had reached their objective.   In the next five years the Thebans, partly by military action, partly by diplomacy, won over nearly all the Bœotian cities and reconstituted the Bœotian confederacy, securing for themselves predominant representation in the counsels of the league and reserving to Thebes alone the right to issue a federal coinage.

Another factor during these years greatly strengthened the anti-Spartan movement in Greece.   The King's Peace, which had for the moment compelled the Athenians to abandon their few maritime alliances, was not strictly observed by them for long.   Before 380 Athens had made new treaties with Chios, Byzantium, Rhodes, and Mitylene.   In 377, when hostile feelings for Sparta were strongest at Athens, the Athenians issued a more general invitation to Hellenic, and even non-Hellenic, states — the Greek subjects of the Great King were specifically excluded, as any attempt to bring them in would have ruined the chances of success — to join a maritime league under Athenian leadership. Great pains were taken in formulating the constitution of this, the so-called Second Athenian Confederacy, to avoid all those features which had been obnoxious in the Confederacy of Delos and might lead potential members to fear a renewal of Athenian imperialism. Each member was completely autonomous; the allied states sent representatives to a congress (*synedrion*), which met at Athens periodically, but from which Athens herself was excluded. The decisions of the league and the determination of its policy rested jointly with the congress of allies and the Athenian council and assembly. Though the executive was from the first in Athenian hands, no regular tribute was to be collected, as had been the case in the Delian League. The allies paid contributions to defray the expenses of the confederacy's operations, but not, so far as we know, at any stated intervals; we are also quite ignorant how the amounts were determined or collected. The financial organization cannot have been left entirely at haphazard; yet there is no trace of any carefully thought out scheme similar to that of Aristeides a hundred years before. It was significant that the Athenians specifically bound themselves to refrain from sending settlers to allied territory, or even from owning land there. For had not the cleruchies been one of the chief grievances of Athens' allies and subjects in the fifth century?

From the archonship of Nausinicus (378–377 B.C.) it shall be unlawful privately or publicly for any Athenian to acquire possessions in the territories of the allies, house or land, either by purchase or by mortgage or in any other way.

Thus the wording of the Athenian inscription that is our main source for the organization of the League.[1] Violations were to be reported to the congress of the allies. It would be interesting to know how differences of opinion between the congress of allies and the Athenian *ecclesia* were composed. The history of the League suggests that, after a few years, the Athenians became less scrupulous in observing the rights of the allies, and we may suspect that the will of the Athenian assembly generally

[1] *Inscript. Graec.* II, 17.

prevailed.   And certainly there are not wanting from the later period of the League instances where the Athenian assembly overruled decrees passed by their allies.   The number of members was at first small.   Besides the four Athenian allies mentioned above and Methymna, Thebes joined in the first year of the League, also the Eubœan communities except Oreus, and a few islands and cities in the northern Aegean.   There were several weaknesses inherent in this organization.   It was a mistake, in view of the rapid shifts that Greek politics underwent, to designate Sparta as the enemy.   A more general formula would have been better, without hostile manifesto against any specific state.   The creation of two sovereign bodies theoretically equal could not in the long run be expected to work together without friction.   Nor is it possible to praise the principle of representation, one city one vote, in the assembly of allies, since they varied so much in their political power and influence. But that was the price to be paid for the fanatical autonomy of the Greek *polis;* and the same factor made impossible what would have been the most satisfactory plan — a single federal council in which both Athens and her allies would have been represented on a proportionate basis.

The avowed purpose of the League was to check the further aggressions of Sparta in the Hellenic world, but this did not preclude offensive operations against the Lacedæmonian state and the Peloponnesian league.   The Spartan reply to the naval activity of Athens was to send a Peloponnesian fleet to interfere with the Athenian grain trade; but in 376 it suffered defeat at the hands of the Athenian admiral, Chabrias, off the island of Naxos. The consequences of this victory in the second year of the Athenian Confederacy were striking.   By this single success Athens recovered her maritime supremacy in the eastern Aegean, and a great number of new members were enrolled in the League. While Chabrias was active among the Cyclades and in Thrace and the Hellespont, Timotheus, the son of Conon, won adherents in northwestern Greek waters.   Among these accessions were most of the Cyclades, the cities of the Chalcidic League which had come into being again a few years after Sparta's intervention, additional cities and islands in the northern Aegean, Corcyra, Acarnania, Cephallenia, and King Alcetas of Epirus.

While the Bœotian Confederacy and Athens' new maritime league were each gaining strength, a short-lived hegemony was established in Thessaly by the genius of one man. Jason, the ruler of Pheræ, had by 374 united all the cities of Thessaly save Pharsalus under his sway, and, by the following year, Pharsalus too was forced to surrender to him. The military strength of this federal realm, as we may describe it, was very considerable, numbering 10,000 hoplites, 6000 cavalry, and abundant light armed troops besides. Exceptionally gifted both as a commander and as an organizer, Jason aimed at widening his political influence beyond the borders of Thessaly. He made friendly alliances with Macedonia and with the Bœotian League; but the efforts of Athens to secure this powerful ally were unsuccessful. This and other circumstances brought about a distinct change in the foreign policy of the leading Athenian statesman, Callistratus, who at no time seems to have been very friendly to Thebes. The financial straits of Athens were very acute; her maritime allies were unwilling or unable to furnish regular subsidies, and measures of coercion, though used by some of the Athenian commanders, were both contrary to the terms and dangerous to the stability of the Confederacy. Thebes, too, though an ally, seems to have given little or no financial help. In addition, the growth of the Theban power aroused the suspicions and fears of a large section of the Athenian people. Thus already in 374 the Athenians made overtures of peace to Sparta, and an agreement was actually reached. Hardly had this been done, when Timotheus was guilty of a technical violation of the treaty. Hostilities were begun afresh, and the war dragged on in a desultory way till 371. By that year the position of Thebes in central Greece was stronger than ever, while Jason of Pheræ was, rightly or wrongly, believed to be planning a naval program that would have been a direct menace to the Second Athenian Confederacy. The Athenians were all the more ready to come to terms with Sparta, when that state took the lead in calling together a congress in the spring of 371, which was attended by all the Greek states and also by a representative of the Great King.

The peace treaty of 371 was a reaffirmation of the King's Peace of 386, but the Athenian Confederacy was recognized as not contravening the provisions for the autonomy of each city-state. Besides this, the Spartan government undertook to withdraw its garrisons from the few places which remained to her of her short-lived empire. These terms were accepted not only by Sparta and Athens, which were chiefly responsible for bringing about the settlement, but by all the lesser *poleis*. But Epaminondas, in his character of Theban representative, claimed the right to sign for the whole Bœotian League. This was peremptorily refused by the president of the congress, the Spartan king, Agesilaus, who went so far as to strike Thebes from the list of signatories, thereby excluding her from the provisions of the peace. This arbitrary action, for which Agesilaus must bear the whole blame, was followed up by an immediate order to the Spartan king, Cleombrotus, who was stationed in Phocis with an army of Peloponnesian troops said to have been 10,000 strong, to invade Bœotia and to attack the Thebans unless they took immediate steps to abandon their control over the Bœotian League. Cleombrotus, following instructions, invaded Bœotia, and, by Leuctra, near the western end of the Theban plain, found himself opposed by a Bœotian army decidedly smaller than his own, perhaps 6000 hoplites and 1000 horse. The decisive victory won by Epaminondas and his Bœotians over a larger force of what had hitherto been regarded as the finest heavy-armed soldiers in the Hellenic world, was due partly to his skillful combination of infantry and cavalry attack, partly to the massed assault by his choicest troops in a column fifty deep, which he directed against the strongest part of the Peloponnesian army, namely, the Lacedæmonian division. No less than four hundred Spartiates, including Cleombrotus himself, were killed; the beaten army, however, retreated in orderly fashion and evacuated Bœotia.

The results of the Bœotian success were of the most far-reaching kind. Thebes was for a decade the most powerful state in Greece, but the period of her military hegemony, though auspiciously begun, only accelerated the general political disintegration of Hellas. The immediate sequel to Leuctra was the enlargement of the Bœotian League by the accession of Eubœa, whose cities seceded from Athens, and of the Acarnanians. Orchomenus, the last Bœotian city to remain outside the league, was now compelled to join. Alliances were concluded with the Phocians, Locrians, and some lesser peoples in central Greece.

In the following year Jason of Pheræ was assassinated, and the Thebans, though they had been on friendly terms with him, can hardly have seriously regretted the passing of so powerful a despot, whose ambitions might in time have threatened their own position in Greece. Meanwhile the Peloponnese was the scene of what was nothing less than a political upheaval. After the heavy losses incurred at Leuctra the number of full Spartan citizens was reduced to 1000 or little more. It was the penalty for the narrowness of the Spartan view in not permitting any modification of the "Lycurgean" institutions and jealously refusing to admit any of the other inhabitants of Laconia or Messenia to the privileges of Spartan citizenship. Nor was it only in her own territory that Sparta was threatened with disruption. Some of her Peloponnesian allies, especially the Arcadians, who had long chafed under Sparta's military demands but had been overawed by her supposedly invincible troops, now openly seceded. Mantinea, destroyed as a city by Sparta in 385, was rebuilt and strongly fortified; then its citizens, with most of the other Arcadian cities, formed a federation of their own. In 370, backed at first by the support of Epaminondas and a Bœotian army, the Arcadians coerced those communities in the country that had so far refused to join them. In 369 they founded a new city, Megalepolis, which was to be the federal capital, and at the same time formed one of the constituent members of the federation. The federal assembly was called the Ten Thousand, a name probably more approximate than exact. We hear also of a council and of a body of fifty persons, called *damiorgoi*; whether the two were identical or separate is a moot point. In any event the council was the body in which the main power and the direction of the League reposed. Representation in it was according to the importance of the constituent towns. The total federal army, to which each of the constituent members contributed a contingent annually, was fixed at five thousand.

Epaminondas in 370 invaded Laconia, thereby preventing Sparta's attempts to stop the formation of the Arcadian League.

Besides ravaging Sparta's home-land he entered Messenia, freed the Helot and Pericecic population, and helped them to form a new and independent state of Messenia. Only a few communities in the extreme south of that district remained faithful to Sparta. On Mt. Ithome, with its unhappy memories of the past, a capital was built. Extensive remains of its town walls and fortified towers are among the finest examples of military architecture in Greece. In 370 Sparta had repelled the attack of the invader on her own city and had maintained her independence; but she was powerless to arrest the formation of two substantial states on her northern and western frontiers. In her need she received some assistance from Dionysius I of Syracuse, with whom she had been in alliance since the beginning of his Tyranny. Various efforts to bring about a peace settlement were made between 369 and 366, and the support of the Persian king was sought by the different groups of belligerents. But, though Thebes, through her representative Pelopidas, secured a Persian rescript in her favor, she was unable to secure its acceptance by Sparta and Athens.

Nowhere did the Thebans succeed in deriving any lasting benefit from their many ephemeral successes. After Jason's death they had been led to intervene more than once in Thessalian affairs, and for a brief space Thessaly was under Theban control. In 366 Epaminondas secured the adherence of Achæa to the Bœotian alliance, but the Theban government followed up this diplomatic success by sending military garrisons there and using force to set up democratic rulers in the Achæan cities. Oligarchic counter-revolutions were the immediate result, and the Achæans, from being allies of Thebes, concluded a treaty with Sparta. Anti-Theban feeling in Greece grew apace. The Arcadian League was trying, not very successfully, to enlarge its territory by warring against several lesser neighbors, but without regard for its late ally and helper. Athens in 366 formed an alliance with the League, while from 366 to 364, after successful operations by Timotheus, her maritime confederacy was enlarged by the accession of Samos, Sestos, and a number of Thracian cities. The Theban reply to this diplomatic and naval activity on the part of Athens was, on Epaminondas' advice, to equip a Bœotian fleet, 100 vessels strong. With it he scored a temporary success by bringing about the defection from the Athenian Confederacy of Byzantium and one or two other states. Nevertheless the Thebans had neither the spare men nor the money to maintain themselves as a naval power in addition to holding on to their military hegemony; therefore after this one year (364) no more is heard of their undertakings on the sea.

War-weary as many or most of the Greeks must have been, no general agreement was possible amid the clash of contending interests and rivalries of party, each advocating a different foreign policy within the cities themselves. The most serious rupture came about in the Arcadian League. Here a strong anti-Theban group was gaining a predominating influence in the councils of the League; in 363 the disagreement had become so acute that the unity of the federation was destroyed. The Mantineans and northern Arcadians contracted alliances with Sparta and the Achæans; they were in friendly relations also with Elis and Athens, from both of which they were to receive military assistance. Tegea and Megalepolis, on the other hand, remained staunch to Thebes and fought on her side when a strong Bœotian army in 362 entered the Peloponnese under command of Epaminondas, with the immediate object of enforcing Theban authority in the recalcitrant cities of Arcadia. The battle fought in the plain to the south of Mantinea would have been a sweeping Theban victory had not Epaminondas been mortally wounded at a critical point in the engagement. Thus the plan of attack which he had evolved was never carried to a finish, and the military results of this encounter were indecisive. Following the counsel given by the dying Epaminondas, the Theban government now convened a congress, and peace was concluded on the basis of the *status quo*. Thereby the Arcadian League was split into two federated groups; Messenian independence was confirmed, though for this reason Sparta held aloof from the agreement; the Bœotian League and the Second Athenian Confederacy remained as before, and the autonomy of each signatory to the peace was guaranteed.

In its political effects the battle of Mantinea was equivalent to a Theban defeat. The loss of Epaminondas was irreparable, though it may well be doubted whether he could ever have succeeded in building up a stable Theban empire. The emi-

nence of his achievement as a military commander and as a tac-
tician, whose innovations introduced important changes into
the methods of land warfare, must not blind us to the fact that
his only acts of constructive statesmanship were the liberation
of Messenia and the part he played in furthering the Arcadian
League.   While it would be unfair to assign all the blame to
him for the complete failure to establish a successful and lasting
hegemony over a great part of Greece, we must admit that not
only the Thebans but Epaminondas himself lacked both the
vision and the experience necessary to emulate a Pericles
or even a Lysander.   Even had this brief empire been more securely established than it was, it is questionable whether the
Thebans would have had the resources to maintain it.   The
death of Epaminondas not only meant the collapse of Thebes
as the leading state in Hellas, but was also disastrous to the
Bœotian League, which rapidly declined in military efficiency and
political influence, and to Thebes' own position in the League.

   If it is difficult to expend much sympathy on the Spartans
themselves for their reduction to the status of a third-rate
power, it is true nevertheless that their decline and the break-
up of the Peloponnesian League was a disaster for the whole of
Greece.   For the passing of that loose but effective organization
signified the destruction of what had been for nearly two centuries the one stable political group in the Hellenic world.
Thus, unwittingly, Thebes prepared the way for the relatively
easy subjugation of Greece by the ruler of a kingdom which,
though its fortunes had for long been partly interwoven with
those of the northern Greeks, was yet regarded as standing
outside the aggregation of Hellenic polities.

2. The Rise of Macedon

   The Macedonians had for centuries been little affected by the
culture and institutions of their Greek neighbors.   They lived
in scattered villages, and there were few fortified places and no
towns of considerable size.   The population was in the main
made up of a powerful landed aristocracy and free peasants.
Monarchic government had continued there without interruption, though with many vicissitudes to the rulers, and the king's
position and authority were not unlike those of the Homeric

chiefs. An absolute ruler in some respects, the Macedonian monarch was, nevertheless, subject to certain restrictions imposed by custom, and was not independent of the good-will of his nobles. Not till the end of the fifth century did a Macedonian sovereign attempt to infuse some measure of Hellenic culture into his subjects and generally to consolidate his loosely knit kingdom. Archelaus (413–399) improved the organization of his army, built forts and roads, and instituted a festival after the model of the Hellenic games, which was held at Dium at the foot of the northeastern slopes of Mt. Olympus. To his court he attracted a number of distinguished artists and poets, the musician and lyric poet, Timotheus, the tragic poets, Euripides and Agathon, and Zeuxis, the most eminent painter of his day.

For forty years after Archelaus' death Macedonia was in so disturbed a condition that most of his work must have been undone. While dynastic quarrels and conspiracies led to frequent changes of kings — one of them, Amyntas III, however, managed to keep his throne for twenty-one years — the Illyrians overran Macedonia, and for a number of years the Macedonian rulers were obliged to buy off these unruly neighbors with an annual tribute. In 359 a desperate crisis ensued. King Perdiccas, with the aim of ending these ignominious payments, attacked the Illyrians; but his army was heavily defeated and he himself was slain. His death was followed by the appearance of several pretenders to the throne, and a large part of the kingdom fell into the hands of the enemy. The legitimate heir to the throne was a child; so his uncle assumed the regency. Philip II, as we may at once call him, although he probably did not set his nephew aside and himself assume the kingly title for several years, was aged twenty-three. As a youth he had spent three years as a Macedonian hostage in Thebes, where he had been well treated, had acquired familiarity with Greek institutions and culture, and, above all, had become thoroughly acquainted with the excellent Theban military organization and tactics, and their chief creator, Epaminondas. On his return home he had held a responsible governorship in Macedonia, so that in 359, in spite of his youth, he had valuable and varied experience. Partly by timely gifts, partly by military action, Philip restored order out of anarchy in his kingdom

and inflicted defeat on his Illyrian neighbors. Then he set himself to secure the most essential prerequisites for the creation of
the greater Macedonia which he aspired to rule — a substantial
source of revenue and a first-class army. Macedonia was still
at this time a loose collection of clans and tribes. By forming
what was virtually a new army Philip also went far toward
creating a Macedonian nation. Earlier kings had in war-time
relied primarily on their cavalry recruited from the landed aristocracy. The foot-soldiers had been of quite secondary importance and had lacked both cohesion and training for war,
though in themselves hardy and brave fighters. Philip's aim
was to make his infantry as effective a military weapon as his
horse, and, by assiduous practice of both, to attain the best
tactical combination of the two. Thus he enrolled his subjects
according to their tribes and clans, and, as far as possible, kept
them together to form territorial divisions or regiments. All
the heavy infantrymen were armed alike, their chief offensive
weapon being a pike or lance (*sarissa*). The characteristic
Macedonian tactical infantry formation, the phalanx, varied
in depth from eight to sixteen men, and was therefore much
shallower than the Theban massed formation favored by Pelopidas and Epaminondas. The men, too, were drawn up in more
open order, whereby more room was ensured for the skillful
use of their pikes, and less reliance was placed on mere shock
tactics and weight of numbers. By an elaborate system of rewards and promotions in all branches of the military service
Philip encouraged healthy ambition and rivalry among his
men; while by constant practising, whether in actual warfare
or in manœuvres, he turned them into the finest standing army
that the world had yet seen — proud of their regiments, loyally
devoted to their king, and proud of their name, without distinction of clan or tribe, of Macedonians.

The needs of his treasury rather than the desire for conquest
dictated Philip's first military operations outside Macedonia.
By the autumn of 357 he had captured Amphipolis, and followed
this up by making himself master of the mining districts of Mt.
Pangæus. There, on the site of an earlier settlement, Crenides,
a larger town soon arose, named Philippi, while the intensive
working of the gold deposits soon produced a copious and steady

flow of bullion into the king's chest. The revenue from this source was estimated at not less than 1000 talents a year. The Athenians, who protested against Philip's activities in Thrace, where they had dependencies, he put off with specious promises which he had no intention of fulfilling. The Athenians for the next three years had too many commitments nearer home to oppose Philip's successful progress in Chalcidice and the Gulf of Therma. Technically, however, they were at war with Macedonia from 357 onwards. Their success in that year in recovering Euboea from Thebes was more than offset by a revolt of three of their strongest allies in the Confederacy — Chios, Rhodes, and Byzantium. These states were soon after joined by Cos, and, as their operations against Athens progressed favorably, by many other members of the maritime league. The cause of these defections is none too clear. In the main, however, the Athenians seem to have had only themselves to blame. During the previous decade they had more than once interfered with the autonomy of this or that ally; forgetful of the original terms of the Confederacy, they were once more striving to substitute imperial domination for the alliance of equals. After three years they were obliged to make peace on terms which reduced the Confederacy to a shadow. Nothing was left of it after 355 save Euboea, a part of the Cyclades, a few communities in Thrace, and the adjacent islands in the northern Aegean. Financially Athens was thoroughly exhausted, since the late war had cost fully 1000 talents, and her income hereafter was greatly shrunken.

During these years Philip had been very active in Thrace and by 353 controlled the whole of Chalcidice directly or, in the case of the Olynthian Confederacy, by alliance. He had also been drawn into the political affairs of Thessaly and central Greece. Simultaneously with the decline of the Boeotian League, their neighbors of Phocis had a brief period of striking military success. The so-called Sacred War originated in the refusal of the Phocians to pay a heavy fine imposed upon them, for an alleged act of sacrilege, by the Council of the Amphictionic League, acting under Theban influence. Rather than submit to the coercion of their neighbors, they decided to resist by force; they were fortunate in being led for several years by military commanders of unusual ability. Carrying on at first as best they could themselves, supported by some mercenaries, they soon found themselves in grave need of funds. They then seized Delphi and did not scruple to use its stored-up treasure to finance the war. They inflicted losses on Bœotia, contracted alliances with Sparta and Athens, though they derived little support from either, and eventually widened their sphere of action by entering Thessaly, whose inhabitants were traditional enemies of Phocis. But they had reckoned without Philip. He, too, had intervened in Thessalian affairs at the request of certain cities, while others, fearing to pass under Macedonian rule, turned to the Phocians for help. The Phocian leader, Onomarchus, had the distinction of beating Philip's troops twice in 353; but in the next year Philip had an ample revenge. For he won a battle against the Phocians, in which not less than 6000 of them were slain, among them Onomarchus. In the summer of that year, after having secured some important bases in Thessaly, Philip advanced toward Thermopylæ. The Athenians, mindful of their alliance with Phocis and seeing an opportunity to checkmate the Macedonian enemy, whose greatness few of them as yet realized, sent a military force to occupy the pass. To force it would have cost Philip more loss and effort than it was worth; so he retired northward again, willing to bide his time.

The energetic intervention of Athens on behalf of her allies was surprising in view of the state of political parties there at this date. The leaders of the war party, who had been largely to blame for the war of 357–355 that had ended so unsatisfactorily, had for that reason lost influence. From 354 the Athenian statesman who gained a remarkable ascendancy over his countrymen was Eubulus. Entrusted with the administration of the Theoric Fund for four years, and very possibly for eight, he exercised a general control over all finances at Athens and was during that period the guiding spirit of Athenian policy.[1] The results of his careful régime were soon evident. State debts were discharged, the fleet was overhauled, defenses and docks

[1] As the ancient authorities are not at one, it is a moot point whether the *Theorica* were already paid to a restricted extent in the Periclean Age, or whether they were not introduced till the fourth century. Originally a small payment was made to the poorest citizens to enable them to attend

that had fallen into disrepair were reconditioned. Over and above this, there was always a sufficient surplus to pay for the pleasure of the people, and from this time revenue that was left over after the year's budget had been balanced was earmarked for this purpose. Thus the material recovery of Athens from the continuous wars of the fourth century, and especially the war with the allies, was marked. But, on the other hand, Eubulus was loath to engage in any new military or naval undertakings, even when the political situation would have made this the wisest course for Athens. By determined action in 352–351 she could have checkmated or seriously retarded the successes of the Macedonian king. It was, moreover, one of the most notable developments of the fourth century that, to a steadily increasing degree, fighting was left to mercenaries. These professional soldiers were drawn from the young men in various Greek cities; to them a life of adventure and the prospect of good pay or ample booty were more attractive than a more settled existence in their native towns. Many, too, were drawn to mercenary service by impoverishment, such as was general in Greece after the Peloponnesian war. The most profitable opportunities were generally open to those who entered the service of the Persian king and his satraps, and the demand from that quarter for Greek professional soldiery was constant. The days when the able-bodied manhood of a Greek *polis* in time of need formed its defense, or when its army and navy in offensive wars were mainly recruited from the citizen body, were passing rapidly away. In a democratic state, like Athens, a further difference between the fifth and the fourth century is noticeable. Whereas in the fifth the business of government and of military command was commonly combined in the same person — we may instance Cimon, Pericles, Alcibiades, and Cleon — in the fourth century the two functions

---

the Greater Dionysia. Then the practice was extended to other festivals, the amount of the payment — originally one drachma — was increased, and the number of recipients was enlarged. From Eubulus' time, at least, the superintendence of the Theoric Fund, in which all surplus revenues were deposited, carried with it a general control over all the state finances. In his time the departments of state were not stinted; yet it was disastrous that all income in excess of what was needed for regular expenditure was diverted to popular amusement thinly disguised as religious observance.

were not united in a single individual. The politicians of fourth-century Athens were not soldiers; her military and naval commanders, as a rule, exercised little or no political influence. In the small city-state of antiquity this division into two classes of professional politicians and professional captains was disastrous. Each played for his own hand; the call of patriotism and the good of the community were too easily forgotten.

To no one were these evils more apparent than to the Athenian politician who, from 351, was the most prominent opponent of Eubulus and the peace party, and the most open denouncer of Macedonia and its king. Demosthenes, who was born in 384, on attaining to manhood was obliged to turn to professional speech-writing to earn a living, since he had been deprived of most of his patrimony by dishonest guardians. Overcoming by assiduous practice certain physical disabilities, he ended by being the greatest orator of his day and of antiquity. Although several of his extant speeches, which were delivered before 351, deal directly or indirectly with political issues, it was not till that year that, in his so-called *First Philippic Oration*, he first clearly enunciated the anti-Macedonian policy which, save for one brief interval, he consistently advocated throughout his life. Philip, after his set-back at Thermopylæ, was once more active in Thrace; his operations in the eastern part of that region, where Athens still had allies or dependencies, and the fact that his warships damaged Athenian interests in the Aegean, caused the Athenians serious alarm. Demosthenes with fine eloquence bade his countrymen keep a fleet of fifty vessels ready at all times to protect the Athenian possessions in the Hellespont and Thracian Chersonese. At the same time he demanded of them, or a portion of them, personal service in army or fleet, and urged them to have done with exclusive reliance on professional soldiery. But the advice of a still young and untried man was not followed. In 349 he repeated his proposals even more pressingly in his three *Olynthiac Speeches*, but the Athenians only acted upon them, and then very imperfectly, when it was too late. A rupture between Philip and the Chalcidic League, of which Olynthus was the head, led this city to appeal for aid to Athens. But, while the Athenians were deliberating, and, after they had made a formal alliance with Olynthus, were failing to send prompt and sufficient help, Philip acted with decision. By the summer of 348 he had, after reducing the lesser Chalcidic cities one by one, finally forced Olynthus itself to capitulate. His treatment of these cities — most of them were razed to the ground and their populations enslaved — was unusually ruthless. As revolted allies the Olynthians, in case of defeat, had, according to Greek usage, to expect harsh punishment; but, in view of the clemency shown by Philip on other occasions — for example in 338 — it is regrettable that we are ignorant of the reasons for his savagery in 348.

Against Athens Philip had scored another success at this time by actively supporting the Eubœan cities in their revolt from Athens; the whole island, with the exception of Carystus, thus passed out of the Athenian Confederacy. By the winter of 347–346 even Demosthenes and the other leaders of the war party saw the imperative need of coming to terms with the Macedonian monarch. Ten envoys were therefore despatched to treat with him. An agreement was reached and, after a good many delays, was signed by both parties by the summer of 346. Each retained such possessions as it held at the time. Hence the peace was all in favor of Philip, while the Phocian allies of Athens had been expressly excluded from the settlement. Their power had been waning for some years, and now Thebes and the Amphictionic League urged Philip to proceed against them. Deserted by all their allies, their main army surrendered to Philip at Thermopylæ, and then their cities submitted one by one. Their punishment was severe, but much less harsh than that accorded to the Chalcidic communities. They ceased to exist as a corporate state; they were disarmed and scattered in villages; they were compelled to repay, in the form of a heavy annual tribute, what they had taken from the Treasure of Delphi. Their votes in the Amphictionic League were taken over by Philip, who thus gained formal admission into what was a Panhellenic institution. In the same year he presided at the Pythian festival held at Delphi. There can be no doubt that this recognition of his Hellenic status was, in spite of the sneers of his enemies at Athens and elsewhere, greatly valued by and valuable to the Macedonian king.

Technically the peace between Philip and Athens lasted for six years. But the former was indefatigable in strengthening his hold on Greece by diplomatic means, and at the same time he now began to plan a war against the hereditary enemy of the Greeks, Persia, in which he would be commander-in-chief of a Panhellenic army. That his attitude to Athens, now the most considerable of the Greek states politically, as well as the artistic and intellectual leader of Greece, was conciliatory was due to the need he felt of either gaining her active support in these ambitious projects or at least of making sure of her friendly neutrality. But the Athenians, ashamed of the peace of 346 and the abandonment of Phocis to Philip, were now far more ready to listen to Demosthenes and his younger supporters, like Hypereides and Lycurgus. In other words, the anti-Macedonian party was gaining the ascendancy in the Athenian *ecclesia*. Thus, when Philip began to intrigue diplomatically in the Peloponnese, the Athenians, at Demosthenes' instigation, sent envoys to warn the Peloponnesian states against Philip's blandishments. By 342 the king had found that the influence of his inveterate enemies in Athens was too strong, and, in the realization that a renewed clash with that city was bound to come, he recommenced operations in eastern Thrace, so as to secure firmly all the region between the Hellespont and the Black Sea. The threat to the Thracian Chersonese was a vital blow at Athens; for the Athenians had been in occupation of this region for many years, and its loss might mean the strangulation of their grain trade with the cities on the Euxine and might even bring them near starvation. The interests at stake, and the need for a supreme effort, were urged upon them by Demosthenes in what, apart from the long *Oration on the Crown*, are his two finest political orations — *On the Affairs of the Chersonese* and the *Third Philippic*. Nor was his success limited to an oratorical triumph. Philip, having unsuccessfully tried to persuade Byzantium and Perinthus to make war on Athens, treated their refusal as a *casus belli*, and in 340 laid siege to Perinthus. But Byzantium, Athens, and the Persian satraps of Asia Minor all sent timely aid; after some months Philip abandoned this enterprise and attempted to take Byzantium by surprise. Here too he was foiled. Thus Athens

and he were again openly at war, and the Athenians, in winning the first round, had scored a decided success. For Demosthenes it was a great personal triumph. At last he was
able to prevail on his countrymen to take a step which he had
advocated for a decade, to devote to war purposes the surplus
revenue which hitherto had been paid into the Theoric Fund.

A new Sacred War, arising out of a trivial incident, led the
Council of the Amphictionic League to invite Philip's intervention once again. It was just such an opportunity as he desired. Passing Thermopylæ, he occupied Elatea in Phocis
which controlled the roads to Thebes and Athens. His envoys
to Thebes demanded that she should support him in an attack
on Athens, or at least remain neutral and permit the passage
of his army through Bœotia. But Demosthenes, as soon as the
occupation of Elatea became known at Athens, persuaded the
Athenians to send to Thebes and offer an alliance, backed by
the promise of immediate military support. The Thebans, to
their credit, accepted the Athenian proposals, and both states
made efforts to win additional help, especially from the Peloponnese. Most of the states there elected to remain neutral, —
awe of Philip and his earlier diplomatic intrigues combined to
bring this about, — so that the only reinforcements that Athens
and Thebes received were from a few smaller states whom
Athens had won over to an anti-Macedonian alliance a year or
two before. Philip did not strike till the summer of 338. After
some initial successes which forced the allies to abandon the
passes from Phocis into Bœotia, he met them in the plain of
Chæronea. Numerically the two armies were fairly equally
matched, each being about 30,000 strong; but Philip's superiority as a general, and the better training and greater
mobility of the Macedonian divisions, combined to bring about
a crushing defeat of the allies, though the Thebans especially
fought bravely and desperately to the last.

With this victory Macedonian hegemony over Greece was
assured. The Peloponnesian states, apart from Sparta, acknowledged Philip's supremacy. Against Thebes he was most
embittered, because her policy toward him had been equivocal
for some time. Some of her chief anti-Macedonian leaders were
executed, the government of the city was intrusted to a pro-

Macedonian oligarchy, and a Macedonian garrison was established in the Cadmeia. Soon after, Philip also placed troops in Chalcis and Corinth. Against Athens he adopted no punitive measures. She lost the Chersonese; she was obliged to disband her Confederacy and to ally herself with Philip; but she was permitted to retain a few extra-Attic possessions, — Lemnos, Imbros, and Scyros, also Samos and Delos.

Before the end of 338 Philip summoned a congress of Hellenic states at Corinth, attended by delegates from all the states of central and southern Greece, except Sparta, and of the Aegean islands. The autonomy and independence of all were proclaimed, and there was formed a federation of *poleis*, whose disputes were hereafter to be referred to a Common Council of the Greeks meeting at Corinth. Internally the several communities were to be governed according to the constitutions existing at the time of the congress. The federated Greeks formed a defensive and offensive alliance with Macedonia, whose king in case of war would be commander-in-chief by land and sea. In that case each member of the League was required to furnish a certain contingent of ships and troops. Severe penalties were fixed against those citizens of any *polis* in the federation who should attempt to subvert its government, or who conspired with, or entered the service of, any foreign power (*e.g.* Persia). Some of these provisions make it clear that Philip, over and above the statesmanly desire of uniting all Greece in harmony, and of substituting arbitration for suicidal conflicts between cities and groups of cities, was also perfecting his plans for an attack on Persia. Whether he aimed merely at the liberation of the Anatolian Greeks, or harbored more ambitious designs of conquest, we do not know. But his intention to lead an expedition into Asia Minor became generally known when, in 337 B.C., he summoned a second Hellenic congress to Corinth. Here the war on Persia was formally determined, and the needful preliminaries arranged. An advance force under Philip's trusted general, Parmenio, set out across the Hellespont in the following spring. It was the king's intention to join him with the main army before the end of 336. But in the summer, shortly before the date fixed for his departure, he was murdered by one of his own officers in the midst of the ceremonies attendant upon his daughter's wedding to Alexander of Epirus.[1]

Philip's premature death occurred at a very critical moment. His work of unifying Hellas had only just been accomplished, and the change from the normal political life of the Greek *poleis* was so fundamental that years were required before all would readily welcome what to many now was as distasteful as it was inevitable. In the world's history, where one man has steadily built up such a political structure as had been raised by Philip, and then almost at once has passed from the scene, his creation has rarely survived his death for long. It was the singular and fortunate experience of Macedonia that, on the death of the greatest ruler whom she had yet experienced, the throne was filled by his still greater son. And though, as we shall see, Alexander was snatched away before his task was finished, he had carried the work begun by Philip many stages farther, and his achievements changed the political, economic, and social aspect of the ancient world.

As for the outcome of the struggle between Greece and Philip, which culminated in the battle of Chæronea and the Congress of Corinth, it is idle and unjustified to brand the Greeks of the fourth century as the degenerate descendants of the victors at Marathon and Salamis, or of the contemporaries of Pericles. Their genius, expressed in material culture, literature, and art, was not inferior to that of their ancestors in the previous century. But their political institutions had proved unadaptable to changed conditions. It was not only political theorists, like Isocrates, who saw the necessity of coöperation and alliance between city-states and strove for Panhellenic unity. The many examples in the fourth century of the formation of federations and leagues are sufficient proof that men of affairs were experimenting in the creation of larger and more composite political organisms than the *polis*. But, interesting and significant as these experiments were, they were only partially successful. Local rivalries and jealousies, which often had their roots

---

[1] The assassination was reported to be an act of vengeance for a private wrong. But it is not improbable that there were political motives behind it, and that the wronged and banished wife of Philip, Olympias, was the real instigator.

in the more than half forgotten past, triumphed over all other considerations. When we remember that from 431 to 338 there was scarcely a year when all the Greeks were at peace, and very few during which whole groups of *poleis* were not engaged in hostilities, we can see how impossible it was for unity to be imposed on Greece from within. Hence, though we may not approve all the methods and acts of Philip and his son, we cannot deprive the former of the credit of having partially solved a difficult political problem, and the latter of the glory of giving a new meaning and mission to Hellenism.

3. The Western Greeks During the Fourth Century

This survey of the political history of the fourth century must conclude with a brief account of the western Greek world. After their triumph against Athens in 413 the Syracusans had sent a squadron to Greece, which for a few years coöperated with the Peloponnesian forces. At home a more extreme form of democratic government became the order of the day; nor was it long before the peace of Sicily was disturbed by the familiar bickering of rival cities. A far greater danger to western Hellenism, however, was the revived lust of conquest and revenge that now filled the Punic state. Not without reason the Carthaginians calculated that Syracuse and the rest of Sicily would be exhausted by their recent struggles against Athens; and, when an appeal from Segesta for help against her old foe, Selinus, reached them, they had an excuse, if one were needed, to intervene in the affairs of the island. A great naval and military expedition was equipped and sailed for Sicily in 409. Selinus was taken after a short siege and destroyed; then Himera in northern Sicily suffered similar treatment. In both cities the Punic armies massacred the inhabitants with indescribable ferocity. In the case of Himera this brutality was the barbarous satisfaction for an old grudge, since it was here that a Carthaginian host had suffered ignominious disaster seventy-one years before. Providentially for the Greeks the Punic commander desisted from further conquests and returned home. Three years later another attack was launched; but in the interval some preparations were made in Syracuse to offer a more effective resistance to the next Carthaginian invasion. In 406 the offensive was renewed; before the end of the year the Carthaginians had taken Acragas. The help given to that city by Syracuse, reinforced by troops from other cities in Sicily and even from southern Italy, was ineffective, apparently owing to the ineptitude of the higher command. It was even whispered that treason had been at work. At all events a new board of *strategoi* was elected, among the new officials being a young and as yet little known citizen, Dionysius. More drastic changes, partly under the influence of the Carthaginian danger, followed quickly. Successful intrigues enabled Dionysius to get his new colleagues deposed and to secure his own appointment as sole *strategos*. It needed only a story, to the effect that his life had been threatened, to persuade his countrymen to assign him a body-guard of 600 men. Thus, within a few months, Dionysius had become a Tyrant in fact, though not in name, since the established constitution was not abrogated. His rise to power had many general points of similarity to that of the sixth-century despots of Greece.

The difficulties which confronted him were tremendous; for, in addition to the precariousness of his own position, there was added the anxiety of the Punic peril. He did not hesitate to sacrifice Sicily, at least temporarily, in order to make sure of his throne. He gave up the defense of two Sicilian cities, which he at first aided against the common enemy, and then came to terms with the Carthaginian general. The Tyrant obtained official recognition by Carthage of his authority; but most of the island, save for Syracuse and a few lesser communities in the East, passed under Punic control.

For the next seven years Dionysius worked unceasingly with two objects in view, to make his own despotism unassailable and to develop Syracuse into a great naval and military state. He converted the acropolis of the city (Ortygia, or the Island) into an impregnable castle, in which he himself resided, guarded by foreign mercenaries and surrounded by friends and supporters on whom he could rely absolutely. Next, he greatly strengthened and augmented the defenses of Syracuse, built new harbor-works, and enlarged the Syracusan navy until, we are told, it numbered not less than 300 vessels. Every branch of the military service was carefully reorganized, and professional soldiery was at all times employed in great numbers. Above all, with the aid of skillful engineers he devised new engines of war for use in siege operations, of which the most famous was a catapult capable of hurling big stones a distance of several hundred yards.

He now set himself to bring all eastern Sicily under his domination. This he effected in the course of three or four years, though on one occasion he came very near to disaster. By 398 he was ready for the task which had been present to his mind from the first, a war of revenge on Carthage, to be attended by the complete expulsion of Phœnicians and Carthaginians from Sicily. Whether his army really numbered 80,000 infantry and 3000 cavalry, as is said, may well be doubted; in any case he was the master of a military and naval strength greater than that controlled by any Greek state up to that time. His first war against Carthage was carried on in 398 and 397, and resumed in 392. The earlier successes of Dionysius were followed by severe set-backs, till finally Syracuse itself was besieged by the enemy on land and sea. It was now that the value of Dionysius' elaborate defenses was fully demonstrated. The strength of the Syracusan walls was proof against all assaults, till at last the enemy, weakened by a plague which decimated their ranks, were completely repulsed. The renewed war in 392 was indecisive, and at the end a treaty was signed between the two combatants, which left Dionysius master of the greater part of Sicily, while the Carthaginian strongholds in the northwestern corner of the island remained intact.

Dionysius next embarked on a policy of conquest in Italy. At the end of six or seven years he had gained control over the greater portion of Magna Græcia, and had established settlements as far afield as Ancona and Hadria on the western, and Pharos and Issa on the eastern, shore of the Adriatic. The two additional wars which he fought with Carthage (in 383–378 and in 368) led to some loss of territory in Sicily, and he suffered more than one naval and military reverse. Yet it was still a wide dominion which passed to his son when Dionysius died in 367.

Dionysius I was indubitably one of the most remarkable

figures of antiquity. Two facts make it difficult to form a full and fair judgment of him. Almost our only source for his reign is the compilation of Diodorus (first century B.C.), who drew on fourth and third century historians but was thoroughly uncritical in his method. Secondly, the Tyranny of Dionysius was unpopular among his contemporaries and execrated by succeeding generations of Greeks, so that the real eminence of the man soon becamed obscured, and he was thought of merely as a type of unconstitutional and ruthless despot. Yet, harsh as some of his actions seem to have been, he was not capriciously cruel; for, first and last, he was a statesman who managed to maintain his authority and a great dominion for nearly forty years. As a general his only equal in Greek history was Philip II, his only superior was Alexander the Great. As a diplomat, as in matters of religion, he had no conscience; and it is perhaps the severest criticism that can be levelled against him that he was prepared to truckle to Carthage for a time and sacrifice Hellenic interests in order to secure his own despotism. He had disregarded Greek conventions by living with two wives at the same time. The eldest son of one of these unions, Dionysius II, succeeded to the throne in 367. But as he had been jealously excluded by his father from any share in the government and was by nature a rather feeble character, it was not surprising that the Syracusan court became the scene for intrigue. At first, the young ruler's kinsman, Dion, exerted a wholesome influence; but after a time Dion's enemies, led by the historian Philistus, gained the upper hand and compassed Dion's downfall and banishment. The latter's attempts to overthrow the Tyranny plunged Syracuse into years of unrest and civil war. Dionysius was expelled for a time, but still matters in Syracuse went from bad to worse, especially after Dion's assassination (354).

The other cities, which had formed part of the realm of Dionysius I, fell into the hands of different petty despots, and the prosperity of the whole country was grievously undermined. Dionysius II returned to Syracuse, and even after the Syracusans in desperation had chosen Hicetas as their general to restore order and defend the city against a new Carthaginian attack, managed to hold the castle of Ortygia. The

Syracusans also sent an urgent appeal for help to Corinth, who listened sympathetically to the prayers of her daughter-city in 344 as she had done in 414. Timoleon was despatched with a small body of volunteers and mercenaries to make common cause with the Syracusan patriots. He soon showed that he was endowed with unusual ability as a general and a statesman. Hicetas had played false and allied himself with Carthage, because his real aim was to become Tyrant of Syracuse himself. But Timoleon overcame all obstacles. He stormed Syracuse and received the Island from Dionysius II, who surrendered to him. In Syracuse and in the other Greek cities, after their despots had been expelled, moderate democratic governments were set up under Timoleon's supervision. A large number of Greeks from the mother country (60,000?) emigrated to the West to help in repopulating the Sicilian *poleis*. Above all, Timoleon inflicted a crushing defeat on a great Punic army in an engagement fought near the River Crimisus in the early summer of 341. Two years later a treaty between Carthage and Syracuse was signed, which reëstablished the boundary between the Greek and Punic spheres in the island that had been fixed after Dionysius I's second Carthaginian war. In 338 Timoleon retired universally honored into private life. Two years later he died; his work was not destined long to survive him.

CHAPTER XVIII

ECONOMIC DEVELOPMENT IN THE FIFTH AND FOURTH CENTURIES

> *One would be justified in the view that Athens
> is situated in the centre of Hellas and of all the
> inhabited world. . . . Although Athens is not
> surrounded by the sea, yet, being accessible to all
> winds like an island, it imports what it needs and
> exports what it wishes; for Athens is near the
> sea. By land, too, it receives much by way of
> commerce, being in fact a mainland city.* —
> Xenophon, *Ways and Means*, i, 1.

IT was noted in an earlier chapter how it is impossible to
form anything more than a very sketchy picture of the economic
life of the Greeks in the archaic period. From the time of the
Persian wars the information to be gleaned from various sources
becomes more copious, but mainly for one state only, Athens.
In the case of other communities it is as scanty, — sometimes
scantier, — for the fifth and fourth centuries as for the seventh
and sixth. Even so basic a question as the size of the population of the Hellenic world, or of any part of it, at this period
must remain unanswered. In the case of Athens alone some
tentative figures may be hazarded. The adult male population
of the Athenian state at the outbreak of the Peloponnesian
war seems to have been approximately 50,000 to 55,000.
Following the normal calculation, which makes these one-
third of the whole citizen body, we arrive at a total figure of
150,000 to 165,000 men, women, and children of civic status.
The resident aliens had steadily increased ever since the
sixth century and, as will be seen, were a most vital factor in the
economic life of Athens. In 431 there were probably not less
than 40,000 to 45,000 of these, one-third of this number being
again reckoned as adult males. The slave population used to be

STATUETTE OF SOCRATES

Plate 21

greatly exaggerated, mainly on the basis of an ill-informed statement by a late writer. But, even at the most conservative estimate, there cannot have been less than 80,000 to 90,000 of them in Attica, and they may have been slightly more numerous.[1] While the total population of the Hellenic world probably did not alter appreciably during the fourth century, the proportion of citizen to non-citizen population in particular city-states did undergo very definite change. An extreme example is furnished by Sparta. Her system was so rigidly exclusive that the normal wastage of citizens was never made good; at the same time not a few not killed in war got into arrears with the contributions that they were expected to make from their allotments, and in consequence forfeited these, and with them their full civic status.[2] In Athens the plague and the Peloponnesian war, especially the Sicilian expedition, had heavily reduced the adult citizen population. To some extent she recovered from these losses; but the proportion of free aliens to citizens steadily rose during the fourth century, until it was as much as 1: 2. The slave population also was greatly augmented in that age.

The importance of the resident foreigners for Athenian trade and commerce was immense. The Athenian state granted these *metoikoi* or denizens little beyond freedom to pursue their calling; on the other hand, it enforced a number of rules with which they had to comply. They were required to pay a small head-tax and to register formally as resident aliens, after they had found an Athenian citizen willing to stand sponsor (*prostates*) for them. Hence in each deme, besides the list of citizens of that deme, there was kept one of resident metics. In most cases of litigation the denizens could only plead indirectly through their sponsor. Non-compliance with these regulations might lead to legal prosecution of the offending metic, and the maximum penalty fixed for the guilty was to be sold into slavery. Furthermore, the denizen was debarred from owning landed property; he was liable to military service, and, provided his wealth was

---

[1] Thucydides (vii, 27) relates that in 414–413 over 20,000 Attic slaves deserted, and he adds that the majority were craftsmen.

[2] Cf. Chapter XXIV for the decline of the Spartan citizens in the third century.

sufficient, he was obliged to bear the same financial burdens as the richer classes of citizens. The grant of citizenship was a privilege or reward only rarely conferred on resident aliens. Somewhat commoner was the bestowal, on those who had deserved well of the state, of what was known as *isoteleia*. The metic so rewarded was exempt from poll-tax, could litigate without the intervention of a *prostates*, and, in the matter of financial and military liabilities, was on a footing of complete equality with the citizens. The greatest privilege of all, which was commonly associated with *isoteleia*, but which is always separately specified on the inscriptions that are our main source of information, was the right of owning landed property. The number of such privileged denizens was not inconsiderable from the end of the fifth century onwards.[1] They formed a class intermediate between the civic body and the ordinary metics.

The majority of denizens were humbler folk engaged in a great variety of occupations. Nor must it be forgotten that many artists, writers, and philosophers, who made Athens their home permanently or for a prolonged period, and whom one consequently tends to think of as Athenians, belonged in fact to the metic class. Such were the speech writer Lysias, the sculptor and engraver Mys, the architect and friend of Pericles, Hippodamus of Miletus, and the philosopher Aristotle. On an inscription recording the names of those employed in 408–407 on the building of the Erechtheum at Athens fifty per cent are those of metics.[2] The numerous persons employed in trade or engaged in commerce, whose litigations are recorded in the *Private Orations* of the Attic Orators, are without exception denizens.[3] These facts are very significant. While no one would suggest that free Athenian citizens did not, both in the fifth and the fourth centuries, to some extent engage in trade and industry, it

[1] One of the best known examples of an *isoteles* was the wealthy Cephalus, the father of the orator Lysias. Cephalus has been immortalized by being introduced as one of the speakers at the beginning of Plato's *Republic*.

[2] To be precise, thirty-five metics out of a total personnel of seventy-one. Twenty names are those of citizens and sixteen those of slaves.

[3] That some of the speeches attributed, for example, to Demosthenes and included in the corpus of Demosthenic orations may not actually be his does not affect the present question. They are genuine and contemporary law-court speeches whoever their author.

seems clear that they formed a minority of the producing class. To the outbreak of the Peloponnesian war agriculture was still the main occupation of the citizens. From the time of Pericles, moreover, the state offered more and more paid employments to its citizens. Though the remuneration was small, little in the way of additional income was needed by the Athenian to eke out an existence. Nor can it be doubted that, had Athens been really a commercial state, in the sense that a majority of her citizens was directly engaged in trade and mercantile pursuits, she would have restricted competing foreigners and even expelled them beyond her borders, instead of encouraging their residence in Athens or Peiræus.

The existence of metics can be proved for more than three score Greek *poleis*, but it is only in the case of Athens that fuller details about their status and activities are available. To deduce, as has been done, that, because the number of denizens was exceptionally great at Athens, their general treatment there must have been better than in other cities is fallacious. The Greeks from other centres who migrated to Athens in preference to Corinth, for example, did so because, from the time of Pericles to the rise of Alexandria, enterprise in trade and commerce at Athens was more profitable than elsewhere.

The distribution of slaves in Greece was geographically very uneven. In Laconia and Messenia, in Crete, and in Thessaly, the large serf population performed the agricultural work for their masters; and, though technically they must be classed as serfs over whom the individual master had only limited control, in fact they were state-owned slaves. Their treatment and the conditions under which they lived were often harder than those of slaves elsewhere, over whom the individual owner had power of life and death. At Sparta it was the deliberate policy of the government from time to time to authorize a secret police of Spartan young men to put to death summarily Helots suspected of insubordination or disloyalty, and thereby to keep this vast subject population in a condition of constant fear. In other regions, where the communities were mainly agricultural or pastoral, for instance in Bœotia or in Arcadia, few slaves seem to have been employed even as late as the second half of the fifth century. In an important city like Thebes, however, their

numbers would be greater and tended to increase.   Thus we
learn that the Thebans, in their last extremity, when dire punishment threatened their city and themselves from Alexander the
Great in 336, emancipated many slaves so that these might
loyally aid in the defense of the city.   The slave class was most
numerous in states like Athens, where there was much mercantile and industrial activity, and where, it may be added, this
human merchandise was most easily come by.   For the great
majority of slaves were acquired by purchase and were of non-
Hellenic race.   Those whose only asset was physical strength
and endurance were employed in the silver mines at Laurium.
That they worked there under appalling conditions, and that
their treatment was brutal, is unhappily beyond dispute.   Much
better was the lot of slaves employed in domestic service, and in
arts and crafts.   If and when a slave was skilled in any occupation, simple self-interest would make the master treat him
reasonably well.   Nor are we justified in doubting that the
average Athenian was decently humane to his servile dependents.   On the other hand, the frequent use of the lash, to which
there are so many semi-humorous references in the comedies
of Aristophanes, and the practice at criminal trials of taking
slave-evidence only under torture, illustrate the darker side of
the institution.   If an Athenian master put his slave to death, he
was liable to be tried not for murder but for manslaughter.
This is an interesting compromise between putting the slave
absolutely in his master's power and setting him on an equality
with free men.   A slave who suffered persistent ill-usage could
seek sanctuary and demand to be sold to another master.   In
ordinary life there was little to distinguish slave from free man
in outward habit, and he was allowed access to most religious
celebrations and festivals.   Manumission was a not infrequent
reward for faithful service.   Sometimes the master freed a slave
during his own life-time; frequently his last will provided for
the manumission of his slaves after his death.   If freed while
his master lived, the slave's status was analogous to that of a
metic.   He was required to take his late master as a patron or
sponsor.   There were many cases, too, where servile craftsmen
were set up in business by their owners, to whom they then
paid a certain percentage of their earnings.

Agriculture had always been, and continued to be, regarded as an honorable occupation, worthy of a citizen. It was one, however, which in the majority of city-states became necessarily more and more difficult to practise profitably. The constant warfare hit the farmers more directly than other members of the community, so that, in Attica, for example, it was the rural population who suffered most severely during the Peloponnesian war. The methods followed in raising field crops continued to be primitive. Good pasturage for cattle was scarce in Greece, large tracts being suitable at best only for sheep and goats. The Greeks, it is true, learnt the value of decayed vegetation and wood-ash for helping to fertilize their fields and knew the advantage of mixing different soils; but, in the absence of artificial or chemical preparations, they had in the main to rely on animal manure. Since this was often difficult to procure owing to the shortage of livestock, it was still the usual procedure in the fifth century for crops to be grown on a particular piece of land only in alternate years, the land lying fallow in the intermediate periods. Even in the fourth century the cultivation of alternating crops seems to have been the exception rather than the rule. The usual procedure, then, was for a farmer to have one half of his land under cultivation in one year and the other half in the next. In existing agreements we find this provided for; the peasant undertook during the last year of his lease not to work more than half his acreage, in order that the next lessee could at once continue the cultivation of the other half. Nor does it seem as if efforts were made to help out the deficiency of pasture lands by growing fodder, like lupines or clover, in the fields that were not planted with cereals in a given year. The absence of machinery — even the plow was of the simplest pattern — made farming a slow and laborious process. The ripe grain was cut by hand with the sickle and was separated from the chaff by the ancient but wasteful method of turning oxen or mules loose to trample on it. Moreover, it is a significant fact that the descriptions of agricultural processes in Xenophon, and still later in Theophrastus, do not substantially differ from those in Hesiod's *Works and Days*. In many parts of Greece, too, the climatic conditions were not favorable to intensive cultivation of wheat or barley. During a large part of the year the rain-fall was too uncertain, a torrential downpour being perhaps succeeded by a prolonged drought. Thus, in Attica, and in many other regions also, it was found that the raising of vines and olive trees was more profitable and more suited to existing conditions; for vines especially could be grown satisfactorily on sloping ground, and the irregularity of the rains in spring and summer was of less consequence. The amount of wheat and barley grown in Attica was only a small part of what was needed to feed the large population, while wine and oil were her two chief articles of export. Many other city-states were similarly dependent on the import of foreign cereals. Bœotia and Thessaly, on the other hand, and much of the Peloponnese, were, under normal conditions, self-sufficient. In the Peloponnese it was only maritime cities with very restricted territory and a large population, like Corinth, which were compelled to import foreign grain.

By far the most important grain-raising region was south Russia; Egypt, Cyprus, and Sicily also grew more cereals than they needed for home consumption. Both in the days of her imperial greatness and in the fourth century it was mainly from the Pontic regions that the Athenians obtained their grain. For this reason the control of the Dardanelles and of Byzantium — or failing this, friendly relations with the last-named city — formed an essential part of Athenian policy. From the last quarter of the fifth century through the greater part of the fourth the Athenians had a commercial agreement with the princes of the Cimmerian Bosporus, by which they were exempted from the payment of export duties at Black sea ports. Not all the grain thus brought to Peiræus was needed to feed the inhabitants of Attica. A portion — the limit fixed by law in the fourth century was one-third — was reshipped from Peiræus to other cities. Yet the government, although it gave constant attention to the safety of the food supply, supplying convoys of war-ships, if necessary, to escort the grain boats from the Black sea, and appointed special officials to regulate the import and export at Peiræus, left the important carrying trade entirely to private enterprise. What is more, if the grain dealers in Lysias' twenty-second speech are, as we have reason to believe, typical, the merchants engaged in this commerce were predominantly non-Athenians, that is to say, denizens. We do not know the outcome of this trial for which Lysias was commissioned to write the prosecuting speech about the year 390; but a passage may at least be cited to show that artificial inflation of prices is no discovery of the modern world: [1]

And yet, you are all aware that the defendants have absolutely no right to speak in this way; for their interests are the very opposite to those of the rest of the population. They make enormous profits on any occasion when news is brought of a national calamity and they sell their grain very dearly. So pleased are they to see your misfortunes that they get information of some of these before other people; others they themselves invent, for example, that the grain-fleet in the Black sea has been wrecked or captured by the Lacedæmonians as it sailed out of the straits, or that the markets have been shut against Athens, or that our treaties are on the point of being cancelled. In fact, so great is their hostility that they use the same opportunities to plot against you as your enemies do. For when your need of grain is greatest, they grab all that there is and refuse to sell, so that we may not dispute about the price but be content to go our way after buying from them at any figure they like to fix. In a word, at times, though Athens is at peace, these fellows reduce her to a state of siege.

The cereals grown in the western Greek world and exported to Greece chiefly supplied Peloponnesian states like Corinth.

Olives and vines, on the other hand, were all but ubiquitous in the Hellenic world. It was a safer undertaking, though it required more capital at first; for vines did not start bearing until the third year and olives not before the tenth. If we hear little about the relative goodness of olives raised in different areas, there was great variety in the wines. The larger islands of the Archipelago — Thasos, Samos, Chios, Lesbos, Rhodes, Naxos, and Cos — were noted for theirs; nor is it without significance that the two-handled wine-cup (*kantharos*) appears on the coins of Naxos and Thasos. To judge by pictorial representations, the vines of ancient, like those of modern, Greece were mostly low-growing dwarf plants needing little artificial support.

The mineral resources of the Greek world, if not ample, seem,

---

[1] Quoted from pages 7–8 of M. L. W. Laistner, *Greek Economics* (London and New York, 1923), where a complete translation of Lysias' speech will be found.

with the help of some imported ores from beyond its confines, to have been adequate. Gold was mined in Thasos and in Mt. Pangæus on the Thracian mainland opposite the island; there was also some, at least in the earlier period, in Siphnos, while the Asiatic Greeks obtained their supply from the interior. The two chief sources of silver in the eastern Mediterranean were Mt. Pangæus and Laurium in southern Attica. There were copper deposits in Eubœa and in some regions in Asia Minor, but the most prolific were still those in Cyprus. Yet this island must sometimes have been an uncertain source of supply for the Greeks, since it was more often than not under Persian control. Iron in small quantities was found in many places; larger deposits existed in · Seriphos, Eubœa, and especially in northeastern Asia Minor and in Laconia. Spain could boast of a wealth of silver and tin, and doubtless the western Greeks looked there for their supply of these metals. How far Spanish ores were exported to the countries bordering the eastern Mediterranean is a matter of great obscurity. Though metals, then, were relatively scarce, there was an abundance of stone. Good limestone could be quarried in various parts of Greece; green porphyry was found in the two mountain ranges — Parnon and Taygetus — that bounded Laconia on the east and west. But, above all, marble abounded, the finest varieties being those from Paros and from Mt. Pentelicus in Attica. There were also rich deposits of clay suitable for bricks, tiles, and vases. The prominence, in regions like Corinthia and Attica, of potters manufacturing the finest ceramic wares was made possible by the exceptionally good raw material at their disposal. As for timber, the process of deforestation in many parts of Greece seems to have begun very early. There was a certain amount in Thessaly, Arcadia, and Crete, but their output was not comparable with the wealth of good lumber available in Macedonia and the interior of Thrace. It was from the hinterland of Chalcidice that the Athenians during the days of their imperial greatness obtained the material necessary for constructing their proud navy.

Although industry and commerce flourished in many Hellenic centres, and the states derived profit therefrom through the customs and harbor dues that they exacted, their scope and

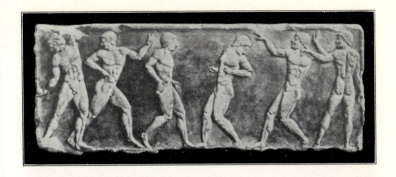

LATE ARCHAIC RELIEF FROM ATHENS

Plate 21a

LATE ARCHAIC RELIEF FROM ATHENS

Plate 21b

character, and the general methods of business in both the fifth and the fourth centuries have often been misunderstood. There is no clear evidence that any Greek government ever legislated for the advantage of, much less subsidized with a view to some important commercial undertaking, its mercantile class. It is true that we now have a Thasian inscription showing that the government of the island in the fourth century interested itself in the wine trade. To prevent speculation it was forbidden to buy up in advance the harvest of a whole vineyard. Strict regulations were enforced to insure that the jars filled with wine were correct measure. Further, no Thasian ship was allowed to load up with foreign wines between two stated points on the mainland coast off Thasos. While it is tempting to interpret these ordinances purely as steps taken by the government to help the local industry in its coastal trade, it seems far more likely — in the absence of any parallel case — to assume that the real reason for this intervention was the expectation of substantial revenue from duties which, with such rigorous supervision, could be most effectively levied. Commercial treaties, of which a number are known from inscriptions, were unlike what is now meant by such. Their object was not to help and extend the trade of the community but solely to facilitate the importation of necessaries, like grain and material for ship-building. Capitalists were forbidden by law to invest capital for the benefit of foreign states. Undertakings for which the government was directly responsible were nevertheless left to private contractors to fulfil. Thus the Athenian treasury derived a royalty from the silver mines at Laurium; but the actual exploitation was left to private lessees, who purchased mining concessions and worked them with slave labor. Similarly, public works were entrusted to private enterprise. On the construction of the Erechtheum free men, metics, and slaves all found work at a uniform wage of one drachma a day.

The production of manufactured articles was in the fifth century carried on by free, metic, and slave craftsmen in their own workshops, with the help of a few subordinates, servile or free. From the end of that century production on a somewhat larger scale, and with a more extensive use of servile labor, became more common, and in the fourth century probably drove

many a master craftsman out of business. Men of means invested capital in small factories in which thirty or forty slaves
might be under a slave or freedman overseer. To the Greeks
of the period this might seem "mass production"; to the modern
it appears as only a slight extension of the older system, coupled
with a greater reliance on servile labor.[1] Moreover, in the rural
districts home production or domestic economy continued the
rule for many articles which in the urban centres were no longer
manufactured in the home.

Master craftsmen owning their own workshops sold their
wares partly directly to buyers, partly through middlemen or
petty traders. The merchant engaged in maritime traffic
regularly accompanied his merchandise, and disposed of it in
person at such centres as he chose to visit. Occasionally we
hear of several men working in conjunction or partnership.
For instance, Lycon of Heraclea had a partner, Cephisiades,
who lived in the island of Scyros, where in addition he engaged
in trade on his own account.[2] Owners of vessels in like manner
used them to carry their own cargoes, though they might also
take another merchant and his commodities with them on their
journeys. But we do not find shippers who made their money
exclusively by the transport of other men's freight. Both the
shipmaster-merchant and the merchant travelling in another's
boat were, in other words, middlemen operating on borrowed
capital. Nothing, in fact, is more noteworthy in the business
life of Greece than this divorce of the capitalist from the
merchant and trader. The latter regularly borrowed money
to purchase the wares in which he traded; he was not himself
the owner of capital. Loans on bottomry are frequently mentioned in the Attic Orators. They were a favorite form of
investment, for they might turn out to be extremely profitable.

---

[1] It is commonly stated that Cephalus, or his son, Lysias, who inherited
the property, employed 120 slaves in a shield factory. This example is
cited as the largest Greek factory of which we have any record. Yet even
for this one case the evidence for so large a number of hands is far from
conclusive. For the statement of Lysias (xii, 8 and 19) does not warrant
the conclusion that the slaves confiscated in 404 by the Thirty were all
factory employés. The list of objects seized embraced all Lysias' effects,
so that some of the 120 slaves are likely to have been those employed on
domestic duties in what had been a large and wealthy household.

[2] Demosthenes, *Orat.* 52.

But the risks were great also; hence the rate of interest exacted was usually very high, and litigation arising out of such transactions was common.[1]

By the fourth century the business of banking had to some extent developed. Money-changing was in any case a complicated matter in view of the innumerable autonomous cities, each of which issued its own coinage. True, there was a tendency among the majority to adhere to one of two standards; but even so they were not all equally conscientious in keeping up the purity of their silver issues. The case of the Attic tetradrachms which were accepted everywhere was all but unique. The Athenian government, moreover, as appears from an inscription, at some date before 421 passed a decree compelling the subjects of the empire to use Attic currency. Another inscription that is of the greatest interest in this connection is a fourth-century decree from Olbia on the Black sea. The government of this city-state, while permitting the free entry of all gold and silver coins, laid down that these must be changed into local currency and in one particular place, obviously in order to enable a proper control to be exercised and the agio to be collected for the state treasury. None but Olbian silver and bronze coins were permitted to circulate within the city. It would be interesting to know how far other Greek *poleis* may have adopted similar measures.

The more successful money-lenders now also received money on deposit and operated on a larger scale with other men's capital, as well as with their own. While, on the one hand, we find prominent bankers, like Pasion and Phormion, engaging in a variety of monetary transactions necessitating, for example, an elaborate system of book-keeping, we observe on the contrary that the ordinary merchant transacted his business on the simplest, not to say on a primitive, plan. Written receipts for loans are nowhere mentioned; sums are deposited or paid in the presence of witnesses. When we find a speaker in one of Demosthenes' speeches putting the question, "Who would be so unwise as willingly to pay money to a person making a written application," we realize how far removed from anything like a developed banking system the Greeks still were.

[1] Cf., for example, Demosthenes, *Orat.* 34 and 56.

In truth, no proper credit system was yet in operation. The transference of sums of money was carried out literally, by the transport of bullion or coin from one place to another. At the same time the type of letter of credit mentioned in the *Trapezi-ticus* (c. 391) of Isocrates was doubtless employed whenever practicable. The plaintiff resided at Athens but had money in Bosporus on the Black sea which he desired to transfer to Athens. He found a certain Stratocles who was going to those parts and needed money while there. So he arranged with Stratocles that the latter should give him money in Athens, while he gave Stratocles a letter to his father in Bosporus, authorizing that gentleman to pay Stratocles an agreed amount when he reached that city. The banker Pasion witnessed the transaction.[1] But in general industry and commerce, though intensive judged by ancient standards, were carried on in the simplest way and differed not only in volume but in kind from what is now commonly understood by those terms.

When we turn to consider the finances of the Greek states, we have once more to admit that only in the case of Athens is it possible to speak with any precision about the financial organization of the state, that is, of income and expenditure, and of the distribution of financial burdens among the inhabit-ants of the country. In fifth-century Athens the chief sources of revenue were the tribute from the subjects and allies, money received for mining concessions in Laurium and royalties from the proceeds of the mines, rents from state-owned property — though this seems to have been small — market dues and harbor dues on all imports and exports, court-fees, fines, and confiscations. But when, as the result of a judicial condemna-tion, the guilty party's estate was confiscated by the govern-ment, it was not retained as state property but sold again to private bidders. In the fourth century the most important of those sources, the tribute, existed no longer. We are almost totally ignorant about the finances of the Second Athenian Confederacy; but, even if the Athenian government in time controlled the contributions of the League members, the amount was paltry compared to the *phoros* of the fifth century, and defrayed only a small part of Athens' heavy expenditure.

[1] Isocrates, *Trapeziticus* §§ 35–6.

There was no regular direct taxation — apart from the head-tax paid by the denizens — but the state was relieved of a considerable portion of the burden which its treasury would otherwise have had to bear by the costly public services known as liturgies. These were undertaken by the wealthier citizens and, save in one case, metics. They were of two kinds, the so-called recurrent liturgies and the trierarchy. The latter, to which citizens only were liable, entailed the cost of equipping and keeping a trireme or ship of war in good condition for one year. The state provided the hull and some tackle, and paid a small sum to the crew; for the rest the trierarch was responsible, and very often he also augmented the sailors' pay. During the fifth century there appears to have been no difficulty in finding the necessary trierarchs to undertake this heavy responsibility singly. But toward the end of the Peloponnesian war it became necessary to divide the cost of a trierarchy between two persons. In the fourth century further modifications were introduced at different times. By the law of a certain Periander, passed in 357–356, the twelve hundred wealthiest persons were divided into twenty companies of sixty. These were further grouped into smaller units, so that a varying number — from two to ten, or even more — would join to defray the cost of keeping one war-ship in fighting trim. The contributions were apparently graduated according to the means of the liable citizens. An enactment, sponsored by Demosthenes in 340–339, introduced certain changes intended to remedy uneven distribution of the financial burden and other abuses which had crept into the system by his day.

Of recurrent liturgies there were many, most of them being connected with religious celebrations and athletic festivals. Thus, for example, the *choregia* entailed the equipping and training of a chorus for the dramatic performances held at the Greater Dionysia or Lenæa; the *gymnasiarchia* similarly took care of athletes in training for the public games. In this way, it will readily be seen, the treasury was quit of a great part of the outlay coincident with the numerous religious celebrations. The performance of these services, at all events in the fifth century, was regarded as a patriotic duty, and the rich citizen commonly made it a point of honor to spend more than the minimum required of him. The opening paragraphs of Lysias' twenty-first oration throw a welcome light both on the variety of the recurrent liturgies and on their relative cost. The defendant, for whom Lysias wrote the speech, is striving to impress on the jury that he has shown himself a generous and public-spirited citizen: [1]

As to the charges against me, gentlemen of the jury, you have been sufficiently instructed; but I ask you to listen also to the rest of what I have to say, so that you may understand what manner of man I am before you pass judgment on me. I was certified as attaining my majority in the archonship of Theopompus (411–410 B.C.). Having been appointed producer of a tragic chorus, I expended thirty minæ; two months afterwards, at the Thargelia, I spent two thousand drachmæ, winning a victory with a men's chorus; and in the archonship of Glaucippus (410–409 B.C.) at the Greater Panathenæa, eight hundred drachmæ on pyrrhic dancers. Furthermore, in the same archonship, I was victorious with a men's chorus at the Dionysia, and I spent, including the setting up of the tripod, five thousand drachmæ; then in the archonship of Diocles (409–408 B.C.) I spent three hundred drachmæ on a cyclic chorus at the Lesser Panathenæa. Meanwhile, for seven years, I acted as trierarch and disbursed six talents. And, while incurring all these expenses and in service abroad risking danger daily on your behalf, I have nevertheless contributed to the war-tax (*eisphora*), thirty minæ on one occasion and four thousand drachmæ on another. As soon as I returned to land, in the archonship of Alexias (405–404 B.C.), I was producing games for the festival of Prometheus, and, having expended twelve minæ, won a victory. Subsequently I was appointed *choregus* for a boys' chorus, and spent over fifteen minæ. In the archonship of Eucleides (404–403 B.C.) I was producer of comedy for Cephisodorus and I was victorious. I disbursed, including the dedication of the equipment, sixteen minæ; and at the Lesser Panathenæa I was *choregus* for a pyrrhic chorus of youths and spent seven minæ. I have won a victory with a trireme in the race at Sunium, expending fifteen minæ; in addition I undertook to defray the cost of sacred embassies, of the procession of the Errephoriæ, and of other similar duties, for which my expenses have amounted to over thirty minæ. Of the sums which I have recounted I should not have disbursed a quarter, had I wished to perform the liturgies merely according to the exact requirements of the law. But while I was acting as trierarch, my ship was the best maintained in the whole fleet.

Even if this case was exceptional, it is surely remarkable that one citizen could spend in a decade as much as 636 minæ on

[1] Lysias, *Orat.* 21, 1–6.

public services.[1] From it we can deduce how vast the total expenditure on religious festivals must have been, and how much of it was, in the absence of direct taxation by the state, borne by a comparatively small number of citizens and denizens. In the succeeding era this frequent drain on their resources was often felt as a burden by those on whom the costly duty fell.

The one direct tax on citizens and resident aliens of means was the *eisphora*. Other states besides Athens occasionally had recourse to this extraordinary tax on property, but it is of the Athenian levy that most is known. It was only sparingly used in the fifth century, the earliest certain instance occurring in 428–427. In the last years of the Peloponnesian war the same means of temporarily easing the urgent financial straits of the treasury were again employed. In the fourth century its use became more and more frequent. By 378–377 a system of collection by companies (symmories) had been introduced, which, owing to abuses and unfair distribution of the required payment among the members of each symmory, had to be revised on more than one occasion. The denizens in all likelihood paid somewhat more heavily than the citizens; for it was one of the privileges sometimes conferred on deserving metics to be classed with Athenians in the payment of this tax. This implies that, without such a concession, a metic of wealth was worse off than a citizen.

The financial difficulties of the Athenian government were almost constant during the first half of the fourth century. The retrenchment and careful supervision of the public income instituted by Eubulus for a time restored an all but bankrupt state to solvency. No less efficient was Lycurgus' administration after 338. When we see how much could be effected by careful management in the days of Athens' political decline, we are forced to assume, even where we have no direct evidence for it, a great deal of wasteful expenditure and inefficient handling of the public purse during earlier decades.

[1] About £2500 ($12,000) in modern currency, but with five or six times the purchasing power.

CHAPTER XIX

THE PROGRESS OF DEMOCRATIC GOVERNMENT AT ATHENS

> *Pallas, Triton-born, Queen Athena, thou and thy sire uphold this city and its citizens without sorrow and revolution and untimely death.* — From an Athenian drinking-song. (*Anthologia lyrica, scol.* 1)

WE are singularly ignorant about the form and methods of government favored by Greek states other than Sparta and Athens. The institutions of Sparta had, as we have seen, become fixed before the end of the sixth century. A short-lived secession of Arcadian cities from the Peloponnesian League was brought to an end by her in 466; but we have no means of determining whether she tried thereafter to compel any of the cities in the League to adopt an oligarchic government. Many were oligarchies already and by their own choice; Mantinea at least was democratic in 421. In the next century, however, the arbitrary and harsh character of the Spartan empire is amply attested.[1] Moderate oligarchies are known to have existed during the fifth century at Thebes and in other Bœotian cities, at Corinth, in Samos until 440, and in Mytilene until 427. On the other hand, Argos was democratically ruled after the Persian wars. In the West tyranny lasted somewhat longer than in Greece or Asia Minor, but there too it ultimately came to an end. Tarentum and most of the Greek communities in Italy were democracies; only the conservative Locrians retained their aristocratic government. Syracuse, after a revolution which followed the death of Hiero in 466, adopted a modified democratic constitution and also an institution similar to ostracism but there called petalism (*petalismos*). Party rivalry in Syracuse appears to have been bitter and the time came

---

[1] Cf. above, p. 288.

when the city again experienced periods of despotic rule.   It would be possible but profitless to prolong this list of names, because we are not in position to form a clear picture of the principles and machinery of government in these numerous city-states.   It is doubtless true that the movement towards a more popular form of government was during the fifth century so wide-spread throughout the Hellenic world as to be all but universal.   But the contrast in that case is only with the despotism or narrow oligarchies of previous centuries; for certainly there were many *poleis* which were ruled as moderate oligarchies and where the citizens as a whole were seemingly quite content with that form of constitution.

In Athens the system of government inaugurated by Cleisthenes remained substantially unaltered for nearly fifty years. In this period, although the sovereignty of the Athenian *ecclesia* was in a sense already accepted as an axiom of the constitution, there was one institution which might be said to be irreconcilable with the principle that the will of the people must prevail.   The ancient Council of the Areopagus still exercised some control. It was described as the guardian of the laws; and, though we are ignorant of its powers, and to what extent it used them, the ancient authorities are agreed that the reduction of the Council to a mere court of justice for trying cases of homicide was a landmark in the history of Athenian democratic government.   This change was effected by Ephialtes and the Progressives in 462–461.   Henceforward there was no one to interfere even indirectly with the will of the people, least of all a rather narrowly oligarchic body of ex-magistrates taken from the wealthy class and continuing their membership of the Council for life.   For such, in spite of its venerable antiquity backed by religious sanctions, the Areopagus must have seemed to all except the most conservative element in the commonwealth.

Five years later the reforming party introduced another innovation, of a sufficiently drastic nature.   A notable change, tending to depress the importance of the archonship, had already been made in 487–486.   Instead of election by the assembly, five hundred eligible persons were now elected by the demes, and from this large number the nine officials were chosen by lot.   As before, only the members of the first and second Solonian classes were eligible for the archonship. But in 457–456 a law was passed which extended the privilege of being a candidate for this magistracy to the third class, the *zeugitai*. Not long afterwards it was enacted that the preliminary choice of candidates should also be made by sortition. Though these posts were hereafter politically of quite secondary importance, since both the preliminary and the final choice depended on the hazard of the lot, while the *strategia* had become the chief executive magistracy, they were still held to confer distinction, if little power, on the holder. After election an inquiry or test of fitness (*dokimasia*) was held to ensure that all necessary requirements had been met and no disabilities existed. Then only could a magistrate or councillor enter on his duties; for the *dokimasia* applied to all holders of office and to the members of the *bule*. However democratic the constitution might be in theory, in practice the possession of some wealth made for greater opportunity to take part in public affairs, so long as magistracies and other services to the state were unpaid. Thus the introduction of payment to the jurors in the *Heliaia*, to the members of the Council of Five Hundred, and to all magistrates other than the *strategoi*, must count as the most radical of the Periclean reforms. Not content with providing this remuneration for performing civic duties, Pericles also introduced a small payment to soldiers and sailors on active service. It remained only to reward the members of the assembly for their attendance at its meetings. But fully half a century passed before this practice, the logical conclusion to Periclean precedents, was adopted. It was introduced by Agyrrhius during the first decade of the fourth century.

The sovereignty of the *ecclesia*, which was composed of all male citizens over eighteen years of age, was ensured in every sphere and by a variety of devices.[1] The responsibility of even the highest magistrates to it was secured by requiring them at the end of their year of office to undergo an official scrutiny (*euthyne*) of their administrative acts. Attempts to subvert the constitution by introducing legislation contrary to the existing

---

[1] In practice youths of 19 and 20 would not attend the *ecclesia*, because, after attaining their majority on the completion of the eighteenth year, they were on military service for two years.

laws rendered the proposer liable to be arraigned on a charge of "unconstitutional action." So important was this means of protecting the Athenian democracy that the person indicted was tried not in the ordinary courts of law but by the *ecclesia*, which for this purpose acted in a judicial capacity. Such trials became rather common in the fourth century, the result of much and often hasty legislation by decrees (*psephismata*) which were subsequently found to conflict with existing statutory law. It was the Athenian practice to hold the proposer of a law or *psephisma* responsible if his proposal was unconstitutional. The politician Aristophon was reputed to have been indicted seventy-five times, and we have actual examples of speeches delivered for the prosecution on two occasions after Aristophon's time in the orations of Demosthenes *Against Timocrates* and *Against Aristocrates*.

There were forty regular meetings of the assembly in the year. Extraordinary meetings could be called by the president of the Council, either as the result of a previous resolution of the *ecclesia*, or if it seemed necessary to the Council or to the board of *strategoi*. The proceedings in the assembly opened with a sacrifice. If the omens were unfavorable, the sitting was at once adjourned; if all was well, the business of the day was at once undertaken. The presiding officers, taken from the Council, brought forward each item of business. A preliminary vote was taken to decide whether the proposal, embodied in the Council's preliminary decree (*probuleuma*), should be accepted as it stood or thrown open to debate. If discussion was voted, the herald called on speakers. Proposals or amendments made by them had to be written down. The final vote on the *probuleuma* was taken by show of hands. Any citizen could bring forward any matter not on the agenda. If a vote approved its consideration, the proposal was referred to the *bule*, which brought a *probuleuma* dealing with it before a subsequent meeting of the assembly.

The Council of Five Hundred was composed of citizens over thirty years of age, who could serve on it not more than twice and then not in successive years. But so large a body could not effectively handle all the detailed business that came before it. Hence it was divided into ten standing committees, each officiating for a tenth part of the year. The order in which these prytanies, as they were called, followed one another was determined by lot. The Council which was, through the system of committees, in continual session, in carrying out its executive functions was not unlike a standing committee of the *ecclesia*. In legislation, as we have seen, the initiative rested entirely with the *bule*, the final decision with the sovereign people. In its executive capacity the Council of course coöperated closely with the board of *strategoi*. In conjunction with them it supervised the upkeep of the navy. Especially important was the control that it exercised in matters of finance; for it checked and supervised financial officials and those magistrates who handled public monies, and one of its duties was to report annually to the assembly on the financial condition of the state. Lastly the *bule* to a limited extent acted also in a judicial capacity. It tried offenses that affected its administrative functions and could fine the offender up to a maximum of five hundred drachmas. In the special class of trial (*eisangelia*) adopted in cases of treason, though a private citizen might lay information in the first place, the direction of the prosecution was undertaken by the Council, while the final judgment rested with the people.[1]

In an ancient democracy, where each adult male citizen took a direct part in the government, it was bound to follow that in practice the control of affairs should devolve mainly on the urban population. The farmers of Attica, especially those who lived at some distance from the capital, could not attend every meeting of the *ecclesia*, whereas the inhabitants of Peiræus and Athens suffered from no such disability. It was inevitable that Athenian policy should most commonly be determined in the interests of the town-dwellers, instead of the civic body as a whole. It was the former who, in all probability, were most jealous of their citizenship, and whose wishes Pericles gratified in 451–450, when he passed an act which we may label reactionary, if we will, but which must be recognized as eminently characteristic of the ancient Greek *polis* and its inhabitants.

---

[1] The actual trial seems sometimes to have taken place before the assembly, sometimes to have been referred by the assembly to one of the regular courts. The latter procedure was apparently the more usual in the fourth century, but clear and definite evidence is unfortunately lacking.

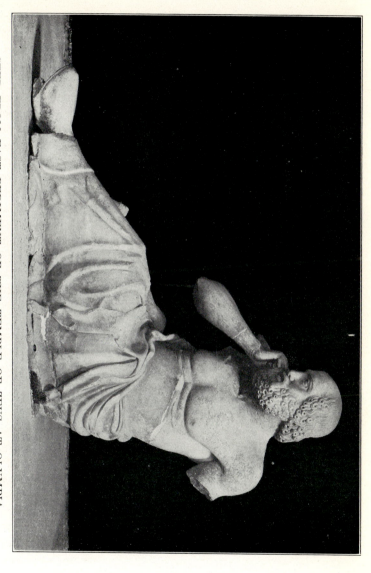

Plate 22

SEER FROM EAST PEDIMENT OF THE TEMPLE OF ZEUS AT OLYMPIA

APOLLO FROM WEST PEDIMENT OF THE TEMPLE OF
ZEUS AT OLYMPIA

Plate 23

correspondingly little say in the formation of policy. Only occasionally do we find the same man — for instance, Eubulus or Lycurgus — occupying an important official position and at the same time exerting a predominating influence on the conduct of affairs.

We know too little of the internal affairs of other Greek states at this period to compare their governments with the Athenian. Yet we have every ground for believing that no considerable *polis* enjoyed a better government than Athens. Thus it was not only disagreement among the various city-states, such as has been described in a previous chapter, but the weakness of their internal government, which led to the eclipse of the Greek *poleis*, and hastened on the era of the great monarchies.

CHAPTER XX

GREEK CIVILIZATION IN THE FIFTH AND FOURTH CENTURIES — PHILOSOPHY, SCIENCE, AND EDUCATION

> *To sum up: I say that Athens is the school of Hellas, and that the individual Athenian in his own person seems to have the power of adapting himself to the most varied forms of action with the utmost versatility and grace. This is no passing and idle word, but truth and fact; and the assertion is verified by the position to which these qualities have raised the state.* — From the funeral oration of Pericles in Thucydides ii, 41 (Jowett's translation).

WHATEVER may be the modern student's final judgment on the political history of Greece, the efficiency and shortcomings of Hellenic constitutions, and the character of the economic life from the Persian wars to the age of Alexander, it is beyond dispute that the intellectual and artistic achievement of Hellas in that era was unique in the history of the world.

In the sixth century by far the most intense intellectual activity had been manifested by the Greeks of Ionia, whether in their own home-land or abroad. The fifth century continued to produce some thinkers who, starting from the philosophical position occupied by the Ionian physicists, speculated on the origin and nature of matter, or who, like Empedocles of Acragas (died *c.* 436 B.C.), evolved a theory in which an effort was made to reconcile the views of Heracleitus with those of the Eleatic school. More radical and of far wider, though not immediate, influence were the speculations of Leucippus (*floruit c.* 450 B.C.) and his disciple, Democritus. Not content with theories which derived all matter or Being from four "elements," Leucippus postulated an indeterminate number of small particles or atoms moving through gravitation in space. With this hypothesis he proceeded to explain the creation of the material Universe, and he also applied it to the mental processes. The system was elaborated by Democritus, and half a century after his death, it was adopted with some modifications by Epicurus and his followers. The philosopher Anaxagoras, who for a time resided at Athens, where he enjoyed the friendship of Pericles, was in some respects more conservative than the atomists in his explanation of the nature of Being; but in teaching that the Universe was ordered and directed by an all-knowing Mind or Intelligence (Nus) he was going greatly beyond anything propounded by previous philosophers; at the same time he rejected a purely mechanical explanation of the Universe such as was taught by Leucippus and his pupil. Anaxagoras' metaphysical doctrine exerted a profound influence on thinkers of the next generation or two, notably on Plato.

Contemporaneous with these developments in philosophy was the rise of scientific medicine, associated with the name of Hippocrates. Little is known of him beyond the fact that he was born *c.* 460 B.C. in Cos, where he became a member of what appears to have been a medical guild, the Asclepiadæ, and in due course himself attained fame as a trainer of physicians. The so-called *Hippocratic Corpus* is a very varied collection of writings, none of which can be attributed with absolute certainty to Hippocrates himself. Also they vary considerably in date — some may even be a little earlier than Hippocrates' time — and in character; for, side by side with formal treatises on medical subjects, are brief clinical records, diaries, and perhaps notes of pupils. It has been suggested with great probability that the *Corpus* represents the remains of a medical library at Cos. These uncertainties about Hippocrates and his writings are, however, of secondary interest compared with the remarkable progress in medical practice made in Cos during the fifth and fourth centuries. Medicine became a part of natural knowledge, freed from beliefs in magic or supernatural agencies. Hippocrates and his fellows recognized disease to be a perversion of nature, that is to say, of the normal functions of the body. Hence they laid the greatest stress on clinical observation, and some of the most interesting portions of the *Corpus* are day by day records of patients' progress. They studied the influence of natural environment on health, more particularly the effect of atmospheric conditions and waters on the inhabitants of different regions and climates. The treatment consisted, as far as possible, in letting nature take her course, combined with a rational diet, exercise, and fresh air. Drugs, bleeding, and other drastic remedies were avoided and used only in special or extreme cases. The diseases of which clinical records have survived in the *Corpus* are those most prevalent in ancient Greece, chiefly fevers of various kinds — doubtless, for the most part, different forms of malaria — consumption and other pulmonary troubles, and both milder and severer kinds of intestinal disturbance. How extremely high the code of medical ethics observed by the Hippocratic school was can be seen from the Hippocratic oath, which with some modification has remained in use by the profession to the present day, and from other passages in the *Corpus*, such as the following: [1]

I urge you not to be too unkind, but to consider carefully your patient's superabundance or means. Sometimes give your services for nothing, calling to mind a previous benefaction or present satisfaction. And if there be an opportunity of serving one who is a stranger in financial straits, give full assistance to all such. For where there is love of man, there is also love of the art. For some patients, though conscious that their condition is perilous, recover their health simply through their contentment with the goodness of the physician. And it is well to superintend the sick to make them well, to care for the healthy to keep them well, but also to care for one's own self, so as to observe what is seemly.

The larger Hellenic public seems to have been little interested or affected by philosophic speculation. The trial and condemnation for impiety of Anaxagoras about the year 450 may have been brought about in part by popular prejudice; but in the main it resulted from the political intrigues of Pericles' opponents. The philosopher avoided the fatal consequences of an adverse verdict by hasty flight, and lived in peace for another two decades at Lampsacus on the Propontis.

Of far more immediate consequence were the activities of a number of men who, though ironically enough many of them

---

[1] *Precepts* 6, in *Hippocrates with an English translation* by W. H. S. Jones (Loeb series), 1, p. 319. A text and translation of the oath will be found in the same volume, pp. 299–301.

had been disciples of the philosophers, led what was really a direct intellectual revolt against their teachers. With the advent of the Sophists, as they were called, the movement for higher education in the Hellenic world began. Their influence, moreover, extended far beyond the boundaries of educational theory and practice; it left a deep mark on political thought, and on literature, especially prose writings, of every kind. The elementary education provided in Greek city-states in the two centuries under consideration was of a simple character. Its purpose was to teach reading and writing to boys from seven to thirteen years of age, and to impart to them some acquaintance with earlier Greek literature. Homer, some portions of Hesiod, and such selections from the early Lyric and Gnomic poets, as might, besides their literary value, help to impress the chief civic and private virtues on the young mind, made up the sum of the authors studied. In this process memorization played a very important part. To this we may add some instruction in the simplest arithmetical calculations, and in singing and playing on the seven-stringed lyre. Provision was also made for the physical training of the boys in wrestling-schools set apart for their use. The schools were, so far as our information goes, uniformly conducted by private persons; consequently their quality varied greatly. It is very possible, though not certain, that the state in general so far concerned itself with the education of the young as to insist that parents should provide their boys with some schooling.[1]

Girls ordinarily were instructed in domestic duties and accomplishments by their mothers in the home. There is no clear evidence before the Hellenistic epoch that they received any school tuition. A woman with any literary training was exceptional, and the majority of Athenian women and girls probably could not read or write. In most Greek states women led a life of semi-oriental seclusion. In Sparta and some other Dorian states, it is true, girls till marriage enjoyed a certain amount of liberty or even license. But the aim of the rulers of Spartan society after all was to ensure a fine, healthy body of women to bear stalwart sons, just as with the boys their one

[1] The Spartan and Cretan systems of training youth had a special character of their own and have been briefly described above, p. 145.

aim was to produce the maximum of physical fitness. Recent
attempts to disprove the commonly assumed seclusion of Athenian and other Greek women, though interesting as a reëxamina-
tion of the evidence, are unconvincing.[1] Oriental influence may
account for woman's retired life in the classical period, and, in
view of the similar phenomenon in the Near East in our own
day, the relative freedom, in fact though not in law, of the
Roman *matrona* is really far more surprising than the seclusion
of her Greek sister. The Greek spent most of his time away
from home. • He married ordinarily to have a home and found
a family of his own. But intellectual companionship, and often
emotional outlet also, he found with persons of his own sex.
The Greek ideal of male friendship, at least in its emotional
aspect, runs counter to the social ideas and customs of our
time. But it cannot be explained away, and it must be accepted
as one of those features of Greek society which it is hard for
a normally minded modern to comprehend. Nor are we justified
in indicting a whole people of moral decadence in this as in any
other era, whose point of view differs from our own. How far
this phenomenon was cause and how far effect of the inferior
position in which most Greek women found themselves, it is
impossible to ascertain. Certainly Homer, and after him the
great tragic poets, could portray the noblest type of womanhood.
But we cannot argue that Greek women in ordinary life were
comparable in influence or strength of character to the heroines
of Sophocles (Antigone, Deianira) and Euripides (Hecuba,
Electra, Medea). Conversely, we can reasonably assume that
the average Greek was a decent husband. But when all the
evidence has been reviewed, we are still faced with the undoubted fact that Greek women played no part in the public,
and very little part in the ordinary social, life of Greece. Two
further points deserve mention. It is only if one remembers the
retirement and absence of education among Greek women that
he realizes fully how radical Plato's proposals in the *Republic*
were. He advocated that in his ideal state the women should,
as far as possible, have the same intellectual and physical training as the men, and, given the same degree of fitness, the same

[1] Cf., for instance, the able but unconvincing article of A. W. Gomme in
Classical Philology XX (1925), pp. 1 ff.

a

b

THE PARTHENON: *a.* WEST FRONT; *b.* EAST FRONT

Plate 24

a

b

a. PARTHENON, SOUTH SIDE; *b.* TEMPLE OF NIKE
Plate 25

or similar responsibilities. On the other hand, feminists who seek for arguments to support their case in Plato generally omit to mention that in his ideal commonwealth there is to be complete community not merely in property but in women and children. And this leads directly to our second point. Plato's great pupil, Aristotle, has often been accused of having a low estimate of women. Granted that in common with most of his contemporaries he regarded them as inferior to men, it is surely in the highest degree noteworthy that one of the main grounds on which Aristotle severely criticized Plato's communism is that it will destroy the family and family life. To Aristotle these are of basic importance, and it is essential to family life that the *mater familias* should be held in honorable esteem by her husband and respected by her children and servants.

In conclusion, the attitude of a typical, well-bred Greek to women and marriage can be studied in one of the smaller works of Xenophon, a treatise on household management containing a chapter on the training of the housewife that is both charming and amusing.[1]

With the completion of elementary schooling the boys of the poorer citizens or metics would be apprenticed to a trade, or go to work on their fathers' farms. For it is essential to bear in mind that the higher or secondary education imparted by the Sophists entailed far more expense for the parent, and in consequence was only within reach of the well-to-do minority. A clear understanding of the general aim of the Sophists will also make clear the chief reason for their rise in the middle of the fifth century. The purpose which they had in view, and which they professed to attain, though not all on precisely the same lines, was to teach the adolescent youth of their day "political excellence"; in other words, to train them so that they might properly fulfil all the duties of citizenship, and take part in public affairs adequately equipped for the task. It was thus the emancipation of a large portion of the Hellenic world after the Persian wars, and the more active political life of a majority of the civic population, especially in democratic states, which created a demand for mental training of a more advanced

[1] Xenophon, *Œconomicus* 7.

decathalon

kind than the schools could provide, together with technical instruction in some subjects with which the public man of the future must needs be familiar. Above all, as will be seen, the scientific study of speech and the right use of words, that is to say the art of rhetoric, would be indispensable alike in political assemblies and in courts of law. The aims of the Sophists being essentially practical, it is natural that they should have disregarded or rejected abstract speculation about the Universe, and should have concentrated on the study of Man. This scepticism toward abstract thought and inquiry into the ultimate reality of things was expressed by several of the Sophists in pregnant sayings, of which the most famous is Protagoras' dictum, "Man is the measure of all things, of those that are that they are, and those that are not that they are not." [1]

Their attention to political theory was noteworthy. The city-state was regarded as the result of a conscious intelligence, being created by Law, not existing by Nature. The antithesis between Nature and Law, on which Protagoras especially insisted, was far-reaching in its effects. It might easily be interpreted as subversive of traditional religion, and, according to one account, Protagoras, the champion of Law — that is, of traditional morality and organized society — was actually arraigned for impiety while at Athens. Again, in discussing different forms of polity, the Sophists were led to pay attention also to non-Hellenic peoples. They contrasted their customs and institutions with those of their own race. By transcending the particularistic views of states and governments held by the average Greek, including most men of affairs, the Sophists became the first exponents of Panhellenic ideas.

These teachers did not establish schools of higher learning in any given place; they were essentially itinerant professors, who visited the numerous cities of the Greek world for short periods. They lectured on various topics to general audiences, and at the same time attached to themselves regular pupils,

---

[1] That is to say, what seems to be true to A is true to A, what seems to be true to B is true to B. Any inquiry must be either for what we know or for what we do not know. To search after the former is absurd, and after the latter is impossible. Since in the second alternative we should not know for what to look; and, even if we found it, how could we recognize that it was the object of our search?

from whose parents they received fees for the instruction that they imparted. Most famous among these Sophists were Protagoras of Abdera, Gorgias of Leontini, Prodicus of Ceos, and Hippias of Elis. Gorgias, who visited Athens in 427 B.C. in the character of envoy from his native city, specialized in the study of rhetoric, and may be regarded as the real founder of artistic Greek prose. Protagoras, in addition to his interest in political science, adapted the antithesis between Nature and Law to educational theory. To get the best results the educator must see that natural gifts in a pupil are guided and brought to fullest flower by training and practice. This threefold division — natural ability, training, and practice — which Protagoras was the first to enunciate, was adopted and developed by all the great educators of the fourth century. Protagoras and Prodicus, again, can claim to be the founders of scientific grammar, which was indeed a necessary preliminary to rhetorical study. Hippias, finally, appears to have been a scintillating personality, who prided himself on the universality of his knowledge and accomplishments. Though brilliant, such a man was necessarily also more shallow; and it is significant that he exerted little influence after his time, whereas Protagoras and Gorgias, each in his sphere, left their mark on the thought and writings of the next generation.

Reckoned by many of his contemporaries as a Sophist, Socrates, son of Sophroniscus, nevertheless differed from those teachers radically in several important respects. He was born in 470–469, but the known facts of his life are few. His father was a stonemason, and he himself for a time appears to have practised the craft. He took part as a hoplite in the siege of Potidæa, and later fought at Delium and Amphipolis. Late in life, in 406–405, he served as a member of the Council of Five Hundred, and alone stood out against the illegalities at the trial of the generals after Arginusæ. His great bodily endurance, simplicity of life, and the fits of abstraction into which he fell from time to time, were as familiar to his contemporaries as his pronouncedly plain features (Plate 21). It is probable that he was for a time a pupil of one of the less known physicist philosophers, Archelaus; and it is in the character of one speculating about the material structure of the Universe that he is burlesqued in Aristophanes' comedy, the *Clouds*, first performed at Athens in 423. Finally, in 399, Socrates was arraigned for impiety and for "corrupting the youth" of Athens, and condemned to drink the hemlock. It is now generally recognized that the trial and the verdict were the result of the strong political, that is to say democratic, reaction against the oligarchs at Athens, some of whom had been intimate, though unworthy, disciples of Socrates. It is also clear that, had Socrates taken any steps to conciliate the jurors, he could have saved his life. It was the last twenty-five years of his career that he devoted to what he regarded as nothing less than a religious mission in the highest sense. His teaching was primarily concerned with human conduct. Convinced that the ethical conceptions and the actions proceeding therefrom of the majority of his fellow-men were erroneous, he set himself the twofold task of eradicating false opinions, and then suggesting a more correct and upright habit of thought. He was no formal teacher. His class-room was the world at large, the market-place, the wrestling-school, the shop, the houses of friends. There he engaged all and sundry in conversation, and by skillful use of question and answer — the dialectic method — strove to convince them of their false thinking and ignorance, and then by the same method to lead them on to ethically right concepts. His personality, perhaps even more than his conversation, must have made a tremendous impression on all with whom he came into contact. He had many disciples, though there was no formal relation of teacher to pupil and no remuneration by the one to the other, as in the case of the Sophists. Socrates' unique position in Greek history is in the first place due to his consistently noble and upright life, and to the fact that he was willing to pay the highest price, his life, rather than recede one iota from his inmost convictions. But scarcely less important than the man himself is the circumstance that, although not strictly a philosopher — in the sense that he elaborated no metaphysical or ethical system — he was the fountain head of some six different philosophical schools. These were founded by disciples, each of whom took over some part of Socrates' teaching, and on that based a systematic philosophy.

By far the greatest of these pupils was Plato. He was born

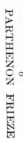

Plate 26

PARTHENON FRIEZE

a

b

a

b

c

THE ERECHTHEUM: *a.* East End; *b.* North Porch; *c.* South Porch

Plate 27

in 427 B.C. After Socrates' death he abandoned his intention of devoting himself to public affairs. For about twelve years after 399 he lived partly in Athens, partly abroad, visiting both Egypt and Sicily. In, or soon after, 387 he started a school of higher education in his own residence.[1] The rest of a long life — he died in 347 — he devoted to teaching and to the composition of many writings in which he set forth his doctrines for the benefit of a larger public. The method of presenting a theory or, conversely, of demolishing false arguments by question and answer, which had been used with such effect by his master, Plato adopted and perfected as a literary form. All his works are composed as dialogues between several speakers, Socrates being generally the principal character.[2] In his earliest dialogues Plato analyzes various moral qualities — for instance, courage, piety, self-control — in order to set out more clearly the principle which was at the root of Socrates' ethical teaching, the equation of virtue with knowledge. It was only about the time that he set up as a teacher in Athens that in the *Phaedo*, and then in the *Republic*, he put forward the doctrine which forms the foundation of his philosophical thought throughout his life, though it underwent sundry modifications and extensions in his later works. In constructing the Theory of Forms or Ideas, Plato contrasted the objects of sense, which are in themselves transitory and unreal, with the general Forms or Ideas from which they derive their name. These alone partake of reality and alone are existent, to be apprehended by the mind alone. They are "the eternal archetype of which the sensible objects are the copies." All learning consists in recollection; for the soul, before it begins its career in the human body, has known the archetype and can be reminded of it when it perceives its imperfect copies in the world of sense. The highest Idea, which is the fountain of all existence and of all knowledge, is the

[1] The name given to it, the Academy, was really the name of a public garden situated nearby, to the northwest of the city, three-quarters of a mile from the Dipylon gate.

[2] Even Plato's latest and longest work, the *Laws*, which he did not live to revise, makes some attempt to keep the dialogue form. But there are lengthy passages where a detailed exposition is entrusted to a single speaker, so that the reader for a time forgets that there are other interlocutors.

Idea of the Good, which is identified with God or the Demiurge,
who created the Universe by imprinting the Forms on the
formless matter of chaos. In a later treatise, the *Timaeus*,
Plato sketched this cosmic creation-process, though he admits
that his picture is no more than an approximation, the absolute
truth of the Demiurge's work being unattainable. Though
even a brief examination of Platonic philosophy is beyond the
scope of this volume, some account of his greatest work may
here be given.

The *Republic* begins with a discussion of the nature of justice.
Various current theories are propounded, but all of them are
found inadequate by Socrates, who is finally called upon to
forsake the rôle of destructive critic and be constructive.
In order to find justice at work — and thereby be better able
to define it — in the human soul and in the political community,
there follows an analysis of human society and the building
up of an ideal state. Plato's psychological tenets are closely
interwoven with his political and educational theories. The
human soul is a living thing, in which there are three elements
striving for the mastery, the appetitive, spirited, and rational.
The first is at the root of purely physical needs and desires,
some of which are necessary (*e.g.* the desire for food in order
to sustain life), some unnecessary. Spirit is the mainspring of
such qualities as courage or righteous indignation, and, provided
it be subordinated to the rational part, is its natural ally. Excess
of spirit will however produce bad developments; for example,
courage will degenerate into pugnacity or cruelty. The rational
or highest part of the soul is the fountain head of intelligence,
and of those emotions which make men susceptible to the beauty
of literature or art. For the soul to function in the best possible
manner it is needful for its three constituents to be adjusted
in perfect harmony, the first and second being in subjection
to the rational part. So, too, in the state there are three classes
of work necessary for its good, and consequently three classes
of persons who are needed to perform it. Lowest in the body
politic, and analogous, as it were, to the appetitive part of the
soul, are the producers of material commodities necessary for
physical existence, the craftsmen, tradesmen, and so forth.
Here Plato advocates a high degree of specialization in craft

and industry; but the producing class is not part of the citizen body, although individual members, in case of special ability, may rise to one of the two higher classes who alone are citizens of the commonwealth.[1] These two, the Auxiliaries and the Guardians, are respectively the younger men, whose task it is to protect the state from its internal and external enemies, and the older men, to whom is assigned the work of legislation and of governing the state. Here, again, the analogy to the spirited and the rational parts of the soul is evident. The main problem of education is the right adjustment of the three parts of the soul in the individual, and Plato devotes his almost exclusive attention to moral training, to the method of developing character, and to the type of character to be developed. The training of the intellect is only undertaken as a primary aim in the case of those who are selected, on attaining to manhood, as fitted to become the future rulers of the state. Their higher education lasts from twenty to thirty years of age, and consists in the main of higher mathematics, that being in Plato's view the most suitable of those studies "which are of universal application." The ablest of the young men so trained will then be chosen to continue their studies for another five years, from thirty to thirty-five, which will be devoted to dialectics and metaphysics. These will in time become the wisest and most responsible of the Guardian class. In order to pursue their education and fulfil their functions in the state without the distraction of material cares or responsibilities, both the Auxiliaries and the Guardians live under a completely communistic régime. There is to be community in property and in women. The last-named are according to their several abilities to be trained in the same manner as the male Auxiliaries and Guardians. Strict eugenic regulations are laid down governing marriages, and the children born of these unions will be reared in state institutions. Toward the end of his great work Plato, who has described his ideal government of the state, proceeds to an examination of various kinds of constitution, and the human characters which correspond to them, these being progressive degenerations of the ideal. His political theories he was to revise and formulate

[1] Cf. on this last point the "myth" or allegory in *Republic*, iii, 414-415.

afresh in two later works, the *Statesman* and the *Laws*. In this last work, realizing that he had portrayed an unattainable ideal in the *Republic*, he has depicted a second-best state. Though this book falls short of the grandeur of conception which permeates the *Republic*, and, owing to its diffuseness and occasional obscurity, has often been neglected, it contains, among much else that is of deep interest, criticisms of existing political systems in Greece, and also Plato's maturest reflections on education, put forward after well-nigh forty years of practical experience as an educator.[1]

We know very little of the inner organization, the curriculum and methods of teaching, the research, carried on in the Platonic Academy; but it can be safely assumed that its working was, as it were, the sublunary counterpart of the education of the Guardians in the *Republic*. In the *Laws* Plato has outlined a scheme by which all instruction and training from earliest youth would be supervised by the state. Suitable buildings and staff would be provided and the various studies from stage to stage, from elementary schooling to what we should call advanced university work, would be graded and brought into proper relation with one another. The radical nature of such proposals will be clear, if it be remembered that all education in Greece had so far been left to private initiative, and that consequently there had been little necessary coördination. If the educational system of the *Republic* found its practical expression in the Academy, the principles advocated by Plato in his last work, that the state or the community should take charge of the education of its citizens, supervise the appointment of teachers, provide proper accommodation, and so forth, were to a great extent realized in the Hellenistic Age, although the character of much of the instruction imparted would not have won the approval of "the god among philosophers."[2]

Aristotle, the greatest of Plato's disciples, was a native of

---

[1] It is not the least fault of most current text-books on the History of Education that Plato's *Laws* are either very summarily dismissed or else passed over. It would be presumptuous, though not difficult, to hazard an explanation for this neglect.

[2] *Deus philosophorum*, as Cicero calls Plato in his treatise, *On the Nature of the Gods*, ii, 32.

Stageirus in Thrace, a Greek town in a "barbarian" region. The early environment in which he thus grew up is not without significance to any one who reads his penetrating analysis of the characteristic attributes of Hellenic and non-Hellenic peoples (*Politics*, iv (7), 7). His father was for a time physician at the Macedonian court, a circumstance to which Aristotle may have owed, at least in part, Philip II's invitation to become the tutor of young Alexander. On attaining manhood Aristotle emigrated to Athens, and was for twenty years a member of the Platonic Academy, first as a pupil, later as a teacher. After Plato's death he was in Asia Minor for a space, and then, in 343, he was summoned to Macedonia. In 335 or 334 he returned to Athens and there set up a philosophical school of his own.[1] When, in 323, Alexander's premature end was the signal for an outburst of anti-Macedonian feeling at Athens, which was extended to any one who had been associated with the late king, Aristotle was forced to retire to Euboea. There he died early in the following year.

Steeped in Platonic doctrines in his earlier life, he had the scientific rather than the creative mind, which led him to modify or reject not a little of his master's teaching. Concerned especially with observing all the processes of nature, he evolved a great philosophical system embracing alike the material world and the world of the mind. We owe a double debt to Aristotle as a mapper out of the sciences and as the inventor of a scientific method. Rigorously applied this process was made up of three stages: first, it was necessary to collect and test current opinions; second, to reach a hypothesis or general law, involving the collection of particulars; third, by deduction, to apply hypotheses to particular instances. The fact that he only partially succeeded in the titanic task which he set himself was inevitable because scientific experimentation was still in its infancy. Though Aristotle himself did much to promote this, and his successors — for instance, Theophrastus — carried on in particular fields of scientific research, his collected evi-

[1] The school was subsequently known as the Lyceum, since he taught in the gymnasium of that name. The alternative appellation, Peripatetics, Peripatetic School, is derived from a Greek word signifying "to walk around," that being the practice of Aristotle while discoursing to his hearers.

dence was at times insufficient for safe generalization. Yet even
so, few men have achieved so much in a lifetime. Not only
did he knit together into his system all the knowledge that the
Greeks up to that time had obtained, but he made his own
contributions to science, which were of much importance, and
greatly in advance of previous investigations. His work on
zoölogy was the first systematic attempt at classifying the various animals into genera and species; and the descriptions of
the habits and character of many of his subjects betray both
first-rate powers of observation and keen powers of reasoning.
It is of great significance that Aristotle enunciates an evolu-
tionary doctrine of progress from the lower to the higher forms
of life; he is still sufficient of a Platonist, however, to explain
this process as due to the design and act of creative Nature.
His philosophical system, following his own division, may be
classified under groups: Speculative Philosophy aiming at
truth, Practical Philosophy aiming at happiness, and Poetic
(*i.e.* Creative) Philosophy aiming at an artistic product. Logic
is not so much a part of the system as the indispensable prerequisite to it. Its proper comprehension must precede inquiry
into any of the three branches of philosophy. His creation of
formal logic is perhaps Aristotle's finest achievement; and
the system expounded in the series of treatises that make up
the *Organon* in all essentials has not been superseded to this day.
Each of the three groups of philosophy can be subdivided, so
that the first includes metaphysics, physics (*i.e.* the natural
sciences), and mathematics; the second, ethics, economics, and
politics; the third, painting, sculpture, and literature. The
extant writings of Aristotle, which, with the exception of the
treatise on the Athenian Constitution, are the lecture notes of
the master, or in some cases perhaps of pupils, can be similarly
grouped, the *Metaphysics* and scientific treatises dealing with
parts of group 1, the *Ethics* and *Politics* with those of group 2,
the *Poetics* and *Rhetoric* with those of group 3. Of the extant
writings the two which are now of the most universal interest,
and which also show the philosopher's wisdom and analytical
power at their best, are the *Ethics* and the *Politics*. The latter
is the profoundest contribution to political science made by
any ancient writer. In Aristotle's thought the *Politics* are a

natural continuation of the *Ethics*, the close connection between the two being clearly expressed thus: [1]

> Since political science makes use of the remaining sciences that are concerned with action, and ordains what men ought to do and what they ought to refrain from doing, the end of political science will include the ends of all the other sciences and this end will, in consequence, be the Highest Good of man. Even if this end to be grasped and cherished is the same for the individual as for the state, nevertheless the end of the state is clearly greater and more complete. For though the Highest Good is a desirable end for the individual, it is even fairer and more divine for a nation and for a state.

That is to say, the Highest Good is the end of both, but ethics is subordinate to politics even as the Highest Good of the individual is merged in the Highest Good of the community. Conduct, Aristotle argues, requires to be regulated by Law, and, like Plato, he was in favor of the kind of supervision of morals found in Sparta. This approach, of course, involves a certain confusion between ethics and politics, which was common to all Greek thinkers before the Stoics. A noticeable feature of Aristotle's ethical system is that he limits his inquiry to the external function of morality. The distinction between virtue and vice is drawn with reference to its outward effect; neither the inward faculty which enables a man to differentiate between the two, nor duty as such is discussed. Again, though voluntary and involuntary actions come up for consideration, the will itself does not. If Aristotle, then, falls short of what modern ethical thinkers would regard as necessary for a complete treatment of ethics, the influence of intervening centuries of Christian theology, with their stress on the Semitic concepts of the will of God and the will of Man, and on the internal aspect of ethics, must in fairness be emphasized.

Virtue aims at a mean between two extremes, or, to give Aristotle's own definition: [2]

> Virtue, then, is a state of character concerned with choice, lying in a mean, *i.e.* the mean relative to us; this being determined by a rational principle, and by that principle by which the man of practical wisdom would determine it.

---

[1] Aristotle, *Nicomachean Ethics* i, 1094a 27 ff.
[2] *Ibid.* ii, 1106b 36.

As might be expected, in view of what has been said above, the virtues and vices are appraised according to the manner in which they affect society rather than the individual, and the emphasis tends to be placed on what we may call civic virtues. Also the intellectual side of virtue weighs most with the philosopher, to the neglect of the emotional. The magnanimous man, for example, is without humility, which, regarded intellectually, would be a fault. Aristotle in his ethical teaching has set himself to inquire what is, in the light of a man's nature and environment, the most desirable plan of life. It is necessary to bear in mind this self-imposed limitation of his subject in order to evaluate justly Aristotle's contribution to the study of moral science.

In Book I of the *Politics* Aristotle begins by tracing the origin of the city-state from the household. The stage intermediate between the two is the village, which arises from a collection of households and is ruled by the eldest progenitor. Originally the *polis* existed merely to minister to life; only gradually it developed to minister to good or noble life. In the theory of the household three forms of association are involved, that of master and slave, husband and wife, and father and child. Aristotle proceeds to analyze the first of these, leaving the other two to the end of the book; for after dealing with slavery, he passes on to consider the origin, meaning, and use of wealth and property. The second Book is composed entirely of criticisms of earlier political theorists, including his master, Plato, and of certain existing social organizations or constitutions. In the Books that follow we find two detailed, but somewhat divergent, classifications of constitutions. In the one, besides the three perfect forms of government, by the one (monarchy), by the few (aristocracy), and by the many (commonwealth), there are the three perversions, tyranny, oligarchy, and democracy. Each of these is better or worse in proportion as it is better or worse adapted to the nature and position of the people. In the other classification Aristotle ignores this very schematic arrangement and contents himself with discussing at length many varieties of constitution. Of great interest are the passages where the philosopher investigates the causes leading to political instability and to revolution. There follows a detailed investigation of the characteristics of monarchies, oligarchies, and democracies. And who was better qualified to generalize on these questions from a large number of particular instances than the author or general editor of one hundred and fifty-eight monographs on existing Greek constitutions? Finally Aristotle constructs for his readers an ideal city and an ideal city-state. The *Politics*, as it has come down to us, is not a homogeneous work; there are repetitions, omissions, and real or apparent contradictions in it. Nevertheless its value as a profound contribution to human thought remains to the present day. As it has been well expressed, "the permanent value of Aristotle's political philosophy consists in its adherence to certain principles found by philosophic reflection, combined with its respect of actual conditions."

We have already seen the valuable function performed in the fifth century by the Sophists as educators, and how the study of rhetoric occupied a leading place in their curriculum. It cannot be gainsaid that there was a dangerous side to this tuition. The scientific study of language and prose composition might be perverted to serve unworthy ends; nor can we doubt that this was sometimes the case. Hence the serious criticisms of the Sophists made by Plato, not only in his earlier works like the *Gorgias*, but in his latest treatise (*Laws*, x, 889e), and the more ebullient attacks of Aristophanes in the *Clouds*, against teachers who merely ruin youth by instructing them how to make the worse argument appear the better. Thus, besides the study of rhetoric proper, two things at least were essential, if the Sophistic education was to fulfil its avowed purpose, to train men to be good and efficient citizens. First, a good knowledge of subjects like history, literature, and jurisprudence was indispensable; for, without that, speeches would perhaps be brilliant or ingenious, but they would be devoid of substantial argument. Secondly, and most important of all, the Sophist must inculcate in his disciples sound ethical principles, the acquisition of which would make it impossible for rhetoric to be used for ignoble purposes.

It is precisely these needs that are stressed by the greatest Sophist of the fourth century, and which he set himself conscientiously and methodically to fulfil in the school of which he was the head for well-nigh half a century. Isocrates, who was born in 436 B.C. in Attica, received as good an education as was then procurable, since his father was a citizen of comfortable means.

He studied for a time with Gorgias, but physical disabilities debarred him from a public career; in addition, he lost his patrimony in the political disturbances at the end of the Peloponnesian war. Hence he was obliged for a few years to eke out a subsistence as a professional writer of law-court speeches. At last, about 387, he set up as a teacher of higher education, continuing at the head of his institution until his death at the advanced age of ninety-eight (338). The normal period of training in his school was three to four years. In the course of his long career he had many hundreds of pupils; a large percentage of them subsequently became noted men in the most divers walks of life. Isocrates' influence as an educator, and as the second founder of rhetoric, was profound and lasted for centuries, affecting not only higher education in the Greek world of the Hellenistic Age, but, in time, Roman writers on the theory of education and rhetoric, notably Cicero.

His service as a teacher was, however, only a part of Isocrates' life-work. He was also a political essayist whose aims have frequently been misunderstood, just as the influence of his political doctrines has been underrated. From the publication in 380 B.C. of his greatest work, the *Panegyricus*, to his last long work, the *Panathenaicus*, which appeared a year before his death, he was a consistent advocate of Panhellenic unity, first under Athenian leadership, later, when he saw that the leader must come from outside the bickering congeries of Hellenic polities, under that of Philip of Macedon. To label Isocrates an "arm-chair" politician is to overlook that his *Panegyricus* certainly contributed to the successful formation of the Second Athenian Confederacy; that his discourse, *On the Peace*, helped to promote the peace policy of Eubulus; and that the influence of his thought on Athenian politicians in the anxious decade from 350 to 340 can still be demonstrated clearly in at least one case, that of Aeschines. Had we the utterances of other members of the philo-Macedonian party at Athens, we should doubtless find many more traces of the Isocratean political program. It is perfectly arguable that Isocrates was wrong and Demosthenes was right in the question of what was Athens' best policy at this juncture; it is indefensible to treat the views on public affairs expressed by the great educator as of no account.

CHAPTER XXI

GREEK CIVILIZATION IN THE FIFTH AND FOURTH CENTURIES: LITERATURE

> *Ought we not, on the contrary, to seek out artists of another stamp, who by the power of genius can trace out the nature of the fair and the graceful, that our young men, dwelling, as it were in a healthful region, may drink in good from every quarter, whence any emanation from noble works may strike upon their eye and ear, like a gale wafting health from salubrious lands, and win them imperceptibly from their earliest childhood into resemblance, love, and harmony with the true beauty of reason?* — Plato, *Republic* iii, 401.

IN the seventh and sixth centuries the poetic genius of the Greeks had manifested itself in lyric, elegiac, and iambic poetry. In contrast to this the greatest poetic artists of the fifth century were, with few exceptions, dramatists; and the four playwrights whose poetic achievement we can still fully appraise from their extant works were all Athenians. With their passing, this form of poetic composition waned also, and the fourth century is preëminently the age of the great prose writers of the Greek world. Again Athens had all but a monopoly of the talents. The life of Simonides (*c.* 553–465 B.C.) is like a bridge from the older to the newer Hellenic world. A native of the island of Ceos, he spent much of his adult life at Athens, first at the court of Hippias and Hipparchus, and then under the Cleisthenic democracy. His association with the despots did him no harm. Indeed, his elegies on those that fell at Marathon and at Thermopylæ are proof that he could be a patriot as well as a courtier. Many stories about him circulated in after years. He was, or he was thought to be, very parsimonious. He had a remarkable memory himself, and, with a view to helping others, invented some kind of mnemonic system. Several sayings attributed to him show that he had

a dry wit. His versatility as a poet was remarkable; for he
was equally at home in choral lyric and in elegiac poetry, being
specially noted for his epigrams and epitaphs. Time has dealt
very unkindly with his work, so that, for example, we have
no means of comparing his epinician odes with those of Pindar.
Some elegiac lines from his pen have been cited above; [1] we
may here add the beautiful lyric fragment in which Danaë,
exposed with her infant child on the ocean, bewails her fate.
The English version by John Addington Symonds, though admirably poetic, is a little too ornate to convey completely the
simple charm of the original.[2]

> When, in the carven chest,
> The winds that blew and waves in wild unrest
> Smote her with fear, she, not with cheeks unwet,
>   Her arms of love round Perseus set,
>   And said: O child, what grief is mine!
> But thou dost slumber, and thy baby breast
>   Is sunk in rest,
> Here in the cheerless brass-bound bark,
> Tossed amid starless night and pitchy dark.
>   Nor dost thou heed the scudding brine
> Of waves that wash above thy curls so deep,
>   Nor the shrill winds that sweep, —
> Lapped in thy purple robe's embrace,
>   Fair little face!
> But if this dread were dreadful too to thee,
> Then wouldst thou lend thy listening ear to me;
> Therefore I cry, — Sleep, babe, and sea, be still,
> And slumber our unmeasured ill!
>   Oh, may some change of fate, sire Zeus, from thee
>   Descend, our woes to end!
> But if this prayer, too overbold, offend
> Thy justice, yet be merciful to me!

But the outstanding lyric poet was Pindar. Though he was
born in the last quarter of the sixth century, his artistic life belongs to the first half of the fifth. His fame now rests on the
Epinician Odes, songs commemorating the athletic victories
won at the four great festivals of Greece by competitors from

---

[1] See above, page 227.

[2] Simonides, *Fragment* 37 (Bergk); J. A. Symonds, *The Greek Poets*,
p. 331.

all parts of the Greek world; for the remains of other Pindaric poetry found during recent years in *papyri* from Egypt, though of great interest to the literary historian, have added nothing to Pindar's poetic renown.

The Bœotians had the reputation of being rustics with few pretensions to education or culture; and certainly since Hesiod's day the land had produced no poet. Pindar himself was sent as a youth to Athens, where he not only received his training in the art of choral composition, but was exposed to all the varying influences of a more refined culture than existed in his homeland. He became friendly with the family of the Alc-mæonidæ, for one of whom, Megacles, he composed the seventh Pythian ode. A late tradition also makes him the friend of his older contemporary, Aeschylus. By 476 his fame as a poet had already been so well bruited abroad, that he was invited to the court of Hiero at Syracuse. His two years' stay in Sicily was rich in poetic output; for the *Epinician Odes*, written to commemorate the athletic victories of Hiero and of Theron of Acragas, are amongst his finest poems.[1] The remainder of his life he appears to have passed in his native land — a bard of Panhellenic reputation whose powers to the very end did not fail him. But though he lived in the days when the Greeks repelled the Asiatic invader and during the momentous decades which saw political and social changes of unparalleled significance, he appears little affected thereby in his poetry. In spirit he belongs to the sixth century; he is full of aristocratic pride, and his ideal manhood is a nobility such as in his time must have all but passed away. He upholds the old traditional religion; at the same time he seeks in many places to rationalize it, and particularly to gloss over those episodes in Greek mythology which were not only repellent to the people of an enlightened age, but might be deemed unworthy of divine beings. The intellectual awakening and scepticism of traditional beliefs that resulted from the philosophic speculations of the sixth and fifth centuries find no echo in his verse. For Delphi and for its god, on the other hand, he had a deep and life-long veneration. Perhaps it was during his visit to Sicily that he

---

[1] *Olympian Ode* 1 and *Pythian Odes* 1, 2, and 3 in honor of Hiero, *Olympian Odes* 2 and 3 in honor of Theron.

became acquainted with Orphism; for in the superb ode to
Theron, which is remarkable for its unusually serious and re-
flective tone, he sets out at some length the doctrines of the
Orphic sect on the rewards and punishments that await man
after death according to the life that he has led on earth.

How that the souls of the wicked, when they have died on this earth,
Forthwith pay the penalty;
For the sins enacted in this realm of God there is one below the earth
    that judgeth,
Delivering the strict account in bitter terms of Doom:
But the souls of the good win a happy life free from hard toil,
Having an equal measure of the sun by night and day,

and he continues to elaborate the contrast between the lot of
the good and of the wicked at some length.[1] The unexampled
richness and variety of Pindar's diction, coupled with his vivid
imagination that pours forth the most varied and unforgettable
imagery of language, render his poetry deserving of being called
sublime. Yet, although his poems abound in moral saws,
these too are of the traditional sort, and exceptions are rare.
And, just as there are moments when we are tempted to call
Pindar a monotheist, only to be confronted a few lines later
with echoes of the old polytheism; so, if we are not wholly
borne away by the purely poetic beauties of his odes, we are
obliged to confess that, save in rare moments, he is lacking in
the deeper insight into religion and into men's hearts which
characterizes, though in different ways, all of the Attic dramatists.

A brief mention must suffice for the younger contemporary
of Pindar, Bacchylides of Ceos. He was little more than a name
until in 1897 nineteen poems or portions of poems by him were
discovered on an Egyptian papyrus. Thirteen are epinician
odes, no less than three of these being in honor of Hiero of
Syracuse, whose guest Bacchylides seems, like so many other
poets, to have been. The remaining six poems are hymns in
praise of gods or heroes. One of these relates at length the
adventures of Theseus on his return from Crete. In it Bacchylides' gift of telling a story simply yet elegantly in verse is

---

[1] *Olympian Ode* 2, 57 ff. The translation is from L. R. Farnell, *The
Works of Pindar*, vol. 1 (1930), p. 12.

abundantly seen, as also in the unique account of Crœsus' fate which has already been quoted in an earlier chapter.[1] Bacchylides was an agreeable minor poet; but he is not in the class of Pindar or even of Simonides.

Next to nothing is known of the drama before the fifth century. It is only when the eldest of the three Attic tragic poets, Aeschylus (524–456 B.C.), had begun his poetic career that the drama as a literary form was fashioned. Seven of his plays are still extant.[2] The earliest of these, the *Suppliants*, cannot be precisely dated, but probably was composed soon after 499, the year in which Aeschylus is said to have begun exhibiting plays at the Dionysiac festival. Tradition attributes to him the introduction of a second actor, an innovation which made possible a proper dramatic dialogue; whereas, before, the lyrics of the Dionysiac chorus had been separated at intervals by dialogues between a single actor and the leader of the chorus. Aeschylus' earlier plays can be performed with only two actors; but when, about 468, a third actor was added — and this remained the fixed number for tragedy — he availed himself of the innovation. Hence a further great advance in dramatic technique became possible. The dramatist's powers are seen at their highest in the great trilogy, *Agamemnon*, *Libation Bearers*, *Eumenides*, which was produced at Athens two years before his death. The subject matter of Aeschylus' tragedies and that of his successors was taken from mythology and heroic legends, familiar to his hearers from youth up, from Homer, and from the poems of the epic cycle. Historical subjects were rarely portrayed, though not wholly unknown. For such was the *Capture of Miletus* by Phrynichus, produced in 493, which so upset the Athenian audience that they fined the poet. Such also is the extant *Persians* by Aeschylus (472). Its setting is in Persia; the persons represented — the queen mother, Atossa, the king's messenger, the chorus of Persian elders, and finally Xerxes himself — are all Persian. But it is first and foremost a noble panegyric on Athens' achievements at Salamis. That, however, is not all. The early part of the play contains more than a hint

---

[1] See above, page 208.
[2] He wrote ninety plays in all, winning the first prize at the dramatic festival at Athens on thirteen occasions.

of the attendant horrors of war, the uncertainty of the issue, the
anguish felt by the relatives of those who have gone to fight.
Over all is the contrast between human endeavor and human
pride and Fate or the Will of God, which can bring one to
nought and humble the other. It is a theme recurrent in Aeschylus' plays. He is not a fatalist as the term is ordinarily
understood; but he believes that there exists a nexus of events
which leads up naturally or inevitably to any great human
misfortune. He is, too, the upholder of Law, Order, and Justice
against tyranny and injustice; it was a dominant theme in the
trilogy of which only the *Prometheus Bound* has survived, and
it is brought impressively before us in the final play of the
Oresteia and its concluding scenes. Of Aeschylus' purely poetic
qualities, the grandeur of his language and the matchless meta-
phors, especially in his choral odes, strike every reader at once.
As a dramatist his power of psychological analysis is profound.
Clytemnestra and Cassandra in the *Agamemnon* are among the
unsurpassed figures of tragedy for all time.

Sophocles (496–406 B.C.) was the son of a well-to-do Athenian
citizen. He himself at different times held important offices in
the Athenian state — he was *strategos* in 440 and one of the ten
probuloi appointed in 412–411 — and he was, judged by the
number of times that he won the first prize at the dramatic
festivals, easily the most successful of the three tragic poets.
His earliest victory occurred in 468; but of the seven extant
plays the earliest, *Antigone*, was produced in 442 or 441, the
latest, *Oedipus at Colonus*, was not performed till some years
after the dramatist's death.[1] Sophocles abandoned the practice
of writing three plays on a single continuous theme; instead,
although at the festivals it was necessary to offer a trilogy in
competition, each of his dramas treated of a separate subject.
In his plays Sophocles takes the heroic legends in their accepted
form. His characters act and speak in strict consistence with
their situation; they do not become, as often in Euripides, the
mouthpieces of the poet's own views. The action in Sophocles'
dramas, too, is steadily directed to one tragic climax, although
the poet shows great diversity in the means which he employs

---

[1] To the seven complete tragedies we may add the considerable fragments of an eighth play, a satyric drama, found on an Egyptian papyrus.

to his end. Thus, *Oedipus the King* is in the matter of plot a masterpiece of intricate construction. From the point of view of dramatic structure it is the greatest of all Greek tragedies; while in the grandeur of its conception it is surpassed alone by Aeschylus' *Agamemnon*. Yet in the *Philoctetes* there is scarcely any plot. The entire interest of the play centres in the psychological analysis of the leading characters, the contrast between them, and the reaction of one upon the other. As a literary artist Sophocles made the Attic Greek language a subtle vehicle of every mood and thought, in a way that was rarely equalled and never surpassed. He is typical of his age and country, Periclean Athens, both in his restraint and detachment, which some critics, contrasting his strictly objective treatment of his characters with the personal note struck here and there by his two rivals, have wrongly interpreted as due to lack of sympathy and understanding, and in his attitude to moral law and to religion. For he strives to bring venerable tradition into harmony with the higher conceptions of morality and beliefs, which were characteristic of the best thought of the age.

Of Euripides (480–406 B.C.), eighteen genuine plays have survived, the *Rhesus*, though included among his works, being of disputed authorship. Of these the earliest is probably the *Alcestis* (438), the latest the *Bacchae* (406), which was not produced till after the poet's death. In more ways than one Euripides was an innovator. His choral odes commonly are mere interludes in the play, and have little connexion with its plot or action. Again, he increased the length and importance of the opening prologue. The result is often somewhat undramatic; but the convention gave the poet greater freedom in the treatment of his actual play, by enabling him to explain fully to his hearers the precise situation at the opening of the dramatic action. It is, however, not merely on the technical side, and in the matter of experiments with metres, that Euripides broke with tradition. While both Aeschylus and Sophocles were, each after his manner, idealists, Euripides is an uncompromising realist in the handling of his themes. His characters often utter views which, but slightly disguised, are the poet's own sentiments on social, ethical, and even political questions. Deeply affected by the Sophistic movement, Euripides frankly questioned the truth of many accepted opinions on religion and morality. His characters are not cast in the heroic mould, but in their good and bad qualities are essentially human. Whether the dictum attributed to Sophocles, "I draw men as they ought to be drawn; Euripides draws them as they are," is a genuine utterance of the older poet or not, it expresses one leading characteristic of Euripides' art. It is noteworthy that his greatest characters are almost without exception women, Medea in the play of that name, Phædra in the *Hippolytus*, Alcestis, Hecuba, Electra, Iphigeneia. In the depth of his understanding and in his sympathy for women he surpassed both his predecessors; yet it was one of the commonest taunts against him in his day that he was a woman-hater. Euripides in this and in other respects was but partially understood in his own time, and, judged by contemporary standards, he was by far the least successful of the three tragic poets. But his innovations, the romantic quality and the "love-interest" in his plays, and the fact that his dramas were in general not typically Athenian, made him the favorite dramatist of later ages.[1]

In the next century tragedies continued to be written, but they were inferior to the works of the three great masters. Plays were written to be read rather than performed; while in the theatres, as Aristotle observes (*Rhetoric*, iii, 1403b), "the actors are now of greater moment than the poets." It became customary to revive one or more of the old masterpieces at the dramatic festivals, in addition to producing new plays, which are lost to us, and which in all likelihood did not survive for any great time in antiquity.

Attic comedy developed more slowly than tragedy. Of the three leading writers of comedy Cratinus seems to have begun his literary career about 450 B.C. Eupolis and Aristophanes (*c.* 448–388) were approximately contemporaries. It is, however, of Aristophanes alone that we can properly judge, since eleven of his plays have come down to us, while those of his

---

[1] Thus, it is significant that the Roman writers of tragedy, both those of the Republican age and Seneca, in borrowing from Greek models, were indebted almost wholly to Euripides. Aeschylus was too archaic and heroic, Sophocles too typical of Periclean Athens to be satisfactorily transplanted.

rivals have not survived. The earliest comedy that we possess, the *Acharnians*, was produced in 425, and appears to have been the third play written by the youthful poet. His latest play was the *Plutus* (388). The feature which perhaps strikes the modern reader of Aristophanes' plays first is their outspokenness. Contemporary personages and institutions were fearlessly attacked or burlesqued. Public opinion approved this license, since the efforts made once or twice in the fifth century to restrict this extreme liberty of speech were unsuccessful. But Aristophanes was far more than a humorist with a knack of composing telling plots and easily flowing dialogue, that is generally witty and occasionally gross. In his choral songs as a whole, and throughout his greatest extant play, he shows himself an imaginative poet of the first rank. That he was a literary critic of a high order is clear to every attentive student of the *Frogs* (405), with its evaluation of the Attic tragedians, as well as from the intensely clever parodies of Euripides' plays introduced into the *Peace* and the *Women at the Thesmophoria*. Three of his comedies are, in effect, pleas for the Peace party, the *Acharnians*, the *Peace* (421), and the *Lysistrata* (411). In the *Clouds* he satirizes certain intellectual movements of the age, Socrates being taken, somewhat unfairly, as typical of a class. In the *Wasps* he makes fun of his fellow countrymen's love for litigation and the law-courts. The *Birds* (414), now generally and rightly conceded to be his masterpiece, is more a play of the imagination, a fantasy full of exquisite poetry mixed with rollicking fun. It depicts the founding of a bird-commonwealth by two Athenians who have grown weary of the life and bustle of their city. Incidentally the play contains much amusing parody of conditions in contemporary Athens.

If the needful allowance be made for exaggeration and burlesque, the Aristophanic comedies are invaluable for the light that they throw on the manners and life of the Athenians of the day. Aristophanes represents for us the older generation who, then, as in all ages, contrast unfavorably the behavior of the young folk with their own in their more decorous youth. He shows us, in the person of Philocleon in the *Wasps*, the varying moods and influences to which the average Athenian, acting as juror in the *Heliaia*, was subject. He depicts, too, the joys of country life, pillories the fashionable way of behaving in the streets or at dinner parties, and in his minor characters brings before us a whole gallery of types familiar to every Athenian in his daily life — tradesmen of all sorts, the informer, the down-at-heels poet, a councillor, an oracle-monger, or one of the Scythian archers who formed the police force of Athens.

Of fourth-century comedy it is difficult to form an adequate judgment, since nothing but the titles of plays and some few fragments have survived. It is clear, however, that the poets of that age had not the same license of speech as their predecessors. Political plays were no longer written, and occasional ridicule of well-known persons was directed not against public men but, for example, against prominent philosophers. The names and characters were fictitious; the poets dealt with types of character and professions. Parodies of literature, philosophy, and even mythology were very popular; the old badinage and invective was replaced by innuendo (cf. Aristotle, *Ethics*, iv, 8). Love intrigue began to be a favorite topic for the plot, and in this respect especially the comedy of the fourth century prepared the way for the comedy of intrigue that flourished in the early Hellenistic Age.

We saw how the spirit of inquiry, which had pervaded the Hellenic world in the sixth century, had among other effects produced the first attempts at a rational presentation of geographical and historical data. The first author to produce a history in a literary form was Herodotus (*c.* 484–425 B.C.), a native of Halicarnassus, whose manhood was spent partly in Samos and Athens, partly in extensive travels, partly, since he joined the colony to Thurii, in the West. This is not the place to enter upon the vexed question of how his history was composed, and whether his primary interest was in geography, while his historical inquiries resulted from a later and secondary phase in his intellectual life. In the *History* as it has come down to us — the division into nine books is a later arrangement — the second half (Books vi to ix) narrates the Persian wars of 490 and 480–479. The earlier half of the work is devoted to a review of the manners, institutions, and history of various oriental peoples included in the vast Persian empire. Herodotus derived his information from oral tradition and local beliefs, from predecessors, especially Hecatæus of Miletus, and, above all, from personal observation on his travels and conversations held with natives of the lands he visited. Hence inevitably the treatment of the various regions is unequal. While, for example, his section on Egypt, which he had himself visited, in addition to having Hecatæus' work, is long and detailed, his observations on Lydia or the Scythians are proportionately a good deal briefer. A similar disparity is observable also in his accounts of earlier Greek history, introduced into different parts of his book. As a story-teller Herodotus is inimitable, and he is a literary artist of the first rank, so that his *History* has enjoyed a deserved popularity throughout the ages. Of his merits as a historian opinions both in ancient and modern times have varied. His weaknesses are undeniable. He has little understanding of military affairs; his natural piety leads him to respect oracles and supposed supernatural phenomena which a more sophisticated writer would have rejected or sought to rationalize; at times — and this is specially noticeable in the Greek portions of his book — he is swayed by political likes and dislikes, so that, for instance, he is partial to Athens and to the Alcmæonid clan, and grossly unfair to Themistocles. Yet we cannot dispute the justice of the title, "the father of history," bestowed on him by Cicero. Herodotus is eminently broad-minded; he has a deep admiration for Eastern civilizations, especially Egypt, and he is capable of doing justice even to the strange customs of uncivilized peoples like the Scythians. Where his statements are the result of personal observation he is highly trustworthy, a fact which modern exploration and research have borne out again and again. Where he depends on others he is naturally at the mercy of his informants; but it would be an error to regard him as quite uncritical. His criticism takes the form of suppressing traditions and statements which he sees cause to reject; or, wherever he himself is in doubt, of giving several traditions of a particular event, leaving the decision to his reader's judgment. Thus, within certain limits, he exercised the function of criticism; he applied it to single questions and details, but he had not yet learnt to apply it to the larger problems of history. He ascertained the truth to the best of his ability, and set down in connected form the traditions and accounts of historical occurrences. Thus, in truth, he fully merits the name bestowed upon him by the Roman writer.

The tremendous intellectual activity, and its rapid progress, during the latter half of the fifth century cannot be illustrated better than by this bald statement of fact, that scarcely more than a quarter of a century separates the *History* of Herodotus from the historical work of Thucydides, son of Olorus. He was born about 471; the known facts of his life are few. He was a victim of the plague in 430–429, and held the office of *strategos* in 425–424, being subsequently banished for his failure to effect the relief of Amphipolis. Exiled for fully twenty years from his native city, he spent the time partly on his ancestral property in Thrace, partly in travel to collect material for his *History*. He returned to Athens in 403, and seems to have died not many years later, leaving his work incomplete. It was of the war, in which so large a part of the Hellenic world was engaged for nearly thirty years, that he set himself to compose a critical narrative. Actually his extant work covers the period from 431 to 411, the first book being in the nature of an introduction, in which he gives a valuable sketch of the earlier development of Hellas, and a summary of Athenian history from 478 to 445, in addition to a detailed examination of the diplomatic and other preliminaries to the Peloponnesian war.

His historical method he has himself very fully explained (i, 21–22); the chapters are worthy of the most careful study, though here only a brief citation can be given.

Of the events of the war I have not ventured to speak from any information, nor according to any notion of my own; I have described nothing but what I either saw myself or learned from others of whom I made the most careful and particular inquiry. The task was a laborious one, because eye-witnesses of the same occurrences gave different accounts of them, as they remembered or were interested in the actions of one side or the other (i, 22).

It is difficult for a modern student to realize how remarkable, indeed how revolutionary, Thucydides' enunciation of what historical writing is, and what it should aim at, must have

seemed in the historian's own day. The points he emphasizes
are: (1) the difficulty of getting reliable information about the
earlier history of Greece; (2) an equal difficulty, though due to
different causes, of obtaining exact information about the
events of the war itself; (3) his purpose and method in introducing speeches into his narrative; (4) the care he took to
obtain accurate data himself. With regard to the first of these
claims, Thucydides, instead of accepting the current legends
and myths, has drawn a picture which, as we now know,
corresponds in all essentials to reality. He knows of a period
of migratory movements, when there were not yet settled political communities in Greece, and of a thalassocracy in the
eastern Mediterranean, which he associates with the name of
Minos. If he accepts the Trojan war as a historical occurrence,
his contention is largely borne out by modern archæological
discoveries. He goes on to trace the gradual evolution of more
settled communities, and sketches the main features of Archaic
Greece. A writer who could thus throw overboard popular
beliefs and legends, and construct a rational account of early
Greek history, in which the main factors are accurately appraised, including the importance of sea-power, commercial
expansion, and the accumulation of wealth, would fill us with
complete confidence in his veracity when he came to deal with
contemporary events, even if we had not other means of check-
ing his unflinching truthfulness. No part of his work has
been so criticized and so misunderstood as the speeches which
he puts in the mouth of the principal actors in the war or of
the spokesmen of particular states. If we are convinced of his
eminent love of truth, we cannot do other than accept his own
statement concerning the speeches: [1]

As for the speeches uttered by the several parties, either when about
to make war, or when already in it, I was at a hard pass for the proper
recollection of their words in simple exactness, whether heard by myself or by sundry others who recounted them to me; they are here expressed according as I supposed each person would have spoken what
was most requisite for treating the actual matters before him; and I
have adhered as closely as I could to the general purport of what
was really said.

[1] Thucydides, i, 22; the translation of these passages is from *Clio En-
throned* by W. R. M. Lamb.

At the same time it is worth remembering that, though Thucydides did not allow literary art to get the better of his conception of historic truth, he was nevertheless profoundly influenced by the Sophistic movement of his day. To show his scrupulous care in narrating events, describing topography and so forth, in short, to demonstrate that he lived up to his own very high standards, it is enough to mention his account of the Plague, which is a model of what such an account should be; his description of Syracuse, which those who have gone over the ground acclaim a work of detailed precision; or the caution that he uses in dealing with figures. When he tells us (v, 68) how and why it is impossible to give the numbers engaged at the battle of Mantinea, we may regret the absence of the information, but we are filled with respect, both for the reasons adduced by the historian for his silence, and for the critical faculty which would have nothing to do with vague guesses or partisan estimates.

Above all, Thucydides was the first to enunciate a philosophy of history. He set himself to determine the causes underlying the political actions of city-states, and of the men who directed their affairs. The motives and characters of the main actors in the war — Pericles, Cleon, Alcibiades, Nicias, Hermocrates of Syracuse — are made clear to us with a masterly hand and a masterly economy of words. So objective is Thucydides' treatment that he gives comments of his own only on the rarest occasions. The facts which he sets out, whether in the narrative or in the speeches uttered by these men, are sufficient clue to the understanding of their psychology. With their personal lives, and the trivialities dear to the biographer, he had no truck; it was their mental attitude, and the actions that sprang from it, which were his concern.

Much of the most modern criticism levelled against Thucydides is futile, and proceeds from the mistaken practice of importing the ideas of the nineteenth and twentieth centuries into the study of the ancients and their works. He is blamed, for example, for neglecting the social and economic history and conditions of his time, or for giving a one-sided account of the origins of the war. His achievement can properly be judged only in the light of the times and circumstances in which he lived. Estimated in this way he is easily the greatest of the ancient historians. Judged by the standards of our own time, his mental attitude and his methods, within the limits of his subject, still stand as a model for the true historical student who would conscientiously combine accurate inquiry with searching and unbiased criticism.

With the passing of Thucydides there was a marked decline in historical writing. What was intended as a continuation of Thucydides' book was given to the world by Xenophon in his *Hellenic History*. It, and his account of the March of the Ten Thousand (cf. p. 284), together record the history of Greece from 411 to 362. There are, however, a number of important omissions, of which one of the most striking is the early history of the Second Athenian Confederacy. From the literary point of view these works, like his minor writings, are agreeable and fluent. The *Anabasis*, moreover, has the vivid charm which only an eye-witness, imbued with the spirit of adventure as well as gifted with an easy pen, could attain. As a historical writer Xenophon is honest, and strives to the best of his power to be accurate. Next to his descriptive power, which is most striking in the record of his personal adventures, he is most successful in the biographical vein. Indeed, the central portion of the *Hellenica* is so dominated by the Spartan king, Agesilaus, for whom Xenophon had an excessive admiration, that the treatment of the years 404–387 is misleading and one-sided. And, in general, he lacks the understanding, the analytical power, and the philosophic detachment of his great predecessor, Thucydides. Hence he fails as a whole to give a coherent picture of the period with which he is dealing, and he is often at a loss to interpret the political motives of the chief persons and governments at that time.

One of the most interesting *papyri* found in recent years contains a portion of a historical work treating in some detail and in a straightforward narrative the events of the year 396–395. It can be used to correct Xenophon's account of several episodes. The authorship is uncertain. Ephorus, Theopompus, Cratippus, and Daimachus of Platæa have all been suggested. But the first two are for various reasons impossible, though it has now been established that Ephorus used the newly dis-covered work. Nor are there satisfactory grounds for assigning

it to Cratippus; while far too little is known about Daimachus
to make the attribution to him anything more than a guess.
As a sample of the new author's method, as well as for the sake
of the unique information that it contains, we may cite chapter 14, where the unsatisfactory character of the Persian ruler as
a paymaster of his mercenary troops is revealed to the reader: [1]

When Cheiricrates, who had arrived to succeed Pollis as admiral,
had already taken over the Lacedæmonian fleet, Conon manned twenty
of his warships and sailed to Caunus. It was because he desired an
interview with Pharnabazus and Tithraustes, and to receive funds
from them, that he went up country to them from Caunus. It happened that many months' wages were due to his men, for they were
badly paid by their commanders. This is quite a usual practice for
those who conduct wars on the Great King's behalf. Thus, in the
Decelean war, when Persia and Sparta were allies, the Persians were
extremely niggardly and elusive in their payments, and the triremes
of the allies would have come to destruction but for the eager energy
of Cyrus. These conditions are the fault of the Great King, who, when
entering on a war, sends a small sum at the beginning to the men in
command; subsequently he neglects them. The men who are in charge
of operations, being unable to defray the cost from their private fortune,
at times allow their forces to be destroyed. This, then, is what used
to happen. Now Tithraustes, when Conon interviewed him and informed him that operations were in danger of disaster owing to lack
of funds for the men to whom those who were conducting the war on
the Great King's behalf were ill advised to refuse it, dispatched certain
Persians of his retinue to pay Conon's men their wages. They had two
hundred and twenty talents, this money having been taken from Tissaphernes' resources. Tithraustes, having stayed at Sardes for a little
while longer, proceeded to the Great King. He appointed Ariæus
and Pasiphernes to take charge of (western) affairs, and handed over
to them for the prosecution of the war the gold and silver that he left
behind. This, they say, amounted to about seven hundred talents.

Other fourth-century historians are known to us directly from
fragments, indirectly through their works being used by compilers of a later age. The chief were Theopompus and Ephorus,
both pupils of Isocrates. Both were greatly influenced by the
political theories and the Panhellenic outlook of their teacher;
but the profounder influence was exerted on their minds by
the rhetorical training that they had received. Theopompus
composed a continuation of Thucydides, covering the years

[1] *Hellenica Oxyrhynchia*, ch. 14.

from 410 to 394; but his greatest work was a history of Philip II of Macedon, which was also in effect a history of the Hellenic world during the middle of the fourth century. Ephorus' work was in one sense more ambitious; it was a general history of the Greeks from the earliest times down to 340 B.C. The scale on which it was written varied; for, while the archaic period of Hellas was sketched rather briefly, the events nearer to the writer's own time were treated with some fullness. Theopompus had what we may call, a strong puritanic strain, perhaps the result of coming under the influence of the Cynic school of philosophy. For it is remarkable how many of the extant fragments contain strictures, many of great severity, on the social customs and morals both of individuals and of whole communities. Both authors were extensively used by later writers, a circumstance at least partly due to the fact that they were attractive and easy to read. The writing of history had now, under the influence of rhetoric, become a literary art; form and expression were the prime consideration, to which historical accuracy, criticism of sources, and unbiased judgment were subordinated. The amusement of the reader, anxiety that he should not be wearied by continuous application to the essential subject of the work, which led to the introduction of amusing or sensational anecdotes, or passages of fine writing empty of content, impaired the dignity and true worth of historical composition, a phenomenon not unfamiliar in our own day. In addition there was often the aim of making historical works serve a didactic purpose, the writer himself being influenced by the teaching of this or that philosophic school. Thus there was every reason why, from time to time, in later centuries, a truly critical mind should group together the trio, Herodotus, Thucydides, and Xenophon, as the three outstanding historical writers of Greece.

The great development in prose writing in the fourth century was the direct outcome of the Sophistic movement. The Alexandrian critics of the following age, in their work of preserving and editing the texts of the great orators, established a canon of ten whom they regarded as of outstanding merit.[1] We have referred elsewhere [2] to the political speeches o͏͏ ͏

---

[1] Cf. below, p. 453.   [2] Cf. above, p. 30͏

thenes and to Isocrates' work as a publicist.   But, when through
the teaching of Gorgias and others eloquence became an art,
it was not merely political or deliberative discourse but the
forensic speech that was brought to a high pitch of perfection.
Fully to understand this development it is necessary to keep in
mind the conception of citizenship held in an ancient democracy
like Athens.   Just as an Athenian was expected to take a direct
part in the government and, as a juror, in the administration
of justice, so he was required, if involved in litigation, to present
his own case, whether as prosecutor or defendant, before a
jury of his fellow-citizens.   The number and activity of the
jury-courts increased rapidly from the Periclean age on.   The
Athenians seem to have had a marked fondness for lawsuits
and for the Heliastic service that they entailed, a weakness that
their countryman, Aristophanes, very effectively satirized.[1]   The
size of these courts varied, 201, 501, 701, 1001, and even larger
panels being mentioned.   Even the lowest was to modern ideas
enormous and unwieldy.   It must, however, be remembered
that the ancient view would be that every citizen ought to be
able to understand the laws of his state.   At the same time it
was believed that the trial of a person before a large group of
his peers would be the most likely means of ensuring that justice
was done.   Such a system, however ideal it might sound in
theory, was in practice liable to break down.   And there are
not wanting instances to show that such large aggregations of
jurors were at times so swayed by the passions and prejudices
of the moment that grave miscarriages of justice resulted.   Obviously not every man who became involved in a suit had either
the education or the wits to present his case adequately.   As
public speaking developed under the influence of the Sophists,
there came into being a class of professional writers of law-
court speeches.   These men were not advocates in the modern
sense; for they did not usually — at least at first — appear in
court on behalf of a client, or, if they did, only in the capacity
of a friend who with the jury's permission would also like to
address them.   But they wrote the speech for their client, and

[1] Primarily in the *Wasps*, produced in 422, a play that centuries later
was to serve Racine as a model for his *Les Plaideurs*. But there are allusions
in other Aristophanic comedies.

the successful writer made it his business not merely to marshal the facts carefully and present his client's case in the most favorable light, but he studied his client's characteristics and manner, so as to produce the illusion, when the speech was delivered, that the client himself was the author. Thus it was not enough for a speech-writer who wished to make his mark to be skilled in oratory and in the law, he must also be something of a psychologist.

Lysias (c. 457–380) excelled in all these qualities. In the most sustained of his extant speeches, *Against Eratosthenes*, a man who had been one of the Thirty and was seeking to regain his full civic status under the restored democracy, the narrative portion is not only of supreme historical importance for the events of 405–403, but is a masterly piece of artistic prose. Lysias' faculty of making his speeches fit the character of his clients is amply apparent in many of the shorter speeches. He strikes the right tone whether the actual speaker is a middle-aged man who, in defending himself against a charge of malicious wounding, frankly admits to his judges that he has been guilty of an amatory indiscretion; [1] or a humble tradesman who is in danger of losing the small pension assigned to him by the state because he is crippled; [2] or a young man of upright character replying to an accusation of having withheld funds belonging to the Treasury.[3] The cases undertaken by Lysias were exceedingly varied. Isæus (c. 410–340), though some of his lost speeches were on behalf of other types of suit, specialized in inheritance cases. His intimate knowledge of the intricate laws of testamentary succession and the admirable clearness of his presentation made him famous in his day and subsequently ensured him a place in the canon of the Attic Orators. Eleven complete speeches have survived, all dealing with his speciality; the fragment of a twelfth is a defense for one, Euphiletus, who was threatened with loss of civic rights.

Demosthenes' fame as the greatest orator of antiquity rests primarily on his political harangues, some of which have already engaged our attention.[4] But, having lost the bulk of his patrimony in his youth, he was for many years a professional speech-writer — the most brilliant pupil that Isæus ever had. A

[1] *Orat.* 3.   [2] *Orat.* 34.   [3] *Orat.* 19.   [4] Cf. above, pp. 303 ff.

sufficient number of speeches written by him for litigants survives to demonstrate his complete mastery of forensic oratory. In a few cases he adopts the practice of suiting his style to his client's character.[1] But for the most part he speaks in his own person. Evidently in the fourth century it was no longer felt necessary to keep up before a jury the fiction that the litigant was his own advocate. Moreover, some of Demosthenes' law-court speeches are so long and intricate that only a master like himself could have delivered them. They partake of the character of deliberative orations.

Thus the fourth century which, as we saw, was singularly poor in poetic output, produced a series of prose authors as eminent in their art as were the Attic dramatists in theirs. Above all, the writings of Plato and Demosthenes remained each in their kind unapproached and unapproachable by the Greeks of later ages.

[1] For instance, in the speeches *Against Conon* (54) and *In Reply to Callicles* (55).

CHAPTER XXII

GREEK CIVILIZATION IN THE FIFTH AND FOURTH
CENTURIES — ART

*Pheidias' representations of gods are said to have
been superior in point of art to his representations
of men; if he had made nothing but the Athena at
Athens and the Olympian Zeus in Elis he would
still have had no rival in ivory. The majesty of the
Zeus so rises to the level of its subject that its beauty
may be thought to have added something to traditional religion.* — Quintilian, *Inst. Orat.* xii, 10.

THERE is a certain irony in the circumstance that one is apt
to judge the outward appearance of cities in the Hellenic world
by the public edifices, sacred or secular, that have survived the
ravages of time or have been uncovered in fair preservation
by the excavator's spade. Actually even a city like Athens
at the height of her glory seems to have presented the extremes
of contrast. The ordinary dwelling-houses were small and
unpretentious. Streets were narrow and insanitary; the relative
dryness of the climate and a southern sun under ordinary conditions prevented serious epidemics. The town sites which modern excavation has laid bare are almost all of Hellenistic date.[1]
Consequently no very precise picture of cities in the classical
picture can be drawn. Moreover, since most of them grew up
very gradually, it is unlikely that they were laid out on any
uniform plan. Athens was no exception. Also, while certain
features and parts of it can be identified with certainty, many
uncertainties still exist. Some of these, it may be hoped, will
be dispelled in the near future, as the projected excavations of
the American Academy in the region of the ancient *agora*
progress. The city was, as we have seen, connected during
the course of the fifth century with its harbor by walls. Between them ran a road from Peiræus to Athens. Another road

[1] See below, page 439.

— the one generally used in peace-time, ran outside the fortifications, and, keeping well to the north, led to one or other of the gates on the northwest side of the city.   Chief of these — and indeed the main gate into Athens — was the Dipylon Gate. Near it was the Potters' Quarter (Outer and Inner Cerameicus) and also the cemetery, from which a number of fine sculptured tombstones — particularly of the fourth century — has been recovered.   The position of several other gates is certain, that of others conjectural, there being probably fourteen in all.   As one passes on from the Dipylon Gate towards the ancient *agora*, the most conspicuous object on the right (south) side is a finely preserved Doric hexastyle temple commonly called the Theseum.   Though slightly later in date than the Parthenon, its proportions are less elegant, the building as a whole making an impression of heaviness that is almost clumsy.   The *agora* in an ancient Greek city was the centre of civic life; that is to say, it was used, at least in early times, for meetings of the citizens, not merely for trade.   At Athens, however, the *ecclesia* held its meetings in the Pnyx.   This may be identified with a large artificial terrace in the form of a semicircle lying on a low hill about a quarter of a mile west of the Acropolis.   In the course of the fourth century this ancient meeting-place was exchanged for the theatre of Dionysus situated on the southern slopes of the same citadel.   On the western side of the Athenian *agora* was the Royal Colonnade (*Stoa basileios*); facing it, on the east side of the market-place, was the Painted Colonnade (*Stoa poikile*), which was ornamented during the fifth century with painted frescoes by Polygnotus and Micon.   On the *agora*, as well as in other quarters of the city, statues of Hermes were set up, and it was these that in 415 were, by a stupid act of vandalism, hacked about and disfigured.[1]   In and round about the *agora*, finally, were many booths and shops, most of them probably temporary structures, that could be removed at will. The barbers' shops, in particular, were popular resorts where townsman and countryman could foregather and exchange gossip.[2]   The Prytaneum, or town-hall, was situated a little

---

[1] See above, page 264.
[2] The speaker in Lysias, *Orat.* 23, 3, refers to a barber's shop which was the favorite haunt of the demesmen of Acharnæ.

Plate 28

TEMPLE OF POSEIDON AT PAESTUM (Southern Italy)

STATUE OF HERMES HOLDING THE INFANT DIONYSUS
(By Praxiteles)

Plate 29

distance away, probably not far from the northern slopes of the Acropolis, which could be ascended only from the west. Immediately opposite, and approximately half way between the *agora* and the Pnyx, was a low hill which can be identified with the Areopagus, the place of assembly of the venerable council to which it gave its name, and from the Periclean age the site of the chief court for the trial of homicide.

The development of sculpture and architecture from the time of the Persian wars was no less rapid and striking than the progress of literature and thought. It is unfortunate that for our knowledge of the works and styles of the greatest artists we depend, apart from literary notices, almost entirely on later copies, which are of very unequal merit. The influence of the athletic festivals showed itself strongly in the predilection of artists for portraying the nude male form. At the same time cult-statues of greater artistic perfection than those of the archaic period were made and dedicated in numerous temples in the Greek world. Both tendencies can be illustrated in the work of three of the most notable predecessors of Pheidias. Pythagoras, whose birthplace is disputed, specialized in athletic statues. His *floruit* can be fixed with fair accuracy because it is known that two such works were made respectively in Olympiad 73 (488–484) and Olympiad 77 (472–468). Even the mythological subjects depicted by him — Apollo fighting the Pytho, the lame Philoctetes, Eteocles and Polyneices in single combat — were clearly only variations on his favorite athletic types. His contemporary, Calamis of Athens, devoted himself with almost equal exclusiveness to statues of divinities, male and female. The most famous of these in antiquity was his Aphrodite Sosandra (Saviour of men), an ancient critic praising especially her "noble and unconscious smile" and "the comely arrangement and order of her drapery." In general this artist seems to have been renowned for the beautiful yet severe simplicity of his art. This quality is found to an eminent degree in the magnificent bronze statue of a charioteer discovered by the French excavators at Delphi. The figure is life-size, representing a young man dressed in the long tunic worn by charioteers. He was evidently portrayed standing in a chariot, for his extended right arm — the left is lost — still holds fragments of

the reins. If the attribution of this bronze to Calamis himself
must be regarded as quite uncertain, its general style at least
makes it highly probable that it was produced by one of his
school or under his influence.

Even more important than these two sculptors, if subsequent
influence be taken as the criterion, was Myron (flourished c. 460).
Copies of several of his works survive. He was a versatile
artist but with a strong leaning towards athletic subjects.
Such was his famous Discobolus, showing an athlete crouching
with tense muscles and weight perfectly balanced at the moment before hurling the discus with his utmost strength. A
similar momentary pose of great physical exertion must have
characterized his statue of the famous runner, Ladas. No
copy of this has been preserved but the admiring words of an
ancient poet give us a hint of its appearance: [1]

> Even as thou wert in life, Ladas, flying before wind-swift Thymus,
> barely touching the earth with the tip of the toes, even so Myron
> made thee in bronze, stamping on all thy body the expectation of the
> Olympian wreath.

Two recent discoveries may here find mention. In 1922 three
four-sided statue bases were turned up in Athens near the
ancient Cerameicus, two being decorated with carved reliefs,
the third with a painted design. On the sculptured panels we
see Athenian youths disporting themselves with handball and
wrestling, while others are practising jumping and javelin-
throwing. Another group of young men is less amiably engaged,
watching the anything but friendly encounter of a dog and
some smaller animal (cat or ferret?). Quite unique is the presentation of some ball-game played with curved sticks (Plates 21a
and 21b). The second set of slabs is in shallower relief and shows
hastier execution than the first. Both, however, are exceedingly
lifelike and spirited compositions. There is much freedom in
the movement and poses of the figures; on the other hand, the
treatment of the face in profile, the eyes and the hair, is still
distinctly archaic. The reliefs, therefore, are likely to date
from the last years of the sixth or the first decade of the fifth
century.

In October, 1928, a bronze statue of somewhat over life-size

[1] *Anthologia Planudea* 54.

was fished up out of the sea off Cape Artemisium. This fine composition (Frontispiece), which on stylistic grounds may be dated to c. 460, probably represents the god Poseidon levelling his trident in his raised right hand as he strides impetuously forward. The arms and hands, though broken off, were also recovered and show the same careful modelling as the torso. Finest of all, however, is the head, with its deep-set eyesockets in which the eyes were once inlaid, as was the case with the Delphi charioteer, and the flowing hair and beard that characterized the immortal ruler of the ocean.[1]

An unusually good index of artistic progress during the fifth century is provided by the sculptural remains of three temples. The pedimental sculptures of the temple of Aphaia in Aegina belong to the first quarter of that century. They represent scenes from the Trojan war. The problem of adapting a group of figures to a triangular space has been successfully solved. The individual figures, though not altogether free from archaic stiffness, are immeasurably in advance of what sculptors of an earlier age had achieved in the lifelike presentation of motion. Every variety of pose is found there — figures at rest, archers kneeling and on the point of discharging their missiles, wounded warriors in the act of falling backwards or already stretched upon the ground in dying agony. Yet by the still somewhat conventional treatment of the faces we are reminded that we are viewing artistic products in the transition stage from lingering archaism to full mastery of an art.

Shortly before 450 B.C. the fine temple of Zeus at Olympia was completed. Of the building itself little remains beyond the ground-plan and the lowest drums of some columns (Plate 17b). It was a Doric temple of normal type, with six columns on the short and thirteen on the long sides. The sculptural decoration consisted of twelve metopes, six at the east and six at the west end, depicting the labors of Heracles. They are fine examples of relief sculpture, in which, however, the spirited presentation of the hero's sundry tasks is to some extent offset by stiffness in the treatment of detail. The author was probably a Peloponnesian artist, but he was certainly not the same who made the

---

[1] This interpretation of the statue is more probable than that it represented Zeus hurling a thunderbolt.

pedimental groups. These — their authorship, too, must remain uncertain — are notably greater in conception and execution, and must be ranked with the finest examples of ancient
art. The scene represented on the eastern pediment was the
chariot race between Pelops and Oenomaus; that on the western, the fight between the Lapiths and the Centaurs. The
magnificent figure of a seer comes from the former, while the
central figure of the west pediment is Apollo, an impressive
portrayal of the nude male figure (Plates 22 and 23). When its
poise and anatomical accuracy are contrasted with the nude
male statues of the previous age, the immense advance, both
artistically and technically, is at once apparent.

The second half of the fifth century was marked at Athens
by great building activity. With the construction of a new
temple in honor of Athena on the Acropolis are linked the
names of two of Athens' most distinguished artists, the
architect Ictinus, and the sculptor Pheidias. This temple,
the Parthenon, was more or less completed by 438, having
been begun nine years before. It was a Doric structure,
with eight columns on the short and seventeen on the long
sides (Plates 24 and 25). The continuous frieze above the
walls of the cella was a non-Doric feature. The ornamentation of this noblest of Greek temples comprised forty-six
metopes, forming part of the normal entablature of a Doric
temple, and depicting scenes from various mythological episodes; the pedimental groups; and, finally, the frieze portraying the Panathenaic procession, to which reference was made in
an earlier chapter (Plate 26). The mythological subjects of
the east and west pediments were both specially appropriate
to Athens and her patron goddess, Athena. On the east, the
birth of Athena in the presence of the Olympian deities, on the
west, the contest between Poseidon and Athena for the lordship
over Attica, were plastically represented. Even in their present
much damaged condition the surviving figures show the complete mastery which the artist had attained in every detail
of his art. We may instance the superb modelling of the nude
male figures, as in the recumbent figure of "Theseus" or the
torso of Poseidon, and the elaborate drapery of the seated female figures. Though Pheidias may not have executed any

part of the Parthenon sculptures himself, it is usually conceded that the general design is his, the execution being left to other artists working under his direction. Pheidias was famous above all for his portrayal of divinities, his two masterpieces being the gold and ivory statues of colossal size of Athena Parthenos, placed in the newly built temple on the Acropolis, and the statue of Zeus Olympios at Olympia. It is impossible to form any adequate conception of either of these works from late and small copies, or from coin representations.[1]

Of Peloponnesian artists who flourished during the fifth century the most renowned was the Argive Polycleitus, the younger contemporary of Pheidias. Polycleitus was the author of a gold and ivory cult-statue of Hera at Argos, which was greatly admired in antiquity. But his forte was the rendering of nude athletes. Two statues especially are known from numerous marble replicas — for the originals were bronze — namely, his Doryphoros, or youth carrying a spear, and his Diadumenos, or youth tying a fillet about his head. The attitude embodied in these works was that of arrested motion. The weight of the body rests on one leg, while the other is lightly poised and drawn back a little way. The head is turned towards the leg on which the weight rests. The ancients praised especially the perfect proportions of the Polycleitan athletes, the result of a profound anatomical study. Even in inferior copies this is apparent. At the same time the type of adolescent or youth is somewhat heavy, almost thick-set. Sculptors of the nude male figure in the next century evolved a type of slimmer build.

We must now pass on to other works by the architect Ictinus. He enlarged the Telesterion at Eleusis, so that the great initiation-hall measured 170 feet square; and it was supported by six rows of seven Doric columns. Contemporary with the building of the Parthenon was the construction of the great entrance gateway to the Acropolis, the so-called Propylæa, the work of Mnesicles, begun in 437 and finished five years later. During the earlier part of the Peloponnesian war there was little further beautification of Athens; but towards the end of the century came the erection of the exquisite little temple to Athena Nike on the southwest corner of the Acropolis and

---

[1] Cf. the quotation from Quintilian at the beginning of this chapter.

of the joint temple to Athena and the hero Erechtheus, called the Erechtheum. In both these buildings the Ionic order was used (Plates 25 and 27). A bold departure from convention was made by Ictinus in the third of his great works, the temple of Apollo near Phigaleia in Arcadia. The architect combined the Doric with the Ionic order by introducing Ionic half-columns in the interior of the cella. Between the last two — there were six on a side — was placed a single Corinthian pillar. Though the effect was impressive, the innovation was not generally copied. The artist Scopas, however, in the next century combined all three orders in the temple of Athena Alea at Tegea in Arcadia.

Among the Greeks of Asia Minor the Ionic order remained the favorite. Although the fifth century seems to have been a period of artistic depression there, the fourth was marked by a great revival of art. The most noble temple erected in that age, and one of the most famous buildings of antiquity, was the new temple, replacing the sixth-century structure, of Artemis at Ephesus. It was an octostyle temple in the Ionic order with columns on the long sides. The lowest drums of the columns on the east front were sculptured in relief. A remarkable building in the Ionic style was the tomb of Mausolus, native prince of Caria, who died in 352. This lofty edifice was composed of a substructure 42 feet in height, a cella surrounded by an Ionic colonnade and resting on the substructure, and a stepped pyramid forming the roof and crowning the whole. Many sculptures adorned this building, in the construction and decoration of which several of the leading artists of Greece were said to have been employed. Room was found for no less than three friezes, depicting a battle of Greeks and Amazons, a Centauromachy, and a chariot race. Between the columns of the peristyle stood equestrian and other statues. Finally, on the summit of the Mausoleum stood a chariot, perhaps containing statues of more than life-size of Mausolus and his queen, Artemisia.[1] Considerable remains of the friezes, the

---

[1] It is, however, doubtful whether the extant statues of Mausolus and Artemisia ever stood in the chariot. Though damaged, their general state of preservation is so good that they are more likely to have been placed in the interior of the building.

statues of the two rulers — unfortunately in a rather damaged condition — and a number of other fragments can still be studied in the British Museum.   The fourth century, like the fifth, produced many sculptors of merit; but three, Praxiteles, Scopas, and Lysippus, surpassed all the others.   The first and second were approximately contemporaries, and their artistic activity belongs to the first half of the century.   From the hand of Praxiteles we possess one undoubted original in the marble statue of Hermes holding the infant Dionysus, which was found by the excavators at Olympia.   Though reckoned a minor work in antiquity, the statue has a unique interest and value for us in being an original.   Contrasted with the athletic statues of Polycleitus, which, it is true, are known only from copies, we note in the Hermes more graceful proportions of the human figure together with a more delicate treatment of the muscles and texture of the flesh.   The head is highly idealized, the perfection of Greek male beauty (Plate 29).[1]   Praxiteles' versatility was notorious in antiquity.   He worked both in bronze and in marble, though more often in the latter material, and the range of subjects depicted by him was unusually diversified. He made many statues of divinities, the most famous of all being his Aphrodite at Cnidus.   It was an innovation to represent the nude female figure, above all in a goddess, who in this work was portrayed as preparing for the bath.   Although the statue is known to us only from replicas, we can still admire the beauty of the head — a worthy peer of the Hermes — and the grace of the pose, the modelling of the flesh, and the skillful treatment of the drapery which the goddess is allowing to glide down on to the hydria at her side.   Praxiteles made no less than three statues of Eros, of which the most admired was the cult-statue at Thespiæ in Bœotia.   The god of love was represented by the artist as a youth on the threshold of manhood and with wings.   A similar conception is found also on Attic red-figure vases; for the portrayal of Eros as a chubby infant belongs to the later Hellenistic and Græco-Roman

---

[1] The genuineness of the statue has recently been questioned, though, in the opinion of the present writer, on insufficient grounds.   For the opinions of various archæologists see *American Journal of Archæology* XXXV (1931), *passim.*

ages. Famous, too, were Praxiteles' statues of the young Apollo
slaying a lizard (Apollo Sauroktonos) and of a youthful satyr.

A fine example, by an unknown artist, of a draped female
figure of the fourth century is provided by a statue of Demeter
now in the British Museum (Plate 30). Some critics have found
in it marks of Praxitelean influence, but the expression of the
beautiful head seems rather to recall the art of Scopas. Of
him, besides his work on the temple at Tegea, far fewer works
are recorded than in the case of his eminent contemporary.
Among the most successful of his creations was a Bacchant
portrayed in a state of Dionysiac frenzy. The ancient writers
stress Scopas' skill in depicting passion and emotional depth
in his figures. He seems to have been, in a sense, the ancestor
of the greater realism in art, sometimes transcending what can
safely be attempted in sculpture without grotesqueness, which
characterized many of the productions of the Hellenistic Age.

Lysippus was the contemporary of Alexander the Great, of
whom he made many portraits in bronze; extant busts of the
great conqueror are probably all to some extent reminiscent of
Lysippean originals (Plate 34). The artist, who is the best
representative of the Peloponnesian art of the fourth century —
Praxiteles was an Athenian, Scopas a native of Paros — was
extremely prolific. His statue of Poseidon became, as it were,
the canonical representation of that deity, even as Pheidias
had made the ideal types of Athena and Zeus, and Polycleitus
of Hera. Poseidon was portrayed standing with one foot resting
on a rock, while in his hand he held the emblem of his power,
the trident. Lysippus was also the author of several statues of
Heracles; one of these, made for Taras in southern Italy, was
of colossal size, and later on was carried off to Rome by Fabius
Maximus. Besides his portraits and his statues of divinities,
Lysippus was the creator of many athletic figures. His Apoxy-
omenos, representing a youth using a strigil, is known only from
an indifferent copy. We can form a better conception of Lysippean art from the marble statue of the Thessalian Agias,
found by the French excavators at Delphi. The original was
bronze, but the surviving copy is contemporary and was perhaps
made under the author's direct supervision. Agias had won
fame by victories at all four national festivals; but the statue

DEMETER
(Original of the Fourth Century)

Plate 30

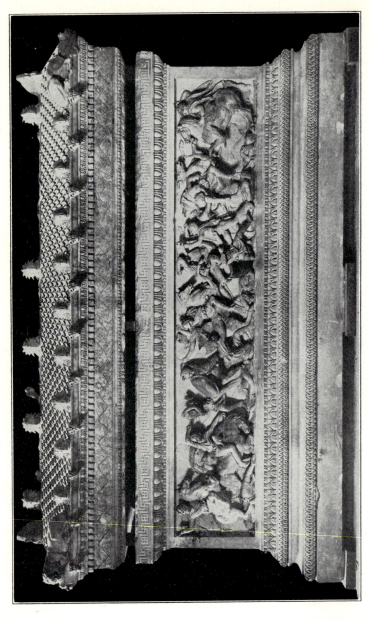

THE ALEXANDER SARCOPHAGUS

Plate 31

is an idealization not a portrait. The muscular development of torso and limbs is finely wrought; the proportions are noticeably more slender than those of Polycleitan athletes. The facial expression is one of concentration and strength; this effect is mainly produced by setting the eyes deep at the inner corners, so that they are rather close together. The authorship of the so-called Alexander sarcophagus (Plate 31) is not known. It was found at Sidon in 1887 and is a glorious specimen of fourth-century work. On the two long sides are represented a battle between Alexander and the Persians, and a lion hunt. The short sides are adorned with a panther hunt and another skirmish between Persians and Greeks. In the gables of the lid are other scenes from war. The whole was elaborately colored, blue, purple, violet, yellow, and two shades of red being employed. This practice, as we have already seen, was followed by the Greeks both for their marble statues and on certain parts of temples.

It is a remarkable fact that the age which saw a great decline in dramatic composition was characterized by more luxurious theatre-building. In the fifth century the masterpieces of the great poets were performed in temporary structures, built mostly of wood. The fine stone theatres, of which a number are still to be seen in Greek lands, belong to the fourth century or to the Hellenistic Age. One of the earliest, and in point of preservation the finest of all, is that at Epidaurus, the work of Polycleitus the younger. The stone theatre at Athens belongs to the second half of the century, although parts of what can still be seen — for instance, the tessellated floor of the orchestra — are of much later, that is to say, of Græco-Roman, date (Plate 32a). Other fourth-century examples are the large theatre at Megalepolis and the smaller structure at Thoricus in Attica. Those at Priene in Asia Minor and at Delos are Hellenistic.

Of the art of the great painters in these centuries — Polygnotus in the first half, Zeuxis and Parrhasius in the second half of the fifth century, Apelles in the age of Alexander — and of many lesser artists besides, it is difficult to form any definite judgment. For, though there is no lack of references to their works and to the general character of their art, such statements do not compensate us for the absence of actual specimens of their painting. True, famous works were sometimes copied in later ages; here and there a surviving fresco at Herculaneum or Pompeii may be imitated from, or reminiscent of, a classical masterpiece. Thus an extant Pompeian wall-painting, representing the sacrifice of Iphigeneia at Aulis, is very probably a reproduction of the most famous work of Timanthes, a painter who lived in the fourth century. Yet to attempt to judge of the one by the other would be not unlike appraising a Rubens from an indifferent oleograph.

Polygnotus (flourished *c.* 470) was famous for the large frescoes, mostly of mythological scenes, that he painted in the Lesche at Delphi and in two public buildings at Athens. He used only a very few colors; there was an absence of light and shade, and but little perspective. But his draughtsmanship must have been highly skilled and subtle, and ancient critics praised especially his transcendent ability to express the character of his human subjects in his portrayal of their faces. Zeuxis and Parrhasius paid more attention to perspective and to shading; they were also pioneers of the new fashion which preferred easel pictures of moderate size to grand frescoes. The female figures of Zeuxis are said to have been executed with unrivalled mastery. Subjects from mythology still predominated. Apelles, too, produced several works of this kind; but his fame rested primarily on his portraits, a type of painting that received little attention before his time. Doubtless the fact that he painted various members of the Macedonian court and made several portraits of Alexander himself helped to spread the artist's renown, even as it certainly did much to popularize portraiture.

But, if we can form only a dim conception of Greek painting in the classical period, the humbler art of the Attic vase-painters can still be studied in all its detail by the specialist. It reached its zenith in the fifth century. The so-called red-figure vases show extreme beauty and great variety in their shapes. The designs were now commonly carried out by a different artist, and are distinguished by marvellous skill in the portrayal of muscles, draperies, and every kind of pose and action. There is, too, an all but infinite diversity of subjects depicted: mythological episodes in endless profusion; scenes from daily life, for example, the school, the palæstra, and the banquet; Dionysiac revels, and other kinds of religious celebrations. The popularity of the works of the Attic potters and vase-painters was maintained throughout the fifth century, but the later specimens, though they exhibit no less skill, in addition to innovations in treatment, brighter coloration by the use of subsidiary colors, and more abundant ornamentation, lack the freshness and naturalism of the best fifth-century works. Then, in the fourth century, the Athenian ceramic industry declined. The most productive and successful centres of manufacture in that century and the next were to be found in the West, in the Greek cities of southern Italy.

CHAPTER XXIII

THE EMPIRE OF ALEXANDER THE GREAT

> *The Stoic state is directed to this one all-embracing principle, that we should not order our lives by cities and by parishes, and our outlook should not be determined by our several private interests, but we should regard all men as fellow citizens and fellow townsmen, and there should be one single life and world, as it were, one gregarious flock reared in common by a common Law. This is the ideal laid down by Zeno, imagined by him as a dream or image of a philosophic good order and state: but Alexander added the deed to the word.*
> — Plutarch, *On the excellence of Alexander* i, 6.

WHEN he succeeded to the throne, Alexander, then only twenty years of age, was faced almost at once with a situation which would have tested to the utmost the resources of a mature man. But over and above his own transcendent natural gifts, he had had the ideal education of a prince and had shouldered responsibility at an exceptionally early age. From the time that he was thirteen he had had Aristotle as his tutor. Thus, besides his training in physical and military exercises and in hunting, in all of which he excelled from early youth, his intellectual education was directed by the profoundest thinker of the age. Already at sixteen Alexander had been entrusted with a position of authority, while at Chæronea he had fought with conspicuous bravery and success. Philip's death was the signal for general unrest in Greece; it needed only the appearance of Alexander at the head of a military force to suppress for the time being the anti-Macedonian feelings there. He was formally elected as his father's successor in the Amphictionic League, and also as commander-in-chief of the League of Corinth. Early in 335 B.C. he conducted difficult campaigns in the interior of Thrace, which took him as far as the Danube,

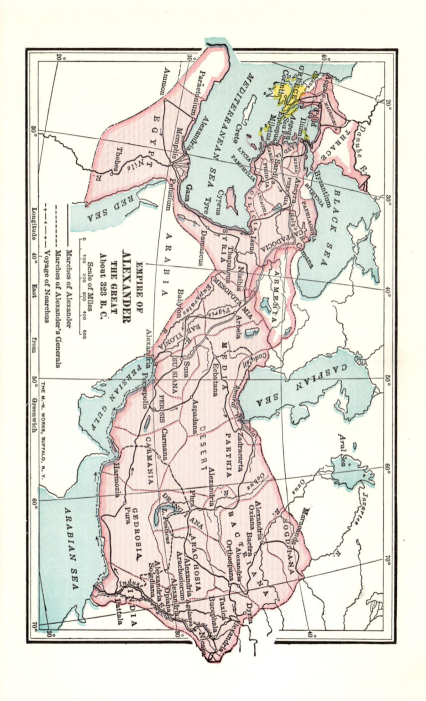

EMPIRE OF
ALEXANDER
THE GREAT
About 323 B.C.

Scale of Miles
0 100 200 300 400 500

———————— Marches of Alexander
------------ Marches of Alexander's Generals
—·—·—·— Voyage of Nearchus

Longitude 40° East from 50° Greenwich 60° 70°

THE M.-N. WORKS, BUFFALO, N. Y.

and he also suppressed an Illyrian rising. A false rumor of his death reaching Greece was at once followed by the revolt of Thebes. Alexander's swift descent on that city stopped the progress of the Greek insurrection. The disloyal city was captured and razed to the ground, the temples and the house of Pindar alone being spared. The people were sold as slaves. Such signal severity could not but intimidate the rest of Greece; also Macedonian garrisons continued as before to be stationed in the Theban Cadmeia, at Chalcis, and at Corinth.

The young ruler now prepared to carry out his father's plans for a war against Persia and for the conquest of Asia Minor. Disaffection had been rife in the western satrapies of the Persian empire throughout the fourth century, while Egypt, which had revolted in 404, had remained for seventy years independent under a succession of native dynasts.[1] They relied largely on mercenaries for fighting material, and on occasion engaged some of the ablest Greek commanders in their service, for example, the Spartan king, Agesilaus, and Chabrias, the Athenian. It will suffice to mention only the most salient episodes in the political disintegration of a once united empire. In 389 the ruler of Salamis in Cyprus, Evagoras, with some Egyptian support, made himself master of practically the whole island. This dominant position he retained till 380 when he finally succumbed to the vastly greater resources of the Great King; but he was granted honorable terms. He reigned until his death (374) as a vassal of Artaxerxes II and was succeeded by his son Nicocles. More formidable to Persian interests was a rebellion in 366 in which the satraps of Phrygia, Armenia, Lydia, and Caria participated. Many of the Anatolian Greek cities were drawn into the revolt as well, while Egypt also lent some support. The authority of the Great King was not reëstablished till 359, and then more owing to the absence of coöperation and of a unified plan among the seditious governors than through the efficiency of the central government. Artaxerxes II died in the following year. His successor, Artaxerxes III, seems to have been a man of decidedly more vigor. After more than one attempt, Egypt was at last recovered by

---

[1] In the classification of Manetho these princes make up the XXVIIIth, XXIXth, and XXXth Dynasties.

him in 343–342; but neither the Egyptians nor the majority of the Phœnician cities, which had previously given some aid to Egypt, were hereafter well disposed to Persia, a fact made sufficiently clear a few years later when the victorious Alexander appeared in the East.

The young ruler now prepared to carry out his father's plans for a war against Persia and for the conquest of Asia Minor. In the spring of 334 he crossed the Hellespont with an army of not less than 30,000 infantry and 5000 cavalry, drawn from Macedonia, the Greek cities of the League, and from some other regions. On the River Granicus he won his first victory against a decidedly smaller Persian army, commanded by the Great King's ablest officer, Memnon. Many of the Greek cities in Asia Minor readily went over to Alexander. In general his approval of democratic governments brought about the downfall of the Tyrants or oligarchies who had ruled under Persian suzerainty. But the conquest of Asia Minor — or the greater portion of it — did not pass off without much fighting. Miletus and Halicarnassus were both captured only after a siege. His fleet, recruited from the allied Greeks, Alexander now dismissed, leaving the Persian navy at large in the Aegean. But his calculation that it would effect little damage to his interests or his lines of communication, and, especially, that Persian attempts to draw the Greek states of the islands and the mainland on to a general anti-Macedonian rebellion would prove futile, was correct. In 333, after conquering Cilicia, he descended into northern Syria, where he found his progress barred by a Persian host, commanded by Darius III in person. This prince, the last of the Achæmenid line of Persian kings, had come to the throne three years before. The size of the forces engaged in this great battle near Issus was greatly exaggerated in antiquity, and cannot be determined with any certainty. Alexander's army must have been slightly smaller than that which fought at the River Granicus. For, though he had received reinforcements, he had also been obliged to leave some garrison troops in Asia Minor. Hence it can hardly have numbered much over 25,000 men all told. The army of Darius, composed partly of orientals, partly of Greek mercenaries, was perhaps 30,000–35,000 strong. Although the Great King had won a tactical advantage in choosing the site where he compelled the Macedonians to fight, neither he nor his staff were Alexander's equals as strategists in the actual battle. The Persian guard and the Greek mercenaries put up a good fight, but the flight of Darius was followed by a general break-up and pell-mell retreat of his army. It was a great victory for Alexander, and its political consequences were far-reaching. The disaffection, which was still latent in Greece and which might well have burst forth into a general revolt against Macedonian overlordship, such as Alexander's regent, Antipater, would have found it difficult to suppress from Macedonia with the limited troops at his disposal, was succeeded by wiser counsels when the news of Alexander's triumph at Issus became known. The Syrian and Egyptian provinces of the Persian empire, for their part, were far from being genuinely loyal to Darius. The realization of this fact must have weighed heavily with Alexander, who, as is probable, now and now only envisaged as a possibility the conquest of the Persian empire.

Save for two places, Syria passed into his hands without resistance. But Tyre and Gaza stood out and had to be reduced by force. The siege of Tyre, which lasted for seven months, was one of Alexander's greatest achievements. The defenders, whose city stood on an island, expended all their skill and ingenuity in beating off the Macedonian attack; but each new defensive measure Alexander countered by fresh devices. Finally, after the Tyrian fleet had been destroyed or captured, a grand assault was made and part of the wall breached. As the men of Tyre had slain some Macedonian prisoners they could expect no mercy at the hands of the victorious enemy. After the slaughter of the fighting men and the sale of the non-combatants into slavery, Tyre was occupied by a Macedonian garrison. Later in the year Gaza also fell after a spirited resistance. Egypt passed into Alexander's power without a struggle; for the Persian governor, knowing that the people were disaffected to Persia, took no risks and surrendered at once to the conqueror. The most momentous event of his visit to Egypt was the foundation of the city of Alexandria on the Egyptian coast, close to the Canopic mouth of the Nile. It was the first, and proved to be the greatest, of the numerous settlements established by, and in this, as in many other cases, named after, Alexander. If, in the first place, the new city was intended to replace Tyre as the great harbor and exchange mart between East and West, it is not unlikely that the founder to some extent foresaw that its admirable situation would quickly make it the foremost port in the whole Mediterranean. Alexander's visit to the desert and oasis, where was situated the oracle of Amen, who was identified with Zeus by the Greeks and whose prophecies were regarded with peculiar veneration, was a romantic episode rather than a profound act of policy. Yet the Egyptian priests, seeing in him the successor of the Pharaohs, acknowledged him as the son of Amen-Ra, in other words, as a god and the son of a god.

Meanwhile the terms which had been proposed by Darius III had been rejected by Alexander; and in the spring of 331 he returned to Syria. From there he advanced to Mesopotamia, crossing the Euphrates at Thapsacus, where Parmenio had carried out orders by constructing a bridge of boats, and then the Tigris without encountering serious opposition. The Great King, instead of trying to bar his progress at the Euphrates, had mustered an army considerably greater than that which fought at Issus in a level plain between the Tigris and a tributary. The third of the engagements between Alexander and the Persians was fought on October 1, 331, and derives its name from the small village of Gaugamela close to the battlefield, or, alternatively, from the more considerable town of Arbela, some miles to the southeast. The battle was stubbornly contested; but, as in the previous year, with the flight of Darius himself, once it became known, the Persian lines gave way and a general pursuit by the victors followed. While the defeated monarch fled into Media, the conqueror marched on Babylon, which opened its gates to him. From there he undertook the invasion of Persis, and, after defeating the satrap Ariobarzanes, captured Persepolis and Pasargadæ. In these royal residences, as in the capital at Susa, which had already submitted, he secured immense quantities of silver and other spoil, the coin and bullion alone being estimated at not less than 180,000 talents. The palace at Persepolis was set on fire by the conqueror, a token that the royal line of Persia had come to an end. In the

spring of 330 he entered Media; having received the submission
of Ecbatana, he hastened on in pursuit of Darius, who was now
the virtual prisoner of Bessus, satrap of Bactria. Soon after,
the Persian king was killed by his companions before Alexander
could seize his person. The assassins escaped.

From 330 to 328 Alexander was fully occupied with the difficult task of conquering the northeastern provinces of the
empire. By the victory at Gaugamela, followed by the death
of Darius, he had been accepted as the successor of the Persian
kings; but in the more outlying regions there was still much
resistance to be overcome. His campaigns in these years took
him as far east as Bactria and Sogdiana, that is to say, to
Afghanistan and Turkestan. His chief opponents were Bessus,
who had assumed the kingly title after Darius' death, and
Spitamenes of Sogdiana, whose military skill gave Alexander
more trouble than that of any other opponent. By the end
of 328 both had been reduced. Alexander's progress through
these distant regions was marked by the foundation of many
new settlements and colonies, whose importance for the subsequent spread of Hellenism was incalculable.

In 327 his restless ambition led him to invade northern
India. A considerable part of this region had once, in the days
of Darius I, been a Persian province; but it had long since passed
out of the control of his successors. Of the many princes in this
country some at once allied themselves with Alexander, others
opposed his passage. Of the latter the most notable was King
Porus who confronted him with a large host on the Hydaspes
(Jhelum) River. He was defeated; but, after surrendering, he
was reinstated in his kingdom and became Alexander's ally.
Soon after, the further progress of the Macedonian conqueror
was brought to an abrupt end by the action of his troops.
Having arrived at the River Hyphasis (Beas) they mutinied.
Wearied by the strain of continuous campaigns in exceptionally
difficult country, and exhausted also by the severity of an unfamiliar climate, they refused to march on into unknown regions.
Alexander remained for three days in retirement in his tent,
hoping that this mark of royal displeasure would change their
minds. But, when they remained obdurate, he could not but
yield, and so he made his way to Patala near the mouth of

the Indus. On the way he fought a campaign against the Malli, in the course of which he contracted a wound which was nearly fatal. From Patala Alexander led his army through the Gedrosian desert (Baluchistan), while his admiral Nearchus was sent, in charge of the fleet, which had been built on the Jhelum at the beginning of the Indian campaign, to explore the sea-route to the head of the Persian Gulf and the mouths of the Tigris and Euphrates. The record of observations, which the admiral took along the whole coast as he skirted it, were of great practical value, as Alexander had intended them to be. For his purpose was to develop for commerce a direct sea route between the estuary of the Indus and the Euphrates. The return of the army was attended by terrible casualties, since, owing to the heat and lack of water, many of his men dropped on the road and failed to rise again. It was but a remnant of his army which at last reached the region of Carmania safely.

During the year 324, which Alexander passed partly at Susa, partly at Opis on the Tigris, and at Ecbatana, he was busy mainly with problems of imperial organization, and under the necessity of rectifying abuses which had crept into the administration during his prolonged absence in the Far East. Early in 323 he moved to Babylon and now elaborated plans for an Arabian expedition. But in June he contracted a fever from which, worn out as he was by his tremendous exertions, not by the intemperance which later detractors with insufficient proof have attributed to him, he never recovered. After nearly a fortnight's illness he died in the thirty-third year of his age.

In all the ancient accounts of Alexander his military achievements are narrated with more or less detail, and, according to the sources used, with very varying degrees of accuracy. Concerning his eminence as a general ancients and moderns are agreed. As one scholar has recently observed, "that he was a great general is certain; Napoleon's verdict suffices." [1] We may cite, too, the verdict of a great nineteenth-century historian of Greece: [2]

We trace in all his operations the most careful dispositions taken beforehand, vigilant precaution in guarding against possible reverse,

[1] W. W. Tarn in *Cambridge Ancient History*, vi, page 425. His chapters are now easily the best account in English of Alexander's career.
[2] G. Grote, *History of Greece*, xii, chapter 94.

and abundant resource in adapting himself to new contingencies. Amidst constant success, these precautionary combinations were never discontinued. His achievements are the earliest recorded evidence of scientific military organization on a large scale and of its overwhelming effects.

Of what Alexander actually accomplished in the way of organizing his huge empire, and of his further plans to weld it together, we hear but little. Even the work of conquest was incomplete at the time of his death; for example, northern Asia Minor as far as the Caspian Sea, together with Armenia, all territory which had formed part of the Persian empire, had been left untouched by him. Nor had there been time for the conqueror to devise any permanent system of imperial government. The absence of this, coupled with the withdrawal of Alexander's unique personality, which alone had held a vast empire together, after his death resulted in the immediate partition of these dominions. Nor can it be said that his temporary measures for ruling the former Persian empire were greatly successful. As in Persian days, the territories were divided into provinces or satrapies, and at first some positions of high authority were entrusted to Persians as well as to Macedonians. But this plan did not work out well, and the king was obliged to replace oriental by western governors. But even the Macedonian officials, whom he left in charge in western Asia and in Mesopotamia during his progress to central Asia and India, proved in many cases unworthy of this trust, having been guilty of peculation and worse forms of misrule. The most notorious offender was Harpalus, who had been left in charge of the royal treasury at Babylon. After a riotous career there, Harpalus, having embezzled a vast sum, retired to Tarsus, and, finally, with the remnants of his spoil fled to Greece. Thus, when Alexander returned from India, he found it necessary to make many changes in his administrative personnel.

In the course of his advance eastward he had founded many new cities, most of them being half Græco-Macedonian, half oriental in population. These, of which there are said to have been no less than seventy, were important for insuring the security of the empire; still more, however, Alexander wished their function to be the dissemination of Hellenic culture in the Ori-

ent. Not a few were named after himself, and, being situated
most favorably for both military and commercial communications, have retained much of their importance to this day.
Such were Alexandreschate (Chodjend) on the Jaxartes, Alexandria Areion (Herat) in the northwest, and Alexandria Aracho-
ton (Candahar) in the south of Afghanistan. His efforts to
fuse the inhabitants of East and West more completely by promoting the intermarriage of Macedonians or Greeks with
Iranians, and by creating corps of oriental troops carefully
trained on the Macedonian model, had little permanent effect.
Such drastic measures were doomed to failure, whereas the
gradual spread of Greek ideas and customs and, in many of the
cities, of Greek law, continued undisturbed in the centuries
that followed. Of immense value for promoting commercial
intercourse between different parts of the empire were his
monetary reforms. He introduced a uniform silver currency
throughout his vast realm, adopting the Attic standard for the
purpose, and abolishing the gold standard of Persia. His silver
coins were issued from a large number of mints in different parts
of the empire; in a few cases he appears to have permitted
older local issues to continue for a space.

There was one aspect of Alexander's policy which gave serious
offense to some of his Macedonian subjects, and which at the
same time had important developments in the Hellenistic Age.
The heroization of dead persons was a very ancient form of
religious practice in Greece; isolated instances are recorded, at
all events in the fourth century, of divine or semi-divine honors
being paid to a living personage, for example, to Lysander by
the people of Samos. But the deification of the reigning monarch, which Alexander demanded of the Greek cities in 324,
when he asked them to honor him as a divine being, was to
introduce into Hellas what was essentially an Eastern conception
and usage. The theocracy of the Egyptian kings has already
been noted; in Persia, though the ruler was not deified, Darius
and his successors described themselves as under the protection
of Ahura-Mazda.[1] Moreover, the servile adoration which they
demanded and received from their subjects would be construed
by Westerners as a mark of divinity. The earlier stages in Alex-

[1] Cf. the citation at the beginning of Chapter XIV above.

ander's progress towards this un-Hellenic claim to divine king-ship, which should be regarded as a matter of considered policy and not the result of vanity, still less of religious exaltation, were the adoption of oriental dress, of Persian court etiquette, and, finally, of the Persian custom of prostration, to which even his Macedonian staff-officers were expected to conform.

In 330 a conspiracy was detected, and Philotas, who com-manded the pick of the Macedonian cavalry, was implicated; after a summary trial he was put to death. While some excuse can be brought forward for this action of the king, his subse-quent order for the execution of Philotas' father, Parmenion, was a crime. For, not only was Parmenion one of the oldest and most trusted of Macedonian commanders, — he had been one of Philip's chief supporters, — but there was no evidence to con-nect him with the attempted treason. The murder, in a fit of passion, of Cleitus, a trusted officer who had once saved Alex-ander's life, and the execution of Aristotle's nephew, Callis-thenes, who was the court historian, for supposed cognizance of a later conspiracy, were other episodes which have marred the fair fame of the conqueror. These abuses of royal power were due to personal rather than political motives; in the case of Philotas it is likely that reasons of state determined Alexander's action.

Many writers have speculated on what might have happened had Alexander's life been prolonged, and it has often been argued that his Eastern conquests would have been followed by the reduction of Carthage and of Italy, where Rome was by that time the leading state. Not only are such speculations futile in themselves, but they presuppose something for which the evi-dence is lacking. For we have no grounds for believing that, even as late as 323, Alexander had ever conceived the notion of becoming a world conqueror. His projected Arabian expedition is thoroughly attested; but, had it taken place, it would only have rounded off his Asiatic conquests. Of any further plans we know nothing.

CHAPTER XXIV

THE GREEK WORLD UNDER THE SUCCESSORS OF ALEXANDER

> *In general, the imperialism of the Hellenes, though they struggled desperately for supremacy, never secured a firm footing beyond the bounds of Hellas herself. They were wonderfully successful in postponing the evil day of defeat and enslavement, but from the time of Philip, son of Amyntas, and Alexander, son of Philip, they appear to me to have had a history of failure which has been unworthy of their past.* — Appian, *History*, Preface.

1. GREECE AND THE NEAR EAST, 323–221 B.C.

THE unity of the empire ceased abruptly on Alexander's death. Nominally the crown passed to his feeble-minded brother, Philip Arrhidæus; a little later the son of Alexander and Roxane was born, and was associated with his uncle as joint monarch. In reality, political power rested with the chief military commanders and provincial governors, the men who had been Alexander's most trusted helpers. Of these the most notable were Antipater, who had been left behind as regent of Macedonia and Greece; Antigonus, governor of Phrygia; and the army commanders at Babylon, — Perdiccas, Ptolemy, Lysimachus, Eumenes, and Craterus. For the moment Perdiccas secured the regency. But there were too many claimants for the chief authority to make a peaceful division of the empire possible, still less to preserve its unity under a single ruler. From the first we can distinguish certain groups which stood together; thus, Antigonus, Ptolemy, and Craterus were in agreement with Antipater, while Eumenes supported Perdiccas. Before the end of 321 fighting had begun. Craterus was slain in battle, and Perdiccas was murdered by his own troops. A partition of provinces and a division of responsibility followed, but it was of short duration. For, two years later, Antipater died at an advanced age, and the struggle was renewed with more intensity than before. It will suffice to indicate very briefly the main stages in the prolonged warfare between the successors of Alexander from 319 to 281.

During the first twenty years of this period the outstanding personality was Antigonus, who gradually built up for himself a position of exceptional strength. Controlling after a few years Asia Minor, Syria, and Mesopotamia, and master of the royal treasury, he was well on the way toward uniting under his single command the greater part of Alexander's empire. But his successes produced a coalition of rival aspirants for power, who might otherwise have played only for their own hands. Chief of these were Cassander, Antipater's son and now ruler of Macedonia; Lysimachus, governor of Thrace and the Propontis; Ptolemy Lagus, viceroy of Egypt; and Seleucus, who in 321 had obtained the satrapy of Babylon, had subsequently been expelled by Antigonus, and who now joined his enemies. In 312 Seleucus recovered Babylon, and, though he did not yet assume the royal title, the dynasty of which he became the founder dated its origin back to that year.[1]

Supported by his son Demetrius, Antigonus carried on against his rivals with varying fortunes to the year 301. His army, commanded by Demetrius, suffered a severe defeat at Gaza in 312, fighting against the forces of Ptolemy. Six years later Demetrius had his revenge; for he beat an Egyptian fleet off Cypriote Salamis, and followed up this success by occupying the whole island. In the same year, and to commemorate this victory, Antigonus assumed the royal title. His rivals followed suit. Finally, in 301, the armies of Seleucus and Lysimachus won a striking victory over Antigonus' hosts at Ipsus in Phrygia. The defeated monarch, rather than live to endure a diminution of his fortunes, took his own life on the field of battle. The five monarchies into which Alexander's empire had thus been broken up were now reduced to four. Of Anti-

---

[1] For the so-called Seleucid Era see above, page 9.

gonus' realm one part, Asia Minor, fell to Lysimachus' share, while Syria was annexed by Seleucus. Demetrius, legitimate heir of Antigonus, remained without a kingdom, but the powerful fleet which he still commanded made him master of the Mediterranean, and enabled him to control the islands and some important seaport towns. Thus there was little chance that the death of Antigonus would be followed by a cessation of war. Actually the struggles were prolonged for twenty years after Ipsus. With the defeat and death of Lysimachus at the battle of Curupedium (Lydia) in 281 Seleucus became master of Asia Minor. Though he himself was assassinated shortly after, his son Antiochus now ruled over what territorially was the greatest of the three remaining Hellenistic kingdoms.

During this half century after Alexander's death the fortunes of the Greeks, both in Hellas and in the West, had been varied and troubled. The mainland states for the most part were now but pawns in the ruthless game played by their more powerful royal neighbors. The discontent of the Greek city-states had been smouldering ever since Philip II's death. We saw how Thebes had received short shrift, and how the success of Alexander at Issus had damped the spirits of even the most ardent anti-Macedonian patriots. An attempted insurrection by Sparta about the same time was a complete failure. At Athens the years following Chæronea were marked by considerable prosperity, mainly owing to the careful financial administration of Demosthenes' younger contemporary, Lycurgus. The prosecution of a certain Ctesiphon for illegality, in proposing that Demosthenes be rewarded with a gold crown for his patriotism in the struggle against Macedonia, was the *cause célèbre* of 330. Demosthenes undertook the defense, while his old antagonist, Aeschines, acted as prosecutor, and his attack was really aimed at Demosthenes, rather than at Ctesiphon. The trial is only of interest now because the speeches of the two rivals have survived, and because Demosthenes' oration, *On the Crown*, which is in reality a defense of his whole political career, is perhaps the finest of all his utterances. Aeschines lost his case, and retiring from Athens, soon after died.

Of a very different character was the scandal which arose at

Athens in 324.   Harpalus, Alexander's dishonest treasurer, on reaching Greece, tried to foment an anti-Macedonian rebellion. The Athenians detained Harpalus and deposited what was left of his treasure, amounting to a very considerable sum, in the Parthenon.   Within a short time Harpalus escaped, and it was further discovered that half of the bullion had disappeared.   Several prominent persons, among them Demosthenes, were arraigned before the court of the Areopagus for accepting bribes.   Demosthenes, with two other leading men, was found guilty and heavily fined, but, being unable to comply, he went into banishment at Aegina.   The circumstances surrounding this trial are very obscure, and the guilt or innocence of the great Athenian patriot cannot now be established with any certainty.   If he did accept money, we can at least feel sure that he did so for political purposes, not for his personal enrichment.   His exile was of short duration.   For, when the news of Alexander's death reached Athens and Greece, a general insurrection broke out through the country, in which the Athenians and the Aetolians took the lead.   For his patriotic exertions on behalf of the allied Hellenic cause Demosthenes was recalled to his native city.   It devolved on Antipater to stamp out this rebellion; but against so large a muster of opponents his forces were inadequate.   He suffered a defeat in the field, and was then driven back on Lamia in southern Thessaly, where he was besieged through the winter of 323–322. But the Greeks failed to make the best of their opportunities. Reinforcements for the Macedonian viceroy arrived from Asia, and within a few months the tables had been turned.   The Athenian navy suffered two defeats, and in the summer of 322 the allies were heavily beaten at Crannon in Thessaly.   For Athens the terms that she was now compelled to accept were bitter.   A Macedonian garrison was sent to occupy Munychia; the democratic constitution was abrogated and replaced by a moderate oligarchy, in which only some 9000 of her propertied citizens had full civic rights.   Finally, she was obliged to surrender the most prominent of her anti-Macedonian leaders, among them Demosthenes.   But he anticipated capture and certain condemnation to death by committing suicide.

The mainland states, being naturally regarded by the rulers

of Macedon as dependents of that kingdom, were now constantly involved in the greater disputes of the successors of Alexander. For the enemies of Cassander found one means of undermining his power in trying to foster an anti-Macedonian coalition in Hellas. After Cassander's death the Macedonian crown passed to several princes in rapid succession, and in these wars, too, at least a part of the Greeks were more than neutral spectators. The political life of Athens was especially stormy during these years. Not long after Antipater's settlement civil disturbances there led to changes of government, until in 317 the city passed under the able administration of Demetrius of Phalerum. He owed his position, and the maintenance of it for ten years, to the close support of Cassander and the continued presence of a Macedonian garrison in Munychia. Though he was regarded by many as a Tyrant under another name, the decade of his administration was one of peace and prosperity for the Athenians. But in 307 the city was taken by Demetrius, nicknamed "the besieger of cities" (Poliorketes), the son of Antigonus. He was hailed by the Athenians as a liberator because he permitted them to restore their democratic régime. The city now became one of the chief prizes in the contest between Demetrius Poliorketes and Cassander for the control of Greece, and its history was correspondingly troubled. In 303, when Demetrius' power was at its height, he revived under the presidency of his father and himself the Hellenic League of Corinth created by Philip II thirty-five years before. The disaster at Ipsus in 301 reacted strongly on the political situation in Greece, and the League rapidly went to pieces. For thirty-eight more years the Athenians, amid varying fortunes, maintained a partial political independence; finally they succumbed before a new Macedonian ruler in the so-called Chremonidean war, — it was named after a leading Athenian politician, Chremonides, — and from 263 their city became virtually a Macedonian outpost in Greece.

Of the greater Hellenistic kingdoms Egypt was the most secure, and its kings, the Ptolemies, though they suffered occasional reverses at the hands of their rivals, were safe in the possession of the country, sheltered by a powerful fleet. For a time they were masters also of southern Syria and overlords over a number of communities in the Aegean. Internally, Egypt, as will subsequently appear, in the third century enjoyed a period of astonishing prosperity, while the capital, Alexandria, besides its commercial preëminence became a centre of scientific and intellectual activity. The great empire of Seleucus and his son Antiochus was too far-flung to endure in its entirety. In Asia Minor several independent states came into being under local princes, although their political fortunes were inevitably linked to some extent with those of their more powerful neighbors. Such minor kingdoms or principalities were Armenia, Pontus, Bithynia, and Cappadocia.

There is a certain element of romance in the meteoric rise to power of Pergamum in northwestern Asia Minor and of its rulers. This strongly fortified city had for a space been held by Lysimachus; but its governor, Philetærus, had gone over to Seleucus in 281, subsequently becoming the acknowledged ruler of the city and a vassal of Syria. Moreover, the Syrian king left him in possession of the abundant treasure stored in the city by Lysimachus. During the eighteen years of his rule Philetærus continued on good terms with Syria; at the same time he used his wealth to cement good relations with his Greek neighbors on the coast and to build up a strong military force composed of mercenaries. His successor, Eumenes, after defeating a Syrian army in the field, attained complete political independence. Under him and later rulers the territory of Pergamum was steadily enlarged, and Pergamum became the strongest, as well as the richest, of the lesser kingdoms of the Near East. It was the shrewd policy of its rulers to watch with care the political moves of the three greater monarchies, Egypt, Syria, and Macedon, and, by their adherence to one side or another, to exert a decisive influence on the course of international affairs.[1]

The far-eastern or central Asiatic portions of the old Persian empire also became separate states by the middle of the third century. Most noteworthy were the kingdom of Bactria, and especially the realm formed out of the old territories of Persis and Media by the Parthians, a half-civilized Iranian people of

[1] Attalus I, the successor of Eumenes, was the first Pergamene ruler to assume the title of king.

whom little is heard before this date. This Parthian kingdom was, however, destined to develop into a great empire, the rival of Rome for the control of the Near and Middle East.

As if the confusion on both sides of the Aegean caused by the warring ambitions of rival monarchs were not enough, a new and unexpected complication in the political situation was produced by the invasions of the Celts or Gauls — the Greeks called them Galatæ — in 279 and the following years. While one horde overran Macedonia in 279, and northern central Greece as far as Delphi in 278, other tribes invaded Thrace and Asia Minor. In Greece the chief credit for defeating and then expelling the enemy belonged to the Aetolians. In Asia Minor the Gaulish marauders tarried longer, and finally settled in northern Phrygia, or, as it now came to be called, Galatia. In Thrace Antigonus Gonatas, son of Demetrius Poliorketes, defeated the Celts in 277. Till then he had only some possessions which his father had held in Greece. But, after his striking victory, he entered Macedonia and secured the throne, which his father had held before him for a brief period, in 276. The founder of a new Macedonian dynasty had to fight hard for a dozen years to maintain his position. At first he was attacked and all but expelled by Pyrrhus of Epirus, a region which, after being a Macedonian dependency for many years, had under the rule of this able prince become a formidable and independent military power.[1] Pyrrhus was killed fighting in Greece in 272; but not long afterward Antigonus' resources were strained to the utmost by a war against Egypt and a coalition of Hellenic states, of which Athens was the chief (266–262), the Chremonidean war to which reference has already been made. Although the later years of his reign — he died in 239 — were seldom free from war, Antigonus made of Macedonia a great and united kingdom, such as it had not been since the days of Philip and Alexander. His suzerainty over a great portion of Greece, secured after the Chremonidean war, did not remain unshaken.

The most formidable obstacle to a united Greek confederation under Macedonian overlordship were two leagues, whose growth in the third century was one of the most interesting

[1] For the Greeks of the West after the time of Timoleon and for Pyrrhus' operations in Italy and Sicily see below, p. 413.

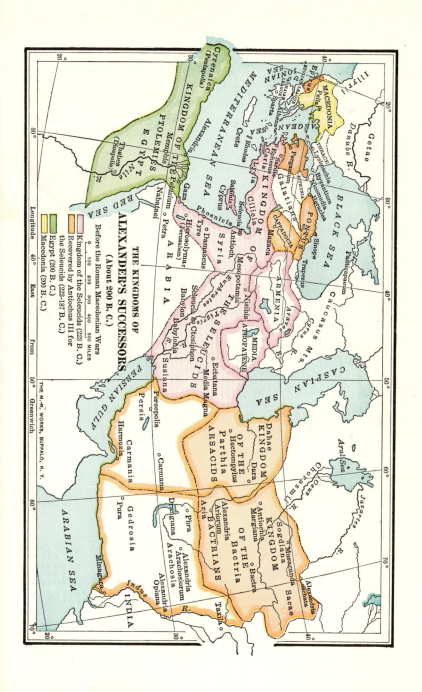

THE KINGDOMS OF
ALEXANDER'S SUCCESSORS
(About 200 B. C.)
Before the Roman Macedonian Wars

0   100   200   300   400   500 MILES

Egypt (200 B. C.)
Macedonia (200 B. C.)
Recovered by Antiochus III for
the Seleucids (223-187 B. C.)
Kingdom of the Seleucids (223 B. C.)

Longitude   40°   East   from   50°   Greenwich

THE M. K. WORKS, BUFFALO, N. Y.

MEDITERRANEAN SEA

AEGEAN SEA

IONIAN SEA

BLACK SEA

CASPIAN SEA

ARABIAN SEA

PERSIAN GULF

RED SEA

ARABIAN SEA

KINGDOM OF THE PTOLEMIES EGYPT

KINGDOM OF EGYPT

THE SELEUCIDS

KINGDOM OF THE ARSACIDS

KINGDOM OF THE BACTRIANS

MACEDONIA

THRACE

PONTUS

ARMENIA

CAPPADOCIA

GALATIANS

CYRENAICA
(Pentapolis)

Cyrene

Alexandria

Memphis

Thebes (Diospolis)

Pelusium

Gaza

Petra

Nabataei

ARABIA

Damascus

Tyre

Sidon

Hierosolyma
(Jerusalem)

Phoenicia

Salamis
Cyprus

Antioch

Seleucia

Crete

Rhodes

Caria

Lycia

Cilicia

Ephesus

Sardis

Pergamum

Byzantium

Nicomedia

Heraclea

Sinope

Trapezus

Caucasus Mts.

Cyrus R.

Araxes R.

ATROPATENE

MEDIA

Nisibis

Mesopotamia

Euphrates R.

Tigris R.

Babylon

Babylonia

Seleucia

Ctesiphon

Echatana

Media Magna

Susiana

Susa

Persepolis

Persis

Carmania

Carmana

Harmozia

Gedrosia

Pura

INDIA

Indus R.

Minagara

Drangiana

Phra

Arachosia

Alexandria
Arachosiorum

Alexandria
Opiana

Taxila

Aria

Alexandria
Ariorum

BACTRIA

Antiochia
Margiana

Alexandria
Margiana

Parthia

Hecatompylus

Dara

KINGDOM
OF THE
Dahae

Sacae

Sogdiana

Maracanda

Alexandria
Eschata

Jaxartes R.

Oxus R.

Chorasmii

Aral Sea

Getae

Danube R.

Illyrii

Epirus

Pella

MACEDONIA

Corinth

Athens

Sparta

Thebes

Argos

political developments in Greek history. Allusion has been made to the Aetolian League, and its services to Greece at the time of the Gaulish invasions. Aetolia, which during the fifth and most of the fourth century was culturally and politically one of the most backward parts of Greece, had even at the time of Alexander's death no considerable towns. The league of its inhabitants, formed originally for military defense, was thus at first composed of a number of cantons or rural districts. Gradually larger towns began to grow up out of the villages, so that when the Aetolian League was at its height, from *c.* 279 onwards, it had to a great extent been converted into a federal union of cities. By the second half of the third century the League controlled either directly, by enlarging its federal membership, or indirectly, by various forms of alliance, all central Greece from the Maliac gulf to the Gulf of Corinth and the mouth of the Achelous, southern Thessaly, and at various times a number of cities lying outside that area.

The Achæan League began in a small way as a federation of a few cities. Of these there were ten in 272; but another quarter of a century elapsed before this federal union began to have much more than local importance. In 251 the city of Sicyon, which had been ruled for some time by a Tyrant, was liberated from despotic misrule through the energy of one of her exiled citizens, Aratus. Sicyon now joined the Achæan League, and her example was followed by other cities outside the geographical area known as Achæa, namely by Megara, Troizen, Epidaurus, and Corinth. Moreover, Aratus became the leading spirit of the enlarged League and remained so for over twenty years, being reëlected every other year to the chief executive magistracy, with which was combined the commandership-in-chief in war.

These two Leagues, and especially the Achæan, about which we are somewhat more fully informed, have deservedly aroused the interest and sympathy of students of history and political science, since they were true examples of federal union, and, as such, can claim to be the most elaborate political organisms known in the ancient world. In the Aetolian League all citizens of the constituent cities or districts were members of the federal assembly, which elected the federal magistrates and officials.

Of these the chief was called *strategos;* he was both the civil and the military head of the League, held office for one year, but could be reëlected after an interval. The assembly was the sovereign power of the League, and remained so throughout, to the extent of performing its electoral functions and deciding questions of peace and war. But for other purposes, as the size of the organization grew, it became impracticable to leave business to a large body which met only twice a year. Hence a small group of persons, called *apokletoi*, collaborated permanently with the *strategos* and the other magistrates. There was also a council, whose members were chosen by the assembly to represent the constituent cities proportionately to their military strength. This council does not appear to have exercised much authority; the *apokletoi*, however, were chosen from among its members.

The Achæan League, too, may originally have had both an assembly and a council. But in the period of its greatest prosperity the two important bodies which decided its affairs were the *synodos* and the *synkletos*. The former seems to have been composed of delegates from all the constituent states, appointed by the respective cities in proportion to their size and importance. Whereas the general policy and business of the League were decided by this meeting of delegates, certain questions involving relations with other states, and decisions about peace and war, were left to the *synkletos*, which was in effect an assembly of all citizens over thirty years of age. The executive was in the hands of the *strategos*, who could be reëlected every other year, but not annually, and some other magistrates, together with ten *demiourgoi*, whose duties must have approximated to those of the Aetolian *apokletoi*. In both Leagues, finally, the constituent communities were independent states with their own constitutions and law-courts. In the Achæan League we even find individual cities issuing their own currency, though there was also a federal coinage.

Unfortunately there were several factors which militated against the efficiency of these two organizations, and prevented them from being politically as influential, and in military affairs as potent, as they should have been. During a great part of their history the two Leagues were hostile to one another;

and, while the Aetolians were for a number of years the allies
of Macedon, it was the policy of Aratus, at least for a time,
to seek the friendship and support of Egypt. Too much
was left to the constituent cities, since there was no adequate
administrative machinery for federal business. Thus, the
fact that it was left to each city in time of war to levy and
maintain its own contingent of troops impaired the League's
military efficiency, and added greatly to the difficulties of the
strategos. In the Achæan League, since peace and war were voted
by the *synkletos*, the soldier under thirty had no voice in deciding
questions in which he was, nevertheless, vitally concerned. Nor
can we praise — though the history of Greek Tyranny makes
us understand the reason for the prohibition — a system of
electing the chief executive for one year only, and of prohibiting
his immediate reëlection, however eminent his abilities.

The personality of Aratus to a great extent surmounted
this difficulty; for he seems to have been strong enough to
insure the continuity of his policy during the alternate years
when he was out of office. Lastly, though our information
on this matter is scanty, the lack of a proper federal organization of finance was bound, in time of war, to involve both
Leagues in frequent difficulties.

The Achæan League steadily grew, especially after the death
of Antigonus Gonatas. For his successor, Demetrius II, almost at once found himself at war with both the Aetolian
and the Achæan Leagues. Though he inflicted some loss on
the former, the latter, thanks in the first place to the energy
of Aratus, was steadily enlarged by the adherence of more
and more Peloponnesian city-states. It was his ambition ultimately to marshal the whole of the Peloponnese to form
a solid anti-Macedonian federation; that it was frustrated was
mainly due to Sparta. Filled with a stubborn pride, which com-
pels our admiration even if we cannot approve its wisdom, the
Spartans had refused to bow to the will of Philip II and Alexander, and had been punished by some loss of territory. Little
is heard of Sparta from the time of her abortive attempt to shake
off Macedonian authority in southern Greece in 331 (cf. p.
402) until 272, when Pyrrhus of Epirus, in the course of a war
against Antigonus Gonatas, invaded Greece. Many of the Hel-

lenic communities received him readily, but Sparta elected to
throw in her lot with the Macedonian king. She evidently believed that a temporary friendship with a power to which she
was otherwise consistently hostile would serve her interests
better than alliance with the brilliant but unstable Epirot. Supported by a Macedonian force sent from Corinth, she repulsed
Pyrrhus' attack on Laconia; the same year saw his death at Argos.
Under her king, Areus, Sparta now enjoyed a few years of
extended political influence in Greek affairs, and concluded alliances with Elis and some of the cities of Arcadia and Achæa.
There followed occasional petty wars with her neighbors for
the next quarter of a century.

When the Achæan League, inspired by Aratus, was rapidly
becoming the most formidable power in Hellas, Sparta concluded an alliance with it. Her internal condition at this
time was, however, marked by acute economic distress. The
rigid conservatism of her citizens, the evil results of which
in the fourth century have already been noted (cf. p. 315),
had not relaxed in the third. Thus, about 245, the total number of Spartiatæ had been reduced to 700, and even of these,
in whose hands the landed property was concentrated, many
were overloaded with debt. The young king Agis, who came
of age in 244, supported and tutored by his uncle Agesilaus,
now projected a radical scheme of reform. Affecting to base
his drastic innovations on the venerable ordinances of Lycurgus, he proposed a cancellation of debts and a redistribution
of the land, so that those Spartans who had forfeited their
full citizenship and lost their allotments could be reinstated.
Furthermore, he aimed to increase the citizen body by the
enfranchisement of 4500 *perioikoi*. These proposals were productive of a violent struggle, leading to the expulsion of the
king's opponents. At this critical juncture Agis was compelled
to fulfil Sparta's obligations as an ally of the Achæan League by
leading a Spartan contingent to coöperate with Aratus against
the Aetolian League, which was now threatening an attack.
On his return from the campaign in 241 Agis found his political
enemies in control at home. He was arraigned for treason and
executed. Once more had the forces of reaction triumphed at
Sparta. The Spartan king, Cleomenes III, who came to the

throne six years later, was more successful.   In 226 with a
mercenary army at his back, he carried out a *coup d'état* at
Sparta.   The ephorate and *gerusia* were abolished, and a new
council was instituted to take the place of those venerable
bodies.   The franchise was extended to several thousand
perioikoi, and a redistribution of the land was effected.   Reforms
were introduced in the army, and the famous Spartan training
of the young, which had fallen into desuetude, was revived.

But Cleomenes was not content to play the rôle of economic
and constitutional reformer.   He set himself, by force or by
diplomacy, to enlarge the political influence of Sparta.   The
program which he aimed to carry through could have but
one outcome in the Peloponnese, a rupture between Sparta
and the Achæan League.   By 227 hostilities had begun; and
both in that year and in 226 Cleomenes inflicted decisive defeats on the forces of the League.   Peace negotiations followed,
and now the Spartan king demanded to be instated as commander-in-chief of the League in time of war.   To Aratus the
acceptance of this condition meant not only that his own
authority would be reduced to comparative insignificance,
but that the Achæan League, and the Peloponnese as a whole,
would pass once again under the general direction of Lacedæmon and its ambitious ruler.   The alternative he saw was to
bring about a foreign intervention.   Since the relations between
Sparta and Egypt were extremely friendly, there remained
only the ancestral enemy of the League, Macedonia, to which
to appeal.   Yet, since Aratus had spent all his life in trying
to create a strong anti-Macedonian power in the Peloponnese,
the step he now contemplated, if taken, would be tantamount
to the destruction of his life-work.   Harsh judgments were
passed on him in antiquity, and have been since.   The action
of the League under his guidance once more illustrates the
bitterness of Greek to Greek, which, throughout Hellenic
history, made any permanent national unity impossible —
the unattainable dream of a few idealist statesmen and political
thinkers.   That a contrary decision, that is to say the acceptance of Cleomenes' demands, would have made any appreciable
difference to the course of Greece's history in the next fifty
years is in the highest degree improbable.

Cleomenes' reply to the Achæan refusal of recognition was a renewal of hostilities. Heavily subsidized by Egyptian gold, he was able to augment his mercenaries, and his military successes brought about the defection from the Achæan League of many Peloponnesian cities. Others he took by force. By the spring of 224 the agreement between Aratus and the Macedonian king, Antigonus Doson, who had succeeded Demetrius II in 229, had been signed, and Antigonus at once marched to the Peloponnese, occupied Corinth and Argos, and compelled Cleomenes to retire to Arcadia. During the winter, when campaigning was at a standstill, the Macedonian reconstituted the Hellenic League from which, apart from the common enemy, Sparta, only the Aetolians kept aloof. Cities which had recently gone over to Cleomenes now as quickly fell away from him; yet for nearly two years he carried on against a stronger foe, until in the spring of 222 he was completely defeated by Antigonus at the battle of Sellasia in Laconia. Cleomenes himself made his escape to the coast, and thence to Egypt. His attempt, two years later, to return with some supporters to Laconia failed, and he committed suicide. His enemy and rival, Aratus, lived till 213, still influential in the counsels of the League, but the dependent of Macedonia. It was said that he was poisoned at the instance of the young Macedonian king, Philip V, who had succeeded Antigonus Doson in 221. The change of ruler in Macedonia at that date seemed to the Aetolians an opportunity for increasing their own power, and they attacked the Achæan League. From this act of aggression there developed a general war between them and Philip with his Hellenic allies, which lasted for three years. Peace was concluded in 217. The Aetolians, who had suffered severe losses, were glad to accept the mild terms imposed by the Macedonian monarch. He, on his side, was anxious for peace in Hellas, so as to have a free hand to undertake a war in which success promised a rich reward. Few men — and certainly Philip was not one of them — at that date realized the strength and endurance of the western power of Rome, which in 217–216 was passing through one of the greatest crises in its history, and among whose active enemies Philip was now to be numbered.

2. The Intervention of Rome in Hellenic Affairs

Political conditions among the western Greek city-states had long been as unstable as among their kinsmen in the eastern Mediterranean. This was in part due to internal dissension, in part to their becoming pawns in the game of two stronger powers, Carthage and Rome. In Syracuse the settlement achieved by Timoleon [1] was of short duration and was succeeded by two decades of civil unrest. From this there at last emerged another autocrat comparable to Dionysius I. Agathocles, a man of humble origin, having established himself as Tyrant with the aid of a faction, was able to maintain his position for nearly thirty years (316–289). During that time, though more than once perilously near to disaster, he brought most of Sicily and parts of southern Italy under his control. In addition he fought with vigor against the hereditary enemy, the Carthaginians. Besieged by them and in danger of being starved into submission, he carried through the bold venture of running the blockade and landing an expeditionary force in northern Africa (310). For three years the war was thus waged in the enemy's country, partly by Agathocles alone, partly in alliance with Ophellas of Cyrene. At last, in 307, a severe defeat forced Agathocles to abandon his transmarine operations. But Carthage, too, was exhausted, and in the following year signed a peace treaty with him by which Sicily was divided into two approximately equal portions, the western passing under Punic control. Some sixteen years later Agathocles made preparations for another war against Carthage, with the immediate object of gaining complete mastery over the island and the further plan of uniting all the western Greeks under his sceptre. He even entered into an alliance with Macedonia; but he did not live to carry out his ambitious plans, as he died in 289. His death occurred at a critical moment, and, as he had no successor, his kingdom at once fell to pieces. When in 281 Tarentum became involved in a dispute with Rome, she appealed to Pyrrhus of Epirus for aid. Brilliant but unstable as this cousin of Alexander the Great was, he seems to have welcomed an invitation that might pave the way for his hegemony

[1] See above, page 313.

over the western Greeks. He landed in Italy in 280 with a force of between 20,000 and 25,000 men, together with a number of elephants. These beasts had been employed with some success at the battle of Ipsus and on other occasions in the wars of Alexander's successors. In Pyrrhus' first two engagements with the Romans — at Heraclea in 280 and at Ausculum in 279 — they contributed not a little to his decisive victories. In 278 Pyrrhus, realizing that Rome could be neither crushed nor overawed enough to accept terms unfavorable to herself, answered an appeal to intervene in Sicilian affairs by crossing over to the island with his army. Here he at first met with an enthusiastic reception from Syracuse and other Greek communities; for, not only had they been disunited since Agathocles' death, but they lived in constant fear of both Carthage and a group of Agathocles' mercenaries who had occupied Messana and converted it into a "free-state of robbers." The Epirot for four years (278–275) waged war against Carthage in the island. He won some striking successes, but the Sicilians after a time became lukewarm in their support, and ultimately came to terms with Carthage independently. They were unwilling to bear indefinitely the heavy demands of men and supplies which he laid upon them, as they realized that his only aim was his personal aggrandizement. Disheartened, Pyrrhus returned to Italy in 275; in the same year a part of his army was heavily defeated at Beneventum by a Roman force. He now abandoned his Italian adventure entirely and withdrew to Epirus, leaving only a garrison behind in Tarentum. That city held out against Rome for some time longer, but in the end was forced to come to terms like the rest of Rome's opponents in southern Italy. The Greek cities were now enrolled as Roman allies and were granted separate treaties with their conqueror. The citadel at Tarentum was converted into a Roman fortress. By 265 Roman authority was supreme throughout the Italian peninsula.

In Syracuse, after the departure of Pyrrhus, faction was again rife. The distress caused by intestinal warfare was aggravated by the raids of the Mamertines in Messana. In Syracuse's hour of need the direction of affairs was entrusted to the *strategos*, Hiero. He inflicted a severe defeat on the Mamertines, and was then accepted by the Syracusans as their king, ruling under the name of Hiero II. He followed up his first military success by an attack on Messana, thereby becoming the unwitting cause of a prolonged struggle between the two leading powers in the western Mediterranean. For, when Hiero blockaded the city, divided counsels prevailed among its inhabitants. One faction sought help from Carthage, another appealed to Rome.

In the First Punic War, which began in 264, Hiero at first concluded a treaty with Syracuse's ancient foe, Carthage. But when a Roman army laid siege to Syracuse, though the city was not taken, Hiero was sufficiently impressed to throw over his Semitic allies and join Rome. For the rest of his long reign — he died in 215 B.C., being then more than ninety years of age — he remained her faithful ally. The Romans next attacked and reduced Agrigentum, in spite of the large mercenary force sent by Carthage for its defense. The sack of the town, and the enslavement of the population by the Roman commander, was an inexcusable act of barbarity, which had the effect of alienating other Sicilian communities from Rome. Yet in the long run their fate depended on the will of Rome; for by the peace treaty signed between Rome and Carthage in 241 Sicily became a Roman province. Syracuse, however, retained its quasi-independent status as a friend and ally of the Roman people. This situation endured until 215 when Hiero died full of years. His young successor, Hieronymus, under the influence of pro-Carthaginian counsellors, declared for Carthage in the life and death struggle then in process of being waged between the African state and Rome. But in 213 the Roman commander, Marcellus, invested Syracuse. The city was taken in the following year and the Syracusan kingdom was thereafter absorbed into the Roman province of Sicily.

Meanwhile Philip V of Macedon had joined the active enemies of Rome. After some vacillation he had in 215 sent envoys to Hannibal and concluded an alliance with him, promising that he would invade Italy. This promise Philip was never able to fulfil; for he was hampered by the lack of an adequate fleet and by the successful if selfish diplomacy of the Roman government, which was able to bring about a strong anti-Macedonian coalition in the Hellenic world. Chief among these allies of Rome were the Aetolian League and Attalus I of Pergamum. The war dragged on without decisive results till 205, when peace was made between the two chief combatants. Each made certain concessions to the other, the allies of either being included in the agreement. But the Greeks of the mainland, and especially the Aetolians, were the real losers in the recent struggle, either through actual deprivation of territory or merely by the long continued drain on their resources. Above all, another great state, Rome, had been added to the number of major powers on whose policy or whims the destiny of the Hellenic cities had long depended. The ink was scarcely dry on the peace protocol of Carthage and Rome, when the victor intervened in the intricate political affairs of the eastern Mediterranean states. The motives and aims of the Roman government at this juncture have been very variously interpreted. Of the three Hellenistic monarchies, Egypt was at the end of the third century the weakest in a military sense. Her relations with Rome before 202 B.C. appear to have been slight. Friendly embassies of the two states had exchanged visits in 273, but there is no evidence that any formal alliance was concluded between them. During the Second Punic War Egypt had supplied Rome with grain — at profiteering rates, as it would seem — at a time when there was considerable danger of famine in Italy. In 203 King Ptolemy IV died, and the throne passed to his infant son. The king of Syria, Antiochus III, had recently recovered some of the eastern territories that had been lost during the reigns of his predecessors. To these he now aimed to add southern Syria, a dependency of the Ptolemies. Philip of Macedon, too, after the very mediocre successes of his recent war against the Greek states, was greedy for further conquests. These two monarchs, seeing Egypt nominally ruled by a child, actually by his corrupt and unwarlike ministers, concluded a pact to deprive Egypt of all her foreign possessions and to divide the spoil. Antiochus took the offensive against her at once in southern Syria; but Philip's task of wresting Egyptian dependencies in the Aegean area was less simple. It aroused at once the enmity of those smaller states, whose interests had not been threatened by the fact that some regions of Thrace and Asia Minor acknowledged Egyptian suzerainty, but who could see only a grave danger to their own political independence in the aggressive tactics of the Macedonian, especially when allied to the Syrian monarch. Rhodes and Pergamum both appealed to Rome to intervene on their behalf. Egypt, too, turned to the western power for support against Antiochus. An Athenian embassy swelled the list of petitioners at Rome; for a quarrel between some of the Greek allies of Philip and Athens had led to an attack on that city.

The Roman senate was in favor of declaring war on Philip and carried its point, mainly by the argument that Philip, if not checked, would try to invade Italy; partly also by playing on the superstitious fears of the masses. But while we may allow for a certain measure of resentment against the Macedonian king for joining the ranks of Rome's enemies in 216, the real fear of the senate was not Philip alone, but what might develop from a coalition between him and Antiochus. The abrupt realization of this by a senate, which so far had little knowledge of the Hellenistic monarchies, determined its action. We shall see that it was not till thirty years later that Roman policy in the Aegean can justly be described as aggressive.

In the so-called Second Macedonian War Rome was from the first supported by the Aetolian League, and by the navies of Pergamum and Rhodes. The other Greek states of any moment were for the present neutral. For nearly two years the war was barren of results; in 198, however, the consul, T. Quinctius Flamininus, took over the command of the Roman armies, and in this year and the next carried out a brilliant offensive. Philip, after a severe defeat on the borders of Epirus and Thessaly, was driven back to the Macedonian-Thessalian frontier. The Achæan League now joined the active enemies of Philip, and that monarch was in sufficient straits to institute negotiations for peace (winter, 198). The terms laid down by Rome were too peremptory for his acceptance; it needed another campaign to compel his submission. In 197 a decisive action was fought in Thessaly at Cynoscephalæ. A stubborn contest in which about 25,000 men were involved on either side, ended in a complete Roman victory. To the student of ancient military history the battle is of special interest because the superiority of the legionary organization over the Macedonian phalanx was here clearly demonstrated.

Forced now to accept the peace terms imposed by Rome, Philip lost all his possessions outside Macedonia, and undertook to enter into no foreign alliances or wars without Roman sanction. His army was reduced in size, and he was called upon to pay a war indemnity of 1000 talents. There was an interesting sequel to the war. The Roman commander-in-chief, Flamininus, attended the Isthmian festival in 196, and there formally proclaimed the independence of the Greek states. That he was a friend and admirer of Greece is clear; it is no less clear that he could not have acted as he did without the approval of the senate. In the general action of the Roman government at this period — the terms dictated to Philip were far less severe than its allies of the Aetolian League desired — we have clear proof of its unwillingness to derive any territorial advantage from the war, or to be drawn any further into Eastern affairs. That a well-known Philhellene carried out the instructions of the Roman senate does not prove that Philhellenism was the motive which determined its decision. The complicated problems arising out of the peace settlement and declaration of Greek autonomy detained Flamininus another two years in Greece. Then, in 194, the Roman garrisons were withdrawn from there.

Meanwhile Antiochus had prosecuted his attack on Egypt with much success. A victory at Mt. Panium in 198 made him master of southern Syria; then he proceeded to annex Greek cities in Asia Minor that had hitherto been Egyptian dependencies. The Rhodians, who declared war on Antiochus and with their fleet prevented him from capturing important bases like Samos, at the same time made urgent representations to the Roman government. But, so long as the Syrian king's activities were confined to Asia Minor, the senate was unwilling to intervene. Even when the king crossed the Hellespont and began to acquire strategic points like Sestos, and to rebuild Lysimacheia, Rome contented herself with diplomatic protests, insisting that Antiochus should abstain from occupying any European territory. Had the issue been a simple one between Rome and Syria, it is possible that hostilities would have been avoided. But certain other factors, or rather persons, intervened to complicate the Near-Eastern situation and make war unavoidable. Shortly before 193 Antiochus was visited by a distinguished exile from Carthage, no less a person than Hannibal. We may surmise that his counsels were not in favor of a peaceful acquiescence in Rome's demands. At the same time, when war had begun, his military genius, as well as his knowledge of Roman tactics, might have been invaluable to his host, had the latter been disposed to accept his advice. The final complication, however, was the action of the Aetolian League in inviting Antiochus to Greece, promising him wide-spread support there as soon as he appeared. The Aetolians, even if the unfavorable estimate of them in Polybius, who, like his father, played a prominent part in the affairs of the Achæan League, be in some degree discounted, were never remarkable for political stability. We have seen that they were dissatisfied with Rome's settlement of 196. With the help of Antiochus they now hoped to become the dominant power in Greece. In 192 Antiochus sailed to Greece with a very moderate force of 10,000, trusting in the Aetolian promises and grossly underestimating the resources of Rome.

A reluctant senate was compelled to go to war, unless it was prepared to stultify its previous action toward the Greeks. A single campaign, and a single Roman victory on the historic site of Thermopylæ, sufficed to drive the Asiatic invader out of Greece (191). But the Romans, having gone so far, and mindful at last of the interests of friendly states like Rhodes and Pergamum, decided to restrict Antiochus' power in Asia. A Roman and Greek allied fleet twice defeated the Syrian navy in the Aegean, and thus prepared the way for the Roman expeditionary force that landed in Asia Minor in the summer of 190. Again the immeasurable superiority of Rome's disciplined legionaries over the numerous but motley host of Antiochus was shown. The king was routed in an engagement fought hard by Magnesia near Mt. Sipylus, and then was driven to make peace on Rome's terms. His possessions in Asia Minor he was forced to give up, the boundaries of his much reduced kingdom being hereafter the Taurus mountains and the Halys River. He undertook not to attack any friends or allies of Rome, and he was required to pay a heavy indemnity within a stipulated time. The allies of Rome, Rhodes and Pergamum, received considerable additions to their respective territories; other communities were enrolled as free and independent allies of Rome. Small kingdoms and principalities in the interior — for example, Bithynia — similarly became client kingdoms of the conqueror. The Aetolians came off more lightly than might have been expected. They had to pay an indemnity, and ceded Cephallenia to Rome. For the rest they, too, were formally enlisted among the free and autonomous allies of Rome, but with the special obligation of furnishing troops when required. It is noteworthy that the Roman government still abstained from making territorial annexations on the Greek mainland.

There was one feature of the Roman settlement which was productive of endless disputes and finally led to drastic action on Rome's part. The Achæan League had been enlarged so as to include most of the communities of the Peloponnese, Sparta not excepted. The adherence of these new members was for the most part forced, not voluntary. Frequent disagreements, and no less frequent appeals to Rome by both parties in a dispute, were the result. A further complication was caused by the divided policies in the states themselves. Generally speaking, the oligarchic or aristocratic party courted the favor of Rome, while the democratic party worked for absolute independence of Roman arbitration in Greek affairs. The senate, whose attitude to Near-Eastern questions was beginning to undergo a marked change, while not intervening directly, now followed the plan of giving the weight of its support to the aristocratic factions in the Hellenic cities.

It was not, however, in Greece only that trouble was brewing. Philip V, in accordance with his treaty obligations, had assisted Rome in her war against Antiochus. So far from being rewarded for his services, as he had hoped, by an extension of territory or a greater degree of autonomy, he received nothing. In 185 he appears to have violated his treaty by invading districts outside Macedonia. Rome peremptorily ordered him to withdraw, a command which he could not but obey. But the last six years of his life were devoted to restoring, as far as possible, the prosperity of his kingdom, with the ultimate aim of trying conclusions with Rome once more when his resources were sufficient.

His bitterness against Rome was inherited by his son, Perseus, who came to the throne in 179. The early years of his reign Perseus spent in strengthening his position by fostering good relations with his neighbors. He formed an alliance with a Thracian prince, Cotys, and came to a secret understanding with King Genthius of Illyria, who was a nominal ally of Rome. Bitter jealousy of Pergamum, which with Roman support had grown great at the expense of Macedonia and Syria, animated Perseus as it had his father. King Eumenes of Pergamum for his part reported the activities of the Macedonian monarch to Rome; finally, in 172 he visited Rome in person to lay before the senate a long list of complaints against Perseus. That body, which had been watching the progress of Perseus for some time, found in the accusations of Eumenes a final justification or pretext for ordering the Macedonian's unconditional submission to Roman demands. When he refused, the Romans declared war (171).

The first three years of the Third Macedonian War were remarkable only for the incompetence of the Roman commanders sent to Greece and the fecklessness of their opponent. By energetic action at the beginning Perseus could probably have brought over a great part of Greece to his side, the Roman force in Epirus at that time being small. As it was, the appearance of additional legions, and the activity of Roman envoys in Greece, deprived him of almost all help from that quarter. Nor did Asiatic states like Bithynia and Syria, with which he had previously entered into friendly relations, now attempt to help him. In 168 the appointment of an able commander-in-chief, Aemilius Paullus, completely changed the military situation. Advancing through Thessaly he gave battle to Perseus close to Pydna in southern Macedonia. Perseus' troops fought bravely; but in the end they were defeated with very heavy loss; for 20,000 are said to have fallen and 11,000 taken prisoners. The king himself escaped, but was subsequently captured and sent to Rome, where he died a few years later.

Even now the Roman government was unwilling to annex the conquered kingdom. Instead, an experiment was tried which cannot be said to have justified itself by results. Macedonia was broken up into four republics, of which only the most

northern, in view of its savage Thracian neighbors, was permitted to have an army. The land-tax formerly paid to the
king was reduced by half, and this sum was collected for the
benefit of the Roman treasury. Estates and mines, which had
been royal property, were confiscated by Rome. To isolate
each of these small states as far as possible, intermarriage and
commercial relations between them were prohibited, Rome
applying the principle that she had already followed in Italy.
During the next two decades internal dissension in the respective governments, and petty disputes between the republics
proved the unwisdom of the Roman experiment. Then, in 149–
146, a pretender appeared, by name Andriscus, who claimed to
be a son of Perseus. His appearance aroused great popular enthusiasm, and he enjoyed some ephemeral successes before the
rebellion was suppressed by Rome. The four republics were
now dissolved, and Macedonia was converted into a Roman
province governed by a Roman viceroy.

The changed attitude of the senate to the Eastern question at
the conclusion of the Third Macedonian War showed itself not
only in its actions in Greece, but in its high-handed treatment of
Rome's old-standing allies, Rhodes and Pergamum. The island
state had been guilty of no hostile act, but had unwisely attempted to mediate in the recent dispute between Perseus and
Rome. After the war the terms of her treaty with Rome were
revised to her disadvantage, so that, from being autonomous,
the Rhodians became dependent allies. At the same time they
were deprived of their possessions on the mainland of southwestern Asia Minor. Worst of all, in view of the fact that
Rhodes was a maritime state, Delos was made a free port by
Roman action, and from this time for fully a century became the
leading mart in the Aegean area. According to a very trustworthy source, the people of Rhodes within a few years could
complain that their receipts from customs dues had sunk from
1,000,000 to 150,000 drachmæ.[1]

Even less justifiable was the manner in which Rome sought
for a pretext to reduce the power of Pergamum. This state had
been valuable to her while Macedonia and Syria were of account.
When this was no longer the case, the senate was anxious to

[1] Polybius xxxi, 7, 12.

humble this Roman ally. Eumenes was accused of hostile designs, and, when he came to Italy to defend himself, was met at Brundisium and sent back to his country. He lost Pamphylia and Galatia, which now became independent principalities, but he was allowed to retain his throne. To complete his chagrin he saw the Roman government showing marked favor to his neighbor, the king of Bithynia. Eumenes' successors, Attalus II and Attalus III, also resigned themselves to the inevitable. On the death of Attalus III Pergamum became a Roman province (133 B.C.). During and after the Third Macedonian War Rome also intervened in the affairs of Syria and Egypt, so that her position as arbiter in the whole Mediterranean was clear to all.

Lastly we must note her policy in Greece after 168. Among the state papers of Perseus, which had been captured by the Romans, were many that incriminated prominent persons with anti-Roman sympathies in Greek states. A number of these the Roman authorities brought to trial and executed. Besides this, numerous hostages were taken from the various cities and sent to Italy. The Achæan League suffered worst of all. One thousand of its prominent men were thus transported into exile, among them Polybius, the historian.[1]

The settlement of Greece in 167 did not pass off without excesses which it is impossible to condone. Civil war in Aetolia was attended by the massacre of several hundred members of the anti-Roman faction, a deed to which the Roman government was privy, if not directly bearing responsibility for it. The punishment of the Epirots for aiding Perseus was not less brutal. Numerous towns in Epirus were destroyed, the widespread ruin of the settlements being accompanied by a wholesale enslavement of the inhabitants. The Roman protectorate over Greece endured for two decades. Then, in 148, a renewed dispute between Sparta and the Achæan League occurred, and the matter was referred to Rome. But before the Roman commission of inquiry appeared on the scene, the Achæan League had taken up arms against their neighbor. The commissioners summoned a congress at Corinth and notified the League that certain members of it would be detached to form

[1] See below, page 456.

independent communities. By 147 the anti-Roman factions in the cities had quite gained the upper hand. They were joined by the communities of Bœotia, Phocis, Locris, and Eubœa, and war was declared on Sparta.

The reply of the Roman government was prompt. While the Roman commander in Macedonia invaded central Greece and suppressed the rising there, L. Mummius was despatched with a naval and military force to southern Greece. The allies were defeated in an engagement near Corinth, and then that city was forced to surrender. It was sacked and burnt; its people were enslaved, and the numerous art treasures, for which this ancient Greek *polis* had long been famous, were deported to Rome. The Greek leagues were now dissolved and the individual cities compelled to enter directly into alliance with Rome. The character of each treaty depended on the past action of the particular city. Those which, like Athens, Sparta, and Argos, had stood consistently on the side of Rome remained autonomous allies. The others became tribute-paying subjects. The governor of Macedonia exercised a general supervision and control in Greece, which was not formally converted into a province until the last quarter of the first century B.C.; for the Greek communities were allowed their own jurisdiction and administration, a privilege not granted to regular provinces, or only to isolated cities in them. At the same time Rome saw to it that the local governments were aristocratic. Thus for more than a century after 146 the fiction of an independent Greece was upheld. The place of Corinth as leading city was taken by Argos, which became the headquarters of Roman and Italian business affairs in Greece.

Here we may fitly close our survey of the political history of the Hellenistic world. Rome was now the arbiter in the Mediterranean, even though more than another century was to elapse before the last of the Hellenistic monarchies was merged in the Roman empire. Already in 133 B.C. Pergamum, on the death of Attalus III, passed into Roman hands, being organized as the Roman province of Asia a few years later. During the sixty years following, Rome, after two prolonged wars with Mithridates of Pontus, secured complete control of Asia Minor, either by annexation or by the enrollment of native principalities as client and allied states.   In 63 Syria became a province and the Roman frontier was thereby advanced to the Euphrates. Finally the annexation of Egypt in 30 B.C. was the postlude to a long and bitter struggle between Rome's two chief aspirants for personal domination over the whole Mediterranean world.

CHAPTER XXV

THE HELLENISTIC AGE

The Museum forms a part of the palaces. It has a promenade, a lounge, and a large hall, in which the learned scholars who belong to the Museum dine in common. This community also owns property in common. A priest, who in former times was appointed by the King, but now by Caesar, is president of the Museum. — Strabo, xvii, i, 8.

1. ECONOMIC AND SOCIAL CONDITIONS

THE Hellenistic Age, that is to say, the period of about two centuries between the death of Alexander and the time when Roman control was firmly established in the eastern Mediterranean, was long regarded as a period of decadence and material decline. Fuller knowledge, the result of extensive excavations, has demonstrated this conception of the Hellenic world after Alexander to be erroneous. At the same time it is now possible to see more clearly the striking differences between this and the preceding age.

The political developments which were sketched in the last chapter caused something little short of revolutionary changes, even though the process of change was gradual, not sudden. Of the innumerable Greek cities, which had for centuries been for the most part autonomous states, the greater number were now dependent on, or actually incorporated in, one or other of the leading monarchies. The old constitutional forms are kept, magistrates are elected, assemblies and councils meet, but they have sunk to the status of municipal officials and town councils. Of the highly developed urban life in the period we have abundant evidence from the inscriptions; the life and conditions in the country districts are less heard of now than before. In spite of the continuous warfare in the period, there is, especially among the smaller cities, a marked

426

disposition to settle disagreements not by the sword but by arbitration. Another method, extensively adopted to restrict the operations of war, was found in declaring many sanctuaries and the lands attached to them inviolable. Gradually the principle was also extended to whole cities and their territories, and to individual members of communities — and these were numerous — which had entered into specific treaty relations with one another. A greater humanity in the relations of man to man was not merely an ideal preached by the adherents of philosophic schools — for example, the Stoics — but found its practical expression in several ways. The treatment of slaves, if we except the wretched inmates of the mines, tended to become gentler, and manumissions were common. Greeks taken prisoner by Greeks were regularly ransomed. The usages of war — again there were some brutal exceptions — were somewhat less harsh than in an earlier age. Such changes arose from a multiplicity of causes, which it is hard to analyze with precision, just as it is often difficult to separate cause and effect. The great increase in intercourse resulting from the altered political conditions, the break-down of the old system of isolated and mutually jealous city-states, and the development of greater facilities for commerce and travel, together with the realization that, whatever local political differences might exist, all Hellenes were the inheritors of a common culture, notably changed the aspect of Greek society.

But there were other and less admirable features. Though there is not sufficient material on which to base even the most tentative statistics, it is clear that the population of Greece, at all events toward the end of the period, was not even stationary but sensibly declining. The epigraphic remains seem to leave no room for doubt that smaller families were the rule in the second century, and that the practice of infanticide, especially of female children, was far from uncommon. The land could support only a limited number of persons, while the development of industry and commerce was not of such a kind as to benefit the majority of the population. The difference between the wealthy few and the impoverished many became much more sharply accentuated than it was in the days of Greek freedom. The social revolution at Sparta, though the best known, is far from being the only instance of civil disturbance arising from the abject poverty of the masses and the demand for better conditions, especially a redistribution of the land. And there are on record cases where such struggles were sufficiently severe to necessitate the intervention of this or that suzerain power.

It is the wealthy who appear most often in the inscriptions. They formed the ruling class in the cities; from among them were chosen officials and counsellors; and, in justice to them, we may add that many of them were lavish with their wealth for the benefit of the community. Many are the inscriptions commemorating public benefactions of divers kinds. For much of the cost of beautifying towns with public buildings, of celebrating public festivals, great and small, of providing for the education of the young and for their proper supervision, was defrayed by private donors. At times, too, the wealthy princes spent large sums on Greek cities with which they were on a friendly footing. No better instance of this can be cited than the munificent patronage extended to Athens by several of the Attalids of Pergamum.[1]

Seleucus and his successors exerted themselves to promote the process of Hellenization, the chief bond to hold together their extensive and heterogeneous empire. Actually, as we have seen, that empire was before long reduced in size, because whole provinces passed into the hands of independent rulers. But even in its more restricted form it was a composite and unstable structure. Large tracts of territory were owned by local princes or magnates who stood in a kind of loose feudal relationship to the royal house. There were many temple properties, some being of great size with thousands of dependents, so that they were veritable miniature states. The most stable element in the empire, as the Seleucids were not slow to recognize, was to be found in the urban community, and so they were most active in fostering the growth of many new cities. These Seleucid foundations thrived in all parts of the realm, as it was at its greatest extent, in the central Asiatic provinces and Mesopotamia, as well as in Syria itself and in Asia Minor. The four chief were Antioch, Seleuceia on the

[1] Cf. below, page 443.

Tigris, Apamea, and Laodicea, but there were many others whose importance, cultural and economic, was scarcely less marked for centuries to come. The growth of Antioch was gradual, until in addition to the Greek it included a large Syrian and Jewish population. So, too, Seleuceia was primarily a Greek city, but contained also a large native population. It became in time one of the largest cities in the world, with well over half a million inhabitants. Even in those urban communities, whose inmates were mostly Asiatics, Greek forms of government and administration were often imitated or directly adopted. In sharp contrast to the semi-independent status of the city-dwellers was that of the rural population. The agricultural workers were serfs, a condition which was of course far older than the Seleucid era, and irrespective of whether the land that they tilled was owned by the monarch or by private persons. There were, however, two exceptions. A good amount of King's Land was utilized for military colonies which were commonly contiguous to some village. The settlers were not time-expired veterans but men who could be mobilized. There is some doubt, indeed, whether they were exempt from taxation, but none at all regarding their liability to military service. On the economic side the value of this system of settlements lay in the fact that it was a means of bringing waste lands under cultivation. Secondly, on the farm-lands belonging to Greek cities many of the tillers appear to have become, even if they were not at first, free peasants.

Very many of the old established Greek cities that had once been autonomous, especially those on the coast, received numerous signs of the royal favor. There is ample epigraphic evidence for this and it was displayed in different ways. Special political privileges might be granted, gifts were bestowed on temples, municipal endowments of various kinds were made, or some relief from taxation or other financial immunity might be given. Thus it was small wonder if the Greek communities repaid such a benefactor by paying him divine honors as Saviour (*Soter*) and instituted festivals in his honor. The worship paid to Seleucid rulers after death, moreover, was general throughout the empire and, next to Hellenization, the most important unifying factor.

Ptolemaic Egypt presents a strong contrast to the Seleucid kingdom. There no such Hellenizing process would have been possible; and the early princes of the royal house, though Græco-Macedonian, made no attempt to imitate their Syrian neighbor. Apart from Alexandria and Ptolemais, a new foundation in Upper Egypt, there were no Hellenic centres in Egypt, for the old settlement at Naucratis languished utterly. Alexandria became in time a composite city of various nationalities. At first the Greek element predominated and remained more or less pure; but gradually, by intermarriage, a more homogeneous Græco-Egyptian population developed to take the place of the earlier and separate ethnic groups. The Jewish colony there, which grew very rapidly, was granted substantial privileges by different Ptolemies; within a century there were many smaller Jewish settlements in different parts of Egypt. They remained distinct, however, from both the Greek and the native population. Alexandria and Ptolemais were organized as Hellenic cities with an assembly, a council, and executive magistrates. However, the presence of royal officials there also probably meant that the authority and the powers of the municipal government were strictly circumscribed. A steady enlargement of many villages under the Ptolemaic *régime* is also noticeable, and a foreign population grew up side by side with, but separate from, the native. The Greeks especially formed separate groups wherever they took up their residence. Not only did they thereby keep up their traditions and customs in general, but the existence of aggregations of Cretans, Bœotians, and so forth, demonstrate that loyalty to their home district remained strong. The national revival in Egypt during the second century was not confined to Alexandria. The foreign groups no longer stayed so exclusive and intermarriage became more frequent; even in the highest official positions Egyptians were occasionally to be found, whereas before these had only been open to Greeks. About the middle of the second century Greek immigration declined rapidly; for wages in Egypt had sunk so appreciably that the Greeks found it more profitable to eke out a living at home. On the other hand, the influx of Syrians appears to have been greater in the second century than in the third.

The Ptolemies, unlike any of their contemporaries, developed a most complicated yet efficient system of state-control in the industrial and commercial life of their country. All important productions and manufactures were royal monopolies. As it has been put, "the king was the first industrial and commercial magnate in the land." To carry out this control by the government, that is to say, by the monarch, over industry and commerce as well as over agriculture, elaborate census statistics were periodically collected. In every village a land register was kept. Records of the whole administrative district were collected in each nome; in addition there was the central registrary for the whole country in Alexandria. Lists were also drawn up of house property and of all draught animals. A vast bureaucracy, grading down from the highest ministers of the king, like the *dioiketes* or chief finance minister, to the humble village headman, was needed to ensure efficient working. The power of the nomarchs declined. At first it was limited by the presence in each nome of a Greek military commander. Later this *strategos* became the chief civil functionary as well. The lot of the mass of the workers was unenviable. Their income rarely rose much above, and sometimes, especially during the second century, fell below, the bare margin of subsistence. Yet their patience was exceptional; for the first serious rebellion does not seem to have occurred till 217. After that riots and strikes took place more frequently, but they could generally be promptly suppressed or else appeased by slight concessions.

Although there is still much that is obscure, particularly in matters of detail, far more is known about the ownership and cultivation of the land in Egypt than in the Seleucid empire. All land was owned by the king, but in practice it is necessary to distinguish between the King's Land, specifically so called, and land held in grant. The King's Land or Royal Land was cultivated by tenant farmers, the King's Peasants, who, after retaining a fixed amount of produce for their own maintenance, were required to turn over the rest to the monarch. Occasionally the actual agricultural work was done by sub-tenants of the chief tenants. The Royal Peasants formed themselves into regular corporations with elders and a secretary in the villages that they inhabited. That they were not in fact wholly free is shown by an oath in a *papyrus* of the late second century, whereby the farmer bound himself not to leave his land between the sowing and the harvest, or till the rent had been paid, nor to retire from agricultural work, nor to enter any one else's service. If enough tenants were not available, the later Ptolemies at least did not hesitate to have recourse to compulsion.

There were several categories of land held in grant. Such were the temple lands; for the legal theory was that this territory was "left to the god" by the king. Also the general administration of temple lands appears to have been under royal control and similar to that in use for the Royal Land. Secondly, there was the land assigned to soldiers, a condition of occupancy being the performance of military or police service. As in the Seleucid kingdom, so in Egypt a double purpose was achieved thereby, defense and reclamation of waste lands. Such land could be recovered by the crown without formality at any time, but actually occupancy tended more and more to become hereditary. Cultivation by sub-tenants was not only permissible but in the case of military chief tenants inevitable, sometimes for considerable periods of time. A third class of land in grant comprised gift lands entrusted by the king to some favorite minister. The estate, extending over several villages, bestowed on Apollonius by Ptolemy II has become a famous example of gift land because of a wealth of *papyri*, in which are recorded the correspondence and business transactions of Apollonius' trusted steward, Zeno, in connection with this property. Land unsuitable for grain we find to some extent leased out for vineyards and small orchards. As some time would elapse before any results could be expected, as much as five years' freedom from taxation might be granted, to be followed by three years of taxes at a reduced rate.

The fullest information with regard to the operation of royal monopolies concerns the production and sale of oils of various kinds. A lengthy *papyrus* informs us about the regulations of Ptolemy II governing this monopoly. With respect to production private competition is absolutely prohibited, but the priests in different temples are allowed, under supervision, to produce sesame oil for their own use. The sale monopoly is absolute, and even the priests are not allowed to sell any of their produce. The law applied to various vegetable oils but not to olive oil; for, although olive trees were cultivated to some extent, the fruit does not seem to have been used for manufacturing oil. There was a rigorous control over the planting of sesame and the other oil-producing plants, and over the amount of land under cultivation, a careful calculation being made of the amount of raw material that a given area was expected to produce. Furthermore, the manufacture of the oil was carried out under the supervision of royal officials. The oil-workers, it is to be observed, though free men, were not permitted to transfer from one district to another. The sale of the manufactured oils was entrusted to a large number of retailers who were obliged to give up their receipts to the royal treasury. The importation of foreign oil was either forbidden or else rendered difficult by heavy protective tariffs. Regulations no less strict governed the royal monopoly of linen fabrics and doubtless all the others as well. Thus, the sale monopoly of linen goods was absolute. As to the production of articles from home-grown flax, the priests again had some privileges, for much of the manufacture was certainly in their hands and they were amongst the most important consumers of the manufactured goods. Yet they could not sell what was surplus to temple requirements, but had to deliver it up to the king's officials. We also hear of private persons being allowed to make linen fabrics. Presumably the privilege was granted to those who were exceptionally skilled in the technical processes involved; but they could only sell to the king, and at a fixed sale-price. In connection with the monopolies must be mentioned the rather elaborate banking system of the Ptolemies. The *papyri* distinguish royal from ordinary banks. The former existed in Alexandria and in the chief administrative districts; in addition some of the villages had sub-offices. The business transacted was entirely concerned with the monopolies. The ordinary banks existed for the citizens to carry out their private transactions more expeditiously, but no one might set up as a banker without a royal patent, or, in the words of a *papyrus*, no one, unless he has leased the right to do so, "may buy, sell, or exchange silver." In short, banking, like the production of most food-products

and articles of daily use — and many luxury goods as well —
was under state control. While it is beyond dispute that the
result of this intensive system was a tremendous development
of all the natural resources available in the country and filled
the royal treasuries with untold wealth, it meant an exploitation
by the Ptolemies of the mass of their subjects, without any
adequate return to them, which it would be difficult either to
parallel or to defend.

Under the energetic rule of the earlier Ptolemies and Seleucids
a remarkable expansion of trade, especially between the Mediterranean world and the East, was seen. The records taken
by men like Alexander's general, Nearchus, which taught the
Greeks much about the Persian Gulf and Indian Ocean, were
of great value to the merchants of the next generations. The
chief avenue of trade from India to the Seleucid kingdom led
by sea to the head of the Persian Gulf; thence it passed up the
Tigris to Seleuceia, and thence by one or other of the caravan
routes across the desert to Antioch, Tyre, or Damascus. Two
overland routes from central Asia and India, a southern one
through Susa and a more northern one through Media, both
led to Seleuceia, which thus became a mart of exceptional importance. The kings of Egypt promoted exploration of the
Red Sea, the Somali coast, and southern Arabia. A voluminous
trade between these regions and Alexandria developed rapidly,
and in time was even extended to southern India. In the Mediterranean area also there was much commercial activity. Merchant boats of larger tonnage were constructed, and many
maritime cities, even those of quite secondary standing, made
a considerable outlay on improving their harbors. While
Alexandria's exports and imports far surpassed those of any
other centre, Corinth, Delos, Ephesus, Cyzicus, and, above all,
Rhodes, prospered exceedingly. Rhodes indeed may be said
to have superseded Peiræus as the nodal point of the carrying
trade in the Aegean. Sporadic evidence suggests that many
smaller communities, proportionately to their size and resources,
did no less well. Nor must the economic importance of the
smaller monarchies be overlooked, especially Pergamum. At
its greatest extent the kingdom of the Attalids included some
thirty Greek allied states, among them the islands of Chios

and Samos, eighteen subject communities, and eleven military colonies; besides these there were several dependent tribes of non-Hellenic stock in the interior of Asia Minor. The royal domains were cultivated by a serf population as in Syria. The territory, moreover, was rich in sundry raw materials — timber and pitch from the vicinity of Mount Ida, silver, and copper. Parchment was a monopoly there as *papyrus* was in Egypt, and there existed royal factories at Pergamum, run by slave labor, for its manufacture and for the weaving of certain kinds of textiles.

Some advance in business methods is another noticeable feature of the age. Letters of credit were now by no means uncommon, and the larger banks at least did important business in loans, not merely to individuals but to city corporations. It must be remembered that a money economy was now practically universal throughout the Hellenic world and was spreading even beyond its confines. If Alexander's measures to secure an international currency were not permanent, at least the amount of money in circulation from his time was vastly greater than before. His Hellenistic successors all gave much attention to currency matters; and, though there was not one single standard, there were only two of real importance. The majority of the Hellenic world followed one or the other, the Alexander drachma (which was on the same standard as the Athenian) or the Phœnician.

No better proof of the universality of Hellenism in this epoch can be found than the following circumstance: Attic Greek, which already in the fourth century had with insignificant exceptions become the regular literary language, now became the universal language of polite intercourse, of diplomacy, and of business. Thus we find it used not merely by the Ptolemies and their officials but by Egyptian peasants — though often incorrectly enough — in appeals and litigation. It was employed by the Roman government when it intervened in the affairs of the Near East; and the study of Greek in Rome and Italy then progressed rapidly, so that by the beginning of the first century B.C. a good working knowledge of that tongue was a necessary part of the equipment of every educated man. Above all, be it noted that for the benefit of the Jews of the Dispersion — that is, the numerous Jewish colonies outside Judæa — their sacred scriptures were translated into Greek. The Pentateuch had been so rendered before the end of the third century; gradually all the books of the Old Testament became available in the common language of intercourse.[1] For long the Greek version was freely used by even the learned Jews and enjoyed high authority, so that the erudite Philo quoted it, and regarded it as of equal value with the original Hebrew text. The existence of this translation and others of a later date also enabled non-Jews to become familiar with Hebrew writings, a fact which was to become of supreme importance to the early Christian communities.

A very notable development of the Hellenistic Age is the spread of education, and the realization by the city governments that this was a matter which should not be left entirely to private initiative and enterprise. There was a general tendency for municipal or town authorities to exercise some control. At the same time much of the money needed for such purposes was provided, not by the treasury, but by grants or bequests of public-spirited citizens. Copious epigraphical material shows that these varied greatly both in size and purpose. In 200–199 B.C. a citizen of Miletus gave no less than ten talents of silver, from the interest of which four school and four gymnastic teachers were to be paid; in addition, a certain proportion of the annual income was earmarked for religious processions and sacrifices, in which the city youth were to take part. At Teos a generous citizen bequeathed 30,000 drachmas. From the interest a number of annually elected instructors were paid, namely: three elementary teachers at 600, 550, and 500 drachmas respectively, two gymnastic instructors at 500 each, one teacher of the *cithara* at 700, and two instructors in military exercises at 250 and 300 drachmas. As the last named was required to teach not less than two months in the year, it is clear that his was only a part-time appointment. In 159 the people of Delphi appealed for financial aid to King Attalus II "on behalf of the teaching of their children." His Majesty

---

[1] To the modern Old Testament scholar this version, called the *Septuagint*, is of superlative importance, because it preserves in translation a text which is about a thousand years older than any extant Hebrew manuscript.

made a donation of 18,000 drachmas for the purpose. The people of Halicarnassus and of Priene were less fortunate when they applied to princes for funds. Promises were forthcoming, but apparently nothing further. Smaller bequests in different towns were intended to support a single teacher or some educational official; to provide for the regular purchase of oil for use in the wrestling-schools; to help to defray the cost of gymnastic competitions; to subsidize new, or pay for the repair of old, school-buildings or equipment; to provide for baths; and, quaintest of all, to pay for a good supply of sponges, as well as for some one to guard the clothes of the bathers.

Though we may now suppose that all boys in the towns, and a good many from the rural districts, received some elementary schooling, and though we have evidence that more attention was paid to teaching the rudiments to girls, more advanced tuition continued to be, as before, only within the reach of the upper class. The word, *ephebeia*, or training of the *ephebi* (young men from eighteen to twenty years of age), which had in the fourth century signified their compulsory military training, in the Hellenistic period acquired a somewhat wider meaning. The institution ceased to be compulsory; it was limited to one year's duration; and, from being military, the training became athletic and intellectual. The general direction of the *ephebeia* was in the hands of a magistrate, called *kosmetes;* he was elected annually and was responsible to the town council before which he laid his yearly report. The teachers appointed by the community to instruct the *ephebi* were all instructors in physical training and athletics. But attendance at the schools of rhetoric and philosophy was a compulsory part of the young men's curriculum during their ephebic year. The life which the students lived was largely communal in character, and its organization was left mainly to the youths themselves. They elected from among themselves a number of the ablest and most popular *ephebi*, who performed various duties and had varying privileges. By analogy with the institutions of the municipality, they were designated by the titles, archon, polemarch, thesmothetes, and so forth. This system, which was of great benefit to the sons of the wealthy, prevailed, as the inscriptions attest, in every larger Hellenic community, not only in Greece but in Asia Minor and Syria, in Alexandria, and as far west as Massilia. The general organization was probably the same everywhere, though in matters of detail there were naturally variations. Thus, the age of admission in Egypt, where boys reached maturity more quickly than in Greece, was appreciably lower. At Athens the Ptolemaion, founded early in the third century by Ptolemy II, was the headquarters of the *ephebeia*. Besides the quarters specially set aside for gymnastic training, it contained a library and lecture-halls. An inscription records the interesting fact that in one year the *ephebi* presented one hundred volumes to the library. Though every city would have its rhetors, there were a few centres which became particularly famous for their teachers of this subject or of philosophy. Such, for example, were Athens, Pergamum, Rhodes, and, particularly at a later date, Antioch. Cities like these in time attracted students from all quarters of the Hellenic world. In conclusion it will not be uninstructive to consider one of the best preserved ephebic inscriptions in somewhat more detail. After the usual preliminaries the activities of the *ephebi* in the past year are set out at some length. We learn that they have taken part in the festival of Artemis Agrotera and in the Eleusinia; also, that they have made sacrifice to Athena Nike and to other divinities. The record then continues:

They have regularly attended the gymnasia throughout the year and have regularly rendered obedience to the director, considering that good discipline was of the greatest importance and most essential. They have incurred no censure in respect of the instructions laid down for them by the people and have obeyed the orders given them by the *kosmetes* and by their teachers. They have punctually attended the classes of Zenodotus in the Ptolemaion and Lyceum, and also of the other philosophers in the Lyceum and the Academy throughout the year.

Guard duties on the Attic frontier are also mentioned, and we are told that the young men "became really familiar with the country and the roads." Then there follows a long list of shrines at which the *ephebi* have made sacrifices, and of festivals in different parts of the country in which they participated in some way or another, sometimes by offerings, sometimes, when there were athletic displays in connection with the festival,

a

b

ATHENS: *a.* Dionysiac Theatre; *b.* Temple of Olympian Zeus

Plate 32

a

b

ATHENS: *a.* MONUMENT OF LYSICRATES; *b.* HOROLOGIUM OF ANDRONICUS (So-called
Tower of the Winds)

by taking a prominent share in these. "They observed," we learn, "good will and friendship towards one another, and, carrying out the plans of the *kosmetes*, indulged in no riots during the whole year." Equipment in the gymnasia which had become worn out was replaced by them at their own expense. Then there follow the usual vote of approval and the resolution conferring a wreath and special seats at festivals on the *ephebi*. The second half of the decree records a vote of thanks to the *kosmetes* and to the teachers. As far as the activities of the past year are concerned it is mainly a repetition of the first part of the decree.[1]

2. ART

The intensity and general prosperity of urban life found its outward expression in carefully planned and well-built towns. The excavation of sites like Delos, Priene, Magnesia, or Miletus, enables one to obtain a far clearer notion of a Hellenistic city than any that can be formed of one in the age of Pericles or Demosthenes. These numerous Greek and Græco-Oriental towns one and all had certain common features; in all there were temples, an *agora*, or market-place, a town hall, a theatre, a gymnasium, and public baths. The lay-out of the streets was as far as possible rectangular; otherwise the plan of different cities varied, being in fact mainly determined by the nature of the territory occupied. The *agora* was in design a court shut off from outside by walls on three sides and adorned on the inside by colonnades. The fourth side of the rectangle was open and bounded by a main street. Paved streets were still the exception; and, though care was taken to ensure an adequate and wholesome water-supply, open drainage was the general rule. Subterranean sewers are mostly an improvement of Roman date. The private houses were adequately comfortable without being at all elaborate. In Delos the dwellings are built around a single court which usually has a colonnade. The chief room of the house is at the farther end of the court, the smaller apartments opening on the sides. Some, at least, of the Delian houses had an upper story. In Priene the colonnades are absent. A long passage regularly leads from the

[1] *Inscriptiones Graecae* II, 1, 471.

street to the courtyard, on three sides of which are various rooms; at the far end of it is a pillared vestibule giving access to the main reception room.

In temple architecture there were no fundamental changes but a great deal of variety in detail. The Doric order was used less and less; where it still occurs the columns have more slender proportions than the examples of the fifth century. The Ionic order retained its wide popularity and at the same time the ornate Corinthian gained rapidly in favor. Seeing that there was great activity in building sacred edifices, varying from massive temples to small shrines, it is not surprising to find much variation in structural detail. Most magnificent of all was the new temple of Apollo at Didyma near Miletus, which, besides its great size, had several uncommon features. It was surrounded by two rows of columns with the unusual number of ten on the short sides. Between the two ends of the ante-chamber walls stood, instead of the usual two pillars, three rows of four columns each. The front row of columns on the east side had sculptured bases, a feature found also in the Artemisium at Ephesus. Again the usual large temple building was replaced at Didyma by a sunken court, at one end of which was a small enclosed shrine containing the cult-image of the god. The court was approached from the vestibule by an impressive stairway of twenty-two steps.

Another novelty in peristyles, which was credited to a second-century architect, Hermogenes, consisted in planning a stylo-bate wide enough for a double row of columns all round and then omitting the inner row, thus creating an unusually wide ambulatory round the cella. It was perhaps because Hermogenes was responsible for the magnificent temple of Artemis Leucophryene at Magnesia on the Mæander that he was wrongly believed to be the originator of this style. For earlier examples of an unusually wide ambulatory are known.[1] The ground plan of the temple at Magnesia shows that it was of this pseudo-dipteral type with eight columns on the short and fifteen on the long sides. The temple of Zeus at Athens, begun in the sixth century but soon discontinued, was taken in hand

---

[1] For instance, the Greek temple at Pompeii, the so-called temple G at Selinus in Sicily, and the temple of Apollo Smintheus in the Troad.

afresh in 174 by Antiochus Epiphanes. It was a true dipteral temple with Corinthian columns; fifteen of these erect and one fallen can still be seen *in situ* (Plate 32*b*). The imposing structure was not finally completed till the time of Hadrian. Decidedly eccentric, at least when judged by earlier standards, was the temple of the Cabeiri in Samothrace. It was a long narrow building with an apsidal end, the only columns being fourteen in front of the vestibule. Occasional innovations are also found in architectural details, for instance in the Ionic capitals or in the practice of fluting only the upper half of columns and leaving the lower half plain. Stone theatres became much commoner than they had been in the fourth century. Municipal buildings, like the council-hall (*buleuterion*) at Miletus, also show the influence of theatral construction; for that edifice consisted of a large square hall, with a single row of columns on three sides forming three aisles, and of a semicircular auditorium with rising tiers of seats beyond.

Two great and costly structures deserve special mention. The harbor of Alexandria, as befitted so important a centre, was the finest in the world. On Pharos island, guarding its entrance, a great lighthouse, reputed to have stood almost 400 feet high, was built by the architect-engineer Sostratus. This impressive as well as useful building deserved to be reckoned, as indeed it was, one of the wonders of the world. A mole, almost a mile in length, connected the island with the mainland, thus making a double sea-harbor; a canal joined the western half to Lake Mareotis, the port to and from which the abundant river traffic flowed. At Pergamum the great altar of Zeus was a splendid monument set up by Eumenes II (197–159). Upon a lofty base stood an Ionic colonnade, which surrounded on three sides a great court. In the middle of this the actual altar was situate. The base in question was decorated with a great frieze, whose total length was fully 400 feet. The subject represented was the battle of the Gods and Titans. The figures were of more than human size and in such high relief that the upper part was sometimes completely detached from the background. In the treatment of this relief, which can still be studied in the Berlin Museum, as in much of the sculpture of the earlier Hellenistic period, the influence of Scopas is still discernible.

In portraiture, similarly, which was a very popular form of art, and in the treatment of athletic or quasi-athletic subjects, the influence of Lysippus and his school lasted for a considerable time. Lysippus, indeed, produced sundry pupils noted in their day. Chares of Lindus, for example, was the author of a colossal bronze statue, about 100 feet high, of Helios, the sun-god, which commemorated the successful defense of Rhodes against the assaults of Demetrius in 305. Another pupil of Lysippus, Eutychides, was commissioned to fashion an allegorical group, representing the Fortune of the city of Antioch in Syria crowned by Seleucus and Antiochus. The central figure, Antioch, was portrayed as a woman seated on a rock, symbolical of the hill on whose slopes the city stood; she was wrapped in a rich cloak and wore a turreted crown on her head, alluding to the city's fortifications. A swimming male figure at her feet symbolized the Orontes, the river on whose banks Antioch stood. Apart from the intrinsic merits of this work, it was important because it established a type of personified figure that was frequently copied in succeeding centuries.

The general characteristics of Hellenistic sculpture are a love of novelty, both in seeking new subjects and in treating old themes in a new way; a constant and even excessive desire for depicting movement; and a realism which contrasts strongly with the art of the classical period, and in time often degenerated into grotesqueness or veritable anatomical studies. This last tendency we see exemplified both in the famous Laocoön group and in the Heracles of the Villa Farnese. Most of the features, good and bad, of Hellenistic sculpture can be studied in the products of the Pergamene school of the late third and the second centuries. Allusion has already been made to the plastic decoration of the great altar of Zeus. The impression left on the spectator by the contending figures in the titanic struggle there represented is one of tremendous strength, great variety in grouping, and consummate technical skill. But closer observation will reveal features less admirable — a certain theatricality in some of the figures, excessive intricacy in the whole design which wearies the eye, making it difficult to envisage either the whole or its parts, and incongruities like the flying draperies of Zeus that are quite out of place in a battle, or his thunderbolt

VICTORY OF SAMOTHRACE

Plate 33a

BUST OF ALEXANDER THE GREAT

Plate 34

which pierces his adversary's leg like any common spear. Attalus I, the father of Eumenes II, had already been a generous patron of the arts; for he commissioned sculptors to create a series of statues in commemoration of his victories over the Gauls. The best known of these, the so-called Dying Gaul, is a marble copy, probably of contemporary Pergamene workmanship, of the bronze original. This is a superb piece of restrained realism, both for the heroic fortitude of the features and the modelling of the torso and legs, which are wonderfully lifelike without being marred by the exaggerated anatomical detail found in so much Græco-Roman work. The same ruler presented a series of bronze statues, somewhat under life size, some representing Gauls and Persians, others gods, giants, and Amazons, to Athens where they were set up on the Acropolis. Again only marble copies of some are preserved. They are technically most skillful and likely to be contemporary replicas; yet these studies of the various attitudes in death, which has come to some more, to some less, violently, are not untouched with some degree of morbid sensationalism.

Among the finest surviving examples of Hellenistic sculpture in the round are the Aphrodite of Melos (2d century?) and the Winged Victory from Samothrace (c. 250? Plate 33a). The Greek mainland appears to have produced few artists of note, if we except Damophon of Messene who flourished in the middle of the second century. Some heads and fragments of drapery from a colossal group by him have been excavated at Lycosura in Arcadia. It was a piece of cult-statuary representing Demeter and Persephone flanked by Artemis and the Titan Anytus. The treatment of the extant heads shows that Damophon was a sculptor of a high order who was consciously influenced by the cult-statues of an earlier age; that is to say, there is some approximation in treatment to the statues of divinities produced in the fifth century. We must also emphasize once more the Hellenistic fondness for *genre* scenes. Some are sculptures in the round, like the popular Boy and Goose by Lysippus' pupil, Boethus, which was subsequently reproduced many times with or without variations; but more common are reliefs with scenes from town or country, or romantic episodes from mythology or real life. In short, the total output of plastic

art in the third and second centuries must have been enormous,
and the copious remains are but a tithe of the total. Much of
what has survived shows great excellence; yet we miss in this
epoch outstanding masters of the art who could be set side
by side with a Pheidias or a Praxiteles.

In painting much the same happened. The art in general,
and especially mural paintings, were exceedingly popular. But
we hear in literature of no Hellenistic peers of an Apelles or a
Zeuxis, although Timomachus of Byzantium (*c.* 150?) enjoyed
a great reputation in his day and after. Moreover, in the
case of sculpture some originals and many first-rate reproduc-
tions have survived in addition to numerous inferior copies;
but in the case of painting there is virtually nothing save the,
for the most part, very indifferent replicas made several centuries
later to decorate the houses of Herculaneum and Pompeii.
Some of these appear to reproduce Greek works of the third,
second, and first centuries B.C., but how faithfully it is difficult
to estimate. The subjects of the larger pictures were taken
chiefly from the epic cycle or from mythology — Heracles as
the slave of Omphale, Achilles on Scyros, Dionysus and Ariadne,
and so forth. The artist's palette appears to have been somewhat more varied than that used by the older generations of
painters, and there was more freedom in the treatment of
subjects because the problems of perspective had been solved.
For smaller surfaces *genre* or still life were much in favor.
Landscape painting for its own sake was not developed; and
the scenes which form the background for figure-subjects, on
which the Hellenistic artist's entire interest was focussed, were
flat and conventional. As for the minor arts, vase painting, it
is true, passed out of fashion, but extant silver vessels with
designs in high relief, either *répoussé* or applied, are proof
that the wealthy could and did obtain for their houses ornaments of superb design and craftsmanship. No less admirable
was the work of the coin-engraver. The rapidly growing popularity of, and skill in, portraiture is reflected very strongly in
the issues of many Hellenistic rulers, which are among the
finest coins ever made in antiquity.

CHAPTER XXVI

THE HELLENISTIC AGE

> *I hate the cyclic poem and take no pleasure in*
> *the trail that leads many hither and thither. I*
> *detest too the lover encircled by a throng, nor do I*
> *drink from the fountain. I loathe all that pertains*
> *to the people.* — Callimachus (*Anthologia Pala-*
> *tina* xii, 43).

1. LITERATURE

THROUGHOUT the Hellenistic and the Græco-Roman eras
Athens remained the headquarters of the philosophic schools
and never lost her premier position in this respect, even when
distinguished philosophers, belonging to this or that sect, for a
while attracted numerous disciples in some other city. Apart
from philosophic studies, however, she ceased to be the intellectual centre of the Hellenic world. Literature, linguistic
and scientific research, flourished in various places; among them
the position of Alexandria was long preëminent and unique. The
credit for this belongs to Ptolemy I, and even more to Ptolemy
II. The so-called Museum (*i.e.* temple of the Muses) of Alexandria was founded as a religious guild. Its buildings included
a spacious mansion in which the members dined in common.
They were nominated by the king, and, besides their subsistence, received salaries and enjoyed certain privileges. Some
gave occasional lectures in public; but this was not obligatory;
for the Museum was not an educational establishment but an
institute for research. Great and successful efforts were made
by the king to attract the most eminent persons in literature
and science to Alexandria. A magnificent library, which by the
middle of the third century seems to have boasted of not less
than half a million manuscripts, was another of the glories of
the city. And, in both that century and the next, a number of
exceptionally able and learned men presided as librarians of this

impressive collection. Ptolemy II appears to have been something more than a patron of science and the arts. He had the
most varied interests. He took part in philological discussions,
he was a good connoisseur of painting, and he spent much money
and labor in forming a collection of rare animals from the
interior of Africa.

It is in one way difficult to evaluate the worth of Hellenistic
literature because the bulk of it has perished. At the same time
its very non-survival cannot be wholly the result of an accident.
We shall, indeed, hardly err in believing 'that, in the main, its
attraction was more ephemeral than, and lacked the enduring
worth of, the earlier literature of Greece. It has already been
pointed out how poetry and the drama declined during the
fourth century, and how its great productions were the philosophical writings of Plato and the speeches of the orators.
One of the features of the early Hellenistic period was a revival
in dramatic writing of a certain type.

The so-called New Comedy had many exponents, of whom the
chief were Diphilus, Menander (c. 342–291), and Philemon
(died in 262). It was rooted in Athens, and after the passing
of its writers in the third century it languished entirely. The
recent recovery of *papyri*, containing considerable fragments of
several plays by Menander, has amplified our knowledge of
compositions which previously could only be appraised from the
Latin adaptations of Plautus and Terence. Having brought
out his first play when he was barely twenty-one, Menander
composed more than a hundred others before he died at a
comparatively early age. About two thirds of his play, *The
Arbitration*, is now available; of the *Shorn Woman* about four
hundred and fifty lines, of the *Woman from Samos* rather more
than three hundred lines survive. Besides these longer fragments
there is a number of shorter pieces; in some cases the plays from
which they come can be identified, in others not. The first
thing that is likely to strike the modern reader is how little these
comedies have in common with the Old Comedy of Aristophanes
and his contemporaries. The second is the close similarity in
plot of one Menandrean comedy to another. Of earlier writers
the one whose influence is most palpable was not a comic poet
at all, but Euripides. His characters, though belonging in

name to the age of heroes, had often been not of heroic but of very human stature. We see in him too — for example, in the *Alcestis* — the beginnings of that parodying of myths which was carried further by the comic poets of the fourth century and left its mark on the New Comedy as well. Thus we may instance the flippant way in which a character in the *Woman from Samos* (244 ff.) alludes to one of the legends about Zeus. The use of coincidence and recognition scenes in the structure of the plot was another Euripidean feature which survived and was adapted by Menander and his fellows for their ends. Finally, it was in Euripides' plays that love romance first found a prominent place. In the New Comedy love intrigues were invariably, as far as we know, the central theme round which the play was built up. On the other hand, that glory of the Old Comedy, the chorus, had all but disappeared in the fourth century as an integral part of the comedy. The choruses in Menander were mere interludes between different scenes. By them the passage of time in the action of the play was marked; but we know that the poet in the published edition of his plays omitted the choral interludes entirely. Gone, too, were public characters from the comic stage. The men and women in the New Comedy were purely fictitious, and, what is more, even the names tended to become stereotyped, so that the audience would know at once that, if Moschion or Chæreas were mentioned, young men were referred to, but if Laches or Demeas were named, the allusion was to elderly citizens.

Menander, in spite of an invitation to Alexandria, remained in Attica all his life, and it is there that his comedies of manners had their setting. Yet, because these stories of disobedient sons and angry fathers, injured wives and designing courtesans were true pictures of a certain class in any Hellenistic city, the plays enjoyed great popularity in the third century wherever Greek was spoken. Since the same names and personages, and even similar situations, appear to have occurred again and again in these comedies, variety was attained by the dramatist in various other ways. Menander was a great artist in language. His sententiousness and pregnant phrases were famous in antiquity. His characterization, as can still be studied in *The Arbitration*, was exceedingly subtle, while his philosophy of life

in an age of suffering and unrest was notably humane. At the
same time there is something almost despairing in such an
utterance as (Fr. 355):

> So unlooked for is advantage, whatever it be, that Fortune produces
> in man's life. She employs no laws according to which she decides the
> circumstances. Nor can any man, while he lives, say, "that experience
> I shall not undergo."

On the other hand, we seem to detect an almost Epicurean echo
in the arguments of the glib slave, Onesimus (*Arbitration*,
624 ff.):

> ONESIMUS. Think you the gods have so much leisure that they
> allot to each mortal man good and ill each day, Smicrines?
> SMICRINES. What mean you?
> ONESIMUS. I will explain to you clearly. All the cities (in the world)
> number a thousand or thereabouts and each has thirty-thousand in-
> habitants. Do the gods destroy or succour each of these, one by one?
> SMICRINES. How so? In that case you mean that the gods have
> an arduous life.
> ONESIMUS. "Do not they take thought for us then?" you will say.
> To each man they have given Character as a commandant to share his
> home. He, ever present, is the undoing of one who seems to use him
> ill, and protects another. He is our god, and he it is whose fault it is
> that one man fares well, the other ill. Him do you appease, by doing
> nothing inept or crude, so that you may fare well.

Whatever our final judgment on the artistic merits of the New
Comedy may be, its influence extended through the centuries.
For it passed to Rome and in its Roman dress became the
literary ancestor of the comedy of manners, a dramatic form
which has enjoyed wide popularity in European literature.
The idyll and the epigram were two much admired literary
forms that were perfected in the Alexandrian period.   The
former, which means a self-contained little picture, is associated
especially with the names of Callimachus and Theocritus. But
their style and subject differed greatly; and, whereas Callimachus was most admired by his contemporaries, posterity has
had no hesitation in reversing that judgment in favor of
Theocritus. Theocritus was a native of Sicily (flourished *c.* 270)
who spent a good part of his adult life in Alexandria.   His
idylls treat a variety of subjects. He was equally successful in

portraying a girl weaving a magic spell to be revenged on a faithless lover (*Id.* 2) and recording graphically the conversation of two Alexandrian women of the people as they watched with the crowd the festival of Adonis (*Id.* 15). But his most exquisite poems are the pastoral idylls in which he sketches the life of the Sicilian shepherds and paints a charmingly naturalistic picture of the joys and trials of rustic life. These bucolic poems have often been imitated — for instance, by Vergil in his earliest work, the *Eclogues* — but never equalled.

The epigram, suitable as it was for a brief and elegant treatment of almost any topic, remained a favorite verse form for many centuries.[1] In the third century B.C. Callimachus was regarded as the greatest master of this form. He was a man of immense learning and a voluminous writer. Comparatively little of his poetry has survived. His longest work, entitled *Aitia* (Causes), ran to four books of elegiac verse. In them the poet discoursed on festivals and games, on various customs, religious and secular, and on the stories connected with the foundation of cities and temples. This choice of themes gave him ample scope for displaying his vast erudition, particularly in the realm of Greek mythology and legendary history. Substantial extracts from this work have come to light in recently deciphered *papyri*. He further composed many hymns and compositions of a courtly kind, like his *Threnody on Arsinoë* and the *Lock of Berenice*, a poem that later found an inspired translator in the Roman poet, Catullus. Felicity of phrase, restraint, and polish were the qualities that chiefly distinguished Callimachus' verse. As the saying attributed to him suggests, "a great book is a great evil," it was chiefly shorter poems which he favored, and in this he set a fashion. In his epigrams alone he sometimes forgets his learning and his habitual reserve to strike a note of genuine emotion or simple pathos.

The age, however, also saw the production of sundry didactic and literary epics, some being of considerable length. To the former class belongs an astronomical poem by Aratus of Soli in

[1] The collection of epigrams made *c.* 920 A.D. by Constantine Cephalas, and now known as the *Palatine Anthology*, because it was discovered early in the seventeenth century by Salmasius in the Palatine Library at Heidelberg, contains poems by more than three hundred writers, extending from the sixth century before to the sixth century after Christ.

Cilicia. In spite of the forbidding nature of the subject this work enjoyed a great vogue. Passages from it were imitated by Vergil in his *Georgics*, and it was translated into Latin first by Cicero and later more successfully by Germanicus, whose version continued long to command attention in medieval Europe among the small band of students of advanced astronomical lore. Of literary or romantic epics the most notable was the *Argonautica* of Apollonius. An Alexandrian by birth, he succeeded Zenodotus in the direction of the great library; he also supervised the studies of the young Ptolemy Euergetes. However, a literary quarrel with Callimachus, and possibly political reasons also, constrained Apollonius to retire to the island of Rhodes. There he became a citizen and passed the remainder of his life. The *Argonautica* in four books runs to some six thousand lines in all. Books 1 and 2 relate with much detail the voyage of the Greek heroes, led by Jason, to Colchis in quest of the golden fleece. The central episode of the story fills Book 3, namely, the romantic passion for Jason of the Colchian princess, Medea, by whose aid the Greeks are enabled to carry out their undertaking. The fourth and longest Book records at somewhat wearisome length the adventures of the heroes on their homeward journey. It is more loosely constructed than the other three and ends quite inconclusively, so that the reader is left in uncertainty about the ultimate fate of the chief characters in the story. The epic is marred all through by the excessive erudition of its author. This was a characteristically Alexandrian fault which we have already observed in the case of Callimachus. On the other hand, Book 3 is distinguished by passages of singular beauty and passion; the poet has been so carried away by his central theme that his pedantic love of learned display is temporarily in abeyance. The *Argonautica* does not seem to have enjoyed much popularity; but, more than two centuries later, it was read by Vergil, who derived some inspiration from it, and did not disdain to imitate some of its episodes in his own greater epic, the *Aeneid*. Of far more modest proportions were miniature epics in which the grand manner was applied half playfully to some slighter theme. This type of poem has a close parallel in those *genre* scenes of which Hellenistic art was especially fond. And, indeed, the best of them, the *Little Heracles* by Theocritus, relates the story how the infant Heracles strangled the serpents that attacked his cradle, a subject also portrayed many times in sculpture and painting.

All this abundance of verse put out in the Hellenistic Age, however much it might vary in quality, at all events was meant only for the educated minority. A less elevated class of composition, the mime, made its appeal to the common man. Little was known about the mime until the publication in 1891 of a *papyrus* of seven such, all but complete, and some fragments of others by Herondas (flourished *c.* 240?).[1] They are all short scenes written in dialogue and in the choliambic metre,[2] dealing with some episode from everyday life. For instance: a mother brings her refractory boy to the schoolmaster for a well-deserved whipping; a jealous woman is restrained with difficulty from cruelly punishing her slave; two women visit the temple of Asclepius to make an offering to the god; two others go to a cobbler's shop and haggle with him, after he has set out his wares before them with all the volubility of a practised salesman. Though marked by a realism that is often sordid and devoid of poetic beauties, these dramatic sketches are executed with considerable humor and a certain terse brilliance which command admiration even where the subject is most objectionable.

The prose literature of the Hellenistic Age was ample and varied, but the bulk of it has not survived. Thus only too often the modern student is confronted with the names of authors and perhaps the titles of their works without being able to obtain a clearer view either of the man or of his writings. It was not for the most part a creative or an imaginative, so much as a technical, literature; for the scientific trend of the age manifested itself also in the realm of letters. The world owes an incalculable debt to the critics and philologists of Alexandria. Zenodotus (*c.* 280), Eratosthenes (*c.* 234), Aristophanes (*c.* 195), and Aristarchus (*c.* 170), all of whom in their

[1] The fifteenth 'idyll' of Theocritus — the women at the festival of Adonis — belongs to the class of mimes, but is less crudely realistic than those of Herondas.

[2] The choliambic line differs from the iambic *senarius* in that the sixth or final foot is not an iambus ($\smile$ —) but a spondee (— —) or trochee (— $\smile$).

turn were keepers of the great library at Alexandria, carried on linguistic researches, and textual criticism and exegesis of the writers of early and classical Greece. Revised texts were prepared of those precious works, spurious writings were distinguished from genuine, careful recensions of the Homeric poems were made, in which supposed interpolations of a later date were marked, learned commentaries were compiled on most of the important classical authors, and, in each branch of literature, certain authors and their works were selected and classed as canonical.[1] Many of the surviving scholia on Greek writers, though put together at a later date, preserve substantial portions of these Alexandrian labors. Granted that these scholars were occasionally arbitrary in their criticisms and in their handling of ancient texts, they in the main did their work wisely and well. But for their indefatigable "cult of the past," many of the masterpieces of Greek literature might never have survived to delight and instruct later generations down to our own time.

Political and forensic oratory declined with the passing of the autonomous city-state, but the study of rhetoric, and with it epideictic oratory, flourished exceedingly. And the rhetorical displays on a set theme or improvised at the moment remained for centuries a most popular form of entertainment in the Greek and then the Græco-Roman world.

No branch of prose literature was more widely cultivated than history. Most of it has perished and our knowledge of it depends on extracts and adaptations in later compilers, like Diodorus Siculus (c. 80 B.C.), and biographers, like Plutarch (c. 45–125 A.D.). Rightly enough the Greeks never forgot that historical composition is an art; for it is only in our own time that the absurdity of regarding or attempting to treat it as a science has prevailed in some quarters. But unfortunately most of the Hellenistic historians failed to keep a just balance. It was one of the undesirable results of rhetorical training that everything was sacrificed to stylistic form and to the desire for entertainment. Accurate presentation of facts and a philosophic

---

[1] The best known is the Canon of the Ten Attic Orators, namely, Antiphon, Andocides, Lysias, Isocrates, Isæus, Aeschines, Demosthenes, Lycurgus, Hypereides, and Deinarchus.

interpretation of movements and events were regarded as of secondary importance. It is not possible here to enumerate more than a few of the historical authors who flourished in the third and second centuries. It is, however, convenient to distinguish three groups. In the first place, the conquests of Alexander and their immediate results gave rise to a large and varied literature. This was, in truth, of very unequal value; for, on the one hand, there was a number of diaries and records kept by persons closely associated with the conqueror. Such were Nearchus, the admiral who sailed with a fleet of one hundred and fifty vessels from the mouth of the Indus to the Persian Gulf, and Ptolemy Lagus, first one of Alexander's trusted lieutenants and afterwards founder of a dynasty in Egypt. On the other hand, the work of the court historiographer, Callisthenes, would seem to have been very untrustworthy, although subsequent writers used it extensively. The lost book of Aristobulus, once a junior officer in Alexander's army, seems to have been apologetic; that is to say, its chief aim was to clear his hero of calumnies that had come into circulation during the quarter of a century after his death. Still somewhat later was Cleitarchus, whose narrative, published about 270, resembled a historical novel more than a critical history. Sober critics, like Cicero, Strabo, or Quintilian, were aware of Cleitarchus' shortcomings; but the book made up in popularity among a wide and less critical public what it lacked in accuracy. Moreover, it probably did not a little to start that Alexander legend which became one of the most persistent and remarkable subjects in all literary history.

The second group of writers consists of those who essayed to give a general account of some portion of Greek history, the emphasis being commonly placed on the events of the author's own day. By far the most eminent of these, judged by modern standards, was Hieronymus of Cardia. He had a long military and administrative career, in the course of which he came into contact with many of the rivals for power in the early Hellenistic Age. His *History of the Diadochs and Successors* covered the period from 323 to 266. It seems to have been a plain but highly accurate account of the political and military developments during a very stirring half-century. Its lack of stylistic adornment was probably the chief reason why it never became popular. Very different was the *History* of Phylarchus from 272 to 222. Outwardly it was a continuation of Hierony-mus' work; but Phylarchus was a typical exponent of the prevailing fashion in historical writing — flowery, full of digres-sions, and especially distinguished by sensational and harassing episodes, reminiscent of the dramatist rather than the historian. The book was used by Plutarch for his *Lives* of Agis and Cleomenes III, and the parts of Phylarchus thus preserved still have a considerable value because of the author's point of view or political bias. For he was friendly to Sparta and hostile to Aratus of Sicyon, so that his presentation is sometimes a use-ful corrective to the pro-Achæan narrative of Polybius. Duris of Samos (*c.* 340–280) was a polymath as well as a man of affairs. Besides his *History* from 370 to 281 he wrote on literary criticism and on art, and also a monograph on Agathocles of Syracuse.

Very ambitious in scope was the work on the Western Greeks, from the earliest times down to 289, by Timæus of Tauromen-ium (*c.* 345–249). His faults appear to have been many, and have been enumerated almost savagely by Polybius. Timæus was a student writing in his study, industrious in gathering materials but without experience of affairs. He catered to popular taste by introducing much anecdotic material — even of an unsavory kind — and numerous digressions. Yet he had certain definite merits. He made an effort to correlate the chronology and methods of reckoning time in the different Greek cities by dating his narrative by the years of the Olympian festival, combining with this the reckoning in use at Sparta, Argos, and Athens. He took pains to ensure accuracy in his geographical data, so that even Polybius wrote a grudging word of approval for this. If the inclusion of dreams, portents, and legends in his narrative was a fault — and it was one which he shared with many ancient historians — he showed interest in cultural and social history — a very unusual trait at that time — by introducing excursuses on ethnology and social customs, as well as notices of important philosophers, poets, and artists. In this respect, as for his chronological scheme, he deserves all the credit due to a pioneer. Taken all in all, and in spite of Polybius' strictures, Timæus' history probably deserved the wide attention that it secured; for the data amassed by him about the Greeks of Italy and Sicily were a storehouse from which later authors borrowed freely.

Thirdly, the fashion set by some of Alexander's generals was imitated by public men in subsequent ages. Memoirs and autobiographies formed a not insignificant branch of historical literature in the Hellenistic Age. One instance must suffice: the memoirs of Aratus, in spite of their natural bias, were an invaluable source of information about the inner history of the Achæan League during the many years that he was its guiding spirit. Polybius has been left to the last. He belongs, indeed, to our second group; but his exceptional merits as a historian, coupled with the fact that substantial portions of his work have been preserved, make it fitting that he should receive separate consideration. He was a member of an old and wealthy family in Arcadian Megalepolis, his father, Lycortas, playing a leading part in the affairs of the Achæan League. Polybius enjoyed the best education available in his day. As a man he gained ample experience both as a soldier and a statesman. In 167, on the conclusion of the Third Macedonian War, the victorious Romans brought numerous Greek hostages to Rome. Amongst them were a thousand prominent persons of the Achæan League, of whom Polybius was one. His residence in Rome, and the happy circumstance that he obtained the acquaintance and then the friendship of many distinguished Romans, produced in him a deep admiration for the new world-power and inspired him to write the history of its growth. This work in its final form covered the period from 221 to 144, with a briefer introductory section which sketched events from 264 to 222. Only Books 1 to 5 have survived entire; of the other thirty-five there remains a considerable collection of extracts and fragments. He, who criticized freely not only Timæus but many other predecessors, laid down very explicitly the three requirements for a historian. They are: the search for and study of original sources, and, in general, the collection of materials. Secondly, personal inspection of countries and important sites, including the noting down of physical peculiarities, distances, and so forth. Lastly, the historian should have ample experience of political life. The purpose of his work was didactic.

It was not intended for the general public — indeed, as a work of art, it is sadly la⸱⸱⸱ — but for politicians and men of affairs, who would be h⸱ by a study of the past in handling the problems of the present and future. Thus, the digressions that he introduces from time to time are strictly utilitarian and relevant to his main subject.[1] Though by no means free from political bias, Polybius was extremely conscientious in verifying all his data and carefully sifting all the evidence that he accumulated. In the speeches, which he introduced only very sparingly, he tries to fulfil to the best of his ability the dictum of Thucydides (1, 22). And, in general, he ranks as a critical historian next to Thucydides among ancient historians. He is his equal in the technique of historical writing, but falls short of him in philosophic detachment and in the deep insight into the affairs of men and states which characterize the Athenian.

2. PHILOSOPHY AND SCIENCE

The most influential philosophic schools in the period were not the Academy and the Lyceum, nor yet the minor sects founded by members of the Socratic circle, though all continued to flourish fitfully, but the Stoics and Epicureans. By the older philosophers the commu⸱⸱ty was considered to be of primary importance; to it the in⸱⸱⸱ ⸱ual and his claims are essentially subordinate. Even to A⸱ ⸱totle, therefore, "Politics" takes precedence over "Ethics." After his time this attitude is entirely reversed.

The Stoic school was founded by Zeno of Citium in Cyprus about 306 B.C. For many years he taught in the Painted Stoa at Athens, and though at first he seems to have had few hearers, he ended by being universally respected and admired. His successor as head of the Stoa was Cleanthes, who died in 231. He, in turn, was succeeded by Chrysippus (c. 280–204), whom later generations regarded as the second founder of this philosophic sect because by his numerous writings he did so much to formulate more clearly and to systematize the Stoic doctrines.

---

[1] For example, the passage on the use of fire signals in time of war (x, 43 ff.) and the comparison of Macedonian armature and tactics with the Roman (xviii, 26 ff.).

During the following century the most eminent Stoic was Panætius of Rhodes; but in his teaching there was already a noticeable tendency towards eclecticism.

Philosophy, which the Stoics identified with virtue, had for them a strictly practical end. Virtue consists, they held, in harmonizing human actions with the general order of the Universe, knowledge of which is therefore entirely needful. They were the first to adopt the threefold division of philosophy into physics or natural philosophy, ethics, and logic or dialectics. Their conception and system of the Universe were extremely materialistic, being also borrowed very largely from earlier thinkers, for example, Heracleitus, Aristotle, and the Cynics. Their ethical system, on the other hand, was highly idealistic. Men's actions should be in accordance with their own particular nature insofar as that nature is in accord with universal Nature. The individual reason of man is a part of the universal Reason. By the help of his reason he must get rid of his irrational impulses which are perversions of it. While there are many such, the four chief are hope, fear, pleasure, and pain. Only he who has freed himself from the trammels of all such beliefs is virtuous or wise. For the earlier Stoics there was no mean between the wise man and the fool, or the good man and the vicious. But such a system was so exacting and austere that later teachers, for example, Panætius, found it necessary to modify some of the Stoic precepts. They then attributed some value at least to progress towards wisdom and to self-control as contrasted with complete freedom from all irrational impulses; and, between the extremes of good and bad, they allowed that of things in themselves indifferent some were preferable to others. Thus, in addition to the absolute good and absolute evil, there were two intermediate classes, of preferable and of undesirable things; in other terms, while the actions of the wise man are perfectly virtuous, the man who is still striving towards wisdom or perfection can perform appropriate actions which have in view, not indeed the absolute good, but some one of the preferable things. In the application of their moral science there are important characteristics which had a far-reaching influence. For the Stoics claimed to have found a substitute for the two main supports which had hitherto upheld men in their daily conduct, the law of the state and the old religion of Greece. In the ideal state of the Stoics all differences of nationality have been merged in the common brotherhood of man. The earlier Stoics, recognizing that such a world-state was an ideal impossible of attainment but one toward which men should strive, believed and taught that men must not neglect either the political life or the life of the family. It was only in a later age, in the days of imperial Rome, that prominent Stoic teachers, influenced by existing political conditions — for the Roman empire was far removed from the Stoic world-state — sometimes betrayed an aversion to the family and the state. If their doctrines exerted no substantial influence on the rulers of the world, they contributed profoundly towards raising moral standards, and promoting a greater and wider humanity.

The Epicureans were out-and-out individualists. Their founder, who set up a philosophic school at Athens in 306, held quite frankly that the state was made for man, and not man for the state. Such a belief, openly expressed in an earlier age, might well have involved him in a prosecution for impiety or treason. He had no interest in science and natural philosophy for its own sake, but studied it only in order to further his ethical teaching. Sensation he regarded as the only criterion of truth; everything must depend on natural causes. When men were cognizant of that, they would be able to follow a right conduct, untrammelled by fear of the gods and superstitious beliefs. Epicurus borrowed his explanation of the material Universe wholesale from Democritus; that is to say, he took over the atomic theory of the earlier thinker, but introduced some modifications into it. Everything is matter; even the soul is composed of atoms, though they are of much greater fineness or rarity than those of the body. He differs from Democritus in asserting the freedom of the human will, a doctrine at variance with the Democritean theory of necessity. For, since Epicurus' first concern was with moral conduct, he must needs insist on the reality of free-will. The concept was applied to the physical world, so that the Epicurean atoms, instead of falling straight downward like the Democritean, could swerve aside and impinge on one another. Epicurus denied that any superhuman power interferes with human affairs, laying down that all things in the world must be referred to mechanical causes. The existence of the gods — they are composed of atoms finer than those of human beings — is not denied. They dwell apart, unconcerned with the working of the Universe or with the affairs of men.

The highest good in his ethical system was happiness which was equivalent to pleasure. But pleasure, as defined by Epicurus, meant not the gratification of the bodily senses but tranquillity, that is to say, freedom from pain and all that is unpleasant and disturbing. Moreover, while this aspect of pleasure was rather negative, the positive pleasure that he advocated was mental or intellectual. This brought hope and memory into play, and for that reason was more lasting and more directly controlled by man. It is important, then, to bear in mind that Epicurus was not a hedonist; his "pleasure," whether in its positive or its negative aspect, has virtue, that is to say, moral excellence, as its indispensable concomitant. Nevertheless it is easy to see how such tenets could become perverted and that they could be readily misinterpreted by the outside world. The most serious fault of Epicureanism, however, is that it is a cowardly and unsocial theory of conduct. Epicurus and his followers, though they believed in friendship among their own group and derived pleasure therefrom, withdrew themselves from public life and from participation in the affairs of the political community in order to attain to an essentially selfish tranquillity.

Research in the natural sciences had been late in developing in the Hellenic world; also, whereas before scientific inquiry was subordinate to speculative philosophy — for instance, higher mathematics was to Plato merely a preparatory discipline for metaphysics — in the Hellenistic Age various sciences were studied for their own sake. It was Aristotle who, more than any other man, by his teaching and by his own investigations, gave an immense stimulus to further inquiries into that vast field of human knowledge. Theophrastus, his successor as head of the Peripatetic school, made invaluable contributions to botanical studies. The researches and classification carried out by these two men in zoölogy and botany remained authoritative for well-nigh two thousand years, and little advance in biology was made after their time. It was different with mathematics and the related sciences. Geometry as a deductive science was at least as old as the time of Pythagoras, and there is little doubt that during the two centuries following great progress in it was made. About 300, Eucleides (Euclid) of Alexandria brought out his *Elements*. This work offered for the first time a systematic treatment of pure geometry; it remained the accepted textbook on the subject until very recent times. While Eucleides seems to have been mainly a collector and systematizer of existing knowledge, Archimedes of Syracuse (*c.* 287–212), the greatest mathematician of the ancient world, made many important discoveries. Moreover, since he was the first to bring experiment into close connection with mathematical theory, he has not unjustly been regarded as the founder of mechanics and hydrostatics. He himself, though he devised many mechanical contrivances, such as the water screw and compound pulleys, regarded this part of his work as secondary. He assigned the first place to his investigations in pure geometry. He was killed by a Roman soldier, ignorant of his identity, immediately after the capture of Syracuse in 212. A century and a half later, his tomb, all overgrown with briers, was discovered by Cicero. On it were engraved a sphere and a cylinder, an allusion to what Archimedes looked upon as his greatest discovery, namely, the ratio of the volume of a sphere to that of a cylinder. In astronomy the outstanding names are those of Aristarchus of Samos (*c.* 310–230) and Hipparchus whose scientific life extended from *c.* 160 to 130. Aristarchus has the distinction of propounding a heliocentric theory of the Universe, making all the planets move in circles about the sun, which he discovered to be many times larger than the earth. The phenomenon that the fixed stars are apparently motionless in face of the earth's motion he correctly attributed to the fact that the distance of the fixed stars was tremendous in comparison with the diameter of the earth's orbit. Later scientists, mainly perhaps because, in the absence of adequate instruments, they were unable to make their practical observations of the heavens tally with Aristarchus' theory, rejected it. Thus the truth remained obscured till the discoveries of Copernicus eighteen centuries later. Hipparchus, although he reverted to the geocentric theory, was a scholar of great eminence. He may be regarded as the founder of trigonometry; he probably deserves the credit for discovering the precession of the equinoxes, and he was responsible for several important astronomical calculations. Thus his estimates that the distance of the moon from the earth is $33\frac{2}{3}$ times the earth's diameter, and that the moon's diameter is one-third of the earth's, are exceedingly close to the true figures.

Eratosthenes (c. 273–192) we have already met as one of the librarians at Alexandria. But his labors as such, though extensive, formed only a small part of his achievement. He deserves to be regarded as the greatest scholar of his age for his diversified work in mathematics, astronomy, chronology, and physical geography. It was in the last named field that he attained the most marked distinction. His calculation of the earth's circumference as 252,000 stades (c. 24,662 miles) is only two hundred miles short of the modern estimate. From observing the similarity of the tides in the Atlantic and the Indian oceans he deduced correctly that it was possible to sail from Spain to India round the southern end of Africa. This was yet another of those discoveries from which no practical results flowed for many a long century.

The researches in physiology and anatomy made by Herophilus and Erasistratus in the first half of the third century were noteworthy. The former stressed the importance of pulsation, and, by his researches on the more important organs of the body and the dissection of animal and human corpses, greatly advanced knowledge of anatomy. While the credit of discovering the nerves also belongs to him, and their connection with the brain, which he regarded as the seat of intelligence, it was probably Erasistratus, not Herophilus, who went a step further and distinguished the motor from the sensory nervous system. The anatomical investigations of these two men of science also made them successful surgeons in their day. But their momentous contributions to knowledge had less effect than might have been expected, since they were, as it would seem, too advanced for their contemporaries.

SELECT BIBLIOGRAPHY

THE following bibliography makes no pretense to offer more than a brief selection of works dealing with ancient history and civilization, or with special aspects thereof. For full bibliographical information the reader is referred to the *Cambridge Ancient History*. Eight volumes of this have appeared to date, carrying the story down to 133 B.C.

For new publications appearing year by year the student should consult the *Annual Bulletin of Historical Literature* of the English Historical Association, in which the first section is assigned to Ancient History, and *The Year's Work in Classical Studies*, published by the Classical Association, which regularly contains chapters on Greek history. More elaborate bibliographical surveys of Greek history are published from time to time in *Bursians Jahresberichte* (Leipzig: Reisland). The most recent on Greek history is by T. Lenschau in Vol. 218, part 3 (1928). It deals with publications issued between 1915 and 1925. Very valuable also is the French publication edited by G. Marouzeau and entitled *L'année philologique* (Paris: Les Belles Lettres). In the *Journal of Egyptian Archaeology* bibliographical articles by various specialists are issued periodically, recording new works on Egypt from the earliest times down to the beginning of the Byzantine period.

A. GENERAL HISTORIES AND WORKS OF REFERENCE

Cambridge Ancient History. *In progress.* Vols. 1 to 8 (Cambridge University Press, 1923–30) and Vols. 1 to 3 of Plates have appeared to date.

Cavaignac, E. *Histoire de l'Antiquité.* Vols. 1 to 3 (Paris: de Boccard, 1913–20).

Daremberg, C. V. and Saglio, E. *Dictionnaire des antiquités grecques et romaines.* (Paris: Hachette, 1877–1919.)

Gercke, A. und Norden, E. *Einleitung in die Altertumswissenschaft.* Ed. 2, 1914; Ed. 3, 1921 — . (Leipzig: Teubner.)

Kubitschek, J. W. *Grundriss der antiken Zeitrechnung.* (Munich: Beck, 1928.)

Lübker, F. H. C. *Reallexikon des klassischen Altertums.* Ed. 8, 1914. (Leipzig: Teubner.)

Meyer, E. *Geschichte des Altertums.* Vols. 1 to 5. Vol. 1, two parts, in the third edition (1910–13), together with *Nachtrag: die ältere Chronologie Babyloniens, Assyriens und Aegyptens* (1925). Vol. 2, part 1 (1928); part 2 (1931). Vols. 3 to 5 (1901–02). (Stuttgart: Cotta.)

Pauly-Wissowa-Kroll. *Realenzyklopädie des klassischen Altertums. In progress.* So far there has appeared A to Mesyros; RA to Symposion; also five *Supplementbände* (1903–31). This is an indispensable work of reference for any detailed study of classical antiquity. (Stuttgart: Metzler.)

Rostovtzeff, M. *History of the Ancient World.* Vol. 1, Ed. 2 (1930); Vol. 2 (1927). (Oxford University Press.) Vol. 1 is devoted to the Orient and Greece, Vol. 2 to Rome.

B. Chapter I

Brown, G. Baldwin. *The Art of the Cave Dweller.* (London: Murray, 1928.)

Burkitt, M. C. *Prehistory.* (Cambridge University Press, 1921.)

Childe, V. G. *The Aryans.* (London: Kegan, Paul; New York: Knopf, 1926.)

Childe, V. G. *The Bronze Age.* (Cambridge University Press, 1930.)

Childe, V. G. *The Dawn of European Civilization.* (London: Kegan, Paul; New York: Knopf, 1925.)

Déchelette, J. *Manuel d'archéologie préhistorique* 1. (Paris: Picard, 1908.)

Ebert, M. *Reallexikon der Vorgeschichte.* Vols. 1 to 14. (Berlin: de Gruyter, 1921–29.) An indispensable work of reference for the prehistoric period.

Forrer, R. *Reallexikon.* (Stuttgart: Spemann, 1907.)

Hoernes, M. *Natur und Urgeschichte des Menschen.* Vols. 1 and 2 (Vienna: Hartleben, 1909).

Hoernes, M. and Menghin, O. *Urgeschichte der bildenden Kunst.* (Vienna: Schroll, 1925.)

Keith, A. *The Antiquity of Man.* Ed. 2, 1925. (Philadelphia: Lippincott.)

Macalister, R. A. S. *Textbook of European Archaeology:* Vol. 1. *The Palaeolithic Period.* (Cambridge University Press, 1921.)

MacCurdy, G. G. *Human Origins.* Vols. 1 and 2 (New York: Appleton, 1924).

Menghin, O. *Weltgeschichte der Steinzeit.* (Vienna: Schroll, 1931.)

Moret, A. *From Tribe to Empire.* (London: Kegan, Paul; New York: Knopf, 1926.)

Myres, J. L. *The Dawn of History.* (London: Williams and Norgate; New York: Holt, 1911, and reprints.)

Osborn, H. F. *Men of the Old Stone Age.* (New York: Scribners, 1916.)

C. CHAPTERS II–V

Breasted, J. H. *Ancient Records of Egypt.* Vols. 1 to 5 (University of Chicago Press, 1906–07).

Breasted, J. H. *History of Egypt.* Ed. 2, 1909 (New York: Scribners).

Childe, V. G. *The Most Ancient East.* (London: Kegan, Paul; New York: Knopf, 1929.)

Cowley, A. *The Hittites.* (Oxford University Press, 1926.)

Delaporte, L. *La Mésopotamie; les civilisations babylonienne et assyrienne.* (Paris: Renaissance du livre, 1923.)

Erman, A. *Life in Ancient Egypt.* (Macmillan, 1894.) This is an English translation of the first German edition of this work. A new and greatly revised edition of the German original appeared in 1925, entitled *Aegypten.* (Tübingen: Mohr.)

Erman, A. *The Literature of the Ancient Egyptians.* (London: Methuen, 1926.)

Gadd, C. J. *The History and Monuments of Ur.* (London: Chatto and Windus, 1929.)

Garstang, J. *The Land of the Hittites.* Ed. 2, 1929 (London: Constable).

Hall, H. R. *The Ancient History of the Near East.* Ed. 6, 1926 (London: Methuen).

Harper, R. F. *Assyrian and Babylonian Literature.* (New York: Appleton, 1901.)

Harper, R. F. *The Code of Hammurabi.* (University of Chicago Press, 1904.)

Hogarth, D. G. *The Ancient East.* (London: Williams and Norgate; New York: Holt, 1914.)

Hogarth, D. G. *Kings of the Hittites.* (Oxford University Press, 1926.)

Jastrow, M. *The Civilization of Babylonia and Assyria.* (Philadelphia: Lippincott, 1915.)

King, L. W. *History of Babylonia.* (London: Chatto and Windus, 1919.)

King, L. W. *History of Sumer and Akkad.* (London: Chatto and Windus, 1923.)

Maspero, G. *The Dawn of Civilization: Egypt and Chaldæa.* (London: S. P. C. K., 1910.)

Meissner, B. *Babylonien und Assyrien.* Vols. 1 and 2 (Heidelberg: Winter, 1920–25). This is now the best and most detailed treatment of the ancient cultures of Mesopotamia.

Meissner, B.   *Die babylonisch-assyrische Literatur.*   (Wildpark-
Potsdam: Akademische Verlagsgesellschaft, Athenaion, 1928.)

Meyer, E.   *Reich und Kultur der Chethiter.*   (Berlin: Curtius, 1914.)

Petrie, W. M. F.   *Arts and Crafts in Ancient Egypt.*   (London: P.
Davies, 1923.)

Petrie, W. M. F.   *Social Life in Ancient Egypt.*   (London: Constable,
1923.)

Rogers, R. W.   *History of Babylonia and Assyria.*   (New York: Abing-
don Press, 1915.)

Smith, S.   *The Early History of Assyria to 1000 B.C.*   (London: Chatto
and Windus, 1928.)

Wiedemann, A.   *Das alte Aegypten.*   (Heidelberg: Winter, 1920.)

Woolley, L.   *Ur of the Chaldees.*   (New York: Scribner, 1930.)

Wreszinski, W.   *Atlas zur altaegyptischen Kulturgeschichte. In progress.*
(Leipzig: Hinrichs.)

D. Chapter VI

Atkinson, T. D. and others.   *Excavations at Phylakopi in Melos.*
(London and New York: Macmillan, 1904.)

Burn, A. R.   *Minoans, Philistines, and Greeks.*   (London: Kegan,
Paul; New York: Knopf, 1930.)

Chadwick, H. M.   *The Heroic Age.*   (Cambridge University Press,
1912.)

Dörpfeld, W.   *Troja und Ilion.*   Vols. 1 and 2 (Athens: Beck und
Barth, 1902).

Dussaud, R.   *Les Civilisations préhelléniques.*   Ed. 2, 1914 (Paris:
Geuthner).

Evans, A. J.   *The Palace of Minos. In progress.*   Vol. 1, 1921; Vol. 2,
parts 1 and 2, 1928; Vol. 3, 1930.   (London and New York: Macmillan.)

Fimmen, D.   *Die Kretisch-mykenische Kultur.*   Ed. 2, 1921 (Leipzig:
Teubner).

Glotz, G.   *The Aegean Civilization.*   (London: Kegan, Paul; New
York: Knopf, 1927.)   The French original of this book appeared
in 1923.

Hall, H. R.   *The Civilization of Greece in the Bronze Age.*   (London:
Methuen, 1928.)

Leaf, W.   *Troy.*   (London and New York: Macmillan, 1912.)

Leaf, W.   *Homer and History.*   (London and New York: Macmillan,
1915.)

Maraghiannis, G. and others.   *Antiquités crétoises. In progress.*
(Candia: Maraghiannis.)

Murray, G. G. *The Rise of the Greek Epic.* Ed. 3, 1924 (Oxford University Press).

Myres, J. L. *Who Were the Greeks?* (University of California Press, 1930.)

Nilsson, M. P. *The Minoan-Mycenean Religion and Its Survival in Greek Religion.* (Oxford University Press, 1927.)

Ridgeway, W. *The Early Age of Greece.* Vol. 1, 1901; Vol. 2 (published posthumously), 1931 (Cambridge University Press).

Rose, H. J. *Primitive Culture in Greece.* (London: Methuen, 1925.)

Seymour, T. D. *Life in the Homeric Age.* (London and New York: Macmillan, 1907.)

Wace, A. J. B. and Thompson, M. *Prehistoric Thessaly.* (Cambridge University Press, 1912.)

Xanthoudides, S. A. *The Vaulted Tombs of Mesará.* Translated by J. P. Droop. (London: Hodder and Stoughton, 1924.)

Important articles will also be found in the cyclopædias of Pauly-Wissowa-Kroll and of Ebert, cited under A and B above.

E. Chapters VII, VIII, and XII

Barton, G. A. *A History of the Hebrew People, from the Earliest Times to the Year 70 A.D., Largely in the Language of the Bible.* (New York: Century Co., 1930.)

Baynes, N. H. *Israel amongst the Nations.* (London: Student Christian Movement, 1927.) An admirable survey with valuable bibliographical annotations.

Browne, E. G. *Literary History of Persia,* Vol. 1 (London: Fisher, Unwin, 1906).

Driver, S. R. *An Introduction to the Literature of the Old Testament.* Ed. 9, 1913 (Edinburgh: Clark).

Huart, C. *La Perse antique.* (Paris: Renaissance du livre, 1925.)

Kittel, E. *Geschichte des Volkes Israel,* Vol. 1, Ed. 5 (1923); Vol. 2, Ed. 4 (1922). (Gotha: Perthes.)

Lods, A. *Israel: des origines au milieu du VIIIe siècle.* (Paris: Renaissance du livre, 1930.)

Macalister, R. A. S. *The Philistines.* (Oxford University Press, 1914.)

Meyer, E. *Die Israeliten und ihre Nachbarstämme.* (Halle: Niemeyer, 1906.)

Olmstead, A. T. *History of Assyria.* (New York: Scribners, 1923.)

Olmstead, A. T. *History of Palestine and Syria.* (New York: Scribners, 1931.)

Peake, A. S. *The Bible.* (London: Hodder and Stoughton, 1914.)

Peake, A. S. (editor). *The People and the Book.* (Oxford University Press, 1925.) A series of essays on the Old Testament by various scholars.

Prasek, J. V. *Geschichte der Meder und Perser.* Vols. 1 and 2 (Gotha: Perthes, 1906–09).

Rogers, R. W. *History of Ancient Persia.* (New York: Scribners, 1929.)

Sellin, E. *Geschichte des Israelitisch-jüdischen Volkes,* Vol. 1, 1924; Vol. 2, 1932. (Leipzig: Quelle und Meyer.)

Stade, B. *Die Entstehung des Volkes Israel.* (Giessen: Ricker, 1899.)

Sykes, P. M. *A History of Persia.* Vols. 1 and 2 (London and New York: Macmillan, 1915). Vol. 1 treats of the history of Persia to the Arab conquest. The work is provided with two admirable maps.

Wellhausen, J. *Prolegomena to the History of Israel.* (London: Black, 1885.)

See also the works of Burn, Hall, Meissner, Rogers, and Smith, listed under C and D.

F. Chapters IX–XI and XV–XIX

Beloch, J. *Griechische Geschichte.* Vols. 1 to 4 (Berlin: de Gruyter, 1914–27).

Berve, H. *Griechische Geschichte.* Part 1. (Freiburg i. B.: Herder, 1931.)

Bilabel, F. *Die Ionische Kolonisation.* (Leipzig: Dieterich, 1920.)

Bonner, R. J. *Lawyers and Litigants in Ancient Athens.* (University of Chicago Press, 1927.)

Bonner, R. J. and Smith, G. *The Administration of Justice from Homer to Aristotle.* (University of Chicago Press, 1930.)

Botsford, G. W. *Hellenic History.* (London and New York: Macmillan, 1922.)

Burns, A. R. *Money and Monetary Policy in Early Times.* (London: Kegan, Paul; New York: Knopf, 1927.)

Bury, J. B. *History of Greece to the Death of Alexander.* Ed. 2, 1922 (London and New York: Macmillan).

Busolt, G. *Griechische Geschichte.* Vols. 1 to 3 (Gotha: Perthes, 1893–1904).

Busolt, G. *Griechische Staatskunde.* Vols. 1 and 2. Ed. 3 (Munich: Beck, 1920–26).

Calhoun, G. M. *The Business Life of Ancient Athens.* (University of Chicago Press, 1926.)

Calhoun, G. M. *The Growth of Criminal Law in Ancient Greece.* (University of California Press, 1927.)

Cary, M. *The Documentary Sources of Greek History.* (Oxford: Blackwell, 1927.) A brief but excellent introduction to the subject.

Cary, M. and Warmington, E. H. *The Ancient Explorers.* (London: Methuen, 1929.)

Casson, S. *Macedonia, Thrace, and Illyria.* (Oxford University Press, 1926.)

Cloché, P. *La Vie publique et privée des anciens Grecs.* Vol. 5: *les classes, les métiers, le trafic.* (Paris: Les Belles Lettres, 1931.)

De Sanctis, G. *Atthis: Storia della repubblica ateniese.* (Turin: Bocca, 1912.)

Ferguson, W. S. *Greek Imperialism.* (New York: Houghton Mifflin, 1913.)

Fowler, W. W. *The City State of the Greeks and Romans.* (London and New York: Macmillan, 1893.)

Francotte, H. *L'Industrie dans la Grèce ancienne.* Vols. 1 and 2 (Brussels: Société Belge de librairie, 1901–02).

Freeman, E. A. *History of Sicily.* Vols. 1 to 4 (Oxford University Press, 1891–94).

Gardner, P. *History of Ancient Coinage, 700–300 B.C.* (Oxford University Press, 1918.)

Glotz, G. *Histoire de la Grèce: des origines aux guerres médiques.* (Paris: Presses Universitaires de France, 1926.)

Glotz, G. *La cité grecque.* (Paris: Renaissance du livre, 1928.) An English translation appeared in 1929.

Glotz, G. (London: Kegan, Paul; New York: Knopf.) *Le Travail dans la Grèce ancienne.* (Paris: Alcan, 1920.) An English translation appeared in 1926 under the title *Ancient Greece at Work.* (London: Kegan, Paul; New York: Knopf.)

Glover, T. R. *From Pericles to Philip.* (London: Methuen, 1919.)

Greenidge, A. H. J. *Handbook of Greek Constitutional History.* (London and New York: Macmillan, 1902.)

Grote, G. *History of Greece.* New Ed. (London: Murray, 1884).

Grundy, G. B. *The Great Persian War.* (London: Murray, 1901.)

Grundy, G. B. *Thucydides and the History of His Age.* (London: Murray, 1911.)

Hasebroek, J. *Griechische Wirtschafts- und Gesellschaftsgeschichte.* (Tübingen: Mohr, 1931.)

Hasebroek, J. *Staat und Handel im alten Griechenland.* (Tübingen: Mohr, 1928.)

Head, B. V. *Historia Numorum.* Ed. 2 (Oxford University Press, 1911).

Heitland, W. E. *Agricola: A Study of Agriculture and Rustic Life in the Greco-Roman World.* (Cambridge University Press, 1921.)

Hill, G. F. *Historical Greek Coins.* (London: Constable, 1906.)

Holm, A. *Geschichte Siziliens im Altertum.* Vols. 1 to 3 (Leipzig: Engelmann, 1870–98).

Laistner, M. L. W. *Greek Economics.* (London: Dent; New York: Dutton, 1923.)

Minns, E. H. *Scythians and Greeks.* (Cambridge University Press, 1913.)

Myres, J. L. *The Political Ideas of the Greeks.* (London: Arnold, 1927.)

Ormerod, H. A. *Piracy in the Ancient World.* (London: Hodder and Stoughton, 1924.)

Pöhlmann, R. von. *Geschichte der sozialen Frage und des Sozialismus in der antiken Welt.* Ed. 3 (Munich: Beck, 1925).

Rostovtzeff, M. *Iranians and Greeks in South Russia.* (Oxford University Press, 1922.)

Roussel, P. *La Grèce et l'orient des guerres médiques à la conquête romaine.* (Paris: Alcan, 1928.)

Schömann, G. F. and Lipsius, J. H. *Griechische Altertümer.* (Berlin: Weidmann, 1897–1902.)

Toutain, J. *L'économie antique.* (Paris: Renaissance du livre, 1927.) An English translation appeared in 1930. (London: Kegan, Paul; New York: Knopf.)

Ure, P. N. *The Origin of Tyranny.* (Cambridge University Press, 1922.)

Vinogradoff, P. *Outlines of Historical Jurisprudence.* Vol. 2 (Oxford University Press, 1922).

Whibley, L. (editor). *A Companion to Greek Studies.* Ed. 3 (Cambridge University Press, 1916).

Whibley, L. *Greek Oligarchies.* (Cambridge University Press, 1896.)

Zimmern, A. E. *The Greek Commonwealth.* Ed. 4 (Oxford University Press, 1924).

G. CHAPTERS XII–XIII AND XX–XXII

Abbot, G. F. *Thucydides: A Study in Historical Reality.* (London: Routledge, 1925.)

Anderson, W. J. and Spiers, R. P. *The Architecture of Ancient Greece.* (London: Batsford, 1927.)

Barker, E. *Greek Political Theory: Plato and His Predecessors.* (London: Methuen, 1918.)

Blass, F. *Die Attische Beredsamkeit.* Vols. 1 to 3. Ed. 2 (Leipzig: Teubner, 1890–93).

Burnet, J. *Early Greek Philosophy.* Ed. 3 (London: Black, 1920).

Burnet, J. *Greek Philosophy: Part 1*. (London and New York: Macmillan, 1914.)

Bury, J. B. *The Ancient Greek Historians*. (London and New York: Macmillan, 1909.)

Buschor, G. *Greek Vase Painting*. (London: Chatto and Windus, 1921.)

Capps, E. *From Homer to Theocritus*. (New York: Scribners, 1901.)

Christ, W. von. *Geschichte der Griechischen Literatur*. Ed. 6 revised by W. Schmid. Vols. 1 and 2 (Munich: Beck, 1920–24).

Cochrane, C. N. *Thucydides and the Science of History*. (Oxford University Press, 1929.)

Collignon, M. *Histoire de la sculpture grecque*. Vols. 1 and 2 (Paris: Didot).

Croiset, A. and M. *Histoire de la littérature grecque*. Vol. 1, Ed. 3 (1909); Vol. 2, Ed. 2 (1898); Vol. 3, Ed. 3 (1914); Vol. 4, Ed. 2 (1899); Vol. 5 (1899). (Paris: Fontemoing.)

D'Ooge, M. *The Acropolis of Athens*. (London and New York: Macmillan, 1908.)

Earp, F. R. *The Way of the Greeks*. (Oxford University Press, 1929.)

Farnell, L. R. *The Cults of the Greek States*. Vols. 1 to 5 (Oxford University Press, 1896–1909).

Field, G. C. *Plato and His Contemporaries*. (London: Methuen, 1930.)

Flickinger, R. *The Greek Theater*. Ed. 3 (University of Chicago Press, 1926).

Freeman, K. J. *Schools of Hellas*. Ed. 3 (London and New York: Macmillan, 1922).

Gardiner, E. N. *Olympia*. (Oxford University Press, 1925.)

Gardner, E. A. *Ancient Athens*. (London and New York: Macmillan, 1902.)

Gardner, E. A. *Handbook of Greek Sculpture*. Ed. 2 (Macmillan, 1915).

Gardner, E. A. *Six Greek Sculptors*. (London: Duckworth, 1910.)

Glover, T. R. *Herodotus*. (University of California Press, 1924.)

Gomperz, T. *The Greek Thinkers*. Vols. 1 to 4 (London: Murray, 1901–12).

Haig, A. E. *The Attic Theatre*. Ed. 3 (Oxford University Press, 1907).

Jaeger, W. *Aristoteles*. (Berlin: Weidmann, 1923.)

Jebb, R. C. *The Attic Orators*. Vols. 1 and 2 (London and New York: Macmillan, 1893).

Judeich, W. *Topographie von Athen*. Ed. 2 (Munich: Beck, 1931).

Livingstone, R. W. (editor). *The Legacy of Greece*. (Oxford University Press, 1922.) A series of essays by different hands.

Murray, G. G. *History of Greek Literature.* (London: Heinemann, 1902.)

Nilsson, M. P. *A History of Greek Religion.* (Oxford University Press, 1925.)

Pfuhl, E. *Meisterwerke Griechischer Zeichnung und Malerei.* (Munich: Bruckmann, 1924.) An English translation, *Masterpieces of Greek Drawing and Painting*, by J. D. Beazley, appeared in 1926. (London: Chatto and Windus.)

Pickard-Cambridge, A. W. *Dithyramb, Tragedy, and Comedy.* (Oxford University Press, 1927.)

Poulsen, F. *Delphi.* (London: Gyldendal, 1920.)

Ridgeway, W. *The Origin of Tragedy.* (Cambridge University Press, 1910.)

Robertson, D. S. *Handbook of Greek and Roman Architecture.* (Cambridge University Press, 1929.)

Ross, W. D. *Aristotle.* (London: Methuen; New York: Scribners, 1923.)

Taylor, A. E. *Plato: The Man and His Work.* (London: Methuen; New York: Kennerley, 1927.)

Tucker, T. G. *Life in Ancient Athens.* (London and New York: Macmillan, 1906.)

Walters, H. B. *History of Ancient Pottery.* Vols. 1 and 2 (London: Murray, 1905).

Warbeke, J. M. *The Searching Mind of Greece.* (New York: Crofts, 1930.)

H. Chapters XXIII–XXVI

Beloch, J. *Griechische Geschichte.* Vol. 4. See under F.

Bevan, E. and Mahaffy, J. P. *A History of Egypt under the Ptolemaic Dynasty.* (London: Methuen, 1927.)

Bevan, E. *The House of Seleucus.* Vols. 1 and 2 (London: Arnold, 1902).

Bevan, E. *Stoics and Sceptics.* (Oxford University Press, 1913.)

Bouché-Leclerq, A. *Histoire des Lagides.* Vols. 1 to 4 (Paris: Leroux, 1903–07).

Bouché-Leclerq, A. *Histoire des Séleucides.* Vols. 1 and 2 (Paris: Leroux, 1913–14).

Bury, J. B. and others. *The Hellenistic Age.* Ed. 2 (Cambridge University Press, 1925). Four suggestive essays on the political history, the literature, the philosophy, and the economic conditions of the Hellenistic Age.

Cardinali, G. *Il Regno di Pergamo.* (Rome: Loescher, 1906.)

Cary, M. *A History of the Greek World from 323 to 146 B.C.* (London: Methuen, 1932.)

Ferguson, W. S. *Greek Imperialism.* See under F above.

Ferguson, W. S. *Hellenistic Athens.* (London and New York: Macmillan, 1911.)

Freeman, E. A. *History of Federal Government.* Ed. 2 revised by J. B. Bury. (Macmillan, 1893.)

Gerkan, A. von. *Griechische Städteanlagen.* (Berlin and Leipzig: de Gruyter, 1924.)

Heath, T. L. *Aristarchus of Samos.* (Oxford University Press, 1913.)

Heath, T. L. *History of Greek Mathematics.* Vols. 1 and 2 (Oxford University Press, 1921).

Hicks, R. D. *Stoic and Epicurean.* (London and New York: Longmans, 1910.)

Hogarth, D. G. *Philip and Alexander of Macedon.* (London: Murray, 1897.)

Jouguet, P. *L'Impérialisme macédonien et L'hellénisation de l'Orient.* (Paris: Renaissance du livre, 1926.)

Kaerst, J. *Geschichte des Hellenismus.* Vols. 1 and 2 (Leipzig: Teubner, 1917–26).

Körte, A. *Hellenistic Poetry.* Translated by J. Hammer and M. Hadas. (Columbia University Press, 1929.)

Lawrence, A. W. *Later Greek Sculpture.* (London: Cape, 1927.)

Mackail, J. W. *Select Epigrams from the Greek Anthology.* (London: Longmans, 1890.)

Niese, B. *Geschichte der Griechisch und Makedonischen Staaten.* Vols. 1 to 3 (Gotha: Perthes, 1893–1903).

Powell, J. U. and Barber, E. A. *New Chapters in the History of Greek Literature.* Series 1, 1921; series 2, 1928. (Oxford University Press.)

Rostovtzeff, M. *A Large Estate in Egypt in the Third Century.* (University of Wisconsin Press, 1922.)

Rostovtzeff, M. *The Economic Policy of the Pergamene Kings.* See in *Anatolian Studies Presented to Sir W. M. Ramsay.* (Manchester University Press, 1923.)

Schnebel, M. *Die Landwirtschaft im Hellenistischen Aegypten.* (Munich: Beck, 1925.)

Singer, C. *Greek Biology and Greek Medicine.* (Oxford University Press, 1922.)

Susemihl, F. *Geschichte der Griechischen Literatur in der Alexandrinerzeit.* Vols. 1 and 2 (Leipzig: Teubner, 1891–92).

Tarn, W. W. *Antigonus Gonatas.* (Oxford University Press, 1913.)

GREEK HISTORY

Tarn, W. W. *Hellenistic Civilisation.* (London: Arnold, 1927.)
Tarn, W. W. *Hellenistic Military and Naval Developments.* (Cambridge University Press, 1930.)
Wendland, P. *Die Hellenistisch-römische Kultur.* (Tübingen: Mohr, 1912.)
Wilcken, U. und Mitteis, L. *Grundzüge und Chrestomathie der Papyruskunde.* Vols. 1 to 4 (Leipzig: Teubner, 1912).
Zeller, E. *The Stoics, Epicureans, and Sceptics.* (London: Longmans, 1880.)
See also the works of Whibley listed under F, and of Blass, Christ-Schmid, and Croiset listed under G.

INDEX

Abd-Ashirta, 66.
Academy, Platonic, 347, 350.
Acarnania, 132.
Achæan League, 407 ff., 416 ff., 423–424.
Achæans, 98, 100, 106.
Acheloos, R., 132.
Acragas, 232, 310.
Acropolis, at Athens, 186, 382 ff.
Acusilaus, 200.
Adab, 21.
Adad-Nirari III, 122.
Admonitions of a Prophet, cited, 81.
Aegina, 150, 223–224, 244, 381.
Aegospotami, battle of, 276.
Aeschines, 402.
Aeschylus, 361–362; cited, 215, 228–229.
Aetolia, 132.
Aetolian League, 406, 407, 412, 416 ff.
Aetolians, 403, 406–408.
Agariste, 155.
Agathocles, 413–414.
Agathon, 298.
Agesilaus, 279, 285, 289, 391.
Agias, statue of, 386.
Agis I, 269, 271.
Agis III, 410.
Agriculture, in Babylonia, 30–31; in Egypt, 74, 431–432; in Greece, 319 ff.; in the Seleucid Empire, 429.
Agyrrhius, 331.
Ahab, 118, 121.
Ahmose I, 56, 63.
Akkad, 18, 19 ff., 23.
Alcæus, 153, 194; cited, 194–195.
Alcetas, 291.
Alcibiades, 261, 263 ff., 271 ff., 276 note, 335.
Alcmæonidæ, 166, 243.
Alcman, 146, 196.
Aleppo, 120.

Alexander Sarcophagus, 387.
Alexander the Great, 308, Chapter XXIII, 402.
Alexandria, 393, 430 ff., 445, 452, 460–461.
Alphabet, Greek, 191.
Alyattes, 206.
Amarna (Akhetaten), 66, 83; documents from, 66, 69.
Amenhotep I, 63.
Amenhotep III, 65, 66, 69.
Amenhotep IV, 65, 67, 69, 83–84.
Ameni, 54.
Amphictionic League, 300, 304, 306.
Amphictiony, 178.
Amphipolis, 250, 299. *See also* Ennea Hodoi.
Amurru, 27.
Amyntas III, 298.
Anacreon, 184.
Anau, 13, 18.
Anaxagoras, 339, 340.
Anaxilas, 233.
Anaximander, 198, 200.
Anaximenes, 198.
Andriscus, 422.
Antalcidas, Peace of. *See* King's Peace.
Anthology, Greek, cited, 380.
Antigonus (general of Alexander), 400, 401.
Antigonus Doson, 412.
Antigonus Gonatas, 406, 409.
Antioch, 429.
Antiochus I, 405.
Antiochus III, 416, 418–419.
Antipater, 400, 401, 403.
Antiphon, 271, 273.
Apella, 147.
Apelles, 388.
Aphaia, temple of, 381.
"Apollo" statues, 187.
Apollonius (minister of Ptolemy II), 432.

INDEX